GRUBER'S

COMPLETE

SAT*

MATH

2nd Edition

WORKBOOK

*SAT is a registered trademark of the College Entrance Examination Board. The College Entrance Examination Board is not associated with and does not endorse this book.

GARY R. GRUBER, PhD

sourcebooks

Copyright © 2009, 2011 by Gary R. Gruber
Cover and internal design © 2011 by Sourcebooks, Inc.

Published by Sourcebooks, Inc.
P.O. Box 4410, Naperville, Illinois 60567-4410
(630) 961-3900
Fax: (630) 961-2168
www.sourcebooks.com

The Library of Congress has catalogued the first edition as follows:

Gruber, Gary R.
  Gruber's complete SAT math workbook / by Gary R. Gruber.
      p. cm.
  1. Mathematics—Examinations, questions, etc. 2. Mathematics—Examinations—Study guides. 3. SAT (Educational test)—Study guides. I. Title. II. Title: Complete SAT math workbook.
  QA43.G742 2009
  510.76—dc22

                          2009008925

Printed and bound in the United States of America.
        SB 10 9 8 7 6 5 4 3 2 1

Recent and Forthcoming Study Aids From Dr. Gary Gruber

Gruber's Essential Guide to Test Taking: Grades 3–5

Gruber's Essential Guide to Test Taking: Grades 6–9

Gruber's Complete SAT Guide 2011 (14th Edition)

Gruber's Complete ACT Guide 2011 (2nd Edition)

Gruber's SAT 2400 (2nd Edition)

Gruber's Complete SAT Critical Reading Workbook (2nd Edition)

Gruber's Complete SAT Writing Workbook (2nd Edition)

Gruber's SAT Word Master (2nd Edition)

Gruber's Complete SAT Guide 2012 (15th Edition)

Gruber's Complete ACT Guide 2012 (3rd Edition)

Gruber's Complete GRE Guide 2012

www.sourcebooks.com

www.drgarygruber.com

www.mymaxscore.com

Contents

PART I

INTRODUCTION   1

PART II

THE 101 MOST IMPORTANT MATH QUESTIONS YOU NEED TO KNOW HOW TO SOLVE   21

PART III

MINI MATH REFRESHER   53

PART IV

DIAGNOSTIC TESTS AND INSTRUCTIONAL MATERIAL   61

PART V

COMPLETE TIME-SAVING STRATEGIES AND SHORTCUTS   245

PART VI

TWO SAT MATH PRACTICE TESTS   307

Purpose of This Book

The mathematics questions on all SAT tests share one thing in common. All the questions test your ability to manipulate math, understand what you are asked to find in a problem, know how to use your math knowledge, and solve the problem in the shortest, simplest way possible. A problem's solution shouldn't have to be long-winded or tedious. It is therefore the purpose of this book to prepare you to effectively attack the math questions on the SAT, to point out important key words and symbols to look for, and to show you how to use shortcuts to quickly solve the problems. In this book there is a wealth of carefully structured material: diagnostic tests, simulated practice tests, complete explanatory answers, strategies, techniques, and shortcuts. Every example is keyed to math instructional material to enable you to quickly strengthen your weaknesses.

You are in excellent hands. Dr. Gary R. Gruber, long known as the leading test preparation authority and the leading mathematics-techniques-and-shortcuts specialist, has, after numerous years of research and field-testing, written this book to prepare you for the math parts of the SAT. You will find special sections of this book dealing with the most powerful strategies and shortcuts for answering the math questions on your SAT. And these strategies and shortcuts can cut your time in answering most of the SAT questions *by a factor of twelve.*

Note that this book can be used effectively for learning shortcuts and for diagnosing and correcting specific types of math problems on any test. The material has been shown to be highly effective and successful for exams like the GRE, GMAT, and GED, and for all school, civil service, and competency exams.

Important Note about This Book and Its Author

This book was written by Dr. Gary R. Gruber, the leading authority on the SAT, who knows more than anyone else in the test-prep market about exactly what is being tested for in the SAT. In fact, the procedures to answer the SAT questions rely more heavily on the Gruber Critical Thinking Strategies than ever before, and this is the only book that has the exact thinking strategies you need to use to maximize your SAT score. Gruber's SAT books are used more than any other books by the nation's school districts and are proven to get the highest documented school district SAT scores.

Dr. Gruber has published more than thirty books with major publishers on test-taking and critical thinking methods, with over seven million copies sold. He has also authored over 1,000 articles on his work in scholarly journals and nationally syndicated newspapers, has appeared on numerous television and radio shows, and has been interviewed in hundreds of magazines and newspapers. He has developed major programs for school districts and for city and state educational agencies for improving and restructuring curriculum, increasing learning ability and test scores, increasing motivation and developing a "passion" for learning and problem solving, and decreasing the student dropout rate. For example, PBS (Public Broadcasting System) chose Dr. Gruber to train the nation's teachers on how to prepare students for the SAT through a national satellite teleconference and videotape. His results have been lauded by people throughout the country and from all walks of life.

Dr. Gruber is recognized nationally as the leading expert on standardized tests. It is said that no one in the nation is better at assessing the thinking patterns of how a person answers questions and providing the mechanism to improve faulty thinking approaches. SAT score improvements by students using Dr. Gruber's techniques have been the highest in the nation.

Gruber's unique methods have been and are being used by PBS, by the nation's learning centers, by international encyclopedias, by school districts throughout the country, in homes and workplaces across the nation, and by a host of other entities.

His goal and mission is to get people's potential realized and the nation "impassioned" with learning and problem solving so that people don't merely try to get a "fast," uncritical answer, but actually enjoy and look forward to solving the problem and learning.

For more information on Gruber courses and additional Gruber products, visit www.drgarygruber.com.

What This Book Contains

Part I—*Introduction*

Part II—*The 101 Most Important Math Questions You Need to Know How to Solve.*

Part III—*Mini Math Refresher.* The purpose of this section is to present the student with a "bird's eye" view of the minimum of math rules and concepts needed for the SAT. Each rule or concept is keyed to the math instructional material in the book, so if the student wants a more comprehensive review, the math instructional part of the book can be used.

Part IV—*Diagnostic Tests and Instructional Material.* Here we have presented diagnostic tests in each area of math encountered on the SAT. You may take these tests to assess your strengths and weaknesses. The diagnostic tests are keyed to specific math instructional material. By referring to the instructional material, you can correct and strengthen your math weaknesses in each area.

Part V—*Complete Time-Saving Strategies and Shortcuts.* This section includes powerful strategies and shortcuts that you can use on your SAT. The methods employed in this section have been constructed and thoroughly field-tested in such a fashion as to cater to individual needs and problems in the SAT math areas. Each technique and shortcut is illustrated with examples that are very similar to the examples found on the most current SATs.

Part VI—*Two SAT Math Practice Tests* (with explanatory answers). Here, two SAT simulated tests are closely patterned after the actual SAT math tests. There are complete explanatory solutions to each of the problems.

How to Use This Book Most Effectively

1. Read Purpose of This Book on page ix.

2. Read What This Book Contains on page xi.

3. Read Introduction on page 1.

4. Read the 101 Most Important Math Questions on page 21.

5. If you feel that you are weak in one or more math areas, take the Diagnostic Tests beginning on page 61. Correct your weaknesses by referring to the Math Instructional Material. Each diagnostic test area is keyed to specific instructions in the Math Instructional Material.

6. Read through the Mini Math Refresher section on page 53. For those concepts and rules that you are unfamiliar with or are unsure of, refer to the Math Instructional Material to which all the rules and concepts are keyed.

7. Read Time-Saving Strategies and Shortcuts beginning on page 245. Make sure that you understand all these techniques and shortcuts.

8. Take the Sample SAT Math Tests beginning on page 307.

9. Score yourself on the sample tests according to the directions at the end of each test. Find out your SAT Scaled Score with the table on page 340. For the questions that you answered wrong or for those questions that gave you difficulty, refer to the explanatory answers. You may also want to refer back to the section on Time-Saving Strategies and Shortcuts, and you may want to retake some Diagnostic Tests.

Part I
Introduction

I. Important Facts about the Math on the SAT

What Is on the Math Part of the SAT?

The math section will include arithmetic, geometry, Algebra I, and some advanced math covering topics in Algebra II, statistics, probability, and data analysis. The test will measure reasoning ability and problem-solving skills.

How Will the Math Test Be Scored?

There will be a range of scores from 200–800.

How Long Will the Math Test Be?

The total time of the math parts will be seventy minutes. There may be an experimental math section of twenty-five minutes that will not count toward your score.

What Math Background Must I Have?

The math part will test first- and second-year algebra (Algebra I and II) and geometry. However, if you use common sense, rely on just a handful of geometrical formulas, and learn the strategies and thinking skills presented in this book, you don't need to take a full course in geometry or memorize all the theorems. If you have not taken algebra, you should still be able to answer many of the math questions using the strategies presented in this book.

Is Guessing Still Advisable?

Although there is a small penalty for wrong answers (one-quarter point for five-choice questions), in the long run, you *break even* if you guess *or* leave the answer blank. So it really will not affect your score in the long run if you guess or leave answers out. And, if you can eliminate an incorrect choice, it is imperative that you not leave the answer blank.

Can I Use a Calculator on the Math Portion of the Test?

Students may use a four-function, scientific, or graphing calculator. While it is possible to solve every question without the use of a calculator, it is recommended that you use a calculator at least at the scientific level for the SAT.

Should I Take an Administered Actual SAT for Practice?

Yes, but only if you will learn from your mistakes by seeing what strategies you should have used on your exam. Taking the SAT merely for its own sake is a waste of time and may in fact reinforce bad methods and habits. Note that the College Board releases SAT answers to students via its Question-and-Answer Service three times a year, usually for the January, May, and October administrations. It is wise to take exams on these dates if you wish to see your mistakes and correct them.

A Table of What's on the SAT Math

Math	
Time	70 min. (Two 25 min. sections, one 20 min. section)
Content	Multiple-Choice Items Student-Produced Response Measuring: Number and Operations Algebra I, II, and Functions Geometry Statistics, Probability, and Data Analysis
Score	M 200–800

Note: There is an experimental section that does not count toward your SAT score. This section can contain any of the SAT item types (writing [multiple-choice], critical reading, or math) and can appear in any part of the test. Do not try to outguess the test maker by trying to figure out which of the sections are experimental on the actual test (believe me, you won't be able to)—treat every section as if it counts toward your SAT score.

A Table of What's on the PSAT Math

Math

Time	50 min. (Two 25 min. sections)
Content	Multiple-Choice Items Student-Produced Responses Measuring: Number and Operations Algebra I and Functions Geometry and Measurement Statistics, Probability, and Data Analysis
Score	20–80

Can I Get Back the SAT with My Answers and the Correct Ones after I Take It? How Can I Make Use of This Service?

The SAT is disclosed (sent back to the student on request for an $18 payment) three of the seven times it is given through the year. You can also order a copy of your answer sheet for an additional $25 fee. Very few people take advantage of this fact or use the disclosed SAT to see what mistakes they've made and what strategies they could have used on the questions.

Check your SAT information bulletin or log on to www.collegeboard.com for the dates this Question-and-Answer Service is available.

Should I Use Scrap Paper to Write on and to Do Calculations?

Always use your test booklet (not your answer sheet) to draw on. Many of my strategies expect you to label diagrams, draw and extend lines, circle important words and sentences, etc., so feel free to write anything in your booklet. The booklets aren't graded—just the answer sheets.

Should I Be Familiar with the Directions to the Various Items on the SAT Before Taking the SAT?

Make sure you are completely familiar with the directions to each of the math item types on the SAT—the directions for answering the Regular Math, and especially the Grid-Type.

What Should a Student Bring to the Exam on the Test Date?

You should bring a few sharpened #2 pencils with erasers, and also your ID.

Bring a calculator to the test, but be aware that every math question on the SAT can be solved without a calculator; in many questions, it's actually easier not to use one.

Acceptable calculators: Graphing calculators, scientific calculators, and four-function calculators (the last is not recommended) are all permitted during testing. If you have a calculator with characters that are one inch or larger, or if your calculator has a raised display that might be visible to other test takers, you will be seated at the discretion of the test supervisor.

Unacceptable calculators: Laptops or portable/handheld computers; calculators that have a QWERTY keyboard, make noise, use an electrical outlet, or have a paper tape; electronic writing pads or stylus-driven devices; pocket organizers; and cell phone calculators will not be allowed during the test.

How Should a Student Pace Himself/ Herself on the Exam? How Much Time Should One Spend on Each Question?

Calculate the time allowed for the particular section. For example, twenty-five minutes. Divide by the number of questions. For example, twenty. That gives you an average of spending one minute and fifteen seconds per question in this example. However, the first set of questions within an item type in a section are easier, so spend less than a minute on the first set of questions and perhaps more than a minute on the last set.

How Is the Exam Scored? Are Some Questions Worth More Points?

Each question is worth the same number of points. After getting a raw score—the number of questions right minus a penalty for wrong answers—this is equated to a "scaled" score from 200 to 800. A scaled score of 500 in each part is considered "average."

It's Three Days Until the SAT; What Can a Student Do to Prepare for the Math Part of the SAT?

Make sure you are completely familiar with the structure of the test (page 19) and the basic math skills needed (pages 53–60). Take the practice tests and refresh your understanding of the strategies and basic skills used to answer the questions.

What Is the Most Challenging Type of Question on the Exam and How Does One Attack It?

Many questions on the test, especially at the end of a section, can be challenging. You should always attack challenging questions by using a specific strategy or strategies and common sense.

What Should a Student Do to Prepare on Friday Night? Cram? Watch TV? Relax?

On Friday night, I would just refresh my knowledge of the structure of the test, some strategies, and refresh some basic skills. You want to do this to keep the thinking going so that it is continual right up to the exam. Don't overdo it; do just enough so that it's somewhat continuous—this will also relieve some anxiety, so that you won't feel you are forgetting things before the exam.

The Test Is Given in One Booklet. Can a Student Skip Between Sections?

No—you cannot skip between the sections. You have to work on the section until the time is called. If you get caught skipping sections or going back to earlier sections, then you risk being asked to leave the exam.

Should a Student Answer All Easy Questions First and Save Difficult Ones for Last?

The easy questions usually appear at the beginning of the section, the middle difficulty ones in the middle, and the hard ones toward the end. So I would answer the questions as they are presented to you, and if you find you are spending more than thirty seconds on a question and not getting anywhere, go to the next question. You may, however, find that the more difficult questions toward the end are actually easy for you because you have learned the strategies in this book.

What Is the Recommended Course of Study for Those Retaking the Exam?

Try to get a copy of the exam that you took if it was a disclosed one—the disclosed ones, which you have to send a payment for, are usually given in October, January, and May. Try to learn from your mistakes by seeing what strategies you could have used to get questions right. Certainly learn the specific strategies for taking your next exam.

What Are the Most Crucial Math Strategies for Students?

All specific math strategies are crucial, including writing and drawing in your test booklet and being familiar with question-type directions. The translations strategy—verbal to math, drawing of lines, etc.—is also important. Also make sure you know the basic math skills cold (see pages 53–60).

I Know There Is an Experimental Section on the Exam That Is Not Scored. How Do I Know Which Section It Is?

The SAT people have now made it so difficult to tell which is the experimental section, I would not take a chance second-guessing them and leaving it out. It will look like any of the other sections. It is true that if you have, for example, two of the same sections, such as two sections that both deal with grid questions, one of them is experimental—but you won't know which one it is. Also, if you have two sections where there is a long double reading passage, one of those sections is experimental, but again you won't know which one it is.

Can I Take the Test More Than Once, and If So, How Will the Scores Be Reported to the Schools of My Choice? Will All Scores Be Reported to the School and How Will They Be Used?

Check with the schools you are applying to to see how they use the reported scores, e.g., whether they average them, whether they take the highest. Ask the schools whether they see unreported scores; if they do, find out how the individual school deals with single and multiple unreported scores.

How Do Other Exams Compare with the SAT? Can I Use the Strategies and Examples in This Book for Them?

Most other exams are modeled after the SAT, and so the strategies used here are definitely useful when taking them. For example, the GRE (Graduate Records Examination, for entrance into graduate school) has questions that use the identical strategies used on the SAT. The questions are just worded at a slightly higher level. The ACT (American College Testing Program), another college entrance exam, reflects more than ever strategies that are used on the SAT.

How Does the Gruber Preparation Method Differ from Other Programs and SAT Books?

Many other SAT programs try to use "quick fix" methods or subscribe to memorization. So-called "quick fix" methods can be detrimental to effective preparation because the SAT people constantly change questions to prevent gimmick approaches. Rote memorization methods do not enable you to answer a variety of questions that appear in the SAT exam. In more than thirty years of experience writing preparation books for the SAT, Dr. Gruber has developed and honed the Critical Thinking Skills and Strategies that are based on all standardized tests' construction. So, while his method immediately improves your performance on the SAT, it also provides you with the confidence to tackle problems in all areas of study for the rest of your life. Remarkably, he enables you to be able to, without panic, look at a problem or question, extract something curious or useful from the problem, and move to the next step and finally to a solution, without rushing into a wrong answer or getting lured into a wrong choice. It has been said that test taking through his methodology becomes enjoyable rather than a pain.

II. The Inside Track on How SAT Math Questions Are Developed and How They Vary from Test to Test

When an SAT question is developed, it is based on a set of criteria and guidelines. Knowing how these guidelines work should demystify the test-making process and convince you why the strategies in this book are so critical to getting a high score.

Inherent in the SAT questions are Critical Thinking Skills, which present strategies that enable you to solve a question by the quickest method, with the least amount of panic and brain-racking, and bring an elegance and excitement to problem solving. Adhering to and using the strategies (which the test makers use to develop the questions) will let you "sail" through the SAT. This is summed up in the following statement:

Show me the solution to a problem, and I'll solve that problem. Show me a Gruber strategy for solving the problem, and I'll solve hundreds of problems.

—Gary Gruber

Here's a sample of a set of guidelines presented for making up an SAT-type question in the math area:

The test maker is to make up a hard math problem, in either the regular math multiple-choice area or the quantitative comparison area, which involves
(A) algebra
(B) two or more equations
(C) two or more ways to solve: one way being standard substitution, the other faster way using the **strategy** of merely *adding* or *subtracting* equations.

Previous examples given to test maker for reference:

1. If $x + y = 3$, $y + z = 4$ and $z + x = 5$, find the value of $x + y + z$.
   (A) 4
   (B) 5
   (C) 6
   (D) 7
   (E) 8

Solution: *Add* equations and get $2x + 2y + 2z = 12$; divide both sides of the equation by 2 and we get $x + y + z = 6$. (Answer C)

2. If $2x + y = 8$ and $x + 2y = 4$, find the value of $x - y$.
   (A) 3
   (B) 4
   (C) 5
   (D) 6
   (E) 7

Solution: *Subtract* equations and get $x - y = 4$. (Answer B)

Here's an example from a recent SAT.

If $y - x = 5$ and $2y + z = 11$, find the value of $x + y + z$.
   (A) 3
   (B) 6
   (C) 8
   (D) 16
   (E) 55

Solution: *Subtract* equation $y - x = 5$ from $2y + z = 11$.
We get $2y - y + z - (- x) = 11 - 5$.
So, $y + z + x = 6$. (Choice B)

III. What Are Critical Thinking Skills?

Critical Thinking Skills, a buzz phrase in the nation, are generic skills for the creative and most effective way of solving a problem or evaluating a situation. The most effective way of solving a problem is to extract some piece of information or observe something curious from the problem, then use one or more of the specific strategies or Critical Thinking Skills (together with basic skills or information you already know) to get to the next step in the problem. This next step will catapult you toward a solution with further use of the specific strategies or thinking skills.

> 1. EXTRACT OR OBSERVE SOMETHING CURIOUS
> 2. USE SPECIFIC STRATEGIES TOGETHER WITH BASIC SKILLS

These specific strategies will enable you to "process" think rather than just be concerned with the end result; the latter usually results in a fast, rushed, and wrong answer. The Gruber strategies have been shown to make one more comfortable with problem solving and make the process enjoyable. The skills will last a lifetime, and you will develop a passion for problem solving. These Critical Thinking Skills show that conventional "drill and practice" is a waste of time unless the practice is based on these generic thinking skills.

Here's a simple example of how these Critical Thinking Skills can be used in a math problem:

> Which is greater, $7\frac{1}{7} \times 8\frac{1}{8} \times 6\frac{1}{6}$ or $8\frac{1}{8} \times 6\frac{1}{6} \times 7$?

Long and tedious way: Multiply $7\frac{1}{7} \times 8\frac{1}{8} \times 6\frac{1}{6}$ and compare it with $8\frac{1}{8} \times 6\frac{1}{6} \times 7$.

Error in doing the problem the "long way": You don't have to *calculate*; you just have to *compare*, so you need a *strategy* for *comparing* two quantities.

Critical Thinking Way:

1. *Observe*: There is a common $8\frac{1}{8}$ and $6\frac{1}{6}$.

2. *Use Strategy*: Since both $8\frac{1}{8}$ and $6\frac{1}{6}$ are just weighting factors, like the same quantities on both sides of a balance scale, just *cancel* them from both multiplied quantities above.

3. You are then left comparing $7\frac{1}{7}$ with 7. The first quantity, $7\frac{1}{7}$, is greater. Thus $7\frac{1}{7} \times 8\frac{1}{8} \times 6\frac{1}{6}$ is greater than $8\frac{1}{8} \times 6\frac{1}{6} \times 7$.

Notice that the Critical Thinking approach gives you a fail-safe and exact way to the solution without superficially trying to solve the problem or merely guessing at it. This book contains all the Critical Thinking Strategies you need to know for the math part of the SAT test.

Dr. Gruber has researched hundreds of SAT tests (thousands of SAT questions) and documented the Critical Thinking Strategies for the math questions (all found in this book) coursing through every test. These strategies can be used for any math problem.

In short, you can learn how to solve a specific problem and thus find the answer to that specific problem, or you can learn a powerful strategy that will enable you to answer hundreds of problems.

IV. Math Strategies for Women

These are questions that women found significantly more difficult than men did. However, after learning the strategies in this book, women scored just as high as men on these sections.

1. Carol has twice as many books as Beverly has. After Carol gives Beverly 5 books, she still has 10 more books than Beverly has. How many books did Carol have originally?

   (A) 20   (B) 25   (C) 30   (D) 35   (E) 40

2.
$$\begin{array}{r} 5\triangle2 \\ \times\quad 9 \\ \hline 5,2\square9 \end{array}$$

   In the correctly computed multiplication problem above, if $\triangle$ and $\square$ are different digits, then $\triangle$ =

   (A) 1   (B) 5   (C) 6   (D) 7   (E) 8

3. If s equals $\frac{1}{2}$ percent of t, what percent of s is t?

   (A) 2%   (B) 200%   (C) 2,000%   (D) 20,000%   (E) 200,000%

Answers, Strategy, and Page in Book for Questions:

Math
1. E	Strategy VIII	276
2. E	Strategy XIII	293
3. D	Strategy VIII	276

V. Multi-Level Approaches to the Solution of Problems

How a student answers a question is more important than the answer given by the student. For example, the student may have randomly guessed, the student may have used a rote and unimaginative method for solution, or the student may have used a very creative method. It seems that one should judge the student by the "way" he or she answers the question and not just by the answer to the question.

Example:

> **Question: Without using a calculator, which is greater:**
> **355 × 356 or 354 × 357?**

Case 1: **Rote Memory Approach** (a completely mechanical approach not realizing the fact that there may be a faster method that takes into account patterns or connections of the numbers in the question): The student multiplies 355×356, gets 126,380, and then multiplies 354×357 and gets 126,378.

Case 2: **Observer's Rote Approach** (an approach that makes use of a mathematical strategy that can be memorized and tried for various problems): The student does the following:
Divides both quantities by 354.

He or she then gets $355 \times \dfrac{356}{354}$ compared with $354 \times \dfrac{357}{354}$.

He or she then divides these quantities by 356 and then gets $\dfrac{355}{354}$ compared with $\dfrac{357}{356}$.

Now he or she realizes that $\dfrac{355}{354} = 1$ and $\dfrac{1}{354}$; $\dfrac{357}{356} = 1$ and $\dfrac{1}{356}$.

He or she then reasons that since the left side 1 and $\dfrac{1}{354}$ is greater than the right side, 1 and $\dfrac{1}{356}$, the left side of the original quantities, 355×356, is greater than the right side of the original quantities 354×357.

Case 3: **The Pattern Seeker's Method** (the most mathematically creative method—an approach in which the student looks for a pattern or sequence in the numbers and then is astute enough to represent the pattern or sequence in more general algebraic language to see the pattern or sequence more clearly):

Look for a pattern. Represent 355×356 and 354×357 by symbols.

Let $x = 354$.

Then $355 = x + 1$, $356 = x + 2$, $357 = x + 3$.

So $355 \times 356 = (x + 1)(x + 2)$ and $354 \times 357 = x(x + 3)$.

Multiplying the factors we get

$355 \times 356 = (x \times x) + 3x + 2$ and $354 \times 357 = (x \times x) + 3x$.

The difference: $355 \times 356 - 354 \times 357 = [(x \times x) + 3x + 2] - [(x \times x) - 3x]$, which is just 2.

So 355×356 is greater than 354×357 by 2.

Note: You could have also represented 355 by x. Then $356 = x + 1$; $354 = x - 1$; $357 = x + 2$. We would then get $355 \times 356 = (x)(x + 1)$ and $354 \times 357 = (x - 1)(x + 2)$. Then we would use the method above to compare the quantities.

—OR—

You could have written 354 as a and 357 as b. Then $355 = a + 1$ and $356 = b - 1$. So $355 \times 356 = (a + 1)(b - 1)$ and $354 \times 357 = ab$. Let's see what $(355 \times 356) - (354 \times 357)$ is. This is the same as $(a + 1)(b - 1) - ab$, which is $(ab + b - a - 1) - ab$, which is in turn $b - a - 1$. Since $b - a - 1 = 357 - 354 - 1 = 2$, the quantity $355 \times 356 - 354 \times 357 = 2$, so 355×356 is greater than 354×357 by 2.

Case 4: **The Astute Observer's Approach** (the simplest approach—an approach that attempts to figure out a connection between the numbers and uses that connection to figure out the solution):

$355 \times 356 = (354 + 1) \times 356 = (354 \times 356) + 356$

$354 \times 357 = 354 \times (356 + 1) = (354 \times 356) + 354$

One can see that the difference is just 2.

Case 5: **The Observer's Common Relation Approach** (this is the approach that people use when they want to connect two items to a third to see how the two items are related):

355×356 is greater than 354×356 by 356.

354×357 is greater than 354×356 by 354.

So this means that 355×356 is greater than 354×357.

Case 6: **Scientific, Creative, and Observational Generalization Method** (a highly creative method and the most scientific method, as it spots a critical and curious aspect of the sums being equal and provides for a generalization to other problems of that nature):

Represent $354 = a$, $357 = b$, $355 = c$, and $356 = d$

We have now that $\boxed{1}$ $a + b = c + d$

$\boxed{2}$ $|b - a| = |d - c|$

We want to prove: $ab < dc$

Proof:

Square inequality $\boxed{2}$: $(b - a)^2 > (d - c)^2$

Therefore: $\boxed{3}$ $b^2 - 2ab + a^2 > d^2 - 2dc + c^2$

Multiply $\boxed{3}$ by (-1) and this reverses the inequality sign:

$-(b^2 - 2ab + a^2) < -(d^2 - 2dc + c^2)$

or

$\boxed{4}$ $-b^2 + 2ab - a^2 < -d^2 + 2dc - c^2$

Now square $\boxed{1}$: $(a + b) = (c + d)$ and we get:

$\boxed{5}$ $a^2 + 2ab + b^2 = c^2 + 2dc + d^2$

Add inequality $\boxed{4}$ to equality $\boxed{5}$ and we get:

$4ab < 4dc$

Divide by 4 and we get:

$ab < dc$

The generalization is that for any positive numbers a, b, c, d when $|b - a| > |d - c|$ and

$a + b = c + d$, then $ab < dc$.

This also generalizes in a geometrical setting, where for two rectangles whose perimeters are the same $(2a + 2b = 2c + 2d)$, the rectangle whose absolute difference in sides $|d - c|$ is *least* has the *greatest* area.

Case 7: **Geometric and Visual Approach*** (this is the approach used by visual people or people who have a curious geometric bent and possess "out-of-the-box" insights):

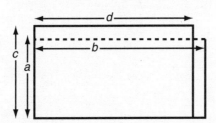

Where $a = 354$, $b = 357$, $c = 355$, and $d = 356$, we have two rectangles: the first one's length is d and width is c, and the second one's length is b (dotted line) and width is a.

Now the area of the first rectangle (dc) is equal to the area of the second (ab) minus the area of the rectangular slab, which is $(b - d)a$ plus the area of the rectangular slab $(c - a)d$. So we get: $cd = ab - (b - d)a + (c - a)d$. Since $b - d = c - a$, we get $cd = ab - (c - a)a + (c - a)d = ab + (d - a)(c - a)$.

Since $d > a$ and $c > a$, $cd > ab$. So $355 \times 356 > 354 \times 357$.

*This method of solution was developed and sent to the author by Dr. Eric Cornell, a Nobel laureate in physics.

Note: Many people have thought that by multiplying the units digits from one quantity and comparing that with the multiplication of the units digits from the other quantity they'd get the answer. For example, they would multiply $5 \times 6 = 30$ from 355×356, then multiply $4 \times 7 = 28$ from 354×357, and then say that 355×356 is greater than 354×357 because $5 \times 6 > 4 \times 7$. They would be lucky. That works if the sum of units digits of the first quantity is the same as or greater than the sum of units digits of the second quantity. However, if we want to compare something like $354 \times 356 = 126{,}024$ with $352 \times 359 = 126{,}368$, that method would not work.

VI. Format of the Math SAT Part

Total time for experimental, pre-test items: 25 minutes—number of questions varies

Note: The following represents a form of the math sections. The SAT has many different forms, so the order of the sections may vary* and the experimental section may not be the third section as we have here. However, the first section will always be the *Essay* and the last section will be a ten-minute Multiple-Choice *Writing* section, neither math.

Ten Sections of the SAT*	Number of Questions	Number of Minutes
Section 2: MATH	**20**	**25**
Regular Math	20	
Section 3: EXPERIMENTAL*	**varies**	**25**
Could be Writing, Critical Reading, or Math		
Section 6: MATH	**18**	**25**
Regular Math	8	
Student-Produced ("grid type")	10	
Section 8: MATH	**16**	**20**
Regular Math	16	

*The order of the sections on the actual test varies, since the SAT has several different forms.

Note: One of the sections is experimental. An experimental section does not count in your SAT score. You cannot tell which of the sections of the test is experimental.

Part II
The 101 Most Important Math Questions You Need to Know How to Solve

Take This Test to Determine Your Basic (as Contrasted with Strategic) Math Weaknesses (Diagnosis and Corrective Measures Follow Test)

101 Math Questions
Answer Sheet

A. Fractions

1.
2.
3.
4.
5.

B. Even–Odd Relations

6.
7.
8.
9.
10.
11.
12.

C. Factors

13.
14.
15.
16.
17.
18.
19.
20.
21.

D. Exponents

22.
23.
24.
25.
26.
27.
28.
29.
30.
31.
32.

E. Percentages

33.
34.
35.

F. Equations

36.
37.
38.
39.
40.

G. Angles
(Vertical, Supplementary)

41.
42.
43.
44.

H. Angles (Parallel Lines)

45.
46.
47.
48.
49.
50.
51.

I. Triangles

52.
53.
54.
55.
56.
57.
58.
59.
60.
61.
62.
63.
64.
65.

J. Circles

66.
67.
68.
69.
70.

K. Other Figures

71.
72.
73.
74.
75.
76.
77.
78.
79.
80.

L. Number Lines

81.
82.

M. Coordinates

83.
84.
85.
86.

N. Inequalities

87.
88.
89.
90.
91.
92.

O. Averages

93.
94.

P. Shortcuts

95.
96.
97.
98.
99.
100.
101.

101 Math Questions Test

Following are the 101 most important math questions you should know how to solve. After you take the test, check to see whether your answers are the same as those described, and whether or not you answered the question in the way described. After a solution, there is usually (where appropriate) a rule or generalization about the math concept just used. Make sure that you understand this generalization or rule, as it will apply to many other questions. Remember that these are the most important basic math questions you need to know how to solve. Make sure that you understand *all of them* before taking any standardized math test such as the SAT.

Do not guess at any answer! Leave answer blank if you don't know how to solve.

A. Fractions

1. $\dfrac{\frac{a}{b}}{c} =$

   (A) $\dfrac{ab}{c}$

   (B) $\dfrac{ac}{b}$

   (C) $\dfrac{a}{bc}$

   (D) abc

   (E) None of these.

2. $\dfrac{1}{\frac{1}{y}} =$

   (A) y

   (B) y^2

   (C) $\dfrac{1}{y}$

   (D) infinity

   (E) None of these.

3. $\dfrac{\frac{a}{b}}{c} =$

   (A) $\dfrac{a}{bc}$

   (B) $\dfrac{ac}{b}$

   (C) $\dfrac{ab}{c}$

   (D) abc

   (E) None of these.

4. $\dfrac{\frac{1}{x}}{y} =$

   (A) xy

   (B) $\dfrac{x}{y}$

   (C) $\dfrac{y}{x}$

   (D) $\left(\dfrac{x}{y}\right)^2$

   (E) None of these.

5. $\dfrac{\dfrac{a}{b}}{\dfrac{b}{a}} =$

 (A) $\dfrac{b^2}{a^2}$

 (B) $\dfrac{a^2}{b^2}$

 (C) 1

 (D) $\dfrac{a}{b}$

 (E) None of these.

B. Even–Odd Relations

6. ODD INTEGER × ODD INTEGER =

 (A) odd integer only
 (B) even integer only
 (C) even or odd integer

7. ODD INTEGER + or − ODD INTEGER =

 (A) odd integer only
 (B) even integer only
 (C) even or odd integer

8. EVEN INTEGER × EVEN INTEGER =

 (A) odd integer only
 (B) even integer only
 (C) even or odd integer

9. EVEN INTEGER + or − EVEN INTEGER =

 (A) odd integer only
 (B) even integer only
 (C) even or odd integer

10. (ODD INTEGER)$^{ODD\ POWER}$ =

 (A) odd integer only
 (B) even integer only
 (C) even or odd integer

11. (EVEN INTEGER)$^{EVEN\ POWER}$ =

 (A) odd integer only
 (B) even integer only
 (C) even or odd integer

12. (EVEN INTEGER)$^{ODD\ POWER}$ =

 (A) odd integer only
 (B) even integer only
 (C) even or odd integer

C. Factors

13. $(x+3)(x+2) =$
 (A) $x^2 + 5x + 6$
 (B) $x^2 + 6x + 5$
 (C) $x^2 + x + 6$
 (D) $2x + 5$
 (E) None of these.

14. $(x+3)(x-2) =$
 (A) $x^2 - x + 6$
 (B) $x^2 + x + 5$
 (C) $x^2 + x - 6$
 (D) $2x + 1$
 (E) None of these.

15. $(x-3)(y-2) =$
 (A) $xy - 5y + 6$
 (B) $xy - 2x - 3y + 6$
 (C) $x + y + 6$
 (D) $xy - 3y + 2x + 6$
 (E) None of these.

16. $(a+b)(b+c) =$
 (A) $ab + b^2 + bc$
 (B) $a + b^2 + c$
 (C) $a^2 + b^2 + ca$
 (D) $ab + b^2 + ac + bc$
 (E) None of these.

17. $(a+b)(a-b) =$
 (A) $a^2 + 2ba - b^2$
 (B) $a^2 - 2ba - b^2$
 (C) $a^2 - b^2$
 (D) 0
 (E) None of these.

18. $(a+b)^2 =$

    (A) $a^2 + 2ab + b^2$
    (B) $a^2 + b^2$
    (C) $a^2 + b^2 + ab$
    (D) $2a + 2b$
    (E) None of these.

19. $-(a-b) =$

    (A) $a - b$
    (B) $-a - b$
    (C) $a + b$
    (D) $b - a$
    (E) None of these.

20. $a(b+c) =$

    (A) $ab + ac$
    (B) $ab + c$
    (C) abc
    (D) $ab + bc$
    (E) None of these.

21. $-a(b-c) =$

    (A) $ab - ac$
    (B) $-ab - ac$
    (C) $ac - ab$
    (D) $ab + ac$
    (E) None of these.

D. Exponents

22. $10^5 =$

    (A) 1000
    (B) 10,000
    (C) 100,000
    (D) 1,000,000
    (E) None of these.

23. $107076.5 = 1.070765 \times$

    (A) 10^4
    (B) 10^5
    (C) 10^6
    (D) 10^7
    (E) None of these.

24. $a^2 \times a^5 =$

    (A) a^{10}
    (B) a^7
    (C) a^3
    (D) $(2a)^{10}$
    (E) None of these.

25. $(ab)^7 =$

    (A) ab^7
    (B) $a^7 b$
    (C) $a^7 b^7$
    (D) $a^{14} b^{14}$
    (E) None of these.

26. $\left(\dfrac{a}{c}\right)^8 =$

    (A) $\dfrac{a^8}{c^8}$

    (B) $\dfrac{a^8}{c}$

    (C) $\dfrac{a}{c^8}$

    (D) $\dfrac{a^7}{c}$

    (E) None of these.

27. $a^4 \times b^4 =$

    (A) $(ab)^4$
    (B) $(ab)^8$
    (C) $(ab)^{16}$
    (D) $(ab)^{12}$
    (E) None of these.

28. $a^{-3} \times b^5 =$

    (A) $\dfrac{b^5}{a^3}$

    (B) $(ab)^2$
    (C) $(ab)^{-15}$

    (D) $\dfrac{a^3}{b^5}$

    (E) None of these.

29. $(a^3)^5 =$
   (A) a^8
   (B) a^2
   (C) a^{15}
   (D) a^{243}
   (E) None of these.

30. $2a^{-3} =$
   (A) $\dfrac{2}{a^3}$
   (B) $2a^3$
   (C) $2\sqrt[3]{a}$
   (D) a^{-6}
   (E) None of these.

31. $2a^m \times \dfrac{1}{3}a^{-n} =$
   (A) $\dfrac{2}{3}a^{m+n}$
   (B) $\dfrac{2a^m}{3a^n}$
   (C) $\dfrac{2}{3}a^{-mn}$
   (D) $-\dfrac{2}{3}a^{mn}$
   (E) None of these.

32. $3^2 + 3^{-2} + 4^1 + 6^0 =$
   (A) $8\dfrac{1}{9}$
   (B) $12\dfrac{1}{9}$
   (C) $13\dfrac{1}{9}$
   (D) $14\dfrac{1}{9}$
   (E) None of these.

E. Percentages

33. 15% of 200 =
   (A) 3
   (B) 30
   (C) 300
   (D) 3,000
   (E) None of these.

34. What is 3% of 5?
   (A) $\dfrac{5}{3}\%$
   (B) 15
   (C) $\dfrac{3}{20}$
   (D) $\dfrac{3}{5}$
   (E) None of these.

35. What percent of 3 is 6?
   (A) 50
   (B) 20
   (C) 200
   (D) $\dfrac{1}{2}$
   (E) None of these.

F. Equations

36. If $y^2 = 16$, $y =$
   (A) +4 only
   (B) −4 only
   (C) + or −4
   (D) + or −8
   (E) None of these.

37. If $x - y = 10$, $y =$
   (A) $x - 10$
   (B) $10 + x$
   (C) $10 - x$
   (D) 10
   (E) None of these.

38. What is the value of x if $x + 4y = 7$ and $x - 4y = 8$?
   (A) 15
   (B) $\dfrac{15}{2}$
   (C) 7
   (D) $\dfrac{7}{2}$
   (E) None of these.

39. What is the value of x and y if $x - 2y = 2$ and $2x + y = 4$?
   (A) $x = 2, y = 0$
   (B) $x = 0, y = -2$
   (C) $x = -1, y = 2$
   (D) $x = 0, y = 2$
   (E) None of these.

40. If $\dfrac{x}{5} = \dfrac{7}{12}$, $x =$
   (A) $\dfrac{35}{12}$
   (B) $\dfrac{12}{35}$
   (C) $\dfrac{7}{60}$
   (D) $\dfrac{60}{7}$
   (E) None of these.

G. Angles (Vertical, Supplementary)

Questions 41–42 refer to the diagram below:

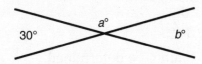

41. $a =$
   (A) 30
   (B) 150
   (C) 45
   (D) 90
   (E) None of these.

42. $b =$
   (A) 30
   (B) 150
   (C) 45
   (D) 90
   (E) None of these.

Question 43 refers to the diagram below:

43. $a + b =$
   (A) 155
   (B) 165
   (C) 180
   (D) 145
   (E) None of these.

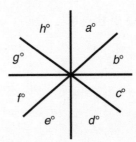

44. What is the value of $a + b + c + d + e + f + g + h$ in the diagram above?
   (A) 180
   (B) 240
   (C) 360
   (D) 540
   (E) None of these.

H. Angles (Parallel Lines)

Questions 45–51 refer to the diagram below:

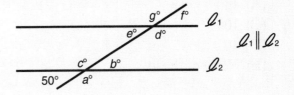

45. $a =$
   (A) 50
   (B) 130
   (C) 100
   (D) 40
   (E) None of these.

46. $b =$
   (A) 50
   (B) 130
   (C) 100
   (D) 40
   (E) None of these.

47. $c =$
   (A) 50
   (B) 130
   (C) 100
   (D) 40
   (E) None of these.

48. $d =$
   (A) 50
   (B) 130
   (C) 100
   (D) 40
   (E) None of these.

49. $e =$
   (A) 50
   (B) 130
   (C) 100
   (D) 40
   (E) None of these.

50. $f =$
   (A) 50
   (B) 130
   (C) 100
   (D) 40
   (E) None of these.

51. $g =$
   (A) 50
   (B) 130
   (C) 100
   (D) 40
   (E) None of these.

I. Triangles

52.

(Note: Figure is not drawn to scale.)

$a =$

   (A) 70
   (B) 40

   (C) $\dfrac{xy}{70}$

   (D) Cannot be determined.
   (E) None of these.

53.

(Note: Figure is not drawn to scale.)

$x =$

   (A) 3

   (B) $\dfrac{50}{3}$

   (C) $3\sqrt{2}$

   (D) Cannot be determined.
   (E) None of these.

54.

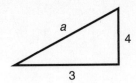

(Note: Figure is not drawn to scale.)

Which is a possible value for *a*?

(A) 1
(B) 6
(C) 10
(D) 7
(E) None of these.

55.

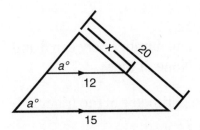

(Note: Figure is not drawn to scale.)

In the triangle above, $x =$
(A) 12
(B) 16
(C) 15
(D) 10
(E) None of these.

56.

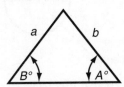

In the triangle above, if B > A, then

(A) $b = a$
(B) $b > a$
(C) $b < a$
(D) A relation between *b* and *a* cannot be determined.
(E) None of these.

57.

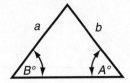

In the triangle above, if $b < a$, then

(A) B > A
(B) B = A
(C) B < A
(D) A relation between B and A cannot be determined.
(E) None of these.

58.

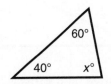

In the triangle above, $x =$
(A) 100
(B) 80
(C) 90
(D) 45
(E) None of these.

59.

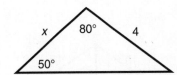

(Note: Figure is not drawn to scale.)

In the triangle above, $x =$
(A) $4\sqrt{2}$
(B) 8
(C) 4
(D) a number between 1 and 4
(E) None of these.

60.

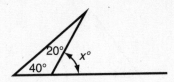

In the diagram above, $x =$
(A) 40
(B) 20
(C) 60
(D) 80
(E) None of these.

61.

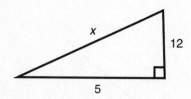

(Note: Figure is not drawn to scale.)

In the right triangle above as shown, $x =$
(A) 17
(B) 13
(C) 15
(D) $12\sqrt{2}$
(E) None of these.

Questions 62–63 refer to the diagram below:

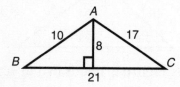

(Note: Figure is not drawn to scale.)

62. The perimeter of the triangle ABC is
(A) 16
(B) 48
(C) 168
(D) 84
(E) None of these.

63. The area of triangle ABC is
(A) 170
(B) 85
(C) 168
(D) 84
(E) None of these.

Questions 64–65 refer to the diagram below:

64. The area of the triangle is
(A) 6
(B) 7
(C) 12
(D) any number between 5 and 7
(E) None of these.

65. The perimeter of the triangle is
(A) 7
(B) 12
(C) 15
(D) any number between 7 and 12
(E) None of these.

J. Circles

Questions 66–67 refer to the diagram below:

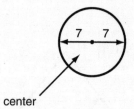

center

66. The area of the circle is
(A) 49
(B) 49π
(C) 14π
(D) 196π
(E) None of these.

67. The circumference of the circle is

   (A) 14π
   (B) 7π
   (C) 49π
   (D) 14
   (E) None of these.

68.

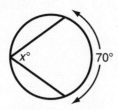

In the diagram above, $x =$
   (A) 70
   (B) 35
   (C) 90
   (D) a number that cannot be determined
   (E) None of these.

69.

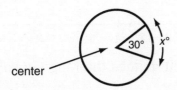

In the diagram above, $x =$
   (A) 30
   (B) 60
   (C) 90
   (D) a number that cannot be determined
   (E) None of these.

70.

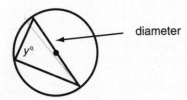

In the diagram above, $y =$
   (A) 145
   (B) 60
   (C) 90
   (D) a number that cannot be determined
   (E) None of these.

K. Other Figures

Questions 71–72 refer to the diagram below:

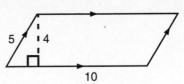

71. The area of the figure is

   (A) 15
   (B) 20
   (C) 40
   (D) 50
   (E) None of these.

72. The perimeter of the figure is

   (A) 15
   (B) 30
   (C) 40
   (D) 50
   (E) None of these.

Questions 73–75 refer to the figure below:

ABCD is a rectangle.

73. What is *BC* if *AD* = 6?

   (A) 4
   (B) 6
   (C) 8
   (D) 10
   (E) 12

74. What is *DC* if *AB* = 8?

   (A) 4
   (B) 6
   (C) 8
   (D) 10
   (E) 12

75. What is *DB* if *AC* = 10?

    (A) 4
    (B) 6
    (C) 8
    (D) 10
    (E) 12

Questions 76–77 refer to the diagram below:

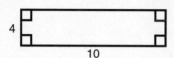

76. The area of the figure is

    (A) 14
    (B) 40
    (C) 80
    (D) 28
    (E) None of these.

77. The perimeter of the figure is

    (A) 14
    (B) 28
    (C) 36
    (D) 40
    (E) None of these.

Questions 78–79 refer to the figure below:

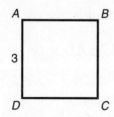

ABCD is a square; *AC* = 3.

78. What is the area of the square?

    (A) 9
    (B) 12
    (C) 16
    (D) 20
    (E) None of these.

79. What is the perimeter of the square?

    (A) 9
    (B) 12
    (C) 16
    (D) 20
    (E) None of these.

80. The volume of the rectangular solid below is

    (A) 48
    (B) 64
    (C) 128
    (D) 72
    (E) None of these.

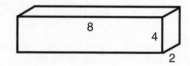

L. Number Lines

Questions 81–82 refer to the diagram below:

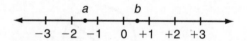

81. Which defines the range in values of *b* best?

    (A) $1 > b > -2$
    (B) $2 > b > 0$
    (C) $1 > b > 0$
    (D) $3 > b > -3$
    (E) $b > 0$

82. Which defines the range in values of *a* best?

    (A) $a > -2$
    (B) $-1 > a > -2$
    (C) $0 > a > -2$
    (D) $-1 > a$
    (E) $0 > a > -3$

M. Coordinates

Questions 83–85 refer to the diagram below:

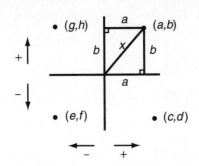

83. How many of the variables $a, b, c, d, e, f,$ g, h are positive?

   (A) 1
   (B) 2
   (C) 3
   (D) 4
   (E) 5

84. How many of the variables $a, b, c, d, e, f,$ g, h are negative?

   (A) 1
   (B) 2
   (C) 3
   (D) 4
   (E) 5

85. If $a = 3$, $b = 4$, what is x?

   (A) 3
   (B) 4
   (C) 5
   (D) 6
   (E) None of these.

86.

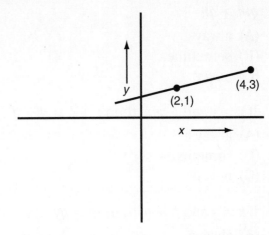

What is the slope of the line above?

   (A) −1
   (B) 0
   (C) +1
   (D) +2
   (E) +3

N. Inequalities

Note: Any variable can be positive or negative or 0.

87. If $x > y$, then $4x > 4y$

   (A) always
   (B) sometimes
   (C) never

88. If $x + y > z$, then $y > z − x$

   (A) always
   (B) sometimes
   (C) never

89. If $-4 < -x$, then $+4 > +x$

   (A) always
   (B) sometimes
   (C) never

90. If $m > n$, where q is any number, then $qm > qn$
    (A) always
    (B) sometimes
    (C) never

91. If $x > y$ and $p > q$, then $x + p > y + q$
    (A) always
    (B) sometimes
    (C) never

92. If $x > y$ and $p > q$, then $xp > qy$
    (A) always
    (B) sometimes
    (C) never

O. Averages

93. What is the average of 30, 40, and 80?
    (A) 150
    (B) 75
    (C) 50
    (D) 45
    (E) None of these.

94. What is the average speed in mph of a car traveling 40 miles for 4 hours?
    (A) 160
    (B) 10
    (C) 120
    (D) 30
    (E) None of these.

P. Shortcuts

95. Which is greater? (Don't calculate a common denominator!)
$$\frac{7}{16} \text{ or } \frac{3}{7}$$
    (A) $\frac{7}{16}$
    (B) $\frac{3}{7}$
    (C) They are equal.
    (D) A relationship cannot be determined.

96. Add: $\frac{7}{12} + \frac{3}{5} =$
    (A) $1\frac{11}{60}$
    (B) $1\frac{13}{60}$
    (C) $1\frac{15}{60}$
    (D) $\frac{10}{17}$
    (E) None of these.

97. Subtract: $\frac{7}{12} - \frac{3}{5} =$
    (A) $-\frac{1}{60}$
    (B) $-\frac{3}{60}$
    (C) $-1\frac{11}{60}$
    (D) $\frac{4}{7}$
    (E) None of these.

98. $\frac{4}{250} =$
    (A) .016
    (B) .04
    (C) .004
    (D) .025
    (E) None of these.

(Note: Do not divide 250 into 4 in the above question!)

99. What is c if

$$200 = \frac{a + b + c}{2} \text{ and } 80 = \frac{a + b}{3}?$$

(A) 160
(B) 140
(C) 120
(D) 100
(E) None of these.

100. What is the value of $95 \times 75 - 95 \times 74$?
(*Don't multiply 95×75 or 95×74!*)

(A) 65
(B) 75
(C) 85
(D) 95
(E) None of these.

101. Find the value of

$$\frac{140 \times 15}{5 \times 7}$$ (*Don't multiply 140×15!*)

(A) 20
(B) 40
(C) 60
(D) 90
(E) None of these.

101 Math Questions: Answers

A. Fractions

1. B
2. A
3. A
4. C
5. B

B. Even–Odd Relations

6. A
7. B
8. B
9. B
10. A
11. B
12. B

C. Factors

13. A
14. C
15. B
16. D
17. C
18. A
19. D
20. A
21. C

D. Exponents

22. C
23. B
24. B
25. C
26. A

27. A
28. A
29. C
30. A
31. B
32. D

E. Percentages

33. B
34. C
35. C

F. Equations

36. C
37. A
38. B
39. A
40. A

G. Angles
(Vertical, Supplementary)

41. B
42. A
43. A
44. C

H. Angles (Parallel Lines)

45. B
46. A
47. B
48. B
49. A
50. A
51. B

I. Triangles

52. A
53. A
54. B
55. B
56. B
57. C
58. B
59. C
60. C
61. B
62. B
63. D
64. A
65. B

J. Circles

66. B
67. A
68. B
69. A
70. C

K. Other Figures

71. C
72. B
73. B
74. C
75. D
76. B
77. B
78. A
79. B
80. B

L. Number Lines

81. C
82. B

M. Coordinates

83. D
84. D
85. C
86. C

N. Inequalities

87. A
88. A
89. A
90. B
91. A
92. B

O. Averages

93. C
94. B

P. Shortcuts

95. A
96. A
97. A
98. A
99. A
100. D
101. C

Basic Skills Math Diagnosis

Math area	Total questions	*If you got any of the answers to the following questions wrong, study answers to those questions.	Page in text for review	Complete Math Refresher: Refer to the sections of the Diagnostic Tests and Instructional Material (Part IV, starting on page 61) shown here for a refresher on the applicable rules.
A. Fractions	5	1–5	41	1-1–1-11
B. Even–Odd Relations	7	6–12	41	1-28, 1-29
C. Factors	9	13–21	42	2-6–2-10, 2-14–2-19
D. Exponents	11	22–32	42–43	1-26–1-27
E. Percentages	3	33–35	43	1-21–1-25
F. Equations	5	36–40	44	2-20–2-25
G. Angles (Vertical, Supplementary)	4	41–44	44–45	3-1
H. Angles (Parallel Lines)	7	45–51	45	3-2
I. Triangles	14	52–65	45–48	3-4, 3-1
J. Circles	5	66–70	48	3-5
K. Other Figures	10	71–80	48–49	3-3
L. Number Lines	2	81–82	49	4-1
M. Coordinates	4	83–86	49–50	4-2, 4-1
N. Inequalities	6	87–92	50	2-37–2-40
O. Averages	2	93–94	50–51	2-34
P. Shortcuts	7	95–101	51	1-8, 2-40

*Answer sheet is on pages 23–24.

Solutions, Generalizations, Rules

A. Fractions

1. (B)

$$\frac{\frac{a}{b}}{c} = a \times \frac{c}{b} = \boxed{\frac{ac}{b}}$$

INVERT TO MULTIPLY

Alternate way:

$$\frac{\frac{a}{b}}{\frac{c}{c}} = \frac{a}{b} \times \frac{c}{c} = \frac{ac}{\frac{b}{c} \times c} = \boxed{\frac{ac}{b}}$$

2. (A)

$$\frac{1}{\frac{1}{y}} = 1 \times \frac{y}{1} = \boxed{y}$$

INVERT TO MULTIPLY

3. (A)

$$\frac{\frac{a}{b}}{c} = \frac{\frac{a}{b}}{c} \times \frac{b}{b} = \boxed{\frac{a}{cb}}$$

4. (C)

$$\frac{1}{\frac{x}{y}} = 1 \times \frac{y}{x} = \boxed{\frac{y}{x}}$$

INVERT TO MULTIPLY

5. (B)

$$\frac{\frac{a}{b}}{\frac{b}{a}} = \frac{a}{b} \times \frac{a}{b} = \boxed{\frac{a^2}{b^2}}$$

INVERT TO MULTIPLY

Alternate way:

$$\frac{\frac{a}{b}}{\frac{b}{a}} = \frac{\frac{a}{b} \times a}{\frac{b}{a} \times a} = \frac{\frac{a^2}{b}}{\frac{b}{a}a} = \frac{\frac{a^2}{b}}{b}$$

$$= \frac{\frac{a^2}{b} \times b}{b \times b} = \boxed{\frac{a^2}{b^2}}$$

B. Even–Odd Relations

6. (A) ODD × ODD = $\boxed{\text{ODD}}$

$3 \times 3 = 9; 5 \times 5 = 25$

7. (B) ODD + or − ODD = $\boxed{\text{EVEN}}$

$5 + 3 = 8$
$5 - 3 = 2$

8. (B) EVEN × EVEN = $\boxed{\text{EVEN}}$

$2 \times 2 = 4; 4 \times 2 = 8$

9. (B) EVEN + or − EVEN = $\boxed{\text{EVEN}}$

$6 + 2 = 8; 10 - 4 = 6$

10. (A) $(\text{ODD})^{\text{ODD}} = \boxed{\text{ODD}}$

$3^3 = 3 \times 3 \times 3 = 27 \text{ (odd)}$
$1^{27} = 1 = \text{odd}$

11. (B) $(\text{EVEN})^{\text{EVEN}} = \boxed{\text{EVEN}}$

$2^2 = 4 \text{(even)}; 4^2 = 16 \text{ (even)}$

12. (B) $(\text{EVEN})^{\text{ODD}} = \boxed{\text{EVEN}}$

$2^3 = 2 \times 2 \times 2 = 8 \text{ (even)}$
$4^1 = 4 \text{ (even)}$

C. Factors

13. (A) $(x+3)(x+2) = x^2 \ldots$

$$(x+3)(x+2) = x^2 + 3x + 2x \ldots$$

$$(x+3)(x+2) = x^2 + 3x + 2x + 6$$

$$(x+3)(x+2) = \boxed{x^2 + 5x + 6}$$

14. (C) $(x+3)(x-2) = x^2 \ldots$

$$(x+3)(x-2) = x^2 - 2x + 3x \ldots$$

$$(x+3)(x-2) = x^2 - 2x + 3x - 6$$

$$(x+3)(x-2) = \boxed{x^2 + x - 6}$$

15. (B) $(x-3)(y-2) = xy \ldots$

$$(x-3)(y-2) = xy - 2x - 3y \ldots$$

$$(x-3)(y-2) = \boxed{xy - 2x - 3y + 6}$$

16. (D) $(a+b)(b+c) = ab \ldots$

$$(a+b)(b+c) = ab + ac + b^2 \ldots$$

$$(a+b)(b+c) = \boxed{ab + ac + b^2 + bc}$$

17. (C) $(a+b)(a-b) =$
$(a+b)(a-b) = a^2 \ldots$

$$(a+b)(a-b) = a^2 - ab + ba \ldots$$

$$(a+b)(a-b) = a^2 - ab + ba - b^2$$

$$(a+b)(a-b) = a^2 - ab + ba - b^2$$

$$\boxed{(a+b)(a-b) = a^2 - b^2} \quad \text{MEMORIZE}$$

18. (A) $(a+b)^2 = (a+b)(a+b)$
$(a+b)(a+b) = a^2 \ldots$

$$(a+b)(a+b) = a^2 + ab + ba \ldots$$

$$(a+b)(a+b) = a^2 + ab + ba + b^2$$

$$\boxed{(a+b)^2 = a^2 + 2ab + b^2} \quad \text{MEMORIZE}$$

19. (D) $-(a-b) = -a - (-b)$
$-(a-b) = -a + b$
$$\boxed{-(a-b) = b - a} \quad \text{MEMORIZE}$$

20. (A) $a(b+c) =$

$$a(b+c) = \boxed{ab + ac}$$

21. (C) $-a(b-c) =$

$$-a(b-c) = -ab - a(-c)$$

$$= -ab + ac = \boxed{ca - ab}$$

D. Exponents

22. (C) $10^5 = 100000$

5 zeroes

23. (B) $107076.5 = 1\,0\,7\,0\,7\,0\,.\,5$

5 4 3 2 1

$$= 1.070765 \times \boxed{10^5}$$

24. (B) ADD EXPONENTS

$$a^2 \times a^5 = \boxed{a^7}$$

$$a^m \times a^n = a^{m+n}$$

25. (C) $(ab)^7 = \boxed{a^7 b^7}$
$(ab)^m = a^m b^m$

26. (A)

$$\left(\frac{a}{c}\right)^8 = \boxed{\frac{a^8}{c^8}}; \left(\frac{a}{c}\right)^m = \frac{a^m}{c^m}$$

27. (A) $a^4 \times b^4 = \boxed{(ab)^4}; a^m \times b^m = (ab)^m$

28. (A)

$$a^{-3} \times b^5 = \boxed{\frac{b^5}{a^3}}$$

$$a^{-m} \times b^n = \boxed{\frac{b^n}{a^m}}$$

29. (C) $(a^3)^5 = \boxed{a^{15}}$

MULTIPLY
EXPONENTS

$$(a^m)^n = a^{mn}$$

30. (A)

$$2a^{-3} = \boxed{\frac{2}{a^3}}$$

$$ax^{-b} = \frac{a}{x^b}$$

Since $a^{-n} = \dfrac{1}{a^n}$

31. (B)

$$2a^m \times \frac{1}{3}a^{-n} = \frac{2}{3}a^m a^{-n}$$

$$= \frac{2}{3}a^{m-n} \text{ or } \boxed{\frac{2a^m}{3a^n}}$$

32. (D)

$$3^2 = 3 \times 3 = 9$$

$$3^{-2} = \frac{1}{3^2} = \frac{1}{9}$$

$$4^1 = 4$$

$$6^0 = 1 \text{ (any number to 0 power} = 1)$$

$$3^2 + 3^{-2} + 4^1 + 6^0 = 9 + \frac{1}{9} + 4 + 1 = \boxed{14\frac{1}{9}}$$

E. Percentages

Questions 33–35

Translate is $\rightarrow =$

of $\rightarrow \times$ (times)

percent (%) $\rightarrow \dfrac{}{100}$

what $\rightarrow x$ (or y, etc.)

33. (B) 15 % of 200 =
↓ ↓ ↓ ↓ ↓

$$15 \frac{}{100} \times 200 =$$

$$\frac{15}{100} \times 200 =$$

$$\frac{15}{100} \times 200 = \boxed{30}$$

34. (C) What is 3 % of 5?
↓ ↓ ↓ ↓ ↓ ↓

$$x = 3 \frac{}{100} \times 5$$

$$x = \frac{3}{100} \times 5$$

$$x = \frac{15}{100} = \boxed{\frac{3}{20}}$$

35. (C) What percent of 3 is 6?
↓ ↓ ↓ ↓ ↓ ↓

$$x \quad \frac{}{100} \quad \times \quad 3 \quad = \quad 6$$

$$\frac{x}{100} \times 3 = 6$$

$$\frac{3x}{100} = 6$$

$$3x = 600$$

$$x = \boxed{200}$$

F. Equations

36. (C) $y^2 = 16$

$$\sqrt{y^2} = \sqrt{16}$$

$$y = \boxed{\pm 4}$$

(Note: $\sqrt{y}$ means the *positive* square root of y; that is, the positive number that when multiplied by itself will give you the value of y.)

$$(\sqrt{y}) \times (\sqrt{y}) = y$$

37. (A) $x - y = 10$

Add y:

$$x - y + y = 10 + y$$

$$x = 10 + y$$

Subtract 10:

$$x - 10 = 10 - 10 + y$$

$$\boxed{x - 10 = y}$$

38. (B) Add equations:

$$x + 4y = 7$$

$$\underline{x - 4y = 8}$$

$$2x + \cancel{4y} - \cancel{4y} = 15$$

$$2x = 15$$

$$\boxed{x = \frac{15}{2}}$$

39. (A) $x - 2y = 2$ $\boxed{1}$

$\quad\quad 2x + y = 4$ $\boxed{2}$

Multiply $\boxed{1}$ by 2:

$$2(x - 2y) = 2(2)$$

We get:

$$2x - 4y = 4$$

Subract $\boxed{2}$ from $\boxed{3}$:

$$2x - 4y = 4 \quad\quad \boxed{3}$$

$$\underline{-(2x + y = 4)} \quad \boxed{2}$$

$$0 - 5y = 0$$

$$\boxed{y = 0} \quad\quad\quad\quad \boxed{4}$$

Substitute $\boxed{4}$ into either $\boxed{1}$ or $\boxed{2}$:

In $\boxed{1}$:

$$x - 2y = 2$$

$$x - 2(0) = 2$$

$$\boxed{x = 2}$$

40. (A) $\dfrac{x}{5} = \dfrac{7}{12}$

Cross-multiply x:

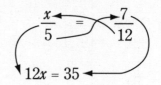

$$12x = 35$$

Divide by 12:

$$\frac{12x}{12} = \frac{35}{12}$$

$$\boxed{x = \frac{35}{12} = 2\frac{11}{12}}$$

G. Angles (Vertical, Supplementary)

This diagram refers to questions 41–42.

41. (B) $a°$ and 30° are supplementary angles (they add up to 180°). So $a + 30 = 180$; $a = \boxed{150}$.

42. (A) $b°$ and 30° are *vertical* angles (vertical angles are equal). So $b = \boxed{30}$.

This diagram refers to question 43.

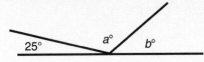

43. (A) $a°$, $b°$, and 25° make up a *straight* angle, which is 180°.
$$a + b + 25 = 180$$
$$a + b = 180 - 25$$
$$a + b = \boxed{155}$$

44. (C) The sum of the angles in the diagram is $\boxed{360°}$, the number of degrees around the circumference of a circle.

H. Angles (Parallel Lines)

This diagram refers to questions 45–51.

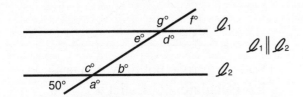

45. (B) $a + 50 = 180$
$a = \boxed{130}$

46. (A) $\boxed{b = 50}$ (vertical angles)

47. (B) $c = a$ (vertical angles)
$= \boxed{130}$

48. (B) $d = c$ (alternate interior angles are equal)
$= \boxed{130}$

49. (A) $e = b$ (alternate interior angles)
$= \boxed{50}$

50. (A) $f = e$ (vertical angles)
$= \boxed{50}$

51. (B) $g = d$ (vertical angles)
$= \boxed{130}$

I. Triangles

52. (A)

(Note: Figure is not drawn to scale.)

If two sides are equal, base angles are equal. Thus $a = \boxed{70°}$.

53. (A)

(Note: Figure is not drawn to scale.)

If base angles are equal, then sides are equal, so $\boxed{x = 3}$.

54. (B)

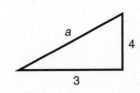

(Note: Figure is not drawn to scale.)

The sum of two sides must be *greater* than the third side. Try choices:

(A) $1 + 3 \not> 4$. (A) is not possible.
(B) $3 + 4 > 6$; $6 + 3 > 4$; $4 + 6 > 3$ ... OK.
(C) $3 + 4 \not> 10$. (C) is not possible.
(D) $4 + 3 = 7$. (D) is not possible.

55. (B) Using similar triangles, write a *proportion*.

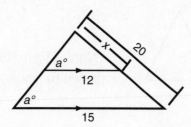

(Note: Figure is not drawn to scale.)

$$\frac{x}{20} = \frac{12}{15}$$
$$15x = 12 \times 20$$
$$x = \frac{12 \times 20}{15}$$
$$x = \frac{\overset{4}{\cancel{12}} \times \overset{4}{\cancel{20}}}{\underset{\underset{3}{\cancel{5}}}{\cancel{15}}} = \boxed{16}$$

In general:

$$\frac{m}{n} = \frac{q}{p} = \frac{r}{r+s}$$

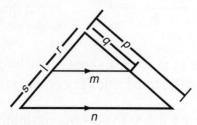

(Note: Figure is not drawn to scale.)

56. (B) The greater angle lies opposite the greater side and vice versa.
If $B > A$, $\boxed{b > a}$

57. (C) The greater side lies opposite the greater angle and vice versa.
If $b < a$, then $\boxed{B < A}$

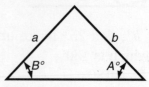

58. (B) Sum of angles of triangle = 180°.
So $40 + 60 + x = 180$.
$$100 + x = 180$$
$$\boxed{x = 80}$$

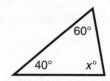

59. (C)

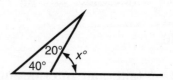

(Note: Figure is not drawn to scale.)
First calculate $\angle C$. Call it y.
$80 + 50 + y = 180$ (Sum of $\angle$s = 180°)
$y = 50$
Since $\angle C = y = 50$ and $\angle B = 50$, side $AB =$ side AC
$AB = \boxed{x = 4}$

60. (C) $x° = 20° + 40°$ (sum of *remote* interior angles = exterior angle)
$$\boxed{x = 60}$$

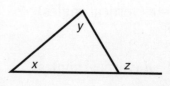

In general,

$z = x + y$

61. (B)

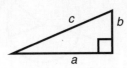

In right $\triangle$, $a^2 + b^2 = c^2$.
So for

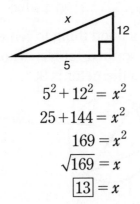

$$5^2 + 12^2 = x^2$$
$$25 + 144 = x^2$$
$$169 = x^2$$
$$\sqrt{169} = x$$
$$\boxed{13} = x$$

(Note: Specific right triangles you should memorize; use multiples to generate other triangles.)
Example of multiple:

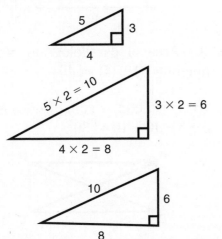

Memorize the following standard triangles:

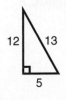

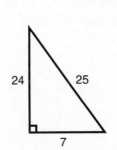

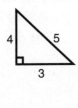

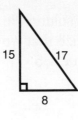

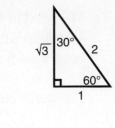

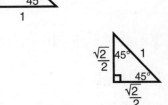

62. (B) Perimeter = sum of sides
$$10 + 17 + 21 = \boxed{48}$$

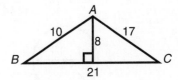

63. (D)
$$\text{Area of } \triangle = \frac{1}{2}hb$$
$$\text{Area of } \triangle = \frac{1}{2}(8)(21) = \boxed{84}$$

64. (A) Area of any triangle $= \frac{1}{2}$ base $\times$ height

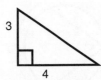

Here 4 is base and 3 is height. So
$$\text{area} = \frac{1}{2}(4 \times 3) = \frac{1}{2}(12) = \boxed{6}.$$

65. (B)

To find perimeter, we need to find the sum of the sides. The sum of the sides is $3 + 4 + x$.

We need to find x. From the solution in Question 61, we should realize that we have a 3-4-5 right triangle, so $x = 5$.

The perimeter is then $3 + 4 + 5 = \boxed{12}$.

Note that you could have found x by using the Pythagorean Theorem:

$$3^2 + 4^2 = x^2; 9 + 16 = x^2; 25 = x^2; \sqrt{25} = x; 5 = x$$

J. Circles

66. (B) Area $= \pi r^2 = \pi (7)^2$
    $= \boxed{49\pi}$

67. (A) Circumference $= 2\pi r = 2\pi (7)$
    $= \boxed{14\pi}$

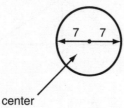

68. (B) Inscribed angle $= \dfrac{1}{2}$ arc

    $x = \dfrac{1}{2} 70$

    $= \boxed{35}$

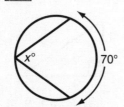

69. (A) Central angle $=$ arc

    $\boxed{30°} = x°$

    Note: The *total* number of degrees around the circumference is 360°. So a central angle of 30° like the one above cuts $\dfrac{30}{360} = \dfrac{1}{12}$ the circumference.

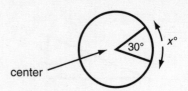

70. (C) The diameter cuts a 180° arc on the circle, so an inscribed angle $y = \dfrac{1}{2}$ arc $= \dfrac{1}{2}(180°) = \boxed{90°}$.

    Here is a good thing to remember: Any inscribed angle whose triangle base is a diameter is 90°.

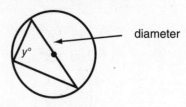

K. Other Figures

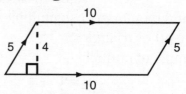

71. (C) Area of parallelogram $=$ base $\times$ height $= (10)(4) = \boxed{40}$

72. (B) Perimeter $=$ sum of sides $=$ $5 + 5 + 10 + 10 = \boxed{30}$

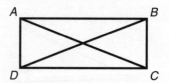

ABCD is a rectangle.

73. (B) In a rectangle (as in a parallelogram) opposite sides are equal. So $AD = BC = \boxed{6}$.

74. (C) In a rectangle (as in a parallelogram) opposite sides are equal.
So $DC = AB = \boxed{8}$.

75. (D) In a rectangle (but not in a parallelogram) the diagonals are equal.
So $DC = AC = \boxed{10}$.

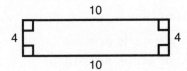

76. (B) Area of a rectangle = length × width $= 4 \times 10 = \boxed{40}$.

77. (B) Perimeter = sum of sides = $4 + 4 + 10 + 10 = \boxed{28}$.

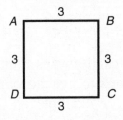

78. (A) Area of a square with side x is x^2. (All sides of a square are equal.) So length = width. Since $x = 3$, $x^2 = \boxed{9}$.

79. (B) Perimeter of a square is the sum of all sides of the square. Since all sides are equal, if one side is x, perimeter = $4x$. $x = 3$, so $4x = \boxed{12}$.

80. (B) Volume of rectangular solid shown below = $a \times b \times c$

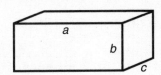

So for:

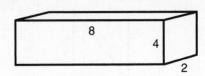

$a = 8, b = 4, c = 2$
and $a \times b \times c = 8 \times 4 \times 2 = \boxed{64}$

Note: Volume of cube shown below = $a \times a \times a = a^3$

L. Number Lines

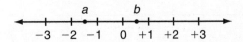

81. (C) b is between 0 and +1, so $\boxed{1 > b > 0}$

82. (B) a is between −2 and −1, so $\boxed{-1 > a > -2}$

M. Coordinates

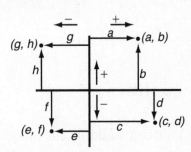

Horizontal right = +
Horizontal left = −
Vertical up = +
Vertical down = −

83. (D) $a, b, c,$ and h are positive (4 coordinates)

84. (D) $d, e, f,$ and g are negative (4 coordinates)

85. (C)

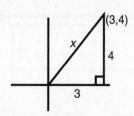

Remember the 3-4-5 right triangle. $\boxed{x = 5}$
You can also use the Pythagorean Theorem:
$3^2 + 4^2 = x^2$; $9 + 16 = x^2$; $x^2 = 25$; $\boxed{x = 5}$

86 (A)

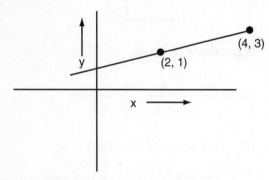

The slope of a line $y = mx + b$ is m. If two points (x_1, y_1) and (x_2, y_2) are on the line then the slope is $\frac{y_2 - y_1}{x_2 - x_1} = m$.

Here $x_1 = 2$, $y_1 = 1$, $x_2 = 4$, $y_2 = 3$

so $\frac{y_2 - y_1}{x_2 - x_1} = \frac{3 - 1}{4 - 2} = 1$.

N. Inequalities

87. (A) You can multiply an inequality by a positive number and retain the same inequality:

$x > y$

$\boxed{4x > 4y}$ $\boxed{\text{ALWAYS}}$

88. (A) You can subtract the same number from both sides of an inequality and retain the same inequality:

$x + y > z$
$x + y - x > z - x$
$\boxed{y > z - x}$ $\boxed{\text{ALWAYS}}$

89. (A) If you multiply an inequality by a minus sign, you *reverse* the original inequality sign:

$-4 < -x$
$(-4 < -x)$
$\boxed{-4 > +x}$ $\boxed{\text{ALWAYS}}$

90. (B) If $m > n$,

$qm > qn$ if q is *positive*
$qm < qn$ if q is *negative*
$qm = qn$ if q is *zero*
So, $\boxed{qm > qn}$ $\boxed{\text{SOMETIMES}}$

91. (A) You can always add inequality relations:

$x > y$
$\underline{+\, p > q}$
$x + p > y + q$ $\boxed{\text{ALWAYS}}$

92. (B) You can't always multiply inequality relations to get the same inequality relation. For example:

$3 > 2$ $\qquad\qquad$ $3 > 2$
$\underline{\times -2 > -3}$ $\qquad$ $\underline{\times 2 > 1}$
$-6 \not> -6$ $\qquad\qquad$ $6 > 2$

However, if x, y, p, q are positive, then if $x > y$ and $p > q$, $xp > yq$.

O. Averages

93. (C) Average of $30 + 40 + 80 =$

$\frac{30 + 40 + 80}{3} = \boxed{50}$

Average of $x + y + z + t + \ldots =$

$\frac{x + y + z + t + \ldots}{\text{number of terms}}$

94. (B) Average speed =
$\dfrac{\text{TOTAL DISTANCE}}{\text{TOTAL TIME}}$

Distance = 40 miles, time = 4 hours

Average speed

$$= \frac{40 \text{ miles}}{4 \text{ hours}} = \boxed{10 \text{ miles per hour}}$$

P. Shortcuts

95. Don't get a common denominator if you can do something more easily:

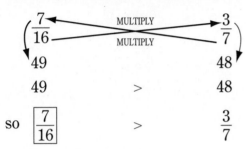

$$49 \qquad > \qquad 48$$

so $\boxed{\dfrac{7}{16}} \qquad > \qquad \dfrac{3}{7}$

96. (A)

$$\frac{7}{12} \underset{\text{MULTIPLY}}{\overset{\text{MULTIPLY}}{+}} \frac{3}{5} = \frac{7 \times 5 + 3 \times 12}{12 \times 5}$$

$$= \frac{35 + 36}{60}$$

$$= \frac{71}{60} = \boxed{1 \frac{11}{60}}$$

97. (A)

$$\frac{7}{12} - \frac{3}{5} = \frac{7 \times 5 + 3 \times 12}{12 \times 5}$$

$$\frac{7}{12} \underset{\text{MULTIPLY}}{\overset{\text{MULTIPLY}}{+}} \frac{3}{5} = \frac{7 \times 5 + 3 \times 12}{12 \times 5}$$

$$= \frac{35 - 36}{60}$$

$$= \boxed{-\frac{1}{60}}$$

98. (A) Don't divide by 250! Multiply both numerator and denominator by 4:

$$\frac{4}{250} \times \frac{4}{4} = \frac{16}{1,000} = \boxed{0.016}$$

99. (A) Get rid of denominators!

$$200 = \frac{a+b+c}{2} \qquad \boxed{1}$$

Multiply $\boxed{1}$ by 2:

$$200 \times 2 = a + b + c \qquad \boxed{2}$$

$$80 = \frac{a+b}{3} \qquad \boxed{3}$$

Multiply $\boxed{3}$ by 3:

$$80 \times 3 = a + b \qquad \boxed{4}$$

Now subtract $\boxed{4}$ from $\boxed{2}$:

$$200 \times 2 - 80 \times 3 = a + b + c - (a + b)$$

$$400 - 240 = \not{a} + \not{b} + c - \not{a} - \not{b}$$

$$400 - 240 = c$$

$$\boxed{160} = c$$

100. (D) Don't multiply 95×75 or 95×74! Factor *common* 95:

$$95 \times 75 - 95 \times 74 = 95(75 - 74)$$

$$= 95(1)$$

$$= \boxed{95}$$

101. (C) $\dfrac{140 \times 15}{5 \times 7}$

Don't multiply 140×15 if you can first *reduce*.

$$\frac{\overset{20}{\cancel{140}} \times 15}{5 \times \cancel{7}_{1}} = \frac{20 \times 15}{5}$$

Further reduce:

$$\frac{20 \times \overset{3}{\cancel{15}}}{\underset{1}{\cancel{5}}} = \boxed{60}$$

Part III
Mini Math Refresher

Use This Section to Get a Concise View of the Minimum Math Rules and Concepts Required for the SAT

Note: Each rule or concept is accompanied by a number in parentheses—for example, (1-25). This number refers to the section in the diagnostic tests and instructional material (page 61) where you can get a more comprehensive review of that particular concept or rule.

1. Rules of Algebra

$$a + b = b + a$$
$$a \times b = b \times a$$

$$(a + b) + c = a + (b + c)$$
$$(a \times b) \times c = a \times (b \times c)$$

(2-6, 2-9)

$$a (b + c) = ab + ab$$
Example: $2 (3 + 4) = 2 \times 3 + 2 \times 4$
$$= \quad 6 \quad + \quad 8$$
$$= \quad 14$$

- -

$$a^2 = a \times a$$
$$a^3 = a \times a \times a$$
$$a^0 = 1$$
$$a^{-n} = \frac{1}{a^n}$$

Example: $2^{-3} = \frac{1}{2^3} = \frac{1}{8}$

$$a^m \times a^n = a^{m+n}$$
Example: $2^3 \times 2^5 = 2^{3+5} = 2^8$
$$a^4 \times a^6 = a^{10}$$

$$\frac{a^n}{a^p} = a^{n-p}$$

Examples: $\frac{2^6}{2^2} = 2^4 ; \frac{2^3}{2^5} = 2^{-2}$

(1-26, 2-9)

$$(a^m)^n = a^{mn}$$
Example:
$$(3^4)^2 = 3^{4 \times 2}$$
$$= 3^8$$
$$(ab)^m = a^m b^m$$
Example: $(2 \times 3)^7 = 2^7 \times 3^7$

(2-9, 2-16)

$$(a + b)(a - b) = a^2 - b^2$$
$$(a + b)^2 = (a + b)(a + b) = a^2 + 2ab + b^2$$
$$(a - b)^2 = (a - b)(a - b) = a^2 - 2ab + b^2$$
$$-(a - b) = b - a$$
$$(a + b)(c + d) = ac + bd + bc + ad$$

(1-27)

$\sqrt{16} = 4$ because $4 \times 4 = 16$

$\sqrt{36} = 6$ because $6 \times 6 = 36$

If $\sqrt{x} = n$, then $n \times n = x$; x cannot be a negative number

2. Fractions

(1-5, 1-10)

$$\frac{a}{b} \times \frac{c}{d} = \frac{ac}{bd} \qquad \frac{a}{b} \div \frac{c}{d} = \frac{a}{b} \times \frac{d}{c} = \frac{ad}{bc}$$

$\dfrac{n}{0}$ is undefined $\qquad \dfrac{n}{n} = 1 \qquad 1 \times n = n$

(1-8)

Common denominators example:

$$\frac{2}{3} + \frac{4}{5} = \frac{2}{3} \times \frac{5}{5} + \frac{4}{5} \times \frac{3}{3} = \frac{10}{15} + \frac{12}{15} = \frac{22}{15} \text{ or } 1\frac{7}{15}$$

(1-8)

Shortcut: $\dfrac{2}{3} + \dfrac{4}{5} = \dfrac{10 + 12}{15}$

$$\frac{a}{b} + \frac{c}{d} = \frac{ad + bc}{bd}$$

SOME GEOMETRY

3. Angles

(3-1)

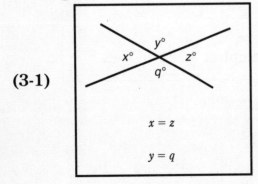

$x = z$

$y = q$

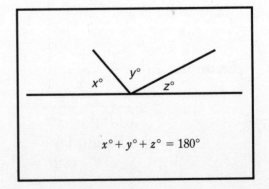

$x° + y° + z° = 180°$

4. Triangles

(3-4)

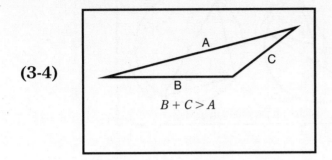

$$B + C > A$$

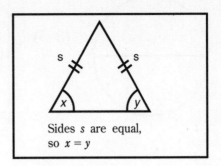

Sides s are equal,
so $x = y$

> **Reminder:** > means "greater than"
> < means "less than"

(3-4)

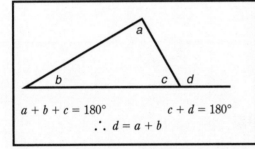

$$a + b + c = 180° \qquad c + d = 180°$$
$$\therefore\ d = a + b$$

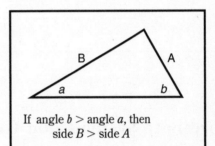

If angle b > angle a, then
side B > side A

(3-4)

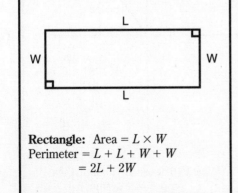

$$a^2 + b^2 = c^2$$

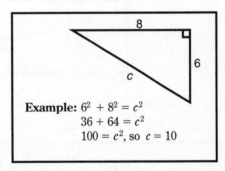

Example: $6^2 + 8^2 = c^2$
$36 + 64 = c^2$
$100 = c^2$, so $c = 10$

5. Areas

(3-6)

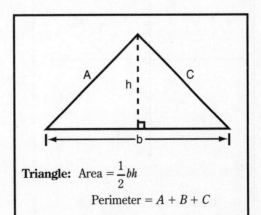

Rectangle: Area $= L \times W$
Perimeter $= L + L + W + W$
$= 2L + 2W$

Triangle: Area $= \dfrac{1}{2}bh$
Perimeter $= A + B + C$

(3-6) 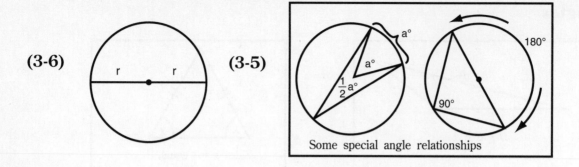 **(3-5)**

Some special angle relationships

Circle : Area = πr^2
Perimeter (circumference) = $2\pi r$ or
πd, where d = diameter = $2r$
π = an irrational constant = 3.14159…

6. Coordinate Systems and Graphing

(4-1)

$$0 < x < 1$$

Number line:

$-2 \quad -1 \quad 0 \quad x \quad 1 \quad 2$

(4-3)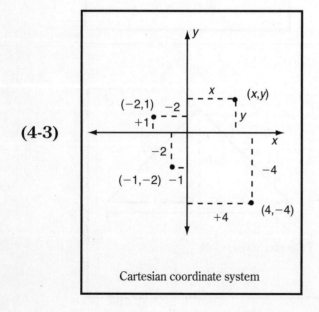

Cartesian coordinate system

(4-5)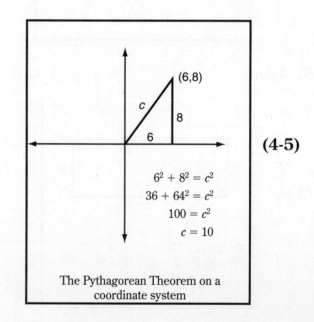

$6^2 + 8^2 = c^2$
$36 + 64^2 = c^2$
$100 = c^2$
$c = 10$

The Pythagorean Theorem on a
coordinate system

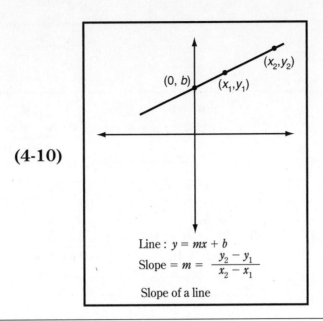

(4-10)

Line : $y = mx + b$

Slope $= m = \dfrac{y_2 - y_1}{x_2 - x_1}$

Slope of a line

7. Solving Equations

(2-20)

Addition Principle: if $a = b$ then $a + c = b + c$	**Multiplication Principle:** if $a = b$, then $ac = bc$

Principle of Zero: if $ab = 0$, then $a = 0$ or $b = 0$

(2-23)

Example: $x^2 - 5x + 6 = 0$
$(x - 2)(x - 3) = 0$
$x - 2 = 0$ or $x - 3 = 0$
$x = 2$ or $x = 3$

Basic Principle

(2-24, 2-25)

$$a + b = c$$
$$\underline{+ \qquad d = d}$$
$$a + b + d = c + d$$

Example:

$$5 + 6 = 11$$
$$\underline{+ \qquad 2 = 2}$$
$$5 + 6 + 2 = 11 + 2$$
$$13 = 13$$

Example: $a + b = 1$
$\underline{+ a - b = 3}$
$2a + 0 = 4$, or $2a = 4$
$a = 2$ **Substitute:** $2 + b = 1$
$b = -1$

8. Inequalities

Basic Principle

$$a > b$$
$$ac > bc \text{ if } c > 0$$

$$a > b$$
$$ac < bc \text{ if } c < 0$$

$$\begin{array}{r} a > b \\ + \quad c > d \\ \hline a + c > b + d \end{array}$$

(2-37, 2-38)

Examples:

$$8 > 7$$
$$8(4) > 7(4)$$
$$32 > 28$$

$$-3 < 9$$
$$-3(-2) > 9(-2)$$
$$6 > -18$$

$$\begin{array}{r} 5 > 4 \\ + \quad 4 > 3 \\ \hline 5 + 4 > 4 + 3 \\ 9 > 7 \end{array}$$

$$\begin{array}{r} 9 > 6 \\ + \quad -5 > -8 \\ \hline 9 + (-5) > 6 + (-8) \\ 4 > -2 \end{array}$$

(2-38)

Another type of inequality:

$$a < b < c$$

$$-2 < x < 5$$
$$2 > -x > -5 \text{ (multiplying}$$
$$\text{by } -1)$$

Relationships: Is it $>$, $<$, $=$?

(2-40)

Example:

$$\frac{3}{4} ? \frac{5}{6}$$

$$\downarrow$$

$$3 \times 6 ? 4 \times 5$$

$$\downarrow$$

$$18 < 20, \text{ so } \frac{3}{4} < \frac{5}{6}$$

(2-39)

Example:

$$a^2 > b^2$$
$$a ? b$$
$$a > b \text{ if } a > 0, b \geqq 0$$

Part IV
Diagnostic Tests and Instructional Material

How to Use the Diagnostic Tests and Instructional Material

Every math area that you will find on the actual SAT is covered in the following pages. For each math area, you have

1. **Diagnostic Test** *followed by*
2. **Solutions for the Test** *followed by*
3. **Instructional Material**

It is important that you take each of these Diagnostic Tests (in any order you wish) in order to find out where your math weaknesses lie. This is the first step in improving your math ability.

After you take a Diagnostic Test, find out how you did by referring to the answers (+ solutions) that follow the Diagnostic Test.

At the end of each solution, there is a hyphenated number (or numbers) in parentheses. This hyphenated number is keyed to the Instructional Material that follows the solutions. The number *before* the hyphen indicates the math area of the problem:

$$1 = \text{Arithmetic}$$
$$2 = \text{Algebra}$$
$$3 = \text{Plane Geometry}$$
$$4 = \text{Analytic Geometry}$$
$$5 = \text{Graphs and Charts}$$
$$6 = \text{Verbal Problems}$$

The number *after* the hyphen gives you the section (within the math area) that explains the rule or principle involved in solving the problem. For example, **1-12** means that the problem deals with decimals (which is part of Arithmetic); **2-20** refers to equations (part of Algebra).

Be sure that for every problem you get wrong, you study thoroughly the rule or principle involved.

Arithmetic
Fractions

Diagnostic Test on Fractions

1. 32 is what part of 96?

   (A) $\frac{32}{64}$ (D) $\frac{96}{32}$

   (B) $\frac{4}{5}$ (E) $\frac{32}{96}$

   (C) $\frac{1}{2}$

2. $17 + \frac{1}{4} =$

   (A) $\frac{17}{4}$ (D) $174\frac{1}{4}$

   (B) $17\frac{1}{4}$ (E) $\frac{1}{4}$

   (C) $4\frac{1}{4}$

3. Change $\frac{37}{5}$ to a mixed number.

   (A) $37\frac{1}{5}$ (D) $7\frac{2}{5}$

   (B) $15\frac{1}{2}$ (E) $5\frac{1}{5}$

   (C) $\frac{5}{37}$

4. Change the mixed number $11\frac{2}{3}$ to a fraction.

   (A) $\frac{35}{3}$ (D) $\frac{13}{3}$

   (B) $\frac{42}{3}$ (E) $\frac{112}{3}$

   (C) $\frac{21}{3}$

5. $\frac{4}{9} + \frac{1}{9} =$

   (A) $\frac{5}{18}$ (D) $\frac{4}{9}$

   (B) $\frac{5}{9}$ (E) $\frac{3}{18}$

   (C) $\frac{3}{9}$

6. Reduce $\frac{36}{90}$ to lowest terms.

   (A) 36   (D) $\frac{8}{10}$

   (B) $\frac{54}{90}$ (E) $\frac{4}{10}$

   (C) $\frac{2}{5}$

7. Find the product of $\frac{3}{8}$ and $\frac{5}{7}$.

   (A) $\frac{15}{56}$ (D) $\frac{3}{7}$

   (B) $\frac{8}{15}$ (E) $\frac{21}{40}$

   (C) 2

8. Find the reciprocal of $\frac{8}{3}$.

   (A) $\frac{4}{14}$ (D) $\frac{1}{3}$

   (B) $2\frac{2}{3}$ (E) 15

   (C) $\frac{3}{8}$

9. $\frac{8}{7}$ is equal to which other fraction?

   (A) $\frac{4}{14}$ (D) $\frac{16}{14}$

   (B) $\frac{21}{14}$ (E) $\frac{3}{14}$

   (C) $\frac{1}{14}$

10. John cut a 10-yard piece of cloth into 3 pieces. The first two pieces were each $2\frac{2}{3}$ yd. long. How long was the other piece?

    (A) $4\frac{2}{3}$ (D) $1\frac{1}{4}$

    (B) $5\frac{1}{3}$ (E) $8\frac{1}{3}$

    (C) $5\frac{2}{3}$

11. Find the sum of $12\frac{1}{5}$, $2\frac{2}{5}$, and $7\frac{4}{5}$.

    (A) $21\frac{1}{5}$ (D) $2\frac{2}{5}$

    (B) $22\frac{2}{5}$ (E) $13\frac{3}{5}$

    (C) $27\frac{7}{15}$

12. $3\frac{1}{4} + 4\frac{1}{3} =$

    (A) $7\frac{7}{12}$ (D) $7\frac{1}{6}$

    (B) $5\frac{1}{2}$ (E) $12\frac{2}{3}$

    (C) $7\frac{1}{12}$

13. $\frac{11}{12} \div \frac{1}{7} =$

    (A) $6\frac{5}{12}$ (D) $1\frac{5}{84}$

    (B) $7\frac{1}{12}$ (E) $\frac{1}{2}$

    (C) $\frac{11}{84}$

14. $\frac{1}{6} + \frac{1}{3} - \frac{1}{2} =$

    (A) 1   (D) 0

    (B) $\frac{1}{7}$ (E) $\frac{5}{6}$

    (C) $\frac{1}{6}$

15. Simplify the following fraction: $\dfrac{\frac{5}{8}}{\frac{1}{2}}$

    (A) $\frac{5}{16}$ (D) $\frac{2}{5}$

    (B) $\frac{1}{2}$ (E) $\frac{3}{4}$

    (C) $1\frac{1}{4}$

16. $12\frac{1}{2} \times \frac{4}{5} =$

    (A) $13\frac{3}{10}$ (D) 10

    (B) $12\frac{2}{5}$ (E) 15

    (C) $2\frac{1}{4}$

17. $\frac{5}{6}$ of $23\frac{2}{3}$ is

    (A) $23\frac{5}{9}$ (D) $17\frac{1}{3}$

    (B) $24\frac{1}{2}$ (E) $19\frac{13}{18}$

    (C) $11\frac{1}{6}$

18. $3\frac{1}{4} - 1\frac{3}{8} =$

    (A) $2\frac{1}{8}$ (D) $4\frac{5}{8}$

    (B) $1\frac{7}{8}$ (E) $1\frac{1}{2}$

    (C) $5\frac{1}{4}$

19. $16\frac{2}{3} \div 6\frac{1}{4} =$

    (A) $2\frac{5}{6}$ (D) $3\frac{5}{6}$

    (B) $1\frac{1}{3}$ (E) $2\frac{2}{3}$

    (C) $2\frac{1}{2}$

20. $\frac{5}{4} \times \frac{4}{10} =$

    (A) $\frac{1}{2}$ (D) $\frac{3}{4}$

    (B) $\frac{1}{4}$ (E) $\frac{1}{5}$

    (C) $\frac{1}{8}$

Solutions for Diagnostic Test

1. **(E)** To find what part of 96 the number 32 is, write a fraction whose numerator is 32 and whose denominator is 96. Thus, 32 is $\frac{32}{96}$ of 96. **(1-1)**

2. **(B)** The sum of an integer and a fraction like $\frac{1}{4}$ can be written as a mixed number, without the plus sign. Thus, $17 + \frac{1}{4} = 17\frac{1}{4}$. **(1-8)**

3. **(D)** To write $\frac{37}{5}$ as a mixed number, divide the denominator into the numerator. $37 \div 5 = 7$, remainder 2. Therefore, $\frac{37}{5} = 7\frac{2}{5}$. **(1-2)**

4. **(A)** The denominator of the fraction is 3. The numerator is $11 \cdot 3 + 2$, or 35. $11\frac{2}{3} = \frac{35}{3}$ **(1-3)**

5. **(B)** To add fractions with the same denominator, add the numerators. $\frac{4}{9} + \frac{1}{9} = \frac{5}{9}$ **(1-8)**

6. **(C)** Both 36 and 90 can be divided by 9, giving $\frac{36}{90} = \frac{4}{10}$. Now 4 and 10 can be divided by 2 giving $\frac{36}{90} = \frac{4}{10} = \frac{2}{5}$ **(1-4)**

7. **(A)** To multiply fractions, multiply the numerators and the denominators. $\frac{3}{8} \times \frac{5}{7} = \frac{3 \times 5}{8 \times 7} = \frac{15}{56}$ **(1-5)**

8. **(C)** To find the reciprocal of a fraction, interchange numerator and denominator. The reciprocal of $\frac{8}{3}$ is $\frac{3}{8}$. **(1-6)**

9. **(D)** To change $\frac{8}{7}$ to a fraction with denominator 14, we multiply $\frac{8}{7}$ by 14 to find the new numerator. $\frac{\frac{8}{7} \times 14}{14} = \frac{16}{14}$ **(1-7)**

10. **(A)** First change to fractions. 10 yards is $\frac{30}{3}$; $2\frac{2}{3}$ is $\frac{8}{3}$, so $2 \cdot 2\frac{2}{3}$ is $2 \cdot \frac{8}{3}$ or $\frac{16}{3}$. $10 - 2 \cdot 2\frac{2}{3} = \frac{30}{3} - \frac{16}{3} = \frac{14}{3} = 4\frac{2}{3}$. **(1-9)**

11. **(B)** One way to do this problem is to add the whole numbers and then the fractions. $12 + 2 + 7 = 21$; $\frac{1}{5} + \frac{2}{5} + \frac{4}{5} = \frac{7}{5}$ or $1\frac{2}{5}$. Now $21 + 1\frac{2}{5} = 22\frac{2}{5}$. **(1-8)**

12. **(A)** We add the whole numbers, then the fractions. $3 + 4 = 7$. 12 is a common denominator since $\frac{1}{4} = \frac{3}{12}$ and $\frac{1}{3} = \frac{4}{12}$ $\frac{1}{4} + \frac{1}{3} = \frac{7}{12}$. Altogether we have $7\frac{7}{12}$. **(1-8)**

13. **(A)** To divide two fractions, multiply the first by the reciprocal of the second. $\frac{11}{12} \div \frac{1}{7} = \frac{11}{12} \times \frac{7}{1} = \frac{77}{12} = 6\frac{5}{12}$ **(1-6)**

14. **(D)** A common denominator is 6. $\frac{1}{3} = \frac{2}{6}$, and $\frac{1}{2} = \frac{3}{6}$. $\frac{1}{6} + \frac{1}{3} - \frac{1}{2} = \frac{1}{6} + \frac{2}{6} - \frac{3}{6} = \frac{0}{6} = 0$ **(1-11)**

15. **(C)** A complex fraction is simplified by division.

$$\frac{\frac{5}{8}}{\frac{1}{2}} = \frac{5}{8} \div \frac{1}{2} = \frac{5}{8} \times \frac{2}{1} = \frac{5}{4} = 1\frac{1}{4}$$

(1-10)

16. **(D)** First change $12\frac{1}{2}$ to the mixed number $\frac{25}{2}$. Now $\frac{25}{2} \times \frac{4}{5} = 5 \times 2$, or 10, cancelling one factor of 5, and one factor of 2. **(1-5)**

17. **(E)** $23\frac{2}{3} = \frac{71}{3}$. "Of" means multiply. $\frac{5}{6} \times \frac{71}{3} = \frac{355}{18} = 19\frac{13}{18}$. **(1-5)**

18. **(B)** $3\frac{1}{4} = \frac{13}{4}, 1\frac{3}{8} = \frac{11}{8}$. A common denominator is 8. $\frac{13}{4} = \frac{26}{8}$.

$\frac{26}{8} - \frac{11}{8} = \frac{15}{8} = 1\frac{7}{8}$. **(1-9)**

19. **(E)** $16\frac{2}{3} = \frac{50}{3}$.

$6\frac{1}{4} = \frac{25}{4}$.

$16\frac{2}{3} \div 6\frac{1}{4} = \frac{50}{3} \div \frac{25}{4} = \frac{50}{3} \times \frac{4}{25}$.

Cancelling, this is $\frac{8}{3}$ or $2\frac{2}{3}$. **(1-6)**

20. **(B)** We cancel a 5 top and bottom to get $\frac{1}{8} \times \frac{4}{2}$. Then we cancel a 4 to get $\frac{1}{2} \times \frac{1}{2}$ or $\frac{1}{4}$. **(1-5)**

Instructional Material on Fractions

1-1 Fractions described

A fraction indicates a division, or a part of a number. Since fractions are numbers, they can be added, subtracted, multiplied, and divided. The numerator of a fraction tells how many parts we have. The denominator tells the total number of parts there are. Thus, in $\frac{3}{4}$, the numerator is 3, the denominator is 4, and the fraction means 3 divided by 4, or 3 parts out of 4.

> Since a fraction is a division, and division by zero is undefined, the denominator of a fraction cannot be zero. If the numerator is zero (and the denominator is not zero), then the fraction equals zero.

When working with fractions, an important rule to remember is:

> The value of a fraction is unchanged when the numerator and denominator are multiplied by the same quantity.

For example:

$$\frac{5}{9} = \frac{5 \times 3}{9 \times 3} = \frac{15}{27}$$

$$\frac{4}{8} = \frac{4 \times \frac{1}{4}}{8 \times \frac{1}{4}} = \frac{1}{2}$$

A number like $5\frac{1}{3}$ is called a mixed number. It means $5 + \frac{1}{3}$.

Practice Exercises for 1-1*

Find the numerator of the following fractions:

1. $\frac{5}{6}$ 2. $\frac{1}{9}$ 3. $\frac{12}{21}$ 4. $\frac{8}{9}$ 5. $\frac{11}{101}$

* Answers for Practice Exercises 1-1 through 1-29 begin on page 108.

6. $\dfrac{17}{19}$ 7. $\dfrac{3}{4}$ 8. $\dfrac{32}{41}$ 9. $\dfrac{201}{202}$ 10. $\dfrac{100}{101}$

Find the denominator of the following fractions:

11. $\dfrac{3}{5}$ 12. $\dfrac{4}{9}$ 13. $\dfrac{12}{21}$ 14. $\dfrac{11}{101}$ 15. $\dfrac{1}{2}$

16. $\dfrac{3}{4}$ 17. $\dfrac{23}{34}$ 18. $\dfrac{17}{31}$ 19. $\dfrac{16}{35}$ 20. $\dfrac{15}{4}$

1-2 To write a fraction as a mixed number

1) If the denominator is larger than the numerator, leave the fraction as it is.
2) If the denominator is smaller than the numerator, divide the numerator by the denominator. The whole number of the mixed number is the quotient. The numerator in the mixed number is the remainder, and the denominator is the same as in the original fraction.

For example: Write $\dfrac{19}{7}$ as a mixed number.

$19 \div 7 = 2$, remainder 5. The mixed number is $2\dfrac{5}{7}$.

Practice Exercises for 1-2

Write the following fractions as mixed numbers:

1. $\dfrac{20}{3}$ 2. $\dfrac{10}{7}$ 3. $\dfrac{7}{4}$ 4. $\dfrac{25}{8}$ 5. $\dfrac{17}{8}$

6. $\dfrac{15}{4}$ 7. $\dfrac{13}{2}$ 8. $\dfrac{18}{10}$ 9. $\dfrac{15}{8}$ 10. $\dfrac{16}{5}$

11. $\dfrac{12}{5}$ 12. $\dfrac{10}{4}$ 13. $\dfrac{9}{4}$ 14. $\dfrac{3}{2}$ 15. $\dfrac{13}{12}$

16. $\dfrac{25}{24}$ 17. $\dfrac{25}{3}$ 18. $\dfrac{17}{9}$ 19. $\dfrac{100}{11}$ 20. $\dfrac{15}{14}$

1-3 To write a mixed number as a fraction

1) The numerator is the whole number times the denominator, plus the old numerator.
2) The denominator is the old denominator.

For example: Express $5\frac{1}{3}$ as a fraction.

numerator: $5 \times 3 + 1 = 16$
denominator: 3
Therefore, $5\frac{1}{3} = \frac{16}{3}$.

Practice Exercises for 1-3

Write the following mixed numbers as fractions:

1. $3\frac{2}{3}$ 2. $16\frac{1}{4}$ 3. $5\frac{7}{8}$ 4. $2\frac{1}{2}$ 5. $3\frac{16}{17}$

6. $7\frac{1}{8}$ 7. $3\frac{1}{2}$ 8. $17\frac{1}{2}$ 9. $3\frac{1}{3}$ 10. $2\frac{5}{8}$

11. $6\frac{7}{8}$ 12. $1\frac{7}{8}$ 13. $1\frac{3}{4}$ 14. $3\frac{1}{9}$ 15. $9\frac{1}{3}$

16. $21\frac{1}{3}$ 17. $27\frac{1}{2}$ 18. $26\frac{2}{3}$ 19. $16\frac{3}{4}$ 20. $15\frac{7}{8}$

1-4 To reduce a fraction to lowest terms

1) Divide both numerator and denominator by whole numbers that divide into both numerator and denominator evenly.
2) If there are no whole numbers that divide both numerator and denominator evenly, the fraction is in lowest terms.

For example: Reduce $\frac{30}{12}$ to lowest terms.

$$\frac{30}{12} = \frac{10}{4} \text{ (dividing numerator and denominator by 3)}$$

$$\frac{10}{4} = \frac{5}{2} \text{ (dividing numerator and denominator by 2)}$$

Now $\frac{5}{2}$ is in lowest terms.

Or, we could have divided the numerator and denominator by 6 right away to get $\frac{5}{2}$.

Practice Exercises for 1-4

Reduce the following fractions to lowest terms:

1. $\dfrac{5}{10}$ 2. $\dfrac{6}{8}$ 3. $\dfrac{30}{100}$ 4. $\dfrac{15}{45}$ 5. $\dfrac{21}{36}$

6. $\dfrac{18}{36}$ 7. $\dfrac{3}{9}$ 8. $\dfrac{63}{99}$ 9. $\dfrac{32}{72}$ 10. $\dfrac{55}{605}$

11. $\dfrac{3}{4}$ 12. $\dfrac{17}{34}$ 13. $\dfrac{21}{30}$ 14. $\dfrac{1}{2}$ 15. $\dfrac{2}{3}$

16. $\dfrac{7}{9}$ 17. $\dfrac{6}{9}$ 18. $\dfrac{3}{5}$ 19. $\dfrac{13}{39}$ 20. $\dfrac{15}{49}$

21. $\dfrac{7}{14}$ 22. $\dfrac{3}{21}$ 23. $\dfrac{8}{15}$ 24. $\dfrac{8}{16}$ 25. $\dfrac{8}{18}$

1-5 To multiply fractions

1) Multiply the numerators to get the numerator of the product.

2) Multiply the denominators to get the denominator of the product.

For example: $\dfrac{3}{5} \times \dfrac{2}{7} = \dfrac{6}{35}$

Another example: Multiply $\dfrac{2}{9}$ by 4

To do this, we represent 4 as $\dfrac{4}{1}$. Then $\dfrac{2}{9} \times 4 = \dfrac{2}{9} \times \dfrac{4}{1} = \dfrac{8}{9}$

To multiply fractions by cancellation:

A shortcut in multiplying is to reduce to lowest terms while multiplying. This is called cancelling or cancellation.

For example: Multiply $\dfrac{3}{14} \times \dfrac{49}{6}$.

The 3 in the numerator and the 6 in the denominator can both be divided by 3.

We are left with $\dfrac{1}{14} \times \dfrac{49}{2}$. Now the 49 and the 14 can both be divided by 7.

This leaves $\dfrac{1}{2} \times \dfrac{7}{2}$. Therefore $\dfrac{3}{14} \times \dfrac{49}{6} = \dfrac{1}{2} \times \dfrac{7}{2}$. Cancelling can take place only between numerators and denominators. Two numbers in the numerator cannot cancel each other. Two numbers in the denominator cannot cancel each other.

The word *of* is sometimes need in problems instead of *times*. For example $\dfrac{1}{3}$ *of* $\dfrac{3}{10}$ means $\dfrac{1}{3} \times \dfrac{3}{10}$ or $\dfrac{1}{10}$.

Practice Exercises for 1-5

Multiply the following fractions *without* cancelling:

1. $\dfrac{3}{4} \times \dfrac{7}{8}$ 　　 2. $\dfrac{2}{3} \times \dfrac{1}{3}$ 　　 3. $8 \times \dfrac{1}{3}$ 　　 4. $\dfrac{3}{7} \times \dfrac{2}{9}$ 　　 5. $\dfrac{4}{7} \times \dfrac{3}{10}$

6. $\dfrac{4}{5} \times 3$ 　　 7. $\dfrac{7}{6} \times \dfrac{6}{7}$ 　　 8. $\dfrac{3}{5} \times \dfrac{2}{3}$ 　　 9. $\dfrac{5}{16} \times \dfrac{1}{8}$ 　　 10. $3 \times \dfrac{9}{2}$

11. $\dfrac{3}{7} \times \dfrac{1}{4}$ 　　 12. $\dfrac{2}{5} \times \dfrac{4}{5}$ 　　 13. $\dfrac{7}{8} \times \dfrac{7}{8}$ 　　 14. $\dfrac{6}{5} \times \dfrac{5}{2}$ 　　 15. $\dfrac{3}{2} \times \dfrac{7}{8}$

Multiply the following fractions, *cancelling* where you can:

16. $\dfrac{3}{4} \times \dfrac{7}{9}$ 　　 17. $\dfrac{3}{16} \times \dfrac{48}{6}$ 　　 18. $\dfrac{7}{15} \times \dfrac{2}{3}$ 　　 19. $\dfrac{3}{5} \times \dfrac{10}{9}$ 　　 20. $4 \times \dfrac{3}{4}$

21. $\dfrac{2}{3} \times 9$ 　　 22. $\dfrac{3}{5} \times \dfrac{25}{27}$ 　　 23. $\dfrac{3}{4} \times \dfrac{4}{3}$ 　　 24. $7 \times \dfrac{1}{7}$ 　　 25. $\dfrac{6}{7} \times \dfrac{14}{36}$

26. $\dfrac{3}{8} \times \dfrac{16}{9}$ 　　 27. $\dfrac{15}{17} \times \dfrac{5}{9}$ 　　 28. $\dfrac{2}{3} \times \dfrac{1}{7}$ 　　 29. $\dfrac{8}{9} \times \dfrac{18}{16}$ 　　 30. $\dfrac{7}{8} \times \dfrac{24}{49}$

31. $\dfrac{2}{7} \times \dfrac{3}{4}$ 　　 32. $\dfrac{5}{7} \times \dfrac{14}{10}$ 　　 33. $1 \times \dfrac{7}{8}$ 　　 34. $2 \times \dfrac{1}{2}$ 　　 35. $\dfrac{1}{3} \times 3$

36. $\dfrac{2}{3} \times \dfrac{9}{5}$ 　　 37. $\dfrac{7}{6} \times \dfrac{3}{14}$ 　　 38. $\dfrac{8}{9} \times 9$ 　　 39. $\dfrac{3}{5} \times 15$ 　　 40. $\dfrac{3}{2} \times \dfrac{2}{3}$

1-6 The reciprocal of a fraction

The reciprocal of a fraction is a fraction with numerator and denominator interchanged.

For example: The reciprocal of $\dfrac{2}{3}$ is $\dfrac{3}{2}$. Since $7 = \dfrac{7}{1}$, the reciprocal of 7 is $\dfrac{1}{7}$.

To divide fractions:

To divide one fraction by another, multiply the first fraction by the reciprocal of the divisor.

For example: Divide $\dfrac{2}{3}$ by $\dfrac{1}{4}$. $\dfrac{2}{3} \div \dfrac{1}{4} = \dfrac{2}{3} \times \dfrac{4}{1} = \dfrac{8}{3}$.

Or, divide $\dfrac{5}{7}$ by 7. $\dfrac{5}{7} \div \dfrac{7}{1} = \dfrac{5}{7} \times \dfrac{1}{7} = \dfrac{5}{49}$.

Practice Exercises for 1-6

Divide (cancel where you can):

1. $\dfrac{3}{8} \div \dfrac{1}{4}$ 2. $\dfrac{7}{16} \div \dfrac{7}{8}$ 3. $\dfrac{1}{3} \div 3$ 4. $\dfrac{6}{7} \div \dfrac{5}{2}$ 5. $1 \div \dfrac{1}{2}$

6. $\dfrac{2}{3} \div \dfrac{3}{2}$ 7. $\dfrac{5}{6} \div \dfrac{5}{6}$ 8. $\dfrac{2}{5} \div \dfrac{4}{5}$ 9. $\dfrac{7}{8} \div \dfrac{14}{24}$ 10. $\dfrac{1}{2} \div 4$

11. $\dfrac{3}{5} \div \dfrac{3}{4}$ 12. $\dfrac{1}{7} \div 14$ 13. $\dfrac{1}{3} \div \dfrac{3}{5}$ 14. $\dfrac{2}{3} \div \dfrac{16}{9}$ 15. $\dfrac{1}{7} \div \dfrac{15}{49}$

16. $\dfrac{3}{4} \div \dfrac{4}{3}$ 17. $\dfrac{3}{4} \div \dfrac{3}{5}$ 18. $\dfrac{3}{4} \div \dfrac{4}{7}$ 19. $\dfrac{3}{4} \div \dfrac{1}{4}$ 20. $2 \div \dfrac{1}{2}$

21. $\dfrac{7}{16} \div 16$ 22. $\dfrac{2}{7} \div \dfrac{16}{21}$ 23. $7 \div \dfrac{2}{7}$ 24. $\dfrac{1}{8} \div 8$ 25. $\dfrac{2}{9} \div \dfrac{9}{16}$

1-7 To change a fraction to an equal fraction with a different denominator

First, decide what denominator you want. Then, find the new numerator. To do this, multiply the original fraction by the new denominator.

For example: Write $\dfrac{4}{5}$ as a fraction with 15 as denominator.

$$\frac{4}{5} = \frac{\left(\dfrac{4}{5} \times 15\right)}{15} = \frac{12}{15}$$

since $\dfrac{4}{5} \times 15 = 12$.

Another example: How many twelfths are there in $\dfrac{4}{5}$?

We must write $\dfrac{4}{5}$ as a fraction with 12 as the denominator. The numerator is $\dfrac{4}{5} \times 12$ or $\dfrac{48}{5} = 9\dfrac{3}{5}$. There are $9\dfrac{3}{5}$ twelfths in $\dfrac{4}{5}$.

Practice Exercises for 1-7

Write the following fractions with the required denominator:

	Fraction	Required Denominator
1.	$\dfrac{1}{4}$	8
2.	$\dfrac{3}{8}$	16
3.	$\dfrac{7}{16}$	32
4.	$\dfrac{2}{3}$	12
5.	$\dfrac{4}{7}$	14
6.	$\dfrac{1}{3}$	9
7.	$\dfrac{1}{2}$	8
8.	$\dfrac{6}{16}$	8
9.	$\dfrac{4}{11}$	22
10.	$\dfrac{50}{102}$	51

1-8 To add fractions

1) If the denominators are the same, simply add the numerators, and leave the denominator alone.
   For example: $\dfrac{2}{5}+\dfrac{1}{5}=\dfrac{3}{5}$.

2) If the denominators are different, we must find a common denominator. One common denominator is the product of the different denominators. Then express both fractions with the common denominator as the denominator. Then just add the numerators.

For example: Add $\dfrac{3}{5} + \dfrac{1}{7}$.

The common denominator is 5×7, or 35.

$$\frac{3}{5} = \frac{\left(\dfrac{3}{5} \times 35\right)}{35} = \frac{21}{35}. \quad \frac{1}{7} = \frac{\left(\dfrac{1}{7} \times 35\right)}{35} = \frac{5}{35}. \quad \frac{21}{35} + \frac{5}{35} = \frac{26}{35}.$$

Here is a tricky way to add two fractions:

$$\text{Add } \frac{3}{5} + \frac{1}{7}$$

Solution:

Multiply 5×7 (the two denominators) to get the *denominator* of the answer. Now to get the numerator of the answer, multiply the denominator, 7, of the second fraction, with the numerator, 3, of the first fraction. We get the number $7 \times 3 = 21$. Now add this number, 21, to the *product* of the denominator of the first fraction, 5, with the numerator of the second fraction, 1. We get $21 + 5 \times 1 = 21 + 5 = 26$. 26 then is the *numerator* of our answer. Since the denominator of the answer is 35 and the numerator is 26, our answer is

$$\frac{26}{35}$$

We are doing the following (shown pictorially):

$$= \frac{7 \times 3 + 5 \times 1}{5 \times 7}$$

$$= \frac{21 + 5}{35} = \frac{26}{35}$$

Therefore $\dfrac{3}{5} + \dfrac{1}{7} = \dfrac{26}{35}$

The least common denominator:

You do not have to use the product of the denominators as the common denominator. Sometimes there is a smaller common denominator. The least common denominator is the smallest number that can be divided by both denominators evenly.

For example: Add $\dfrac{2}{7} + \dfrac{1}{14}$.

The least common denominator is 14. $\dfrac{2}{7} = \dfrac{\left(\dfrac{2}{7} \times 14\right)}{14} = \dfrac{4}{14}.$

Therefore, $\dfrac{2}{7} + \dfrac{1}{14} = \dfrac{4}{14} + \dfrac{1}{14} = \dfrac{5}{14}.$

Another example is: If Mary bought $\frac{5}{3}$ yards of blue cloth, $\frac{2}{9}$ yard of green cloth, and $\frac{8}{3}$ yards of yellow cloth, how many yards did she buy in all?

We must add $\frac{5}{3}+\frac{2}{9}+\frac{8}{3}$. First, $\frac{5}{3}+\frac{8}{3}=\frac{13}{3}$. Then add $\frac{13}{3}+\frac{2}{9}$. The least common denominator is 9. $\frac{13}{3}=\frac{\frac{13}{3}\times 9}{9}=\frac{39}{9}$. $\frac{39}{9}+\frac{2}{9}=\frac{41}{9}$.

Therefore $\frac{5}{3}+\frac{2}{9}+\frac{8}{3}=\frac{41}{9}$. Mary bought $\frac{41}{9}$, or $4\frac{5}{9}$ yards of cloth.

Practice Exercises for 1-8

Add (reduce answer where you can):

1. $\frac{2}{3}+\frac{1}{3}$

2. $\frac{1}{5}+\frac{3}{5}$

3. $\frac{1}{3}+\frac{1}{6}$

4. $\frac{1}{7}+\frac{3}{8}$

5. $\frac{2}{7}+\frac{3}{21}$

6. $\frac{7}{16}+\frac{3}{32}$

7. $\frac{5}{6}+\frac{6}{7}$

8. $\frac{2}{3}+\frac{3}{2}$

9. $\frac{7}{8}+\frac{3}{16}$

10. $\frac{1}{3}+\frac{1}{2}+1$

11. $\frac{2}{3}+\frac{1}{6}+\frac{1}{9}$

12. $\frac{1}{7}+\frac{1}{3}+\frac{1}{6}$

13. $\frac{1}{7}+\frac{1}{9}$

14. $\frac{2}{5}+\frac{4}{9}$

15. $\frac{3}{5}+\frac{7}{10}$

16. $\frac{8}{9}+\frac{9}{8}$

17. $\frac{2}{7}+\frac{3}{4}+\frac{1}{2}$

18. $\frac{3}{4}+1+2\frac{1}{4}$

19. $3\frac{1}{2}+2\frac{1}{4}+\frac{1}{9}$

20. $\frac{2}{3}+\frac{4}{7}+\frac{3}{5}+\frac{2}{5}$

21. $\frac{1}{2}+\frac{1}{3}+\frac{1}{4}+\frac{1}{5}$

22. $\frac{7}{8}+\frac{8}{7}+\frac{9}{8}$

23. $\frac{1}{2}+\frac{1}{4}+\frac{1}{6}$

24. $1+\frac{1}{4}+\frac{1}{8}$

25. $\frac{3}{4}+\frac{3}{5}+\frac{3}{7}$

1-9 To subtract fractions

1) If the denominators are the same, subtract numerators and keep the denominators the same.

For example: $\frac{5}{7}-\frac{3}{7}=\frac{2}{7}$.

2) If the denominators are different, express both fractions with a common denominator, and then subtract numerators.

For example: Find $\dfrac{2}{3}-\dfrac{1}{6}$.

The least common denominator is 6. $\dfrac{2}{3}=\dfrac{\left(\dfrac{2}{3}\times 6\right)}{6}=\dfrac{4}{6}$. Then,

$\dfrac{2}{3}-\dfrac{1}{6}=\dfrac{4}{6}-\dfrac{1}{6}=\dfrac{3}{6}$.

Another example: One-third less than 5 is _____ .

We must find $5+\dfrac{1}{3}$. The common denominator is 3, since 5

means $\dfrac{5}{1}$. $\dfrac{\overset{5}{1}\times 3}{3}=\dfrac{15}{3}$. Then, $5-\dfrac{1}{3}=\dfrac{15}{3}-\dfrac{1}{3}=\dfrac{14}{3}=4\dfrac{2}{3}$.

Practice Exercises for 1-9

Subtract (reduce answer where you can):

1. $\dfrac{5}{8}-\dfrac{3}{8}$

2. $\dfrac{4}{7}-\dfrac{2}{7}$

3. $\dfrac{5}{6}-\dfrac{1}{12}$

4. $\dfrac{3}{8}-\dfrac{1}{4}$

5. $\dfrac{1}{7}-\dfrac{1}{8}$

6. $\dfrac{3}{2}-\dfrac{2}{3}$

7. $\dfrac{3}{4}-\dfrac{4}{7}$

8. $\dfrac{1}{2}-\dfrac{1}{4}$

9. $\dfrac{1}{3}-\dfrac{1}{9}$

10. $\dfrac{3}{5}-\dfrac{2}{5}$

11. $\dfrac{2}{3}-\dfrac{3}{5}$

12. $\dfrac{15}{16}-\dfrac{1}{8}$

13. $\dfrac{1}{2}-\dfrac{1}{3}$

14. $\dfrac{7}{16}-\dfrac{3}{32}$

15. $\dfrac{3}{5}-\dfrac{2}{6}$

16. $\dfrac{1}{3}-\dfrac{1}{5}$

17. $\dfrac{3}{4}-\dfrac{7}{16}$

18. One-half less than four

19. One-third less than three

20. $\dfrac{1}{5}-\dfrac{1}{8}$

21. $\dfrac{16}{17}-\dfrac{1}{34}$

22. $\dfrac{5}{8}-\dfrac{3}{10}$

23. $\dfrac{7}{6}-\dfrac{6}{7}$

24. $1\dfrac{2}{3}-\dfrac{1}{3}$

25. $1\dfrac{2}{3}-1\dfrac{1}{6}$

26. $\dfrac{2}{9}-\dfrac{1}{8}$

27. $\dfrac{1}{5}-\dfrac{1}{6}$

28. $\dfrac{17}{18}-\dfrac{3}{10}$

29. $\dfrac{2}{11}-\dfrac{2}{33}$

30. $\dfrac{8}{7}-\dfrac{24}{49}$

1-10 Complex fractions

A complex fraction is a fraction whose numerator or denominator is itself a fraction.

For example: $\dfrac{\frac{2}{3}}{\frac{5}{7}}$ is a complex fraction. A complex fraction may be

simplified by division.

Thus, $\dfrac{\frac{2}{3}}{\frac{5}{7}} = \dfrac{2}{3} \div \dfrac{5}{7} = \dfrac{2}{3} \times \dfrac{7}{5} = \dfrac{14}{15}$.

Practice Exercises for 1-10

Simplify the following complex fractions:

1. $\dfrac{\frac{1}{2}}{\frac{1}{6}}$ 2. $\dfrac{\frac{3}{4}}{\frac{7}{8}}$ 3. $\dfrac{\frac{2}{3}}{\frac{7}{8}}$ 4. $\dfrac{\frac{7}{16}}{\frac{3}{8}}$ 5. $\dfrac{\frac{1}{3}}{\frac{1}{4}}$

6. $\dfrac{\frac{2}{5}}{\frac{5}{6}}$ 7. $\dfrac{\frac{2}{5}}{\frac{3}{10}}$ 8. $\dfrac{\frac{1}{9}}{\frac{1}{18}}$ 9. $\dfrac{\frac{3}{7}}{\frac{9}{21}}$ 10. $\dfrac{\frac{3}{4}}{\frac{4}{3}}$

1-11 To add, subtract, multiply, or divide mixed numbers, or mixed numbers and fractions

First change all mixed numbers to fractions, and then use the rules for operating with fractions.

For example: Multiply $3\dfrac{1}{3} \times \dfrac{1}{10}$.

$3\dfrac{1}{3} = \dfrac{10}{3}$, so $3\dfrac{1}{3} \times \dfrac{1}{10} = \dfrac{10}{3} \times \dfrac{1}{10} = \dfrac{1}{3}$.

In doing problems with fractions on a multiple-choice test, remember that you must obtain the answer in the right form. For example, if the choices given are mixed numbers, then you must convert your answer to a mixed number; if the choices are in lowest terms, you must reduce your answer to lowest terms.

Practice Exercises for 1-11

Multiply (reduce answer where you can):

1. $2\frac{1}{2} \times \frac{1}{8}$ 4. $3\frac{1}{3} \times 2$

2. $3\frac{1}{4} \times \frac{1}{9}$ 5. $3\frac{1}{2} \times 4\frac{1}{8}$

3. $1\frac{1}{2} \times 2\frac{1}{2}$

Divide (reduce answer where you can):

6. $3\frac{1}{3} \div \frac{3}{4}$ 9. $1 \div 2\frac{1}{2}$

7. $2\frac{1}{8} \div 3\frac{1}{4}$ 10. $3\frac{1}{3} \div 3$

8. $1\frac{1}{2} \div 3\frac{1}{2}$

Decimals

Diagnostic Test on Decimals

1. What fraction equals .201?

   (A) $\dfrac{1}{201}$ (C) $\dfrac{20}{100}$

   (B) $\dfrac{3}{10}$ (D) $\dfrac{201}{1000}$

   (E) $\dfrac{201}{110}$

2.* 3.29×1000 equals

   (A) .329
   (B) 32.9
   (C) 329
   (D) 3290
   (E) none of the above

3.* $.18 + 1.19 + 2.3$ equals

   (A) 4.01   (D) 3.86
   (B) 3.67   (E) 2.87
   (C) 3.40

4.* 1.3×13.4 equals

   (A) 41.18   (D) 17.42
   (B) 274.2   (E) 1.353
   (C) 411.8

5.* $.024 \div 100$ equals

   (A) 24   (D) .76
   (B) .00024   (E) 240
   (C) .24

6. A shirt costs $3.75. If Jay buys 3 shirts, how much change does he get from a $20 dollar bill?

   (A) $8.75   (D) $9.50
   (B) $9.00   (E) $9.75
   (C) $9.25

7.* Write $\dfrac{11}{25}$ as a decimal.

   (A) .11   (D) .36
   (B) .44   (E) .0375
   (C) .25

8. Add $\dfrac{1}{3}$, .2, and .75.

   (A) 5.25   (D) .1275
   (B) 1.3   (E) $\dfrac{77}{60}$
   (C) $\dfrac{4}{15}$

9.* $(.3)(.3)(.3)$ equals

   (A) .001
   (B) .003
   (C) .027
   (D) .333
   (E) none of the above

10.* Write $\dfrac{170}{272}$ as a decimal.

   (A) .170   (D) .625
   (B) .102   (E) .127
   (C) .375

Solutions for Diagnostic Test (without a calculator)

1. **(D)** To write .201 as a fraction, we multiply .201 by the power of 10 needed to turn it into a whole number. $.201 \times 1000$ equals 201, so $.201 = \dfrac{201}{1000}$.   **(1-14)**

2.* **(D)** To multiply by 1000, we move the decimal point three places to the right, first adding a zero at the end of 3.29. $3.29 \times 1000 = 3290$.   **(1-13)**

* Note: These problems can also be done with a calculator.

3.* **(B)** First align the numbers as follows, and then add:

$$.18$$
$$1.19$$
$$+2.3$$
$$\overline{3.67}$$ **(1-15)**

4.* **(D)** Multiply as if they were whole numbers. There are two decimal places in the answer.

$$13.4$$
$$\times 1.3$$
$$\overline{402}$$
$$\underline{134}$$
$$17.42 \qquad \textbf{(1-17)}$$

5.* **(B)** We must move the decimal point two places to the left, first putting two zeroes in front of .024: 00.024 ÷ 1000 = .00024. **(1-13)**

6. **(A)** 3 × \$3.75 = \$11.25. Writing \$20 as \$20.00 and subtracting,

$$\$20.00$$
$$-\$11.25$$
$$\overline{\$\ 8.75} \quad \textbf{(1-17, 1-16)}$$

7.* **(B)** $\dfrac{11}{25} = \dfrac{11 \times 4}{25 \times 4} = \dfrac{44}{100}$ or .44. **(1-19)**

8. **(E)** Convert to fractions: $.2 = \dfrac{1}{5}$, $.75 = \dfrac{3}{4}$; now

$$\frac{1}{3} + \frac{1}{5} + \frac{3}{4} = \frac{20}{60} + \frac{12}{60} + \frac{45}{60} = \frac{77}{60}$$
(1-20)

9.* **(C)** (3)(3)(3) = 27. We need three decimal places, so we get .027. **(1-17)**

10.* **(D)** We divide 272 into 170, bringing down zeroes as we need them:

$$\begin{array}{r} .625 \\ 272\overline{)170.0} \\ \underline{163\ 2} \\ 6\ 80 \\ \underline{5\ 44} \\ 1\ 360 \\ \underline{1\ 360} \\ 0 \end{array}$$
(1-18)

Instructional Material on Decimals

1-12 Decimals described

A decimal fraction is a fraction whose denominator is a power of 10—that is, the denominator is 10, 100, 1000, etc.

For example: $\dfrac{313}{1000}$ is a decimal fraction. It can also be written .313; the first digit after the decimal point stands for tenths, the second digit stands for hundredths, and the third stands for thousandths, etc. Thus, $.313 = \dfrac{3}{10} + \dfrac{1}{100} + \dfrac{3}{1000}$ or $\dfrac{313}{1000}$. Also .007 means $\dfrac{7}{1000}$, or $\dfrac{0}{10} + \dfrac{0}{100} + \dfrac{7}{1000}$. A number of the form 17.36 means $17 + .36$, or $17\dfrac{36}{100}$.

* Note: These problems can also be done with a calculator.

> Adding zeros on the *right* side of a decimal fraction does not change the value of the decimal fraction.

Thus, .3 = .30, since the first decimal means $\frac{3}{10}$ and the second means $\frac{30}{100}$.

Practice Exercises for 1-12

Write the following as *decimal fractions:*

1. .425   2. .07   3. .3   4. .045   5. .325

Write the following as *decimals:*

6. $\frac{21}{100}$ 7. $12\frac{3}{10}$ 8. $1\frac{6}{10}$ 9. $3\frac{33}{100}$ 10. $21\frac{1}{1000}$

1-13   To multiply a decimal by a power of 10

Move the decimal point to the right, one place for each zero in the power of 10.

For example: What is 100×32.812?
Since 100 has two zeros, we must move the decimal point two places to the right: $100 \times 32.812 = 3281.2$.

Another example: Find 1000×37.68.
We can write $37.68 = 37.680$, and now we can move the decimal point three places to the right. $1000 \times 37.680 = 37680$.

To divide a decimal by a power of 10

We must move the decimal place to the left, one place for each zero in the power of 10.

For example: What is $17.23 \div 100$?
Moving the decimal point two places to the left, we get $17.23 \div 100 = .1723$.

Another example: What is $11.4 \div 10000$?
Before we move the decimal point four places to the left, we write $11.4 = 0011.4$; now $0011.4 \div 10,000 = .00114$.

Practice Exercises for 1-13*

Multiply:
1. $10 \times .32$
2. 100×2.16

Divide:
6. $13.25 \div 100$
7. $1.76 \div 1000$

* Note: These problems can also be done with a calculator.

3. 1000×12.11
4. 100×1.0762
5. $10,000 \times .7534$

8. $21.36 \div 10$
9. $170.3 \div 1000$
10. $1.14 \div 10,000$

1-14 To convert a decimal to a fraction

1) The numerator of the fraction is found by multiplying the decimal by the power of 10 required to make the decimal a whole number.

2) The denominator of the fraction is the power of 10 you multiplied by.

For example: Change .812 to a fraction.

We must multiply .812 by 1000 to make it a whole number. Therefore $.812 = \frac{(.812 \times 1000)}{1000}$ or $\frac{812}{1000}$. This could be reduced if required.

Practice Exercises for 1-14

Change the following decimals to fractions:

1. .7
2. .73
3. .735
4. .7355
5. .620

6. 1.21
7. 100.01
8. 2.17
9. .001
10. .015

1-15 To add decimal numbers*

1) Align the numbers so that the tenths are written under tenths, the hundredths are written under hundredths, etc.

2) The decimal point goes right under the decimal point in the numbers being added. Then, add as you add whole numbers.

For example: Add 10.9, 15.73, and 22.001.

Write the sum like this:

$$
\begin{array}{r}
10.9 \\
15.73 \\
+\,22.001 \\
\hline
48.631
\end{array}
$$

Practice Exercises for 1-15

Add:

1. $5.6 + 17.89 + 10.001$
2. $4.32 + 16.15 + 2.65$
3. $1.1 + 1.505 + .032$
4. $3.114 + 2.176 + .001$
5. $8.6 + 9.27 + 10.314$

6. $7.5 + 3.5$
7. $3.2 + 2.14 + 2.60$
8. $1.17 + 1.117 + 1.1117$
9. $8.6 + 6.2 + 3.5$
10. $2.14 + 1.15 + 1.16$

* Note: These problems can also be done with a calculator.

11. .001 + .01 + .1

12. .12 + .24 + .36

13. 1.5 + 3.5 + 4.5

14. 2.718 + 2.61 + 1.63

15. 3.51 + 4.002 + 6.0786

16. 7.14 + 4.17 + 1.47

17. 8.65 + 6.24 + 7.36

18. 9.21 + 7.65 + 4.62

19. 3.143 + 2.145 + 3.716

20. 4.761 + .01 + .001

1-16 To subtract decimal numbers*

1) If one number has more decimal places than the other, add zeros at the right end so that there are the same number of decimal places in the two numbers.

2) Align the numbers, tenths under tenths, etc. Put the decimal point under the decimal point in the numbers being subtracted. Subtract as with whole numbers. For example: What is 17.19 − 8.4?

First write 8.4 as 8.40 and then subtract:

$$\begin{array}{r} 17.19 \\ -\ 8.40 \\ \hline 8.79 \end{array}$$

Another example: If one store sells a shirt for $10 and another sells it for $3.35 less, how much does it cost in the cheaper store?

We must subtract $3.35 from $10, so write $10 as $10.00 and then subtract:

$$\begin{array}{r} \$10.00 \\ -\ 3.35 \\ \hline \$\ \ 6.65 \end{array}$$

Practice Exercises for 1-16

1. Subtract: 15.4 − 7.9

2. Subtract: 20.13 − 13.76

3. Subtract: 150.21 − 129.90

4. What is the difference in price of an item that sells for $30.23 and an item that sells for $27.67?

5. In 12 hours Bill can mow 6.3 lawns. In 12 hours John can mow 3.7 lawns. In 12 hours how many more lawns can Bill mow than John?

6. How much more is a coat costing $125.64 than a coat costing $101.75?

7. Subtract: 207.654 − 76.234

8. Subtract: 175.42 − 75.527

9. What discount am I getting off the list price of an item that lists for $125.00 if I get the item for $96.50?

10. How much more weight is a 36.4 kilogram object than a 28.6 kilogram object?

11. Subtract 36.3 from 101.8

12. Subtract 1.76 from 10

13. How many more centimeters is 2.54 centimeters than 1.76 centimeters?

* Note: These problems can also be done with a calculator.

14. What is the difference in length of two objects, one whose length is 24.1 meters and the other whose length is 10.7 meters?
15. Subtract: 170.012 − 69.015
16. Subtract: 7.3 − 6.41
17. How much more interest would I make in a year from a bank that gives $20.75 yearly on my deposit, than from a bank that gives $18.65 yearly on my deposit?
18. How much longer is a rod of 12.34 meters than a rod of 11.65 meters?
19. Subtract: 16.35 − 15.72
20. Subtract: 180.621 − 24.379

1-17 To multiply two decimal numbers*

1) Just multiply the numbers as if they were whole numbers.
2) The number of decimal places in the answer is the sum of the number of decimal places in the factors.

For example: What is 3.1 × 2.7?
There will be two decimal places in the answer:

$$
\begin{array}{r}
3.1 \\
\times 2.7 \\
\hline
217 \\
62 \\
\hline
8.37
\end{array}
$$

Another example: Multiply .75 by 3.2.
There will be three decimal places in the answer:

$$
\begin{array}{r}
.75 \\
\times 3.2 \\
\hline
150 \\
225 \\
\hline
2.400
\end{array}
$$

Practice Exercises for 1-17

Multiply:

1. 3.3 × 1.2
2. .75 × 2.1
3. .6 × 70
4. .325 × .25
5. 8.6 × 6.8
6. 21.5 × 31.4
7. 1.07 × 9
8. 1.06 × 2.1
9. 1.05 × 2.34
10. .35 × 7
11. 1.21 × 1.21
12. 3.54 × .9
13. 7 × 8.6
14. 6.54 × 3.2
15. 18.3 × .04
16. 7.5 × 7.6
17. 1.1 × 1.1
18. 8.5 × 5.8
19. 2.01 × 2.01
20. 3.12 × 2.13

* Note: These problems can also be done with a calculator.

1-18 To divide decimal fractions*

1) Multiply the divisor by the power of 10 required to make it a whole number.
2) Multiply the number being divided by the same power of 10.
3) The decimal point in the quotient is right above the decimal point in the number being divided.
4) Add zeros at the end of the number being divided to express the remainder as a decimal.

For example: What is $51 \div 1.2$?

To make 1.2 a whole number, we multiply by 10. We must multiply 51 by 10 also. We now divide $510 \div 12$. We add one zero after the decimal point.

$$
\begin{array}{r}
42.5 \\
12\overline{)510.0} \\
48 \\
\hline
30 \\
24 \\
\hline
60
\end{array}
$$

Therefore, $51 \div 1.2 = 42.5$.

Note: Sometimes the remainder cannot be expressed as a decimal, no matter how many zeros are added after the number being divided. In this case, the remainder is usually expressed as a fraction.

Practice Exercises for 1-18

Divide:

1. $25 \div 1.2$
2. $50 \div 1.8$
3. $125 \div 6$
4. $2.2 \div .5$
5. $1.7 \div 8$

6. $32.4 \div 1.6$
7. $2.7 \div 1.5$
8. $1.5 \div .05$
9. $7.5 \div .25$
10. $8.32 \div 4.1$

1-19 To convert a fraction to a decimal*

1) Write the numerator with a decimal point and zeros after it.
2) Divide the numerator by the denominator.

For example: Write $\frac{2}{125}$ as a decimal.

We write 2 as 2.000 and then divide:

$$
\begin{array}{r}
.016 \\
125\overline{)2.000} \\
1\ 25 \\
\hline
750 \\
750
\end{array}
$$

Therefore $\frac{2}{125} = .016$.

* Note: These problems can also be done with a calculator.

Problems with decimals will not usually involve messy arithmetic. The important point is to keep track of where the decimal point belongs.

Sometimes we can multiply the numerator and denominator by the same number, which will enable us to quickly convert the fraction into a decimal:

For example: Convert $\frac{1}{5}$ into a decimal.
We multiply both numerator and denominator by 2.

$$\frac{1}{5} \times \frac{2}{2} = \frac{2}{10}$$

We know that $\frac{2}{10} = .2$, so .2 is our answer.

Here's another example: Convert $\frac{3}{25}$ to a decimal.

We multiply both numerator and denominator by 4:

$$\frac{3}{25} \times \frac{4}{4} = \frac{12}{100}$$

Now $\frac{12}{100} = .12$, so .12 is our answer.

On some occasions you may want to convert fractions to decimals.
For example: If a boy ran 1.33 miles one day, 1.25 miles the next day, $\frac{1}{4}$ mile the third day, and 1.2 miles the fourth day, how many miles did he run during the four days?

To do this, express $\frac{1}{4}$ mile as a decimal:

$$\frac{1}{4} = .25$$

Thus, we add

$$\begin{array}{r} 1.33 \\ 1.25 \\ .25 \\ +1.2 \\ \hline 4.03 \end{array}$$

Therefore he ran a total of 4.03 miles.

Practice Exercises for 1-19

Convert the following fractions to decimals:

1. $\dfrac{1}{25}$ 6. $\dfrac{1}{4}$ 11. $\dfrac{1}{3}$

2. $\dfrac{21}{40}$ 7. $\dfrac{3}{8}$ 12. $\dfrac{2}{5}$

3. $\dfrac{3}{50}$ 8. $\dfrac{4}{25}$ 13. $\dfrac{3}{250}$

4. $\dfrac{9}{4}$ 9. $\dfrac{21}{100}$ 14. $\dfrac{4}{500}$

5. $\dfrac{3}{125}$ 10. $\dfrac{8}{200}$ 15. $\dfrac{1}{15}$

1-20 How to attack problems involving fractions and decimals*

For example: If a boy ran .3 miles one day and $\dfrac{1}{3}$ mile the next, how many miles did he run in all?

To do this, express .3 as $\dfrac{3}{10}$ and then add: $\dfrac{1}{3}+\dfrac{3}{10}=\dfrac{19}{30}$.

Practice Exercises for 1-20

1. Add: $\dfrac{1}{4}+.25+1$

2. Add: $\dfrac{2}{5}+.2+1.5$

3. If a car traveled 1.4 kilometers in one day, $1\dfrac{3}{5}$ kilometers the next day, and 1.6 kilometers the third day, how many kilometers did it travel in the three days?

4. The length of a field can be gotten by adding 10 yards, 20.36 yards, and $15\dfrac{1}{4}$ yards. What is the length of the field?

5. Add $\dfrac{3}{5}+1.7+\dfrac{1}{3}$

---

* Note: These problems can also be done with a calculator.

Percentages

Diagnostic Test on Percentages

1. Change the fraction $\frac{7}{8}$ to a percent.

   (A) $87\frac{1}{2}$%   (D) 75%

   (B) $\frac{7}{8}$%   (E) 87%

   (C) 78%

2. If the attendance of a class is 100%, which statement is true?

   (A) The whole class is present.
   (B) Half of the class is present.
   (C) A fourth of the class is present.
   (D) One hundredth of the class is present.
   (E) None of the above is true.

3. 65% is equivalent to which of the following?

   (A) 65
   (B) 6.5
   (C) .65
   (D) .065
   (E) .0065

4. Change .1% to a decimal.

   (A) 1
   (B) .1
   (C) .01
   (D) .001
   (E) .0001

5. What is .73 expressed in percent?

   (A) 7%   (D) .73%
   (B) 73%   (E) 27%
   (C) 7.3%

6. What is $4\frac{1}{6}$% as a fraction?

   (A) $\frac{1}{6}$ (D) $\frac{2}{3}$

   (B) $\frac{1}{48}$ (E) $\frac{1}{24}$

   (C) $\frac{1}{18}$

7. 38 is 20% of what number?

   (A) 760   (D) 190
   (B) 380   (E) 7.6
   (C) 58

8. What is 16% of 80?

   (A) 12.8   (D) 24
   (B) 96   (E) 16
   (C) 1280

9. If a man has $1,500 in the bank and the annual interest rate is 5%, how much money will he have in the bank after 1 year?

   (A) $1,515
   (B) $1,505
   (C) $1,425
   (D) $1,575
   (E) $1,625

10. The original price of a car is $3000. What is the new price if the original price is reduced by 10%?

    (A) $2800
    (B) $2700
    (C) $2100
    (D) $600
    (E) $1200

Solutions for Diagnostic Test

1. **(A)** To change $\frac{7}{8}$ to a percent, change $\frac{7}{8}$ to an equivalent fraction with 100 as the denominator.

$$\frac{7}{8} = \frac{87\frac{1}{2}}{100}$$

The answer is the numerator with the sign "%" added, or $87\frac{1}{2}$%. **(1-22)**

2. **(A)** 100% of something means all of something. So, the entire class is present. **(1-21)**

3. **(C)** To change 65% to a decimal, remove the percent sign and move the decimal point two places to the left. 65% = .65 **(1-22)**

4. **(D)** To change .1% to a decimal, remove the percent sign and move the decimal point two places to the left. In this case two 0s must be added.

$$.1\% = .001 \qquad \textbf{(1-22)}$$

5. **(B)** To change .73 to a percent, move the decimal point two places to the right and add the percent sign. .73 = 73% **(1-22)**

6. **(E)** To change $4\frac{1}{6}$% to a fraction, remove the percent sign and form a fraction with the resulting number as the numerator and 100 as the denominator. Then reduce the fraction.

$$4\frac{1}{6}\% = \frac{4\frac{1}{6}}{100} = \frac{1}{24} \qquad \textbf{(1-22)}$$

7. **(D)** 20% is $\frac{1}{5}$. To find the number divide 38 by $\frac{1}{5}$. $38 \div \frac{1}{5} = 38 \times 5 = 190$. **(1-25)**

8. **(A)** 16% is .16. To find the number, multiply 80 by .16. $80 \times .16 = 12.8$ **(1-25)**

9. **(D)** Interest =
Principal × Rate × Time

Interest = $1500 × .05 × 1 = $75,

since 5% is .05.
The total amount of money he will have is $1500 + $75 = $1575. **(1–24)**

10. **(B)** Amount reduced =
Original price × Rate

Since 10% = .1, amount reduced = $3000 × .1 = $300. The new price is $3000 − $300 = $2700. **(1-24)**

Instructional Material on Percentages

1-21 Percents described

Percent is another method of describing parts of a whole; other ways of doing so are fractions and decimals. In a fraction, the denominator can be any number, and it is sometimes hard to compare fractions such as $\frac{1}{286}$ and $\frac{3}{597}$. Percents are like fractions whose denominator is always 100; thus, percents describe parts of a hundred or the number of hundredths.

Suppose a student does 80 problems correctly out of 100 problems in an exam. There are several ways to describe the part of the whole exam he has done correctly: $\frac{80}{100}$ (fraction) or .80 (decimal) or simply 80 hundredths. The word "hundredths" is replaced by the symbol "%" when we use percents. The part of the exam the student has correct is 80%, read "80 percent." Note that $1 = \frac{100}{100} = 100\%$. 100% of a number equals the entire number.

Practice Exercises for 1-21

1. A student scored 85 questions correct from a total of 100 questions. What percent did he get on the exam?

2. A man pays only $60 for an item that originally sells for $100. What percent of the original price does the man pay for the item?

3. $\frac{8}{10}$ of the class of juniors are females. What percent of the junior class is female?

4. If $\frac{1}{5}$ of all lawyers are self-employed, what percentage of lawyers are self-employed?

5. If 1 out of 20 persons live to 85, what percent of people live to 85?

1-22 Conversion of percents, decimals, and fractions

Since percents, fractions, and decimals are equivalent in describing parts of a whole, it is possible to convert a percent into a decimal and a fraction, and a decimal or fraction into a percent. It is convenient to do so because in doing calculations involving percents, it is not so easy to work with percents directly. Normally, one changes percents to either fractions or decimals since they are easier to work with.

1) To change decimals into percents, the rule is to multiply the decimal by 100 (move the decimal point two places to the right) and then add the sign "%" at the end.

For example: Change .365 into a percent.
Multiply .365 by 100: .365 × 100 = 36.5
Therefore, .365 = 36.5%.

2) To change a fraction into a percent, there are two methods:

a) Change the fraction into an equal fraction whose denominator is 100. Then the percent is the numerator with the sign "%" at the end.

For example: Change $\frac{4}{25}$ into a percent.

Change $\frac{4}{25}$ into an equal fraction with 100 as the denominator. (Multiply both numerator and denominator by 4.)

$$\frac{4}{25} \times \frac{16}{100}$$

Therefore, $\frac{4}{25} = 16\%$.

b) First change the fraction into a decimal by dividing the denominator into the numerator. Then change the decimal into a percent.

For example: Change $\frac{4}{25}$ into a percent.

First change $\frac{4}{25}$ into a decimal.

$$\frac{4}{25} = 4 \div 25 = .16$$

Then change .16 into a percent.

$$.16 \times 100 = 16$$
$$.16 = 16\%$$

Therefore, $\frac{4}{25} = .16 = 16\%$.

3) To change a percent into a decimal, remove the percent sign and divide the number by 100.

For example: Change 25% into a decimal.
Remove the percent sign in 25% to get 25. Then divide 25 by 100.
$25 \div 100 = .25$
Therefore, 25% = .25.

4) To change a percent into a fraction, remove the percent sign and form a fraction using the remaining number as the numerator and 100 as the denominator. Reduce the fraction if necessary.

For example: Change 25% into a fraction.
Remove the percent sign in 25% to get 25. Then form the fraction with 25 as the numerator and 100 as the denominator, or the fraction $\frac{25}{100}$. $\frac{25}{100}$ reduces to $\frac{1}{4}$. Therefore, 25% = $\frac{1}{4}$.

Practice Exercises for 1-22

Change the following to percents:

1. .214

2. 2.2

3. $\frac{2}{25}$

4. $\frac{3}{4}$

5. $\frac{3}{8}$

6. .12

7. 3.36

8. .74

9. $\frac{1}{3}$

10. $\frac{1}{2}$

11. $\frac{2}{3}$

12. $\frac{7}{8}$

13. .001

14. .01

15. 1.01

Change the following to decimals:

16. 72%

17. 65%

18. 34.3%

19. 4.2%

20. .3%

21. 1.1%

22. 10%

23. 8.65%

24. $2\frac{1}{4}\%$

25. $11\frac{1}{2}\%$

26. 75.5%

27. 8.3%

28. $\frac{1}{2}\%$

29. 5%

30. 117.6%

Change the following to fractions:

31. 26%

32. 12.5%

33. 15%

34. 13.5%

35. $2\frac{1}{4}\%$

36. 12.25%

37. 75%

38. $66\frac{2}{3}\%$

39. $14\frac{2}{7}\%$

40. 10%

41. 18.6%

42. $\frac{1}{2}\%$

43. 50%

44. 9%

45. 111.2%

1-23 Fraction and decimal equivalents

The following table is a list of common percents and their equivalent fractions and decimals.

Percent	Fraction	Decimal
100%	1	1.0
50%	$\frac{1}{2}$	.5
25%	$\frac{1}{4}$	.25
75%	$\frac{3}{4}$	.75
80%	$\frac{4}{5}$	.8
60%	$\frac{3}{5}$	.6
40%	$\frac{2}{5}$	.4
20%	$\frac{1}{5}$	.2
10%	$\frac{1}{10}$	.1
5%	$\frac{1}{20}$	.05
$12\frac{1}{2}\%$	$\frac{1}{8}$	.125
$87\frac{1}{2}\%$	$\frac{7}{8}$	.875
$33\frac{1}{3}\%$	$\frac{1}{3}$	.333...*
$66\frac{2}{3}\%$	$\frac{2}{3}$	.666...*
$16\frac{2}{3}\%$	$\frac{1}{6}$	.1666...*

*Note: These are called repeating decimals and will never "come out even." When these occur, use fractions instead of decimals to solve problems.

Practice Exercises for 1-23

Fill in the missing boxes relating percent to fraction to decimal.

	Percent	Fraction	Decimal
1.	40		.4
2.		$\frac{1}{6}$	
3.			.875
4.	5		
5.		$\frac{1}{8}$	
6.	$33\frac{1}{3}$		
7.		$\frac{4}{5}$	
8.	100		
9.			.25
10.			.65

1-24 Interest and discount problems

The two most common types of percent problems are interest problems and discount problems. To solve these problems, first change the rate (if the rate is given, it is usually given in percent) from a percent to either a decimal or a fraction, and then substitute into the formulas.

1. For simple interest problems, the formula used to solve the problems is

$$\text{Interest} = \text{Rate} \times \text{Principal} \times \text{Time}$$

For example: Mr. Jones has $1400 in the bank. If the interest rate is 5%, how much money does he have in the bank after 1 year?

The total amount he has in the bank after 1 year is the money he had originally plus the interest.

Principal = $1400
Rate = 5%
Time = 1 year

First, change 5% to a decimal.
5% = 5 ÷ 100 = .05

Write down the formula for interest.

Interest = Rate × Principal × Time
= .05 × $1400 × 1
= $70

The amount of money he has after 1 year is $1400 + $70 = $1470.

2. For the discount problems, the formula is

Amount of Discount = Rate of Discount × Original Price

For example: The original price of a painting is $40. If the discount price is $36, find the rate of discount.

The amount of discount is the original price minus the discount price.
Amount of Discount = $40 − $36 = $4
Original Price = $40
Write down the formula for discount problems.
Amount of discount = Rate of Discount × Original Price
$4 = Rate of Discount × $40
Rate of Discount = $4 ÷ $40 = .1
Since the rate is normally expressed in percent, change .1 to a percent.
.1 × 100 = 10
.1 = 10%
Therefore, the rate of discount is 10%.

Practice Exercises for 1-24

1. What is the simple interest on $1500 for one year at 6% interest per year?

2. What is the difference in simple interest in one year between two loans, one for $6000 at 10.2% yearly interest, the other for $4000 at $12\frac{1}{4}$% yearly interest?

3. A man buys a painting for $150. The original selling price of the painting was $200. What rate of discount (of the original selling price) did the man get?

4. An item originally sells for $250. A woman gets a 20% discount on the original selling price. How much does the woman pay for the item?

5. An item originally sells for $300. A man gets *two* successive discounts of 10% and 20% on the selling price of the item. How much does the man pay for the item, and what *single* discount was the man really getting?

6. The only interest on a deposit left for one year in a bank is 8%. Suppose Mary put $1000 in the bank for one year, then decided to reinvest the $1000, plus the interest she received, for another year. At the end of the two years, how much money will Mary have (principal + total interest)?

7. The term "40-10 discount" means that on an item, you first get a 40% discount and then get a 10% discount. How much would you pay for an item originally costing $100 if you get a 40-10 discount?

8. A woman buys an item for $80. The original cost of the item was $100. What discount did she get on the original cost of the item?

9. A man pays $\frac{4}{5}$ of the original price for an item. What discount (percent) did the man receive on the item?

10. What is the simple interest on $250 at $10\frac{1}{4}$% per year for five years? (Do not compound interest.)

1-25 More percent problems

In general, problems involving percent fall into three categories. Consider the following statement:

$$15 \text{ is } 50\% \text{ of } 30$$

Whenever any two of the numbers given above are known, the third one can be found. The three types of problems involving percent are then to find one of the three numbers. The possible problems relating to the statement above are:

1) What is 50% of 30?

To find the answer, change 50% to either a fraction or a decimal, and then multiply by 30.

$$50\% = \frac{1}{2} = .5$$
$$\frac{1}{2} \times 30 = 15 \quad .5 \times 30 = 15$$

Both give the same answer.

2) 15 is what percent of 30?

To find the answer, either divide 15 by 30 to give a decimal or form the fraction with 15 as the numerator and 30 as the denominator. Then change either to a percent.

$$15 \div 30 = .5 \quad \frac{15}{30} = \frac{1}{2}$$
$$\frac{1}{2} = 50\%$$
$$.5 = 50\%$$

3) 15 is 50% of what number?

To find the answer, first change 50% to either a fraction or decimal, and then divide 15 by that number.

$$50\% = \frac{1}{2} = .5$$
$$15 \div \frac{1}{2} = 15 \times 2 = 30 \quad 15 \div .5 = 30$$

To do a problem involving percent, it is really a question of figuring out which of the three types of percent problems it is. Once you know the correct type, you just follow the rules to find the answer.

For example: John weighs 165 pounds. If Jack weighs 10% less than John, how much does Jack weigh?

To find out Jack's weight, we must first find out how many pounds lighter Jack is than John. Since we know that John weighs 165 pounds and Jack weighs 10% less than that, we are involved with a type 1 problem.

What is 10% of 165?
$$10\% = .1$$
Multiply .1 by 165: $.1 \times 165 = 16.5$
So, Jack weighs 16.5 pounds less than John.
$$165 - 16.5 = 148.5$$
Jack weighs 148.5 pounds.

Practice Exercises for 1-25

1. 20 is 40% of what number?

2. What is 25% of 240?

3. 18 is what percent of 50?

4. Harry can carry 200 pounds of weight. John can carry 80% of what Harry can carry. How much weight can John carry?

5. John made $225 in the first week of his business. The second week, he made $300. By what percent did his business income increase from the first to the second week?

6. 18 is 30% of what number?

7. 24 is 10% of what number?

8. What is 10% of 20?

9. What is 5% of 50?

10. 15 is 80% of what number?

11. 20 is what percent of 10?

12. 15 is what percent of 50?

13. Mary swam 5 laps on Monday, 10 laps on Tuesday, and 15 laps on Wednesday. What percentage of laps on Wednesday did Mary swim on Tuesday? On Monday?

14. John is 30% taller than Jack. If Jack is 5 feet tall, how tall is John?

15. 16 is 50% of what number?

16. 18 is what percent of 40?

17. The temperature rose from 60° to 80° in one day. By what percentage did the temperature increase in one day?

18. John made $100 the first week and $80 the second week. By what percentage did his earnings decrease from the first week to the second?

19. 12 is what percent of 12?

20. 8 is what percent of 4?

21. 3 is 6% of what number?

22. 2 is 4% of what number?

23. What is 25% of 8?

24. What is 15% of 200?

25. What is 24% of 150?

Exponents and Roots

Diagnostic Test on Exponents and Roots

1. Which of these is $7 \times 7 \times 7 \times 7$?

   (A) 4^7
   (B) 7^4
   (C) 4^3
   (D) 14^2
   (E) none of the above

2. $(5^0)(8^1)$ equals

   (A) 5
   (B) 8
   (C) 40
   (D) 3
   (E) 13

3. $(11^3)(11^5)$ equals

   (A) 88
   (B) 11^8
   (C) 11^2
   (D) 22^8
   (E) none of the above

4. $\sqrt{12} + \sqrt{24}$ equals

   (A) $2\sqrt{6} + 2\sqrt{3}$ (D) $6 + \sqrt{3}$
   (B) $\sqrt{36}$ (E) $6\sqrt{2}$
   (C) $\sqrt{288}$

5. $15^5 \div 15^2$ equals

   (A) 30^3 (D) 3^5
   (B) 5^7 (E) 15^3
   (C) 10^5

6. Find $\sqrt{100} + \sqrt{49}$.

   (A) $\sqrt{149}$ (D) 23
   (B) $\sqrt{490}$ (E) $\sqrt{10} + \sqrt{14}$
   (C) 17

7. $\sqrt{147} =$

   (A) $7\sqrt{3}$ (D) 14
   (B) 21   (E) $2\sqrt{98}$
   (C) $3\sqrt{7}$

8. Find a cube root of 64.

   (A) 2   (D) 16
   (B) 3   (E) 32
   (C) 4

9. $2^{-3} \times 16 =$

   (A) 1
   (B) 4
   (C) 128
   (D) .5
   (E) none of the above

10. $\dfrac{1}{3^{-3}} =$

   (A) $\dfrac{1}{27}$ (D) $\dfrac{1}{6}$

   (B) 27   (E) $-\dfrac{1}{9}$

   (C) -6

Solutions for Diagnostic Test

1. **(B)** 7 is used as a factor 4 times. We can write this 7^4.   **(1-26)**

2. **(B)** A number raised to the zero power is 1; a number raised to the first power is itself. Therefore, $(5^0)(8^1) = 8$.
   (1-26)

3. **(B)** To multiply, we add exponents (providing the numbers being raised to powers are the same). Thus, $(11^5)(11^3) = 11^{5+3} = 11^8$.   **(1-26)**

4. **(A)** The square root of a product is the product of the square roots of the factors.
$$\sqrt{12} + \sqrt{24} = \sqrt{4}\sqrt{3} + \sqrt{4}\sqrt{6}$$
$$= 2\sqrt{3} + 2\sqrt{6} \qquad \textbf{(1-27)}$$

5. **(E)** To divide, we subtract exponents:
$15^5 \div 15^2 = 15^3.$ **(1-26)**

6. **(C)** Since $10 \times 10 = 100$, and $7 \times 7 = 49$, $\sqrt{100} \times \sqrt{49} = 10 + 7 = 17.$ **(1-27)**

7. **(A)** The square root of a product is the product of the square roots of the factors. $\sqrt{147} = \sqrt{49}\sqrt{3} = 7\sqrt{3}.$ **(1-27)**

8. **(C)** $64 = 2 \cdot 2 \cdot 2 \cdot 2 \cdot 2 \cdot 2$ or $4 \cdot 4 \cdot 4$ or $4^3.$ Thus 4 is a cube root of 64.   **(1-26)**

9. **(E)** 2^{-3} is $\dfrac{1}{2^3}$ or $\dfrac{1}{8}$. $\dfrac{1}{8} \times 16 = 2$, which is not listed.   **(1-26)**

10. **(B)** $\dfrac{1}{3^{-3}} = \dfrac{1}{\left(\dfrac{1}{3^3}\right)} = \dfrac{1}{\left(\dfrac{1}{27}\right)} = 27.$ **(1-26)**

Instructional Material on Exponents and Roots

1-26   Exponents described

An exponent tells how many times a number is to be used as a factor. For example, in the expression 4^3, the exponent 3 means that we are to multiply $4 \times 4 \times 4$. The expression 5^4 means $5 \times 5 \times 5 \times 5$. If the exponent is zero, the value of the expression is always 1. Thus, $3^0 = 10^0 = 1$. If the exponent is 1, the value of the expression is the number whose exponent is 1. Thus, $3^1 = 3$, and $7^1 = 7$.

Problems with exponents can be done by remembering that exponents just count factors. For example: Evaluate $3^4 \times 3^3$. Since 3^4 means "use 3 as a factor four times," and 3^3 means "use 3 as a factor three times," and since we then multiply the results, we are using 3 as a factor $3 + 4$, or 7, times. Therefore $3^4 \times 3^3 = 3^7$. Similarly, $4^5 \div 4^2 = 4^3$, because we are dividing out two of the five factors of 4, leaving three factors of 4, or 4^3.

A negative exponent indicates the reciprocal of a positive exponent. Thus, $5^{-2} = \dfrac{1}{5^2}$. Note that $5^2 \times 5^{-2} = 5^0 = 1$.

SUMMARY

I.   If two numbers have the *same* base (e.g., 3^2, 3^5 or 7^2, 7^6) when we *multiply*, we *keep* the *base* and *add* the exponents:

      Examples: $3^2 \times 3^3 = 3^5$
                  $2^{-1} \times 2^{-2} = 2^{-3}$
                  $3^2 \times 3^{-2} = 3^0 = 1$
                  $2^5 \times 2^{-3} = 2^2$
                  $7^6 \times 7^{14} = 7^{20}$

II.   If two numbers have the *same* base (e.g., 3^2, 3^5 or 7^2, 7^6) when we *divide*, we *keep* the *same base* and *subtract* the exponents:

Examples: $3^2 \div 3^1 = 3^1$

$7^5 \div 7^3 = 7^2$ $\qquad$ $\dfrac{7^5}{7^4} = 7^1 = 7$

$7^5 \div 7^6 = 7^{-1}$ $\qquad$ $\dfrac{8^9}{8^3} = 8^6$

$2^{-1} \div 2^{-2} = 2^1$

$6^8 \div 6^{-3} = 6^{11}$ $\qquad$ $\dfrac{8^7}{8^7} = 8^0 = 1$

$6^{-2} \div 6^2 = 6^{-4}$

III. Examples of products of exponents:

$$(3^2)^3 = 3^2 \times 3^2 \times 3^2 = 3^{2 \times 3} = 3^6$$
$$(4^2)^4 = 4^8 \; (= 4^2 \times 4^2 \times 4^2 \times 4^2)$$

When you have a number such as 3^2 and raise that number to a power [e.g., $(3^2)^3$], you *multiply exponents* and *keep the base*: $(3^2)^3 = 3^6$.

IV. When multiplying two different bases with the same powers, *multiply the bases* but *keep the power*.

Examples: $2^4 \times 3^4 = (2 \times 3)^4 = 6^4$

$3^5 \times 4^5 = (3 \times 4)^5 = 12^5$

$7^1 \times 6^1 = (7 \times 6)^1 = 42^1 = 42$

When dividing two different bases with the same powers, *divide the bases* but keep the power.

Examples: $2^4 \div 3^4 = \left(\dfrac{2}{3}\right)^4$

$$\dfrac{7^5}{8^5} = \left(\dfrac{7}{8}\right)^5$$

$$\dfrac{6^7}{3^7} = \left(\dfrac{6}{3}\right)^7 = 2^7$$

Practice Exercises for 1-26

1. Write the product of 2^3 and 2^7 as a power of 2.

2. $4^7 \div 4^2 = ?$

3. $2^5 = ?$

4. $2^{-3} = ?$

5. $3^{-1} \times 2^3 \times 4^0 = ?$

6. $7^{-1} \times 7^3 \div 7^5 = ?$

7. $\dfrac{4^7}{4^4} = ?$

8. $\dfrac{3^2}{3^5} = ?$

9. $7^{-1} \times 7^{-2} \div 7^{-3} = ?$

10. $(6^2)^3 = ?$ (Write as power of 6)

11. $(4^{-2})^{-3} = ?$ (Write as power of 4)

12. $\dfrac{6}{6^5} = ?$ (Write as power of 6)

13. $6 \times 6^4 \times 6^{-3} = ?$

14. $2^{-1} \times 4^{-2} \times 3^5 = ?$

15. $1^{-100} = ?$

16. Evaluate: $8^4 \div 4^4$

17. Evaluate: $2^3 \times 3^3$

18. Evaluate: $\dfrac{3^3}{9^3}$

19. What single number raised to a power is $\dfrac{7^5}{4^5}$?

20. What single number raised to a power is $62^{15} \times 2^{15}$?

1-27 Square root of a number described

The square of a number is the number multiplied by itself. For example, $4^2 = 4 \times 4 = 16$. The square root of a given number is a number whose square is the original number. Thus, the square root of 16, written $\sqrt{16}$, is 4 since $4 \times 4 = 16$. (The $\sqrt{}$ symbol always means a positive number.)

Note: The square root of any number, times itself, is the number. Examples: $\sqrt{4} \times \sqrt{4} = 4$; $\sqrt{16} \times \sqrt{16} = 16$

> The key relationship in simplifying the square root of a product is the product of the square roots of the factors.

To simplify a square root, try to find a factor of the number under the square root sign that is a perfect square (4, 9, 16, 25, etc.). If such a factor can be found, then we can simplify.

For example: $\sqrt{32} = \sqrt{16 \times 2} = \sqrt{16} \times \sqrt{2} = 4\sqrt{2}$; this cannot be simplified further.

Similarly the sum $\sqrt{3} + \sqrt{2}$ cannot be simplified. We can add expressions with square roots only if the numbers inside the square root sign are the same.

For example: Add $\sqrt{50} + \sqrt{2}$.
First, $\sqrt{50} = \sqrt{25 \times 2} = \sqrt{25} \times \sqrt{2} = 5\sqrt{2}$. Then, $\sqrt{50} + \sqrt{2} = 5\sqrt{2} + \sqrt{2} = 6\sqrt{2}$.
   Note: Just as $\sqrt{25} \times \sqrt{2} = \sqrt{50}$,

$$\frac{\sqrt{25}}{\sqrt{2}} = \sqrt{\frac{25}{2}}$$

That is, when we divide square roots, we can divide the numbers *inside* the square roots and then take the square root of the result.

Division examples: $\dfrac{\sqrt{15}}{\sqrt{3}} = \sqrt{5}$

$$\frac{\sqrt{25}}{\sqrt{5}} = \sqrt{5}$$

$$\frac{\sqrt{36}}{\sqrt{6}} = \sqrt{6}$$

Multiplication examples: $\sqrt{20} \times \sqrt{3} = \sqrt{60}$
$$\sqrt{4} \times \sqrt{6} = \sqrt{24}$$
$$\sqrt{16} \times \sqrt{2} = \sqrt{32}$$

Similarly, the cube of a number is the number multiplied by itself three times. For example, since $8 = (2)(2)(2)$, 8 is the cube of 2. A cube root of a given number is a number whose cube is the given number. Thus, 2 is a cube root of 8, written $\sqrt[3]{8} = 2$.

Note: $\sqrt[3]{8}$ can be written as $8^{\frac{1}{3}}$. Similarly $\sqrt{2}$ can be written as $2^{\frac{1}{2}}$, and so forth.

Rationalizing the denominator:

Sometimes we wish to have the square root of a number in the numerator instead of in the denominator.

Example: Convert the fraction $\frac{1}{\sqrt{2}}$ so that the denominator does not contain a square root.

Solution: Multiply both denominator and numerator by $\sqrt{2}$:

$$\frac{1}{\sqrt{2}} \times \frac{\sqrt{2}}{\sqrt{2}} = \frac{\sqrt{2}}{\sqrt{2}\ \sqrt{2}} = \frac{\sqrt{2}}{2}.$$

Notice that by multiplying the denominator by $\sqrt{2}$, we "rationalize" the denominator.

Practice Exercises for 1-27

1. What is the value of the square root of 36?
2. Simplify: $\sqrt{700}$
3. Add: $\sqrt{50} + \sqrt{18} + \sqrt{32}$
4. What is the value of $\sqrt[3]{64}$?
5. Evaluate: $\frac{\sqrt{5} \times \sqrt{10}}{\sqrt{2}}$
6. Simplify: $\sqrt{8} + \sqrt{2} + \sqrt{16} + \sqrt{32}$
7. Evaluate: $64^{\frac{1}{2}}$
8. Convert the fraction $\frac{3}{\sqrt{2}}$ so it has a simplified denominator. (Hint: Rationalize denominator so denominator does not have $\sqrt{2}$ in it.)
9. Simplify: $\sqrt{5} + \sqrt{80} + \sqrt{25}$
10. What is $\sqrt{32} \times \sqrt{4}$?
11. What is $\frac{\sqrt{27}}{\sqrt{3}}$?
12. Evaluate: $\frac{\sqrt{5} + \sqrt{20} - \sqrt{45}}{\sqrt{70}}$
13. Simplify: $\frac{\sqrt{3} + \sqrt{27} - \sqrt{6}}{\sqrt{3}}$
14. What is $\sqrt{49} + 64^{\frac{1}{2}} + \sqrt[4]{81}$?
15. If $\sqrt{2}$ is approximately equal to 1.4142, approximate $\frac{1}{\sqrt{2}}$.

Whole Numbers

Diagnostic Test on Whole Numbers

1. 148 is divisible by

   (A) 37   (D) 43
   (B) 21   (E) 89
   (C) 17

2. If the sum of two consecutive numbers is 15, the smaller number is

   (A) 7   (D) 6
   (B) 1   (E) 8
   (C) 12

3. If a number is odd, then it can *never* be divisible by

   (A) 3   (D) 5
   (B) 1   (E) 7
   (C) 2

4. Which of the following are consecutive even numbers?

   (A) 2, 3, 4, 5   (D) 32, 34, 36
   (B) 1, 1½, 2   (E) .1, .2, .3
   (C) 1, 3, 5

5. An even number is always divisible by

   (A) 1   (D) 4
   (B) 2   (E) 0
   (C) 3

6. Which of the following is a factor of 21?

   (A) 7   (D) 14
   (B) 42   (E) 15
   (C) 0

7. 17 is a multiple of

   (A) 5   (D) 11
   (B) 2   (E) 34
   (C) 17

8. Which of the following is an even prime number?

   (A) 0   (D) 3
   (B) 1   (E) 4
   (C) 2

9. Factor 176 into prime factors.

   (A) (1)(4)(11)   (D) (1)(2)(2)(11)
   (B) (2)(2)(2)(2)(11) (E) (1)(176)
   (C) (1)(2)(11)

10. Which number is divisible by both 4 and 9?

    (A) 2,178   (D) 3,536
    (B) 1,311   (E) 5,256
    (C) 8,519

Solutions for Diagnostic Test

1. **(A)** Divisible means able to be divided without any remainder.
   $148 = 37(4)$ or $148 \div 37 = 4$ **(1-28)**

2. **(A)** If n is the smaller number, then the other number is $n + 1$.
   So $n + n + 1 = 15$
   $n = 7$ **(1-28)**

3. **(C)** An odd number can never be divided by 2. **(1-28)**

4. **(D)** Even numbers are 2, 4, 6, 8, etc. So, 32, 34, and 36 are consecutive even numbers. **(1-28)**

5. **(B)** An even number is a number that is divisible by 2. **(1-28)**

6. **(A)** One number is a factor of a given number if it divides into the given number exactly. **(1-28)**

$$21 \div 7 = 3$$

So, 7 is a factor of 21.

7. **(C)** Any whole number is a multiple of itself. So, 17 is a multiple of 17. **(1-28)**

8. **(C)** A prime number is a number that has exactly two factors. The only even prime number is 2. **(1-28)**

9. **(B)** To factor 176 into prime factors, factor out the smallest prime and repeat the process until all the factors are prime numbers.

$$176 = 2(88)$$
$$= 2(2)(44)$$
$$= 2(2)(2)(22) = 2(2)(2)(2)(11)$$

(1-28)

10. **(E)** 5256 is divisible by 4, since 56 is divisible by 4 ($56 \div 4 = 14$); and is divisible by 9, since the sum of the digits is divisible by 9: $5 + 2 + 5 + 6 = 18$. **(1-29)**

Instructional Material on Whole Numbers

1-28 Whole numbers described

The whole numbers (integers) are 0, 1, 2, 3, 4, and so on. The whole numbers have some special definitions and properties. In this section, the word "number" refers only to whole numbers.

1) A number is *divisible* by another number if the second number divides into the first number without any remainder. For example: 10 is divisible by 5.
2) A number that is divisible by 2 is called an *even* number. Examples of even numbers are 0, 2, 4, 6, and 8.
3) A number that is not even is an *odd* number. Examples of odd numbers are 1, 3, 5, 7, and 9.
4) *Consecutive* means following in the natural order. For example: 15, 16, 17, and 18 are consecutive whole numbers. 2, 4, and 6 are consecutive even numbers. 11, 13, and 15 are consecutive odd numbers.

Note:
(a) Consecutive numbers differ by 1, consecutive even numbers differ by 2, and consecutive odd numbers differ by 2.
(b) In the whole numbers, the even numbers and odd numbers alternate. In other words, an even number is followed by an odd number and an odd number is followed by an even number.

5) A number is a *multiple* of another number if it is divisible by the second number. For example: 10 is a multiple of 5, and 10 is a multiple of 2.

6) A number is a *factor* of another number if the second number is divisible by the first number. For example: 2 is a factor of 10, 5 is a factor of 10, and 1 and 10 are also factors of 10.

> Note: Any number is always a multiple of itself and 1. 1 and the number itself are always factors of that number.

7) A *composite* number is any number that has more than two factors. Examples of composite numbers are 10 and 12: 10 has four factors (1, 2, 5, and 10) and 12 has six factors (1, 2, 3, 4, 6, and 12).

8) A *prime* number is any number that has exactly two different factors, itself and 1. The first 10 prime numbers are 2, 3, 5, 7, 11, 13, 17, 19, 23, and 29.

> Note:
> (a) 2 is the only even prime number. Every other even number has at least 3 factors: 1, 2, and itself.
> (b) 1 is neither a prime number nor a composite number since it has only one factor: 1.

9) If a factor of a number is a prime number, it is a *prime factor*. For example: Of the factors of 10, the prime factors are 2 and 5.

10) To factor is to express the number as the product of its factors, excluding 1 and itself. For example: To factor 10, write 10 as (2)(5). In this case the factors 2 and 5 are prime factors, so 10 is factored into prime factors.

To factor a number into prime factors:
First factor out the smallest prime factor, and then factor out the next smallest prime factor, and so on. Continue to factor out the prime factors until it is not possible to factor any further (until all the factors are prime factors).

For example: Factor 200 into prime factors.

First factor the 2s out of 200.

$$200 = (2)(100)$$
$$= (2)(2)(50)$$
$$= (2)(2)(2)(25)$$

The next smallest factor is 5.

$$200 = (2)(2)(2)(5)(5)$$

Since all the factors are prime numbers, 200 cannot be factored any further.

Practice Exercises for 1-28

1. What is the sum of the first five consecutive odd numbers?

2. What is the sum of the first five consecutive even numbers? (Start with 2.)

3. Which is an even number?

   (A) The product of two odd numbers

   (B) The product of two even numbers

   (C) The product of an odd and an even number

   (D) The sum of two odd numbers

   (E) The sum of an odd and an even number

   (F) The difference between two odd numbers

   (G) The difference between an odd and an even number

4. What are the prime factors of 132?

5. Why is an even number that is not 2 never prime?

6. What is the greatest prime factor of 110?

7. Why is 2 a prime number?

8. Which is greater: The sum of the first three odd numbers or the sum of the first three even numbers? (Do not use 0.)

9. What is the fifth prime number? (Start with 2.)

10. Factor the number 63 into prime factors.

1-29 To find out whether or not a number is prime

See whether the number has any factor other than itself and 1; if it does not have any, then it is a prime. To find the factors of a number, the following divisibility tests will be helpful:

Division tips:

1) A number is divisible by 2 if its last digit is even.

   For example: 342 is divisible by 2, since the last digit, 2, is even. 356,771 is not divisible by 2 since its last digit, 1, is odd.

2) A number is divisible by 3 if the sum of its digits is divisible by 3.

   For example: 528 is divisible by 3, since $5 + 2 + 8 = 15$, which is divisible by 3. 721 is not divisible by 3, since $7 + 2 + 1 = 10$, which is not divisible by 3.

3) A number is divisible by 4 if the number formed by the last two digits is divisible by 4.

For example: 987,528 is divisible by 4, since the number formed by the last two digits, 28, is divisible by 4. 926 is not divisible by 4, since 26 is not divisible by 4.

4) A number is divisible by 5 if its last digit is either 0 or 5.

For example: 340 is divisible by 5, since the last digit is 0. 344 is not divisible by 5, since the last digit is 4.

5) A number is divisible by 6 if it is divisible by both 2 and 3.

For example: 546 is divisible by 6, since it is divisible by 2 (its last digit is even) and by 3 (5 + 4 + 6 = 15, which is divisible by 3). 521 is not divisible by 6, since it is not divisible by 2.

6) A number is divisible by 8 if the number formed by the last 3 digits of the number is divisible by 8.

For example: 5064 is divisible by 8, since 64 is divisible by 8. 5121 is not divisible by 8, since 121 is not divisible by 8.

7) A number is divisible by 9 if the sum of its digits is divisible by 9.

For example: 1782 is divisible by 9, since 1 + 7 + 8 + 2 = 18, which is divisible by 9. 782 is not divisible by 9, since 7 + 8 + 2 = 17, which is not divisible by 9.

Practice Exercises for 1-29

1. Which of the following numbers is exactly divisible by 3?

   (A) 214   (B) 345   (C) 721

2. Which of the following is exactly divisible by 4?

   (A) 212   (B) 724   (C) 865

3. Which number is exactly divisible by 5?

   (A) 264   (B) 325   (C) 710

4. Which number is exactly divisible by 9?

   (A) 2164   (B) 3123   (C) 2178

5. Which number is exactly divisible by 8?

   (A) 20,896   (B) 41,324   (C) 21,642

Answers to Practice Exercises in Arithmetic
(1-1 through 1-29)

1-1

1. 5	5. 11	9. 201	13. 21	17. 34
2. 1	6. 17	10. 100	14. 101	18. 31
3. 12	7. 3	11. 5	15. 2	19. 35
4. 8	8. 32	12. 9	16. 4	20. 4

1-2

1. $6\frac{2}{3}$	5. $2\frac{1}{8}$	9. $1\frac{7}{8}$	13. $2\frac{1}{4}$	17. $8\frac{1}{3}$
2. $1\frac{3}{7}$	6. $3\frac{3}{4}$	10. $3\frac{1}{5}$	14. $1\frac{1}{2}$	18. $1\frac{8}{9}$
3. $1\frac{3}{4}$	7. $6\frac{1}{2}$	11. $2\frac{2}{5}$	15. $1\frac{1}{12}$	19. $9\frac{1}{11}$
4. $3\frac{1}{8}$	8. $1\frac{8}{10}$	12. $2\frac{2}{4}$	16. $1\frac{1}{24}$	20. $1\frac{1}{14}$

1-3

1. $\frac{11}{3}$	5. $\frac{67}{17}$	9. $\frac{10}{3}$	13. $\frac{7}{4}$	17. $\frac{55}{2}$
2. $\frac{65}{4}$	6. $\frac{57}{8}$	10. $\frac{21}{8}$	14. $\frac{28}{9}$	18. $\frac{80}{3}$
3. $\frac{47}{8}$	7. $\frac{7}{2}$	11. $\frac{55}{8}$	15. $\frac{28}{3}$	19. $\frac{67}{4}$
4. $\frac{5}{2}$	8. $\frac{35}{2}$	12. $\frac{15}{8}$	16. $\frac{64}{3}$	20. $\frac{127}{8}$

1-4

1. $\frac{1}{2}$	6. $\frac{1}{2}$	11. $\frac{3}{4}$	16. $\frac{7}{9}$	21. $\frac{1}{2}$
2. $\frac{3}{4}$	7. $\frac{1}{3}$	12. $\frac{1}{2}$	17. $\frac{2}{3}$	22. $\frac{1}{7}$
3. $\frac{3}{10}$	8. $\frac{7}{11}$	13. $\frac{7}{10}$	18. $\frac{3}{5}$	23. $\frac{8}{15}$
4. $\frac{1}{3}$	9. $\frac{4}{9}$	14. $\frac{1}{2}$	19. $\frac{1}{3}$	24. $\frac{1}{2}$
5. $\frac{7}{12}$	10. $\frac{1}{11}$	15. $\frac{2}{3}$	20. $\frac{15}{49}$	25. $\frac{4}{9}$

1-5

1. $\dfrac{21}{32}$

2. $\dfrac{2}{9}$

3. $\dfrac{8}{3}$

4. $\dfrac{2}{21}$

5. $\dfrac{12}{70}$ or $\dfrac{6}{35}$

6. $\dfrac{12}{5}$ or $2\dfrac{2}{5}$

7. $\dfrac{42}{42}$ or 1

8. $\dfrac{6}{15}$ or $\dfrac{2}{5}$

9. $\dfrac{5}{128}$

10. $\dfrac{27}{2}$ or $13\dfrac{1}{2}$

11. $\dfrac{3}{28}$

12. $\dfrac{8}{25}$

13. $\dfrac{49}{64}$

14. $\dfrac{30}{10}$ or 3

15. $\dfrac{21}{16}$ or $1\dfrac{5}{16}$

16. $\dfrac{7}{12}$

17. $\dfrac{3}{2}$ or $1\dfrac{1}{2}$

18. $\dfrac{14}{45}$

19. $\dfrac{2}{3}$

20. 3

21. 6

22. $\dfrac{5}{9}$

23. 1

24. 1

25. $\dfrac{1}{3}$

26. $\dfrac{2}{3}$

27. $\dfrac{75}{153}$

28. $\dfrac{2}{21}$

29. 1

30. $\dfrac{3}{7}$

31. $\dfrac{3}{14}$

32. 1

33. $\dfrac{7}{8}$

34. 1

35. 1

36. $\dfrac{6}{5}$ or $1\dfrac{1}{5}$

37. $\dfrac{1}{4}$

38. 8

39. 9

40. 1

1-6

1. $\dfrac{3}{2}$

2. $\dfrac{1}{2}$

3. $\dfrac{1}{9}$

4. $\dfrac{12}{35}$

5. 2

6. $\dfrac{4}{9}$

7. 1

8. $\dfrac{1}{2}$

9. $\dfrac{3}{2}$

10. $\dfrac{1}{8}$

11. $\dfrac{4}{5}$

12. $\dfrac{1}{98}$

13. $\dfrac{5}{9}$

14. $\dfrac{3}{8}$

15. $\dfrac{7}{15}$

16. $\dfrac{9}{16}$

17. $\dfrac{5}{4}$ or $1\dfrac{1}{4}$

18. $\dfrac{21}{16}$ or $1\dfrac{5}{16}$

19. 3

20. 4

21. $\dfrac{7}{256}$

22. $\dfrac{3}{8}$

23. $\dfrac{49}{2}$ or $24\dfrac{1}{2}$

24. $\dfrac{1}{64}$

25. $\dfrac{32}{81}$

1-7

1. $\dfrac{2}{8}$

2. $\dfrac{6}{16}$

3. $\dfrac{14}{32}$

4. $\dfrac{8}{12}$

5. $\dfrac{8}{14}$

6. $\dfrac{3}{9}$

7. $\dfrac{4}{8}$

8. $\dfrac{3}{8}$

9. $\dfrac{8}{22}$

10. $\dfrac{25}{51}$

1-8

1. 1
2. $\dfrac{4}{5}$
3. $\dfrac{1}{2}$
4. $\dfrac{29}{56}$
5. $\dfrac{9}{21}$ or $\dfrac{3}{7}$

6. $\dfrac{17}{32}$
7. $\dfrac{71}{42}$ or $1\dfrac{29}{42}$
8. $\dfrac{13}{6}$ or $2\dfrac{1}{6}$
9. $\dfrac{17}{16}$ or $1\dfrac{1}{16}$
10. $1\dfrac{5}{6}$

11. $\dfrac{17}{18}$
12. $\dfrac{27}{42}$ or $\dfrac{9}{14}$
13. $\dfrac{16}{63}$
14. $\dfrac{38}{45}$
15. $\dfrac{13}{10}$ or $1\dfrac{3}{10}$

16. $\dfrac{145}{72}$ or $2\dfrac{1}{72}$
17. $\dfrac{43}{28}$ or $1\dfrac{15}{28}$
18. 4
19. $\dfrac{211}{36}$ or $5\dfrac{31}{36}$
20. $2\dfrac{5}{21}$

21. $\dfrac{77}{60}$ or $1\dfrac{17}{60}$
22. $3\dfrac{1}{7}$
23. $\dfrac{11}{12}$
24. $1\dfrac{3}{8}$
25. $\dfrac{249}{140}$ or $1\dfrac{109}{140}$

1-9

1. $\dfrac{1}{4}$
2. $\dfrac{2}{7}$
3. $\dfrac{3}{4}$
4. $\dfrac{1}{8}$
5. $\dfrac{1}{56}$
6. $\dfrac{5}{6}$

7. $\dfrac{5}{28}$
8. $\dfrac{1}{4}$
9. $\dfrac{2}{9}$
10. $\dfrac{1}{5}$
11. $\dfrac{1}{15}$
12. $\dfrac{13}{16}$

13. $\dfrac{1}{6}$
14. $\dfrac{11}{32}$
15. $\dfrac{4}{15}$
16. $\dfrac{2}{15}$
17. $\dfrac{5}{16}$
18. $\dfrac{7}{2}$ or $3\dfrac{1}{2}$

19. $\dfrac{8}{3}$ or $2\dfrac{2}{3}$
20. $\dfrac{3}{40}$
21. $\dfrac{31}{34}$
22. $\dfrac{13}{40}$
23. $\dfrac{13}{42}$
24. $1\dfrac{1}{3}$ or $\dfrac{4}{3}$

25. $\dfrac{1}{2}$
26. $\dfrac{7}{72}$
27. $\dfrac{1}{30}$
28. $\dfrac{29}{45}$
29. $\dfrac{4}{33}$
30. $\dfrac{32}{49}$

1-10

1. 3
2. $\dfrac{6}{7}$

3. $\dfrac{16}{21}$
4. $\dfrac{7}{6}$ or $1\dfrac{1}{6}$

5. $\dfrac{4}{3}$ or $1\dfrac{1}{3}$
6. $\dfrac{12}{25}$

7. $\dfrac{4}{3}$ or $1\dfrac{1}{3}$
8. 2

9. 1
10. $\dfrac{9}{16}$

1-11

1. $\dfrac{5}{16}$
2. $\dfrac{13}{36}$

3. $\dfrac{15}{4}$ or $3\dfrac{3}{4}$
4. $\dfrac{20}{3}$ or $6\dfrac{2}{3}$

5. $\dfrac{231}{16}$ or $14\dfrac{7}{16}$
6. $\dfrac{40}{9}$ or $4\dfrac{4}{9}$

7. $\dfrac{17}{26}$
8. $\dfrac{3}{7}$

9. $\dfrac{2}{5}$
10. $\dfrac{10}{9}$ or $1\dfrac{1}{9}$

1-12

1. $\frac{425}{1000}$ 3. $\frac{3}{10}$ 5. $\frac{325}{1000}$ 7. 12.3   9. 3.33

2. $\frac{7}{100}$ 4. $\frac{45}{1000}$ 6. .21   8. 1.6   10. 21.001

1-13

1. 3.2   3. 12110   5. 7534   7. .00176   9. .1703

2. 216   4. 107.62   6. .1325   8. 2.136   10. .000114

1-14

1. $\frac{7}{10}$ 3. $\frac{735}{1000}$ 5. $\frac{620}{1000}$ or $\frac{62}{100}$ 7. $100\frac{1}{100}$ 9. $\frac{1}{1000}$

2. $\frac{73}{100}$ 4. $\frac{7355}{10000}$ 6. $1\frac{21}{100}$ 8. $2\frac{17}{100}$ 10. $\frac{15}{1000}$

1-15*

1. 33.491   5. 28.184   9. 18.3   13. 9.5   17. 22.25
2. 23.12   6. 11   10. 4.45   14. 6.958   18. 21.48
3. 2.637   7. 7.94   11. .111   15. 13.5906   19. 9.004
4. 5.291   8. 3.3987   12. .72   16. 12.78   20. 4.772

1-16*

1. 7.5   5. 2.6   9. $28.50   13. .78 centimeters   17. $2.10
2. 6.37   6. $23.89   10. 7.8 kilograms   14. 13.4 meters   18. .69 meters
3. 20.31   7. 131.42   11. 65.5   15. 100.997   19. .63
4. $2.56   8. 99.893   12. 8.24   16. .89   20. 156.242

1-17*

1. 3.96   5. 58.48   9. 2.457   13. 60.2   17. 1.21
2. 1.575   6. 675.1   10. 2.45   14. 20.928   18. 49.3
3. 42   7. 9.63   11. 1.4641   15. .732   19. 4.0401
4. .08125   8. 2.226   12. 3.186   16. 57   20. 6.6456

1-18*

1. $20.8\frac{1}{3}$ 3. $20.8\frac{1}{3}$ 5. .2125 7. 1.8 9. 30

2. $27.7\frac{7}{9}$ 4. 4.4 6. 20.25 8. 30 10. $2\frac{12}{410}$ or $2\frac{6}{205}$

1-19*

1. .04 4. 2.25 7. .375 10. .04 13. .012

2. .525 5. .024 8. .16 11. .33333... 14. .008

3. .06 6. .25 9. .21 12. .4 15. .06666...

1-20*

1. 1.5 or $1\frac{1}{2}$ 2. 2.1 or $2\frac{1}{10}$ 3. 4.6 kilometers 4. 45.61 yards 5. $\frac{79}{30}$ or $2\frac{19}{30}$

1-21

1. 85% 2. 60% 3. 80% 4. 20% 5. 5%

1-22

1. 21.4% 10. 50% 19. .042 28. .005 37. $\frac{75}{100}$ or $\frac{3}{4}$

2. 220% 11. $66\frac{2}{3}$% 20. .003 29. .05 38. $\frac{2}{3}$

3. 8% 12. 87.5% 21. .011 30. 1.176 39. $\frac{1}{7}$

4. 75% 13. .1% 22. .1 31. $\frac{26}{100}$ 40. $\frac{1}{10}$

5. 37.5% 14. 1% 23. .0865 32. $\frac{25}{200}$ or $\frac{125}{1000}$ 41. $\frac{186}{1000}$

6. 12% 15. 101% 24. .0225 33. $\frac{15}{100}$ 42. $\frac{1}{200}$

7. 336% 16. .72 25. .115 34. $\frac{135}{1000}$ or $\frac{27}{200}$ 43. $\frac{1}{2}$

8. 74% 17. .65 26. .755 35. $\frac{9}{400}$ or $\frac{225}{10000}$ 44. $\frac{9}{100}$

9. $33\frac{1}{8}$% 18. .343 27. .083 36. $\frac{49}{400}$ or $\frac{1225}{10000}$ 45. $1\frac{112}{1000}$

*Note in **1-15** through **1-20**, these problems can be solved with a calculator.

1-23

	Percent	Fraction	Decimal
1.	40	$\frac{4}{10}$ or $\frac{2}{5}$	.4
2.	$16\frac{2}{3}$	$\frac{1}{6}$	.1666…
3.	$87\frac{1}{2}$	$\frac{7}{8}$	.875
4.	5	$\frac{5}{100}$ or $\frac{1}{20}$	.05
5.	$12\frac{1}{2}\%$	$\frac{1}{8}$	.125
7.	$33\frac{1}{8}$	$\frac{1}{3}$	.333…
6.	80	$\frac{4}{5}$	.8
8.	100	$\frac{1}{1}$ or 1	1.0
9.	25	$\frac{1}{4}$	.25
10.	65	$\frac{65}{100}$ or $\frac{13}{20}$	.65

1-24

1. $90
2. $122
3. 25%
4. $200
5. $216; 28%
6. $1166.40
7. $54
8. 20%
9. 20%
10. 128.12\frac{1}{2}$ or $128.13 (rounded off)

1-25

1. 50
2. 60
3. 36%
4. 160 pounds
5. $33\frac{1}{3}\%$
6. 60
7. 240
8. 2
9. $\frac{25}{10}$ or $2\frac{1}{2}$
10. $18\frac{3}{4}$
11. 200%
12. 30%
13. $66\frac{2}{3}\%$; $33\frac{1}{3}\%$
14. $6\frac{1}{2}$ feet
15. 32
16. 45%
17. $33\frac{1}{3}\%$
18. 20%
19. 100%
20. 200%
21. 50
22. 50
23. 2
24. 30
25. 36

1-26

1. 2^{10}	5. $\frac{8}{3}$ or $2\frac{2}{3}$	9. 1	13. 6^2 or 36	17. 6^3 or 216
2. 4^5	6. 7^{-3} or $\frac{1}{7^3}$	10. 6^6	14. $\frac{243}{32}$ or $7\frac{19}{32}$	18. $\left(\frac{1}{3}\right)^3$ or $\frac{1}{27}$
3. 3^2	7. 4^3 or 64	11. 4^6	15. 1	19. $(1.75)^5$
4. $\frac{1}{8}$	8. 3^{-3} or $\frac{1}{27}$	12. 6^{-4} or $\frac{1}{6^4}$	16. 2^4 or 16	20. 124^{15}

1-27

1. 6	4. 4	7. 8	10. $8\sqrt{2}$	13. $4-\sqrt{2}$
2. $10\sqrt{7}$	5. 5	8. $\frac{3\sqrt{2}}{2}$	11. 3	14. 18
3. $12\sqrt{2}$	6. $7\sqrt{2}+4$	9. $5\sqrt{5}+5$	12. 0	15. $\frac{1.4142}{2}$ or .7071

1-28

1. 25
2. 30
3. (B), (C), (D), (F)
4. $11 \times 3 \times 2 \times 2$
5. Because any even number is divisible by 2, an even number (except 2, since 2 is prime) cannot be prime.
6. 11
7. Because it is exactly divisible only by itself and 1.
8. $2 + 4 + 6$ is greater than $1 + 3 + 5$.
9. 11
10. $7 \times 3 \times 3$

1-29

1. (B) 345
2. (A) 212 and (B) 724
3. (B) 325 and (C) 710
4. (B) 3123 and (C) 2178
5. (A) 20896

Algebra

Signed Numbers

Diagnostic Test on Signed Numbers

1. $6 - 8$ equals

   (A) 9   (D) 4

   (B) -2 (E) -14

   (C) -4

2. $(+8) + (-3)$ equals

   (A) -5 (D) -11

   (B) 11   (E) 5

   (C) 10

3. $(+2) + (-5)$ equals

   (A) 7

   (B) -7

   (C) 3

   (D) -3

   (E) none of the above

4. $(-3) - (-7)$ equals

   (A) 10   (D) -4

   (B) -10 (E) 21

   (C) 4

5. During an experiment, temperature was measured three times. The second reading was 10 degrees lower than the first, and the third was 15 degrees lower than the second. If the first reading was 5 degrees, what was the last?

   (A) 0 degrees   (D) -10 degrees

   (B) 10 degrees   (E) -20 degrees

   (C) -5 degrees

6. $(-1)(-2)(-3)(-4)$ equals

   (A) -10

   (B) -24

   (C) 24

   (D) 8

   (E) none of the above

7. $(-3) - (+3) + (+3)$ equals

   (A) 9   (D) -6

   (B) -9 (E) -3

   (C) 6

8. $(-15) \div (+3)$ equals

   (A) 12   (D) -5

   (B) -12 (E) 5

   (C) 45

9. $(-3)^7$ equals

   (A) 3^7 (D) -3

   (B) -21 (E) 3^{-7}

   (C) -3^7

10. Which of the following equals $\left(-\dfrac{3}{4}\right) \div \left(\dfrac{1}{2}\right)$?

    (A) $\dfrac{-3}{2}$ (D) $\dfrac{-3}{-2}$

    (B) $-\dfrac{3}{8}$ (E) $\left(-\dfrac{3}{2}\right)$

    (C) -1

Solutions for Diagnostic Test

1. **(B)** When a positive number is subtracted from a smaller positive number, the result is negative. $6 - 8 = -2$. **(2-2)**

2. **(E)** We subtract 3 from 8. Since 8 is larger than 3, the result is $+5$. **(2-2)**

3. **(D)** We subtract 5 from 2. Since 2 is smaller than 5, the result is -3. **(2-2)**

4. **(C)** We change the sign of -7 and then add 7 and -3, getting 4. **(2-2)**

5. **(E)** Since the temperature decreased both times, we must subtract twice. $5 - 10 - 15 = -5 - 15 = -20$. **(2-2)**

6. **(C)** There are four (an even number) minus signs. The product must be positive. $1 \cdot 2 \cdot 3 \cdot 4 = 24$. **(2-3, 2-5)**

7. **(E)** First, $(-3) - (+3)$ equals -6, changing the sign of $+3$ and adding. Now $(-6) + (+3)$ equals -3. **(2-2)**

8. **(D)** $15 \div 3$ is 5. Since we have one minus sign, we get $(-15) \div (+3) = -5$. **(2-4)**

9. **(C)** There are seven factors (an odd number) and therefore seven minus signs. Thus $(-3)^7 = -(3^7)$. **(2-5, 1-26)**

10. **(A)** $\left(-\dfrac{3}{4}\right) \div \left(\dfrac{1}{2}\right) = -\left(\dfrac{3}{4} \times \dfrac{2}{1}\right) = -\dfrac{3}{2}$. We can put the minus sign in the numerator. $-\left(\dfrac{3}{2}\right) = \dfrac{-3}{2}$. **(2-4)**

Instructional Material on Signed Numbers

2-1 Signed numbers described

When a larger positive number is subtracted from a smaller positive number, the result is a negative number. For example, $5 - 10 = -5$, read "minus 5." A signed number is a number with a plus or minus sign associated with it. In dealing with signed numbers, if the sign is omitted, the number is understood to be positive. Thus $+10 = 10$.

Practice Exercises for 2-1*

Subtract:

1. $4 - 8$	8. $6 - 12$	15. $32 - 34$
2. $6 - 7$	9. $13 - 14$	16. $16 - 33$
3. $9 - 12$	10. $15 - 25$	17. $15 - 40$
4. $27 - 36$	11. $12 - 14$	18. $2 - 10$
5. $16 - 32$	12. $1 - 2$	19. $5 - 8$
6. $3 - 4$	13. $5 - 7$	20. $25 - 50$
7. $4 - 7$	14. $15 - 17$	

* Answers for Practice Exercises 2-1 through 2-40 begin on page 169.

2-2 To add two signed numbers

1) If the numbers have the same sign, add them as if they were unsigned numbers, and then use the sign they both had. For example, $(+3) + (+4) = +7$. Or, $(-2) + (-4) = -6$.

2) If the numbers have different signs, subtract them as if they were unsigned numbers. If you subtract a smaller number from a larger one, the result is positive. For example, $(-2) + (+5) = 5 - 2 = +3$. If you subtract a larger number from a smaller one, the result is negative. For example, $(+3) + (-6) = 3 - 6 = -3$.

Another example: Find $(+1) + (-2) + (+3) + (-4) + (+5)$.
We add all the numbers with the same sign. $(+1) + (+3) + (+5) = +9$.
$(-2) + (-4) = -6$.
We now have to add $(+9) + (-6) = 9 - 6 = +3$.

To subtract two signed numbers:

Just change the sign of the number being subtracted and then add.

For example: $(-3) - (+6) = (-3) + (-6) = -9$.
Or, $(-5) - (-3) = (-5) + (+3) = 3 - 5 = -2$.

Practice Exercises for 2-2

Evaluate:

1. $1 + 4 - 5$
2. $3 - 7 - 6 + 5$
3. $2 + (+4) - (+6)$
4. $3 + (+5) + (+7)$
5. $6 - (-3) + (-2)$
6. $-7 - (-7) - 7$
7. $6 - (-8) + (-3) - (+3)$
8. $+2 - 2 + (-6) + (-6) - (-3)$
9. $+9 - 3 - 7 - (-3)$
10. $2 + (-2) - (+2) + (+2)$
11. $3 + (-3) - 4 + (-7)$
12. $-8 + 8 + 4 - 4$
13. $2 - 2 - (-2) + (-2)$
14. $6 - 15 - (-13) - (-12)$
15. $8 - 5 + (-4) - (+5)$
16. $7 - 8 - (-4) - 3$
17. $6 - 2 - (13) - (-14)$
18. $+8 - 7 - (-7) - (-8)$
19. $2 - 12 - (-12) + (-12)$
20. $-1 - (-3) - (-4) + 5$

2-3 To multiply two signed numbers

1) The sign of the answer is given by the following rule: If the numbers have the same sign, the product is positive. If the numbers have different signs, the product is negative.

2) Then just multiply the numbers as if they were unsigned.

For example: Since $3 \times 5 = 15$, we have $(+3) \times (+5) = +15$, $(+3) \times (-5) = -15$, $(-3) \times (+5) = -15$, and $(-3) \times (-5) = +15$.

Practice Exercises for 2-3

Multiply:

1. $(+2) \times (+3)$
2. $(+6) \times (-2)$
3. $(-3) \times (-7)$
4. $(-2) \times (+4)$
5. -2×4
6. $(-6) \times (-4)$
7. $(-5) \times 3$
8. $(-5) \times (+3)$
9. $(-5) \times (-3)$
10. $(+5) \times (-3)$

11. $(+5) \times (+3)$
12. $(-8) \times 7$
13. $(-7) \times (-8)$
14. $(-6) \times (+4)$
15. $(-13) \times (-2)$
16. $(+13) \times (-2)$
17. $(-12) \times 3$
18. $3 \times (-4)$
19. $4 \times (-3)$
20. $4 \times (+3)$

2-4   To divide two signed numbers

1) Find the sign of the quotient just as in the rule for multiplication.
2) Then just divide the numbers as if they were unsigned numbers.

For example: $(+25) \div (-5) = -5$, but $(-25) \div (-5) = +5$.
The rules for division of signed numbers stipulate that a fraction is positive if its numerator and denominator have the same sign, and a fraction is negative if its numerator and denominator have different signs.

Thus, $\dfrac{-1}{+2} = \dfrac{+1}{-2} = -\dfrac{1}{2}$, but $\dfrac{-1}{-2} = +\dfrac{1}{2}$.

Practice Exercises for 2-4

Divide:

1. $15 \div (-3)$
2. $-15 \div (-3)$
3. $+20 \div (+4)$
4. $\dfrac{-15}{-5}$
5. $\dfrac{18}{-3}$
6. $-20 \div (-4)$
7. $-15 \div 3$

8. $\dfrac{-36}{12}$
9. $\dfrac{36}{-12}$
10. $\dfrac{-36}{-12}$
11. $9 \div (-3)$
12. $-9 \div (-3)$
13. $+9 \div (+3)$
14. $\dfrac{-6}{2}$

15. $\dfrac{6}{-2}$
16. $\dfrac{-6}{-2}$
17. $-6 \div (+2)$
18. $25 \div (-5)$
19. $\dfrac{-25}{-5}$
20. $\dfrac{+25}{-5}$

2-5   To multiply or divide strings of numbers

1)   Multiply and divide as if the numbers were unsigned.
2)   The sign of the result is positive if there is an even number of minus signs. The sign is negative if there is an odd number of minus signs.

For example: What is $(-2)^5$?
Since the exponent is odd, there is an odd number of minus signs in the product, and the sign of $(-2)^5$ is $-$. Since $2^5 = 32$, $(-2)^5 = -32$.

Another example: What is $-2 \times (-4) \times (+3) \times (-2)$?
Multiply $2 \times 4 \times 3 \times 2$. We get 48. There is an *odd* number of minus signs, so our answer is -48.

Practice Exercises for 2-5

Evaluate:

1. $(-3)^4$

2. $(+2)^4$

3. $\dfrac{(-2)^8}{(+2)^3}$

4. $(-2)^3 \times (-3)^2$

5. $(-2) \times (-4) \times (+3)$

6. $(-5) \times (-1) \times (-3)$

7. $6 \times (+4) \times (+2) \times (-3)$

8. $(-2) \times (-3) \times (-2) \times (-2)$

9. $(-1) \times (+1) \times (-1) \times (+1)$

10. $(-1) \times (+1) \times (-2) \times (+2)$

11. $(-1) \times (-1) \times (-2) \times (-2) \times (-2)$

12. $4 \times 3 \times (-2)$

13. $4 \times 3 \times (-2) \times (-2)$

14. $6 \times (-4) \times (-2) \times (-1) \times (+5)$

15. $(-1)^{21} \times (-1)^{20}$

Algebraic Expressions

Diagnostic Test on Algebraic Expressions

1. $7a^2 + 3b^2 + 2a^2 =$

    (A) $9a^2 + 3b^2$ (D) $a^{18} + b^6$

    (B) $11a^2b^2$ (E) $7(a^2 + 3b^2)$

    (C) $9a^4 + 3b^2$

2. $4x - (3y - x) =$

    (A) $3x + 3y$ (D) $5x - 3y$

    (B) 0 (E) $4(3y - x)$

    (C) $2x$

3. Multiply $3ax^2$ and $4ay^2$.

    (A) $12xy$

    (B) $12a^2$

    (C) $12a^2xy$

    (D) $(12axy)^2$

    (E) none of the above

4. $3m + (2n - 5m) =$

    (A) $8m - 2n$ (D) $4mn$

    (B) $2n + 2m$ (E) $2(m + 3n)$

    (C) $2n - 2m$

5. Simplify $\dfrac{7}{y} + \dfrac{y}{7}$.

    (A) 1 (D) $\dfrac{14 + 2y}{7y}$

    (B) 2 (E) $7y$

    (C) $\dfrac{49 + y^2}{7y}$

6. $(x + 1)(3x - 2) =$

    (A) $3x^2 + x - 2$ (D) $x^2 + 4x + 2$

    (B) $4x + 1$ (E) $-x^2 - 2$

    (C) $3x^2 - 2$

7. $(6by^3 + 3ay^2) \div 2y^2 =$

    (A) $4y^2 + ab$ (D) $(3by)\left(\dfrac{3}{2}a\right)$

    (B) $3by + \dfrac{3}{2}a$ (E) $b + 3a$

    (C) $\dfrac{9}{2}aby$

8. $\left(\dfrac{5xy}{3ab}\right)\left(\dfrac{4a^2}{7x^2}\right) =$

    (A) $\left(\dfrac{20}{21}\right)\left(\dfrac{ay}{bx}\right)$

    (B) $(xy - a^2)(5b - 3y)$

    (C) $\left(\dfrac{20}{a}\right)\left(\dfrac{21}{b}\right)(xy)$

    (D) $\left(\dfrac{a}{x}\right)\left(\dfrac{y}{3}\right)$

    (E) $\dfrac{5x^3}{7b^2}$

9. A number, x, is divided by 3. Four more than the result would be represented by

    (A) $\dfrac{x}{7}$ (D) $\dfrac{x}{3} + y$

    (B) $\dfrac{x + 3}{4}$ (E) $\dfrac{x}{3} - 4$

    (C) $\dfrac{x}{3} + 4$

10. $(a + b)(f + 2g) =$

    (A) $(af + bg)^2$

    (B) $af + bf + 2ga + 2gb$

    (C) $4abfg$

    (D) $ab + 2fg$

    (E) $ag + 2bf$

11. The sum of two numbers is $\dfrac{3}{2}$ times the difference of the numbers. An equation that states the same thing is

    (A) $x = \dfrac{3}{2}y - y$

    (B) $x + \dfrac{3}{2}y = x - \dfrac{3}{2}y$

    (C) $(x + y) = \dfrac{3}{2}(x - y)$

    (D) $x + y = \dfrac{2}{3}x - \dfrac{2}{3}y$

    (E) $xy = x + y + \dfrac{2}{3}$

12. If $x = 1$, $y = 2$ and $m = 3$, then $(xym^5 \div m^3) - 2xy =$

(A) 12   (D) 19
(B) 14   (E) 22
(C) 16

13. If $a \# b = a^2 + b^2$, then $(1 \# 1) \# 1$ equals

(A) 1   (D) 4
(B) 2   (E) 5
(C) 3

14. When $y = -2$ and $x = -3$, what does $-3y - 2x$ equal?

(A) -1 (D) 5
(B) 1   (E) 12
(C) -5

15. If $x * y = \dfrac{(x+y)^2}{(x-y)^2}$, then which of the following equals 1?

(A) $0 * 0$ (D) $2 * 1$
(B) $1 * -1$ (E) $2 * 2$
(C) $-1 * 0$

Solutions for Diagnostic Test

1. **(A)** We can add only terms with the same base raised to the same power. $7a^2 + 3b^2 + 2a^2 = (7a^2 + 2a^2) + 3b^2 = 9a^2 + 3b^2$. **(2-7)**

2. **(D)** We remove parentheses, changing the signs because the sign preceding the parentheses is minus.

$$4x - (3y - x) = 4x - 3y + x$$
$$= (4x + x) - 3y = 5x - 3y. \quad \textbf{(2-7)}$$

3. **(E)** We multiply numbers and different letters separately.

$(3ax^2)(4ay^2) = (3 \cdot 4)(a \cdot a)x^2y^2 = 12a^2x^2y^2$. This choice is not listed. **(2-9)**

4. **(C)** We remove parentheses, keeping signs the same.

$3m + (2n - 5m) = 3m + 2n - 5m = 2n + (3m - 5m) = 2n - 2m$ **(2-7)**

5. **(C)** $7y$ is a common denominator.
$$\frac{y}{7} = \frac{y^2}{7y}, \frac{7}{y} = \frac{7^2}{7y} = \frac{49}{7y},$$
$$\frac{y}{7} + \frac{7}{y} = \frac{y^2}{7y} + \frac{49}{7y} = \frac{y^2 + 49}{7y} \quad \textbf{(2-8)}$$

6. **(A)** Using the distributive law,
$$(x + 1)(3x - 2) = x(3x - 2) + 1(3x - 2)$$
$$= 3x^2 - 2x + 3x - 2$$
$$= 3x^2 + x - 2. \quad \textbf{(2-9)}$$

7. **(B)** $(6by^3 + 3ay^2) \div 2y^2 = \dfrac{6by^3}{2y^2} + \dfrac{3ay^2}{2y^2}$
$$= 3by + \frac{3}{2}a \quad \textbf{(2-10)}$$

8. **(A)** $\left(\dfrac{5xy}{3ab}\right)\left(\dfrac{4a^2}{7x^2}\right) = \left(\dfrac{5y}{3b}\right)\left(\dfrac{4a}{7x}\right)$, cancelling an a and an x.
$$\left(\frac{5y}{3b}\right)\left(\frac{4a}{7x}\right) = \left(\frac{5 \cdot 4}{3 \cdot 7}\right)\left(\frac{ay}{bx}\right) = \left(\frac{20}{21}\right)\left(\frac{ay}{bx}\right)$$
(2-9)

9. **(C)** x divided by 3 is represented by $\dfrac{x}{3}$. Four more than this is $\dfrac{x}{3} + 4$. **(2-11)**

10. **(B)** Using the distributive law, $(a + b)(f + 2g) = a(f + 2g) + b(f + 2g) = af + 2ag + fb + 2gb$. Rearranging, we get choice (B). **(2-9)**

11. **(C)** If the two numbers are x and y, then their sum and difference are $x + y$ and $x - y$. Saying that the first is $\dfrac{3}{2}$, the second is the same as writing $x + y = \dfrac{3}{2}(x - y)$. **(2-11)**

12. **(B)** First simplify. $(xym^5 \div m^3) = xym^2$. $xym^2 - 2xy = (1)(2)(9) - 2(1)(2) = 14$. **(2-10, 2-12)**

13. **(E)** $1 \# 1 = 1^2 + 1^2 = 2$. Now, $2 \# 1 = 2^2 + 1^2 = 5$. **(2-13)**

14. **(E)** If $y = -2$ and $x = -3$, then $-3y - 2x = -3(-2) - 2(-3) = (+6) - (-6) = +6 + 6 = 12$. **(2-12, 2-2)**

15. **(C)** If $y = 0$, $x * y$ reduces to $\dfrac{x^2}{x^2}$, or 1, as long as x is not 0. Therefore $-1 * 0 = 1$. **(2-13)**

Instructional Material on Algebraic Expressions

2-6 The use of algebraic expressions

If we want to express arithmetical rules, or geometrical facts, or everyday formulas in general terms, we use algebra. In algebraic expressions we use letters to represent numbers. (Algebraic expressions can contain both letters and numerals.) To indicate that the area of a rectangle is its base multiplied by its height, we write $A = bh$. The "A" stands for the area, the "b" stands for the length of the base, and the "h" stands for the height. When two letters are written together without a symbol between them (or with a dot between them), they are to be multiplied. Thus $2x$ means 2 times x, and $7b^2$ means 7 times b squared, or 7 times b times b. If we wanted to express the fact that, in general, the order in which numbers are added does not matter, we could write $x + y = y + x$.

Since algebraic expressions represent numbers, we can add, subtract, multiply, and divide them.

Practice Exercises for 2-6

Write as an algebraic expression:

1. The area of a square is the square of its side.

2. The area of a triangle is one-half the product of the height and the base.

3. Twice a quantity.

4. Five plus a quantity.

5. The perimeter of a square is four times its side.

6. The order in which two numbers are multiplied does not matter.

7. One quantity divided by another quantity.

8. One quantity added to twice that quantity.

9. Five times a quantity, plus 2.

10. Distance is equal to rate of speed times time.

2-7 To add and subtract algebraic expressions

The addition and subtraction of algebraic expressions is possible only if the letters in the expressions are the same, and have the same exponents. (Expressions such as these are called "like terms," and adding and subtracting them is called "combining like terms.") Thus $2x + x = 3x$, and $y^2 - 3y^2 = -2y^2$, but $3x + 2y^2$ cannot be simplified. Note: In an expression like $2y^3$, the 2 is called a coefficient, and combining like terms involves adding coefficients.

> The important rule to remember in adding and subtracting algebraic expressions is the rule for removing parentheses: If the sign before the parentheses is +, just remove the parentheses. If the sign before the parentheses is −, change the sign of every expression inside the parentheses and then remove the parentheses.

For example: Simplify $x - (-x + 1)$
Remove the parentheses in $x - (-x + 1)$. We change the $-x$ to $+x$, and the $+1$ to -1, and then write $x - (-x + 1) = x + x - 1 = 2x - 1$.

Another example: Simplify $(x + 2y) - (x - 3y)$.
We remove the first parentheses, but before we can remove the second parentheses we must change signs: x becomes $-x$, and $-3y$ becomes $+3y$. Now, $(x + 2y) - (x - 3y) = x + 2y - x + 3y = 5y$.

Practice Exercises for 2-7

Evaluate:

1. $y - (y - 1)$

2. $(x + 3y) - (x + 2y)$

3. $2x^2 - x^2$

4. $3x^2 - (2x^2 + y)$

5. $-2x^2 - (x^2 + 3x^2) - (-2x^2)$

6. $-(-x - 2y) - (y - 2x)$

7. $(x + 3y) + (x - 2y)$

8. $2x - y - (2x + y)$

9. $a^2 + 2ab + b^2 - (a^2 - 2ab + b^2)$

10. $a - b - (a + b)$

11. $x^2 - y^2 - (y^2 - x^2)$

12. $x^2 - 2x^2 + 3y^2 - 2y^2$

13. $y^2 - 3y^2 - 5y^2 + 2y^2$

14. $(y + 2y) - (y - 2y) + y$

15. $x^2 - y^2 + (x^2 + y^2) - (x^2 - y^2) + x^2$

2-8 To add algebraic expressions that are fractions

Proceed just as in adding regular fractions. The product of the different denominators is a common denominator.

For example: Add $\dfrac{2}{x} + \dfrac{3}{y}$.

The common denominator is xy. $\dfrac{2}{x} = \dfrac{2y}{xy}$ and $\dfrac{3}{y} = \dfrac{3x}{xy}$.

Therefore, $\dfrac{2}{x} + \dfrac{3}{y} = \dfrac{2y}{xy} + \dfrac{3x}{xy} = \dfrac{2y + 3x}{xy}$.

Remember we can always use the shortcut in adding fractions (See **1-8**).

For example: Add $\dfrac{2}{x} + \dfrac{3}{y}$.

Solution:

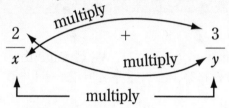

Multiply $2 \times y$ and then
multiply $3 \times x$. Now add the results:
$$2y + 3x$$
Now multiply $x \times y$.
We get xy.
Thus, the answer is

$$\frac{2y + 3x}{xy}$$

In general,

$$\frac{a}{b} + \frac{c}{d} = \frac{ad + bc}{bd}$$

Practice Exercises for 2-8

Add or subtract:

1. $\dfrac{3}{x} + \dfrac{4}{y}$

2. $\dfrac{3}{x} - \dfrac{4}{y}$

3. $\dfrac{2}{3x} + \dfrac{6}{2x}$

4. $\dfrac{2}{3x} - \dfrac{6}{2x}$

5. $\dfrac{a}{b} + \dfrac{c}{d}$

6. $\dfrac{2}{y} - \dfrac{1}{y}$

7. $\dfrac{a}{3} + \dfrac{b}{4}$

8. $\dfrac{a}{4} + \dfrac{4}{b}$

9. $\dfrac{a}{4} + \dfrac{4}{a}$

10. $\dfrac{2}{a} - \dfrac{a}{2}$

11. $\dfrac{2}{a} - \dfrac{2}{b}$

12. $\dfrac{2}{a} - \dfrac{b}{2}$

13. $\dfrac{a}{10} - \dfrac{a}{5}$

14. $\dfrac{x^2}{y^2} + \dfrac{x}{y}$

15. $\dfrac{x^2}{y^2} - \dfrac{x}{y}$

2-9 To multiply simple algebraic expressions

Do the numerical and letter multiplication separately, and then multiply the results.

For example: Multiply $2x$ by $3x^2$.
First, $2 \times 3 = 6$, and then $x^2 \times x = x^3$. Altogether, $(2x)(3x^2) = 6x^3$.

> The key in multiplying algebraic expressions is the distributive law. In general, it says $a(b + c) = ab + ac$. Also, $a(b - c) = ab - ac$.

For example: Multiply $(x + 2)(x + 3)$.
First, $(x + 2)(x + 3) = (x + 2)x + (x + 2)3$, by the distributive law. Using the distributive law again, $(x + 2)x = x^2 + 2x$, and $(x + 2)3 = 3x + 6$. Altogether, $(x + 2)(x + 3) = x^2 + 2x + 3x + 6 = x^2 + 5x + 6$.

Another example: Multiply $(2y + 1)(y - 5)$.
We use the distributive law to get
$$\begin{aligned}
(2y + 1)(y - 5) &= (2y + 1)y - (2y + 1)5 \\
&= 2y^2 + y - (10y + 5) \\
&= 2y^2 + y - 10y - 5 \\
&= 2y^2 - 9y - 5
\end{aligned}$$

Practice Exercises for 2-9

Multiply:

1. $(3x)$ by $(2x^2)$
2. $(2x)(7x^3)$
3. $(-2x)(-3x)$
4. $2x(2x + 1)$
5. $2x(1 - 2x)$

6. $(x + 1)(x - 1)$
7. $(x + 1)(x + 2)$
8. $(x + 1)(x - 2)$
9. $(2x + 2)(x - 1)$
10. $(3y - 1)(3y + 3)$

11. $(a + b)(a - b)$

12. $(-2x)(3x^2)$

13. $(2x - 1)(2x + 1)$

14. $(-1 - y)(-1 + y)$

15. $(y^2 - 1)(y^2 - 1)$

16. $(x + 2)(x^2 + 2)$

17. $(x - 3)(x - 5)$

18. $(x + 3)(x - 5)$

19. $(x + 3)(x + 5)$

20. $(x - 3)(x + 5)$

2-10   To divide simple algebraic expressions

Divide the numerical and letter parts of the expressions separately. Thus, $15x^2y^2 \div 5xy = (15 \div 5)(x^2 \div x)(y^2 \div y) = 3xy$. Dividing is like reducing a fraction. We simply divide numerator and denominator by the factors they have in common.

For example: Divide $21a^2b^3$ by $14a^2b^5$.

We form the fraction $\dfrac{21a^2b^3}{14a^2b^5}$. Since the numerator and denominator both contain the factors 7, a^2, and b^3, we can divide numerator and denominator by these factors. We are left with 3 in the numerator, and 2 and b^2 (from $b^5 \div b^3 = b^2$) in the denominator. Therefore, $21a^2b^3 \div 14a^2b^5 = \dfrac{3}{2b^2}$.

> To do other division problems, we can use the distributive law. For division, the distributive law is $\dfrac{a+b}{c} = \dfrac{a}{c} + \dfrac{b}{c}$ and $\dfrac{a-b}{c} = \dfrac{a}{c} - \dfrac{b}{c}$.

For example: Divide $72y^3 + 16y^2$ by $8y$.
First, we use the distributive law, so that $\dfrac{72y^3 + 16y^2}{8y} = \dfrac{72y^3}{8y} + \dfrac{16y^2}{8y}$. Now $72y^3 \div 8y = 9y^2$, and $16y^2 \div 8y = 2y$. Therefore, $(72y^3 + 16y^2) \div 8y = 9y^3 + 2y$.

There are other division problems, such as $(x^2 + 7x + 12) \div (x + 3)$, that require the ability to factor more complicated algebraic expressions. If we can factor the expressions involved, then we can use the procedures outlined above. (See the next section on factoring.) If we cannot factor the expressions, then the division process is similar to the division of whole numbers, and this is generally not tested.

Practice Exercises for 2-10

Divide:

1. $\dfrac{20x^3y^2}{4xy}$

2. $\dfrac{15a^2b^2}{5ab^3}$

3. $\dfrac{36a^3 + 12b^2}{12ab}$

4. $\dfrac{24a^3 - 16a^4}{8a}$

5. $\dfrac{(x+3)(x-2)^2}{(x-2)}$

6. $\dfrac{16x^3 - 4x}{4x}$

7. $(24y^3 - 16y^2) \div 8y^2$

8. $15x^2y^3z^4 \div 5xyz$

9. $(36y - y^2) \div y$

10. $\dfrac{y - y^2}{y^2}$

11. $\dfrac{2a^2b^3}{4a^3b^4}$

12. $\dfrac{8 - 8y}{8 - 8x}$

13. $\dfrac{32y^5 - 24x^2y^2}{8y^3}$

14. $\dfrac{24xy - 6x^2y^2}{3xy}$

15. $\dfrac{x^2yz + xy^2z + xyz^2}{xyz}$

2-11 Converting words into algebraic expressions

Some problems involve converting words into algebraic expressions. In this case, the important thing is to let some letter stand for the words "a number." The choices after the problem will tell you which letter.

For example: How would one represent 12 more than four times a certain number? Say we let n stand for that certain number. Then four times the number is $4n$, and 12 more than that is $4n + 12$.

Another example: Represent the amount by which 22 exceeds 7 times a number. Let the number be n. Then 7 times the number is $7n$; 22 exceeds $7n$ by the amount $22 - 7n$.

Practice Exercises for 2-11

Represent the following in algebraic terms (use n or x or y for the algebraic letters).

1. Six more than three times a number.
2. The amount by which 3 exceeds twice a number.
3. Five less than three times a number.
4. Half of 20% of a number.
5. Six years more than twice the age of Mary.
6. Twice the sum of two numbers.
7. The reciprocal of a number.
8. Four times a number subtracted from 5.
9. The amount by which 24 is greater than sixteen times a number.
10. A number is multiplied by 2. The result is added to three times the original number. What is the final result?

2-12 Evaluating algebraic expressions

Since the letters in an algebraic expression stand for numbers, and since we add, subtract, multiply, or divide them to get the algebraic expression, the algebraic expression itself stands for a number. When we are told what value each of the letters in the expression has, we can evaluate the expression.

> In evaluating algebraic expressions, place the value you are substituting for a letter in parentheses. (This is important when a letter has a negative value.)

For example: What is the value of the expression $a^2 - b^3$ when $a = -2$, and $b = -1$? $a^2 - b^3 = (-2)^2 - (-1)^3 = 4 - (-1) = 5$.

> If you can, simplify the algebraic expression before you evaluate it.

For example: Evaluate $\dfrac{32a^6b^2}{8a^4b^3}$ if $a = 4$, and $b = -2$.

First we divide:

$\dfrac{32a^6b^2}{8a^4b^3} = \dfrac{4a^2}{b}$. Then $\dfrac{4a^2}{b} = \dfrac{4(+4)^2}{-2} = -32$.

Practice Exercises for 2-12

1. Find the value of the expression
$$a^2 + ab + b^2$$
when $a = 1$ and $b = -1$

2. Evaluate:
$$\frac{x^2 - x}{x + 2}$$
when $x = 2$

3. Evaluate:
$$\frac{24x^2y^3}{6xy}$$
when $x = 2$, $y = 3$

4. Find the value of
$$\frac{x - y}{x + y} + \frac{x + y}{x - y}$$
when $x = 2$ and $y = -1$

5. Evaluate:
$$\frac{15a^2b^3}{5a^3b}$$
when $a = 10$ and $b = 5$

6. Find the value of
$$\frac{x^2 + xy - y}{x + y}$$
when $x = -2$ and $y = -1$

7. Find the value of

$$\frac{39a^2b^3c^4}{13a^3b^2c}$$

when $a = -1, b = -2, c = +3$

8. What is the value of

$$\frac{a^3b^2}{a^2b^4} - (a^2 - b^2)^2$$

when $a = 2$ and $b = -2$?

9. If $x = 2$ and $y = -1$, evaluate

$$x^2 - y^3 + x - y$$

10. If $x = 2$ and $y = -1$, evaluate

$$\frac{(x + y)^2 - (x - y)^2}{x + y}$$

2-13 Operations defined by algebraic expressions

Sometimes problems about evaluations are presented differently. Addition and multiplication are two examples of operations: We take two numbers and "operate" on them to get a third number. Many different operations could be defined (we could operate on one, two, or more numbers). These operations are defined by an algebraic expression. To invent an operation *, we might say $a * b = ab + a + b$. Then, to find 3 * 4, we evaluate $ab + a + b$ with $a = 3$ and $b = 4$. Thus, 3 * 4 = $3 \cdot 4 + 3 + 4 = 19$.

> An operation is undefined if the denominator of an algebraic expression defining it is zero.

For example: Say $a \& b = \dfrac{a^2 - b^2}{ab}$. Find $x \& x$. When is $x \& x$ undefined?

Since $a \& b = \dfrac{a^2 - b^2}{ab}$, $x \& x = \dfrac{x^2 - x^2}{x^2} = \dfrac{0}{x^2} = 0$, if x is not 0. If $x = 0$, then $x \& x$ is undefined because the denominator would be zero.

Practice Exercises for 2-13

1. If $a * b = \dfrac{a}{b} + \dfrac{b}{a} + ab$

   Find the value of $(2) * (-3)$

2. Evaluate $(-1) ! (-1)$
   if $a ! b = a^2b + b^2a$

3. If $m * n = mn + mn^2$

   evaluate $(-1) * \left(\dfrac{1}{2}\right)$

4. If $x * y$ means the largest integer greater than x but an integer less than y, evaluate

   $$2 * 10$$

5. If $x ! y = x - y - xy - xy^2 - x^2y$, which is greater, $(2) ! (-1)$ or $(-1) ! (2)$?

Factoring

Diagnostic Test on Factoring

1. What is the largest common factor of the expression $4ab + 20a^2$?

   (A) a (D) $4ab$

   (B) a^2 (E) 1

   (C) $4a$

2. Factor $3ab + ac + ad$.

   (A) $a(3b + c + d)$

   (B) $3a(a + b + c)$

   (C) $a(b + c + d)$

   (D) $(a + b + c)(3a + b + c)$

   (E) none of the above

3. Factor $m^2 + m^3n + m^2n^2$.

   (A) $m(m + mn + mn^2)$

   (B) $mn(1 + m + m^2)$

   (C) $m(m^2 + m^2n + mn^2)$

   (D) $m^2(1 + mn + n^2)$

   (E) $n(m^2 + m^3 + m^2n)$

4. Which of the following is a perfect square?

   (A) $3x^2$ (D) y^5

   (B) $2y + 1$ (E) xy

   (C) $4x^4y^4$

5. Factor $a^2 - b^2$.

   (A) $(a - b)(a - b)$ (D) $a(a - b)$

   (B) $(a + b)(a + b)$ (E) $(a + b)(a - b)$

   (C) $(a^2 + b^2)(a - b)$

6. Factor $81y^4 - z^2$.

   (A) $(9y - z)(9y^3 + z)$

   (B) $(9y^2 - z)(9y^2 + z)$

   (C) $(3y - z)(27y^3 + z)$

   (D) $(9y^2 + z)(9y^2 + z)$

   (E) $(81y^2)(y^2 - z^2)$

7. Factor $a^2 - 11a + 10$.

   (A) $(a - 1)(a - 5)$ (D) $(a - 1)(a - 10)$

   (B) $(a + 1)(a + 10)$ (E) $(a + 1)(a + 5)$

   (C) $(a - 2)(a + 5)$

8. Factor $b^2 + 2b - 35$.

   (A) $(b + 5)(b + 7)$ (D) $(b - 5)(b + 7)$

   (B) $(b - 5)(b - 7)$ (E) $(b - 1)(b + 35)$

   (C) $(b + 5)(b - 7)$

9. Factor $15a^3 - 15ab^2$ completely.

   (A) $a(15a^2 - 15b^2)$

   (B) $15a(a + b)(a - b)$

   (C) $a(15a + b)(a - b)$

   (D) $3ab(5a^2 - 5ab)$

   (E) $5a(3a + 3b)(3a - 3b)$

10. Factor $m^3 - m^2 - 20m$ completely.

    (A) $m(m - 5)(m + 4)$

    (B) $(m^2 - 5m)(m + 4)$

    (C) $m(m + 2)(m + 10)$

    (D) $m(m - 4)(m + 5)$

    (E) $m(m - 20)(m - 1)$

Solutions for Diagnostic Test

1. **(C)** A common factor is an expression that divides into all the terms of the given expression. The largest common factor of $4ab + 20a^2$ is $4a$.   **(2-15)**

2. **(A)** a is the largest common factor of $3ab + ac + ad$. Divide $3ab + ac + ad$ by a to get the other factor. So, $3ab + ac + ad = a(3b + c + d)$.   **(2-15)**

3. **(D)** m^2 is the largest common factor of $m^2 + m^3n + m^2n^2$. Divide $m^2 + m^3n + m^2n^2$ by m^2 to get the other factor. So, $m^2 + m^3n + m^2n^2 = m^2(1 + mn + n)$. **(2-15)**

4. **(C)** $4x^4y^4 = (2x^2y^2)^2$ is a perfect square. **(2-16, 2-15)**

5. **(E)** The factors of the difference of two squares are the sum and difference of the square roots. So, $a^2 - b^2 = (a + b)(a - b)$. **(2-16)**

6. **(B)** $81y^4 - z^2$ is the difference of two squares. It is factored into the sum and difference of the square roots.

    So, $81y^4 - z^2 = (9y^2 + z)(9y^2 - z)$. **(2-16)**

7. **(D)** $a^2 - 11a + 10$ is a trinomial. The first term in each factor must be a. By trial and error, $a^2 - 11a + 10$ is factored into $(a - 10)(a - 1)$. **(2-17)**

8. **(D)** $b^2 + 2b - 35$ is a trinomial. The first term in each factor must be b. By trial and error, $b^2 + 2b - 35$ is factored into $(b - 5)(b + 7)$. **(2-17)**

9. **(B)** To factor $15a^3 - 15ab^2$ completely, first factor out the largest common factor, $15a$.

    $$15a^3 - 15ab^2 = 15a(a^2 - b^2)$$

    Then factor the difference of two squares to get $15a(a + b)(a - b)$. **(2-19, 2-17)**

10. **(A)** To factor $m^3 - m^2 - 20m$ completely, factor out the largest common factor m.

    $$m^3 - m^2 - 20m = m(m^2 - m - 20)$$

    Then factor the trinomial to get $m(m - 5)(m + 5)$. **(2-19, 2-17)**

Instructional Material on Factoring

2-14 Factors of an expression

The factors of an expression are two or more expressions whose product is equal to the first expression.

For example: The factors of $x^2 + xy$ are x and $x + y$, since their product $x(x + y)$ is equal to $x^2 + xy$.

To factor any expression is to write the expression as the product of its factors. There are three special types of factoring, which we shall discuss soon.

Practice Exercises for 2-14

Find the factors:

1. $x^2 + x$
2. $5x + 5$
3. $a^2 - ab$
4. $a^2 + ab$
5. $5x - 5$
6. $x^2 - x$
7. $ab + ab^2$
8. $3xy - 3x$
9. $2x - x^2$
10. $x^2 - xy^2$

2-15 Common factors

A factor that divides into each term of the expression is called a common factor.

For example: For the expression $x^2 + xy$, x divides into each term of the expression. So x is a common factor.

To factor an expression with a common factor:

1) Find the largest common factor of all the terms in the expression. This is one of the factors of the expression.
2) Divide the expression by the largest common factor. The quotient is the other factor.
3) Write the answer as the product of the two factors.

For example: Factor $4x^2 + 2x$.

Step 1: $2x$ is a factor of both $4x^2$ and $2x$, and it is the largest common factor.

Step 2: Divide the expression by the largest common factor.

$$(4x^2 + 2x) \div 2x = 2x + 1$$

Step 3: Write the answer as the product of the factors.

Therefore, $4x^2 + 2x = 2x(2x + 1)$.

Practice Exercises for 2-15

Factor:

1. $x^3 - x^2$
2. $x^3 + x^2$
3. $x + xy$
4. $a^2b - b^2a$
5. $yx - xy^2$

6. $a^2b + b^2a$
7. $3xy - 3x^2y^2$
8. $4xy - 4$
9. $4xy - 4x$
10. $4xy - 4x^2y$

2-16 The difference of two perfect squares

If an expression has two terms and the expression consists of one perfect square minus another perfect square, the expression is a difference of two squares. For example, $x^2 - y^2$ is a difference of two squares, and so is $4m^2n^2 - 4$. The second case is a difference of two squares, since $4m^2n^2$ is a perfect square ($4m^2n^2 = [2mn]^2$) and 4 is a perfect square ($4 = 2^2$).

To factor a difference of two squares:

1) Take the square root of each of the perfect squares.
2) One of the factors is the sum of the square roots. The other factor is the difference of the square roots (the first minus the second).
3) Write the answer as the product of the two factors.

For example: Factor $4m^2n^2 - 4$.

Step 1: Take the square root of each perfect square.

$$\sqrt{4m^2n^2} = 2mn \qquad \sqrt{4} = 2$$

Step 2: One factor is the sum of the square roots, $2mn + 2$. The other factor is the difference of the square roots, $2mn - 2$.

Step 3: Write the answer as the product of the factors. Therefore, $4m^2n^2 - 4 = (2mn + 2)(2mn - 2)$.

Practice Exercises for 2-16

Factor:
1. $a^2 - b^2$
2. $4a^2b^2 - x^2y^2$
3. $16x^4y^4 - 4$
4. $(100)^2 - 1$
5. $(x + a)^2 - (x + b)^2$

6. $16x^2y^2 - 16$
7. $x^4 - y^4$
8. $(100)^2 - 4$
9. $9x^2 - 4y^2$
10. $4x^2y^2 - 9x^4y^4$

2-17 Factoring trinomials into binomials

The next type is the factoring of trinomials into binomials. A trinomial is an expression with three unlike terms, such as $x^2 + 2x + 1$ and $mn + n + 1$; a binomial is an expression with two unlike terms, such as $x + 2$ and $m + n^2$.

For example: $x^2 + 3x + 2 = (x + 2)(x + 1)$ is an example of a trinomial, $x^2 + 3x + 2$, factored into factors, $x + 2$ and $x + 1$, that are binomials.

> Not all trinomials can be factored into binomials. Examples of unfactorable trinomials are $mn + n + 1$ and $x^2 + 3x + 1$. It is not easy to determine whether a trinomial can be factored or not without actually attempting to factor the expression.

Even with trinomials that can be factored, there is no definite method of finding the factors directly. The method used here requires trial and error.

To factor a trinomial of the form $x^2 + bx + c$, where b and c are numerals:

1) First, write down the first term of each factor, which is x. $(x +)(x +)$
2) To find the second term of each factor, find two numbers whose product is equal to c and whose sum is equal to b. (This requires trial and error.)
3) Write the answer as the product of the two factors.

For example: Factor $y^2 - 5y + 6$.

Step 1: Write down the first term of each factor, which is y.
$$(y +)(y +)$$

Step 2: To find the other term of each factor, find two numbers whose product is 6 and whose sum is -5. The following pairs of numbers have 6 as their product:

$$1, 6 \qquad\qquad\qquad 2, 3$$
$$-1, -6 \qquad\qquad\qquad -2, -3$$

Of these, the only pair of numbers whose sum is -5 is -2 and -3. So, -2 and -3 are the second terms of the factors. Therefore, the factors are $y - 2$ and $y - 3$.

Step 3: Write the answer as the product of the factors.
$$y^2 - 5y + 6 = (y - 2)(y - 3)$$

> *Note:* (i) Whenever you have a form such as $x^2 - ax + b$, where a and b are positive numbers, the factors take the form $(x -)(x -)$.
> Example: Factor $x^2 - 4x + 4$.
> Solution: $(x - 2)(x - 2) = x^2 - 4x + 4$
>
> (ii) Whenever you have a form $x^2 + ax + b$, where a and b are positive numbers, the factors take the form $(x +)(x +)$.
> Example: Factor $x^2 + 3x + 2$.
> Solution: $(x + 2)(x + 1)$
>
> (iii) Whenever you have a form $x^2 + ax - b$ or $x^2 - ax - b$, where a and b are positive numbers, the factors take the form $(x +)(x -)$.
> Example: Factor $x^2 + x - 2$.
> Solution: $(x + 2)(x - 1) = x^2 + x - 2$
> Example: Factor $x^2 - x - 2$.
> Solution: $(x + 1)(x - 2) = x^2 - x - 2$

Practice Exercises for 2-17

Factor:

1. $x^2 + 4x + 4$ 6. $x^2 + 2xy + y^2$
2. $x^2 + 2x + 1$ 7. $x^2 - 2xy + y^2$
3. $x^2 - 6x + 8$ 8. $x^2 - 5x + 6$
4. $x^2 + 2x - 8$ 9. $x^2 + 5x + 6$
5. $x^2 + 6x + 8$ 10. $x^2 + x - 6$

2-18   Factoring a trinomial of the form $ax^2 + bx + c$, where a, b, and c are numbers:

1) Find all possible pairs of binomials in which the product of the first terms is equal to ax^2 and the product of the second terms is equal to c.

2) Of these pairs, find the pair of binomials whose product is equal to the trinomial by multiplying each pair.

For example: Factor $2x^2 - 7x - 4$.

<u>Step 1</u>: Find all possible pairs of binomials in which the product of the first terms is equal to $2x^2$ and the product of the second terms is equal to -4. $2x - 2$ and $x + 2$ is a possible pair, since the product of the first terms, $2x$ and x, is $2x^2$, and the product of the second terms, -2 and 2, is -4.

All possible pairs are:

$2x - 2$ and $x + 2$ $2x + 2$ and $x - 2$
$2x - 1$ and $x + 4$ $2x + 4$ and $x - 1$
$2x + 1$ and $x - 4$ $2x - 4$ and $x + 1$

<u>Step 2</u>: Multiply these pairs of binomials to find the pair whose product is $2x^2 - 7x - 4$. The only correct pair is $2x + 1$ and $x - 4$. Therefore, $2x^2 - 7x - 4 = (2x + 1)(x - 4)$.

> Note: In a multiple-choice test, it is sometimes easier to multiply in each choice given to find the answer, rather than try to find the factors.

Practice Exercises for 2-18

Factor:

1. $2x^2 + 4x + 2$ 3. $9x^2 - 6x + 1$
2. $3x^2 + 2x - 1$ 4. $4x^2 - 4x - 3$

5. $2x^2 + 3x + 1$
6. $4x^2 + 4x + 1$
7. $2x^2 - x - 1$

8. $2x^2 + x - 1$
9. $9x^2 - 8x - 1$
10. $9x^2 - 10x + 1$

2-19 Complete factoring of an expression

To factor an expression completely is to factor the expression into expressions that cannot be factored any further.

To factor an expression completely:

1) Look for any common factor. If there is any common factor, factor it out.
2) Factor the resulting expressions until they cannot be factored any further.

For example: Factor completely $10y^2 - 40$.
Step 1: Factor out the common factor 10.

$$10y^2 - 40 = 10(y^2 - 4)$$

Step 2: $y^2 - 4$ is a difference of two squares and can still be factored into $(y + 2)(y - 2)$. Therefore, $10y^2 - 40 = 10(y + 2)(y - 2)$.

Another example: Factor completely $x^2 - 5x + 4$.
There is no common factor. So "factor completely" simply means "factor the expression." $x^2 - 5x + 4$ is factored $(x - 1)(x - 4)$. Therefore, factored completely, $x^2 - 5x + 4 = (x - 1)(x - 4)$.

Practice Exercises for 2-19

Factor completely:

1. $8y^2 - 32$
2. $2x^2 - 4x - 6$
3. $x^2 - 4x + 3$
4. $4y^2 + 4y - 8$
5. $4x^2 - 4$

6. $3x^2 + 6xy + 3y^2$
7. $3x^2 - 6xy + 3y^2$
8. $25y^2 - 25$
9. $4x^2 + 8x + 3$
10. $4x^2 + 4x - 3$

Equations

Diagnostic Test on Equations

1. If $x = y$, then
   (A) $x - 2 = y + 2$ (D) $x = x + y$
   (B) $2x = 3y$ (E) $xy = x + y$
   (C) $x + y = 2y$

2. Solve the equation $x + 5 = 12$.
   (A) $x = 5$ (D) $x = 7$
   (B) $x = 12$ (E) $x = -12$
   (C) $x = -10$

3. Solve the equation $5x + 12 = 77$.
   (A) $x = 11$ (D) $x = 8$
   (B) $x = 12$ (E) $x = 16$
   (C) $x = 13$

4. Solve the equation $4y + 9 = 5y + 17$.
   (A) $y = 10$ (D) $y = -5$
   (B) $y = 13$ (E) $y = -8$
   (C) $y = 6$

5. Solve the quadratic equation $y^2 - 4y + 3 = 0$.
   (A) $y = 3, y = -1$ (D) $y = 3, y = 1$
   (B) $y = 3$ (E) $y = 1$
   (C) $y = -3, y = -1$

6. Find the solutions to the equation $x^2 - 16 = 0$.
   (A) $x = 4, x = -4$ (D) $x = 2, x = -2$
   (B) $x = 4$ (E) $x = -2$
   (C) $x = 16$

7. For the equation $x + y = 2y + 5$, solve for x in terms of y.
   (A) $x = 3y + 5$ (D) $x = y$
   (B) $x = y + 5$ (E) $x = 5 - y$
   (C) $x = 5 - 3y$

8. If $x = 4y - 5$, then $y =$
   (A) $\dfrac{x-5}{4}$ (D) $\dfrac{x-5}{2}$
   (B) $x - 5$ (E) $\dfrac{x+5}{4}$
   (C) $x + 5$

9. If $x = y + 5$ and $y = 10$, then $x =$
   (A) 5 (D) 50
   (B) -5 (E) 25
   (C) 15

10. If $x + y = 11$ and $2y = 6$, then $x =$
    (A) 7 (D) 8
    (B) 14 (E) 3
    (C) 5

Solutions for Diagnostic Test

1. **(C)** Since the equality does not change if y is added to both sides, $x + y = y + y = 2y$.
   (2–20)

2. **(D)** $x + 5 = 12$
   Subtract 5 from both sides to get $x = 7$.
   (2-22)

3. **(C)** $5x + 12 = 77$
Subtract 12 from both sides to get $5x = 65$.
Divide both sides by 5 to get $x = 13$.
(2-22)

4. **(E)** $4y + 9 = 5y + 17$
Subtract $4y + 17$ from both sides to get
$-8 = y$ or $y = -8$. **(2-22)**

5. **(D)** Factor the expression in $y^2 - 4y + 3 = 0$
to get $(y - 3)(y - 1) = 0$. So, either $y - 3 = 0$
or $y - 1 = 0$. Therefore, $y = 3$ or $y = 1$.
(2-23)

6. **(A)** $x^2 - 16 = 0$
Factor $x^2 - 16$ to get $(x - 4)(x + 4) = 0$.
Either $x - 4 = 0$ or $x + 4 = 0$. So, $x = 4$
or $x = -4$. **(2-23)**

7. **(B)** $x + y = 2y + 5$
Subtract y from both sides to get
$x = y + 5$. **(2-24)**

8. **(E)** $x = 4y - 5$
Add 5 to both sides to get $x + 5 = 4y$.
Divide both sides by 4 to get $y = \dfrac{x+5}{4}$.
(2-24)

9. **(C)** $x = y + 5$ and $y = 10$.
Substitute 10 for y to get $x = 10 + 5 = 15$.
(2-25)

10. **(D)** $x + y = 11$ and $2y = 6$.
Solve for y in the second equation to get
$y = 3$.
Substitute 3 for y to get $x + 3 = 11$, or
$x = 8$. **(2-25)**

Instructional Material on Equations

2-20 Description of equations

An equation is a statement that two expressions are equal. The reason for learning to solve equations is that knowing how to solve equations makes solving problems easier. Some examples of equations are $10 + 5 = 15$, $4x - 5 = 10$, formulas such as $A = l \times w$ (area = length × width), and proportions.

In the equation $4x - 5 = 10$, the equals sign indicates that the expression to the right of it is to have the same value as the expression to the left of it ($4x - 5$ is to have the same value as 10). There are four properties of equations that you will use later to solve equations with unknowns:

1) If the same expression is added to both expressions of an equation, the resulting expressions are still equal.

   For example: $10 + 5 = 15$
   Add 6 to the left expression $10 + 5$ to get $10 + 5 + 6$, and add 6 to the right expression 15 to get $15 + 6$. The two resulting expressions, $10 + 5 + 6$ and $15 + 6$, have equal values.

$$10 + 5 + 6 = 15 + 6$$

   This, of course, can be checked by adding the numbers to get $21 = 21$.

2) If the same expression is subtracted from both expressions of an equation, the resulting expressions are still equal.

For example: $10x + 5x = 15x$
Subtract $5x$ from the expression $10x + 5x$ to get $10x + 5x - 5x$, and subtract $5x$ from the expression $15x$ to get $15x - 5x$. The resulting expressions have the same value.

$$10x + 5x - 5x = 15x - 5x$$

Combining the terms shows that the two expressions are equal.

$$10x = 10x$$

3) If both expressions of an equation are multiplied by the same expression, the resulting expressions are equal.

For example: $5x^2 + 2 = 10$
Multiply the expression $5x^2 + 2$ by 6 to get $6(5x^2 + 2)$, or $30x^2 + 12$, and multiply the expression 10 by 6 to get 60. The resulting expressions have the same value.

$$30x^2 + 12 = 60$$

4) If both expressions of an equation are divided by the same nonzero expression, the resulting expressions are still equal.

For example: $7y = 14$
Divide the expression $7y$ by 7 to get $\dfrac{7y}{7}$, or y, and divide the expression 14 by 7 to get $\dfrac{14}{7}$, or 2. The resulting equation is equivalent to the original equation.

$$y = 2 \text{ is equivalent to } 7y = 14$$

Practice Exercises for 2-20

1. If $5x = 10$, find what $10x$ is equal to.
2. If $5y + 1 = 9$, what is the value of $10y + 2$?
3. If $8y = 16$, what does y equal?
4. If $25x^2 + 15 = 30$, what is $75x^2 + 45$?
5. $x + 1 = 4$. Find x.

2-21 Finding missing values of the unknown quantity in an equation

In algebra, the expressions consist of both constants, such as 0, 15, or any other number, and variables, which are represented by letters. The variables in an equation stand for unknowns. Solving an equation that has unknowns means finding values for the unknowns that, when substituted into the equation, will make the two expressions in the equation equal.

For example: Consider the equation $2x = 10$.

To solve the equation is to find a value or values for x that will make the equation true. In this case, only when $x = 5$ does the equation hold.

$$2x = 10$$

When 5 is substituted for x,

$$2(5) = 10$$
$$10 = 10, \text{ which is obviously true.}$$

With any other value such as $x = 6$, the equation does not hold. When 6 is substituted into the equation,

$$2(6) = 10$$
$$12 = 10, \text{ which is not true.}$$

Practice Exercises for 2-21

Find the value of x for each of the equations by finding a value of x that will make the equation true:

1. $2x = 14$
2. $3x = 18$
3. $x + 5 = 10$
4. $x - 3 = 6$
5. $2x + 1 = 2$
6. $x - 4 = 4$
7. $x + 4 = 4$
8. $2x = 2$
9. $2x = 0$
10. $x = 8 - x$

2-22 Solving equations with one unknown

The simplest kind of equation to solve is an equation with only one unknown and in which the exponent of the unknown is no larger than 1. Such an equation is called a linear equation with one unknown. Examples of this kind of equation are $5x = 20$, $10y - 6 = 4$, $x + 1 = 0$, and $2x + 2 = 3x$.

To solve a linear equation with one unknown:
1) Use properties 1 and 2 (see Section 2-20) to put all terms involving the unknown on one side of the equation and all constant terms on the other side.
2) Combine the like terms, if necessary.
3) Use properties 3 or 4 (see Section 2-20) to isolate the unknown—that is, to have only the unknown on one side of the equation. (Make the coefficient of the variable 1.) When the unknown is isolated, the equation is solved because the value of the unknown is on the other side of the equation.

For example: Solve the equation $3x = 15$.
Step 1 is already completed, since the only term involving the unknown is on one side of the equation and the constant term is on the other side.
Step 2 is already completed also.
Step 3: To isolate x in the equation $3x = 15$, apply property 4 (see Section 2-20).

Divide both expressions of the equation by 3. The resulting expressions, $\dfrac{3x}{3}$ and $\dfrac{15}{3}$, are equal.

$$\frac{3x}{3} = \frac{15}{3}$$
$$x = 5$$

Therefore the value for x is 5.

> After solving an equation, the answer should be checked to make sure that it is correct. To check the answer, substitute the value found for the unknown into the original equation, and then simplify to see if the expressions are equal.

To check the above example, substitute 5 for x in the equation.

$$3x = 15$$
$$3(5) = 15$$
$$15 = 15$$

Thus, the answer is correct.

Another example: Solve the equation $10x + 17 = 3x - 4$.
Step 1: Put all terms involving x on one side and the constant terms on the other.
Subtract 17 from both sides of the equation.
$$10x + 17 - 17 = 3x - 4 - 17$$
$$10x = 3x - 21$$

Subtract $3x$ from both sides of the equation.
$$10x - 3x = 3x - 21 - 3x$$
$$7x = -21$$

Step 2 has already been done.
Step 3: Isolate the unknown.
Divide both sides by 7.

$$\frac{7x}{7} = \frac{-21}{7}$$
$$x = -3$$

To check that -3 is the correct value for x, substitute -3 into the equation.

$$10x + 17 = 3x - 4$$
$$10(-3) + 17 = 3(-3) - 4$$
$$-30 + 17 = -9 - 4$$
$$-13 = -13$$

Therefore, the answer checks out.

> Note: Sometimes an equation such as $x^3 + 3x = x^3 + 6$ may not look like a linear equation, since there are x^3 terms in it. However, if the equation is simplified by subtracting x^3 from both sides, the resulting equation is $3x = 6$, which is a linear equation and can be solved.

Practice Exercises for 2-22

Solve for x:

1. $7x = 14$
2. $7x + 3 = 24$
3. $12x + 2 = 10x + 8$
4. $9x - 16 = 3x - 10$
5. $\dfrac{x}{5} = 20$

6. $3x - 2 = 2x + 1$
7. $x - 5 = 2x - 5$
8. $2x + 3 = 3x + 2$
9. $6x = -12$
10. $\dfrac{3}{x} = -15$

2-23   Description of a quadratic equation

A quadratic equation is an equation in which the unknown's highest power is 2. Examples of quadratic equations with one unknown are $3x^2 + 8x + 5 = 0$, $x^2 = 3x + 4$, and $y^2 + 2y = 4y - 1$.

A method for solving quadratic equations is factoring. This method is based on a principle for multiplying numbers.

> If the product of two factors is zero, then at least one of the factors is zero.

For example: $(x + 3)(x - 1) = 0$

Since the product of the two factors is zero, then either $x + 3 = 0$ or $x - 1 = 0$.

To solve quadratic equations by factoring:

1) Use properties 1 and 2 (see Section 2-20) to put all terms on one side of the equation, while the other side is 0.
2) Combine the like terms, if necessary.
3) Factor the expression.
4) Since the product of the factors is 0, the equation will hold if at least one of the factors is equal to zero. So set the factors equal to 0.
5) Solve the resulting equations.

For example: Solve the equation $x^2 - 25 = 0$.

<u>Steps 1 and 2</u> have already been taken.

<u>Step 3:</u> Factor the expression $x^2 - 25$.

$x^2 - 25$ is factored into $(x + 5)(x - 5)$. So,

$$(x + 5)(x - 5) = 0$$

<u>Step 4:</u> Set each factor equal to 0.

$$x + 5 = 0 \quad \text{or} \quad x - 5 = 0$$

<u>Step 5:</u> Solve the resulting equation.

$$x + 5 = 0$$
$$x = -5$$
$$x - 5 = 0$$
$$x = 5$$

The answer is either $x = -5$ or $x = 5$.

To check whether the answer is correct, substitute $x = -5$ and then $x = 5$ into the original equation.

First, $x = -5$,

$$x^2 - 25 = 0$$
$$(-5)^2 - 25 = 0$$
$$25 - 25 = 0$$
$$0 = 0$$

Then, $x = 5$,

$$x^2 - 25 = 0$$
$$5^2 - 25 = 0$$
$$25 - 25 = 0$$
$$0 = 0$$

Therefore, the answer is correct.

Another example: Solve the equation $y^2 = 5y - 4$.

<u>Step 1:</u> Put all terms on one side of the equation. Subtract $5y$ from both sides and add 4 to both sides.

$$y^2 - 5y + 4 = 5y - 4 - 5y + 4$$
$$y^2 - 5y + 4 = 0$$

<u>Step 2</u> has already been taken.

<u>Step 3:</u> Factor the expression $y^2 - 5y + 4$.

$y^2 - 5y + 4$ is factored into $(y - 1)(y - 4)$.

So,

$$(y - 1)(y - 4) = 0$$

<u>Step 4:</u> Set each factor equal to 0.

$$y - 4 = 0 \quad \text{or} \quad y - 1 = 0$$

<u>Step 5:</u> Solve the resulting equations.

$$y - 4 = 0 \qquad\qquad y - 1 = 0$$
$$y = 4 \qquad\qquad\qquad y = 1$$

Therefore, the answer is either $y = 4$ or $y = 1$. To check the answer, substitute first $y = 4$ into the original equation and then $y = 1$.

First, $y = 4$:

$$y^2 = 5y - 4$$
$$4^2 = 5(4) - 4$$
$$16 = 20 - 4$$
$$16 = 16$$

Then, $y = 1$:

$$y^2 = 5y - 4$$
$$1^2 = 5(1) - 4$$
$$1 = 5 - 4$$
$$1 = 1$$

Therefore, the answer is correct.

Practice Exercises for 2-23

Solve for x:

1. $x^2 - 2x + 1 = 0$

2. $x^2 - 5x + 6 = 0$

3. $x^2 + x = 2$

4. $x^2 = 36$

5. $x^2 = x + 2$

6. $x^2 - 49 = 0$

7. $x^2 - 4x = -3$

8. $x^2 + 5x + 6 = 0$

9. $x - x^2 = -12$

10. $25 - x^2 = 0$

11. $x^2 - 100 = 69$

12. $2x^2 = 3x - 1$

13. $4x^2 + 4x + 1 = 0$

14. $2x^2 + x = 1$

15. $9x^2 = 1$

2-24 Solving equations with more than one unknown

An equation may have more than one unknown. In this case, there is generally no specific solution for the unknowns; each unknown can have almost any value depending on the values of the other unknowns. Examples of equations with more than one unknown are $x + 2y = 56$, $m + n + p = 0$, and $3x + 7y + z = 2$. In problems that have equations with more than one unknown, you are usually asked to solve for one unknown in terms of the others.

The method used in solving for one unknown in terms of the others in a linear equation is basically the same as the method used in solving a linear equation with only one unknown.

For example: Solve the equation $2x + 3y = 6$ for x.

<u>Step 1:</u> Use properties 1 and 2 (see Section 2-20) to put all terms involving x on one side of the equation and all the other terms on the other side. Subtract $3y$ from both sides of the equation, and then combine terms:

$$2x + 3y - 3y = 6 - 3y$$
$$2x = 6 - 3y$$

<u>Step 2:</u> Use property 4 (see Section 2-20) to isolate x.
Divide both sides by 2.

$$\frac{2x}{2} = \frac{6-3y}{2}$$
$$x = \frac{6-3y}{2}$$

Once x is alone on one side of the equation and does not appear on the other side, the problem is really finished; x is equal to the expression on the other side, which is in terms of y and constants.

Practice Exercises for 2-24

Solve for x (in terms of y):

1. $3x - 2y = 2x$

2. $3x - 2y = 2x + y$

3. $2x + y = 6$

4. $y - x = 3y$

5. $y - x = 2y + x$

6. $\dfrac{x}{y} = 2$

7. $x - y = y - x$

8. $3x + 3y = 3$

9. $\dfrac{x+1}{y} = 2$

10. $3x + 4y = 4x + 3y$

2-25 Using solution of one equation to solve another

Sometimes, we must use the solution of one equation to solve another.

For example: If $xy + \dfrac{y}{x} = 10$, and $x + 3 = 5$, find y.
First, we solve $x + 3 = 5$, to get $x = 2$.
We then substitute 2 for x in the equation $xy + \dfrac{y}{x} = 10$ to get $2y + \dfrac{y}{2} = 10$.

Combining like terms, we get $\dfrac{5}{2}y = 10$. Now we multiply both sides of the equation by 2 to get $5y = 20$. Dividing both sides by 5, we get $y = 4$.

Another example: If $x - y = 1$ and $x + y = 2$, solve for x.

Solution: Write the equations as follows:

$$x - y = 1$$
$$x + y = 2$$

Add both equations:

$$x - y = 1$$
$$\underline{+(x - y = 2)}$$
$$x + x - y + y = 1 + 2$$

Notice that the ys cancel and we are left with

$$x + x = 1 + 2$$
$$\text{or} \quad 2x = 3$$

$$\boxed{x = \frac{3}{2}.}$$

To find the value of y, we substitute back into one of the equations:

$$x - y = 1 \text{ where } x = \frac{3}{2}$$

We get

$$\frac{3}{2} - y = 1$$

$$-y = 1 - \frac{3}{2}$$

$$-y = -\frac{1}{2}$$

$$\boxed{y = \frac{1}{2}}$$

Practice Exercises for 2-25

Solve for y and x.

1. $x + 2 = 3$; $\dfrac{x}{y} + x = 4$

2. $x + y = 3$; $-x - 2y = 4$

3. $x + 2y = 2x$; $y + 6 = 9$

4. $x + 2y = 2x$; $x - y = 1$

5. $\dfrac{x}{y} = 1$; $x + y = 1$

6. $x + y = 2x$; $2x - y = 2$

7. $\dfrac{1}{y} + \dfrac{1}{x} = 1$; $x + 1 = 3$

8. $5 - y = 4$; $x + y = 9$

9. $x - 2y = y - 2x$; $\dfrac{x}{y + 1} = 2$

10. $y + 2 = 4$; $xy + \dfrac{x}{y} = \dfrac{5}{2}$

Ratio and Proportion

Diagnostic Test on Ratio and Proportion

1. Which represents the same ratio as $7 : 5$?

   (A) $5 : 7$ (D) $6 : 6$

   (B) $3 : 1$ (E) $17 : 15$

   (C) $14 : 10$

2. Which ratio equals $10 : 6$?

   (A) $3 : 8$

   (B) $3 : 5$

   (C) $3 : 3$

   (D) $3 : 16$

   (E) none of the above

3. How many times the ratio $3 : 4$ is the ratio $6 : 1$?

   (A) 1 (D) 8

   (B) 3 (E) 18

   (C) 5

4. If x is to 8 as 15 is to 12, then x equals

   (A) 10 (D) 14

   (B) 8 (E) 6

   (C) 12

5. Write a proportion that means the same as $sr = tq$.

   (A) $\dfrac{s}{r} = \dfrac{t}{q}$

   (B) $sr + tq = 1$

   (C) $sr - tq = 1$

   (D) $\dfrac{s}{t} = \dfrac{q}{r}$

   (E) $st = rq$

6. If the side of a square is doubled, the perimeter of the square is

   (A) unchanged

   (B) doubled

   (C) halved

   (D) multiplied by 4

   (C) divided by 4

7. On a map, 1 inch represents 25 miles. Two cities 150 miles apart would be separated on the map by

   (A) 3 inches   (D) 6 inches

   (B) 4 inches   (E) 7 inches

   (C) 5 inches

8. If there are 1.15 land miles in a nautical mile, how many land miles are there in 10 nautical miles?

   (A) 15

   (B) 12.3

   (C) 8.8

   (D) 11.5

   (E) none of the above

9. How many ounces are there in 4 lbs 5 ounces?

   (A) 4.31 (D) 69

   (B) 6.18 (E) 60

   (C) 53

10. x is to y as 4 is to 5.   Then $y : x$ equals

    (A) $3 : 5$ (D) $5 : 2$

    (B) $5 : 4$ (E) $9 : 1$

    (C) $-4 : 5$

Solutions for Diagnostic Test

1. **(C)** Since ratios only deal with relative size, doubling both parts of a ratio does not affect the value of the ratio. $7 : 5 = 14 : 10$. **(2-26)**

2. **(E)** $10 : 6 = 5 : 3 = 3 : \left(\dfrac{9}{5}\right)$. This is not a listed choice. **(2-26)**

3. **(D)** $x(3 : 4) = 6 : 1$

   $\dfrac{3}{4}x = \dfrac{6}{1}$. $3x = 24$. $x = 8$.

   (2-26, 2-22)

4. **(A)** $x : 8 = 15 : 12$

   $\dfrac{x}{8} = \dfrac{15}{12}$. $12x = 120$. $x = 10$ **(2-28)**

5. **(D)** $sr = tq$. $\dfrac{sr}{tr} = \dfrac{tq}{tr}$. Cancelling,

   $\dfrac{s}{t} = \dfrac{q}{r}$. **(2-28)**

6. **(B)** Let the side of the original square be s. Then the perimeter of the old square is $4s$. The side of the new square is $2s$, and its perimeter is $4(2s)$, or $8s$. $8s : 4s = 2 : 1$. The perimeter doubles. **(2-27)**

7. **(D)** $\dfrac{1\,\text{in}}{x\,\text{in}} = \dfrac{25\,\text{miles}}{150\,\text{miles}}$. $25x = 150$, $x = 6$ **(2-29)**

8. **(D)** $\dfrac{1.15\,\text{land}}{x\,\text{land}} = \dfrac{1\,\text{naut}}{10\,\text{naut}}$. $x = 10(1.15)$
   $= 11.5$ **(2-29)**

9. **(D)** 1 lb = 16 ounces. 4 lbs = 64 ounces. 4 lbs 5 ounces = 64 + 5 = 69 ounces. **(2-33)**

10. **(B)** Using the product of the means equals the product of the extremes, $x : y = 4 : 5$ becomes $5x = 4y$

    $\dfrac{5x}{4x} = \dfrac{4y}{4x}$. **(2-28)**

Instructional Material on Ratio and Proportion

2-26 A ratio described

A ratio is a comparison between two numbers or between two measurements with the same units. For example, $2 : 3$ and 2 feet : 3 feet are both ratios. However, 1 yard : 3 gallons is not a ratio, because yards and gallons are not the same units. $2 : 3$ is read "the ratio of 2 to 3."

A ratio can be considered a fraction. The ratio $2 : 3$ could be written as the fraction $\dfrac{2}{3}$. Since, when we consider ratios, we are interested only in the relative size of the two numbers or quantities, ratios can be reduced just like fractions. For example, $6 : 9$ is equal to $2 : 3$ because $\dfrac{6}{9} = \dfrac{2}{3}$. Other operations are performed just as they are with fractions. For example, what ratio is twice the ratio $3 : 4$? $3 : 4$ is $\dfrac{3}{4}$. Twice $\dfrac{3}{4}$, or $2 \times \dfrac{3}{4}$ equals $\dfrac{3}{2}$. Therefore the ratio $3 : 2$ is twice the ratio $3 : 4$.

Practice Exercises for 2-26

Write the following ratios as fractions:

Write the following fractions as ratios:

1. $4:7$ 3. $4:9$ 5. $3:2$ 7. $1:1$ 9. $2:1$ 11. $\dfrac{5}{6}$ 13. $\dfrac{2}{3}$ 15. $\dfrac{2}{1}$ 17. $\dfrac{1}{2}$ 19. $\dfrac{3}{1}$

2. $8:3$ 4. $6:5$ 6. $2:3$ 8. $1:2$ 10. $10:11$ 12. $\dfrac{2}{3}$ 14. $\dfrac{1}{2}$ 16. $1\dfrac{2}{3}$ 18. $1\dfrac{2}{3}$ 20. $\dfrac{9}{10}$

2-27 The effect of the change of one quantity on another

If two quantities are related by a formula, a change in one quantity might cause the other quantity to change. We could be required to find the change in one quantity given the change in the other. To do this:

1) Pick a letter to stand for the original value of the quantity whose change we are given.
2) Find the ratio of the following—New value : Original value.

For example: The area of a circle is πr^2, where π is a constant and r is the radius of the circle. What happens to the area if the radius is doubled?

Let x equal the original radius. Then πx^2 is the original value of the area. The new radius is double the original, or $2x$. The new area is $\pi(2x)^2$ or $4\pi x^2$. The ratio of New area : Original area is $4\pi x^2 : \pi x^2$, or $4:1$. Doubling the radius multiplies the area by 4.

Another example: Light intensity is found by the formula $\dfrac{I}{d^2}$, where I is a constant, and d is the distance from the light. If the distance from the light is tripled, what happens to the intensity?

Let the original distance be x. Then the original intensity was $\dfrac{I}{x^2}$. The new distance is $3x$ and the new intensity is $\dfrac{I}{(3x)^2}$, or $\dfrac{I}{9x^2}$. The ratio of new intensity : original intensity is $\dfrac{I}{9x^2} : \dfrac{I}{x^2}$, or $\dfrac{1}{9} : 1$. The intensity was multiplied by $\dfrac{1}{9}$ when the distance tripled. In these problems, the formulas are well known, or they will be given.

Practice Exercises for 2-27

1. The area of a circle is πr^2 where π is a constant, and r is the radius. What happens to the area if the radius is tripled?

2. The circumference of a circle is $2\pi r$, where π is a constant and r is the radius. What happens to the circumference if the radius is doubled?

3. If $y = \dfrac{2}{x}$, what happens to y if x is doubled?

4. If $y = n(n - 1)$, what happens to y if n is increased by 1?

5. The distance an object falls is given by the formula

$$y = at^2$$

where y is the distance it falls, and t is the time it takes to fall (a is a constant). What happens to y if the time t is tripled?

6. If $y = x + 3$, what happens to y if x is increased by 2?

7. The volume of a cube is s^3, where s is the length of a side of the cube. What happens to the volume if the side of the cube is tripled?

8. The area of a rectangle is $l \times w$ where l = length and w = width. If both the length and width are doubled, what happens to the area?

9. The perimeter of a rectangle is $2l + 2w$, where l is the length and w is the width. What happens to the perimeter if both the length and width are doubled?

10. If $\dfrac{x}{y} = 2$, what happens to y if x is tripled?

2-28 Proportions described

A proportion is simply a statement that two ratios are equal. An example of a proportion is $4 : 5 = 8 : 10$, which is read "4 is to 5 as 8 is to 10." Since ratios are fractions, problems with proportions generally involve equations with fractions. These can be solved by clearing the equation of fractions.

For example: What number is to 12 as 3 is to 4?

We are asked to solve the proportion $x : 12 = 3 : 4$. This can be written $\dfrac{x}{12} = \dfrac{3}{4}$. We multiply both sides of the equation by 12, and we get $x = 12 \times \dfrac{3}{4}$, or $x = 9$.

In general, proportions can be solved by using the rule: "The product of the extremes equals the product of the means." In the proportion $a : b = c : d$, the extremes are the outside terms, a and d. The means are the inside terms, b and c. The rule says that $ad = bc$. By dividing both sides of $ad = bc$ by two of the terms of the proportion, we can get various proportions equivalent to $a : b = c : d$.

For example: If x is to y as m is to n, then x is to m as _____.
We are given that $x : y = m : n$. Using "the product of the extremes equals the product of the means" rule, we get $xn = my$. Dividing both sides of this equation by mn, we get $\dfrac{x}{m} = \dfrac{y}{n}$. Therefore, x is to m as y is to n.
Another example: If 3 pounds of apples cost 57¢, how much do 10 pounds of apples cost?
We set up the proportion $\dfrac{3\,\text{lbs}}{10\,\text{lbs}} = \dfrac{57¢}{x¢}$. The units cancel out. Using "the product of the extremes equals the product of the means," we get $3x = 570$, or $x = 190$. 10 pounds cost 190¢, or $1.90.

Practice Exercises for 2-28

1. Solve for x: $x : 3 = 4 : 6$

2. What number is to 15 as 1 is to 3?

3. 2 pounds of apples cost 50¢. What do 5 pounds of apples cost?

4. How many pounds of peaches can I get for $1.25 if 1 pound of peaches costs 25¢?

5. If a car can go 15 miles per gallon, how many miles can the car go on 10 gallons?

6. What number is to 10 as 25 is to 75?

7. If 3 pencils cost 10¢, how much do 300 pencils cost?

8. 5 gallons of gasoline costs $4.50. How much would $8\dfrac{1}{2}$ gallons of gasoline cost?

9. Solve for x: $2 : x = 5 : 8$

10. 8 is to what number as 12 is to 15?

2-29 To solve scale problems, express the given information as a proportion

For example: If 1 inch on a map represents 10 miles, then 2 inches represent 20 miles, etc. This can be expressed in a proportion,

$$\frac{1\,\text{inch}}{2\,\text{inches}} = \frac{10\,\text{miles}}{20\,\text{miles}}$$

In a problem, one of the terms in the proportion may be unknown.

For example: If one inch on a map represents 30 blocks, how many inches would be needed to represent 135 blocks?
We set up the proportion

$$\frac{1\,\text{inch}}{x\,\text{inches}} = \frac{30\,\text{blocks}}{135\,\text{blocks}}$$

The units cancel, and we must solve the proportion $\dfrac{1}{x} = \dfrac{30}{135}$. The product of the means equals the product of the extremes, so

$$30x = 135$$
$$x = 4\frac{1}{2}$$

Therefore $4\dfrac{1}{2}$ inches are required to represent 135 blocks.

Practice Exercises for 2-29

1. If one inch on a map represents 15 miles, how many inches represent 20 miles?

2. If 1 centimeter on a map represents 2.5 kilometers, how many kilometers do 2 centimeters represent?

3. If 1 square inch represents 3 square miles, what does 1.5 square inches represent?

4. If 1 foot length represents 500 miles on a map, then what is the greatest number of miles that can be represented on a paper of length 1 yard?

5. $2\frac{1}{2}$ inches represent 1 mile on a map. How many miles are represented by 10 inches?

2-30 To convert from one unit of measurement to another, we use proportions

(This makes sense only if the different units are measuring the same thing.)

For example: How many inches are there in 100 centimeters if there are 2.5 centimeters in 1 inch?

We set up the proportion

$$\frac{1\,\text{inch}}{x\,\text{inches}} = \frac{2.5\,\text{centimeters}}{100\,\text{centimeters}}$$

The units cancel and we have

$$\frac{1}{x} = \frac{2.5}{100}$$

or $2.5x = 100$. $x = 40$. Therefore, there are 40 inches in 100 centimeters.

Practice Exercises for 2-30

1. If there are 2.5 centimeters in an inch, how many centimeters are there in 20 inches?

2. There are 12 inches in a foot. How many inches tall is a 6-foot man?

3. 4 quarts equal 1 gallon. How many quarts equal 3.5 gallons?

4. There are 5280 feet in a mile. How many feet are there in $1\frac{1}{2}$ miles?

5. If 1 kilometer $= \frac{5}{8}$ of a mile, how many kilometers are there in 1 mile?

Rate and Work

Diagnostic Test on Rate and Work

1. A trip takes 5 hours in a car moving 40 miles per hour. How long would the trip take in a 100-mile-per-hour train?

   (A) 1 hour   (D) 4 hours

   (B) 2 hours   (E) 5 hours

   (C) 3 hours

2. In still water, a boy rows 5 miles an hour. With the aid of a current, he can make a 21-mile trip in 3 hours. How fast is the current?

   (A) 2 miles per hour

   (B) 4 miles per hour

   (C) 6 miles per hour

   (D) 3 miles per hour

   (E) 5 miles per hour

3. It takes Bill 4 hours to do a job. It takes Joe 2 hours to do the same job. How many such jobs could they do together in 4 hours?

   (A) 1   (D) 7

   (B) 3   (E) 9

   (C) 5

4. For the first 5 hours of a flight, a plane is assisted by a 100-mile-per-hour wind. For the next 3 hours, it is hindered by a 100-mile-an-hour wind. If the total distance traveled is 3400 miles, how fast is the plane in windless conditions?

   (A) 150 miles per hour

   (B) 300 miles per hour

   (C) 400 miles per hour

   (D) 500 miles per hour

   (E) 1000 miles per hour

5. Jane can bake a cake in 2 hours. Jill can bake a cake in 5 hours. Working together, how long would it take to bake the cake?

   (A) $2\frac{1}{2}$ hours   (D) $3\frac{1}{4}$ hours

   (B) $3\frac{1}{2}$ hours   (E) $\frac{4}{5}$ hours

   (C) $1\frac{3}{7}$ hours

Solutions for Diagnostic Test

1. **(B)** Distance equals rate multiplied by time. $5 \cdot 40 = 100x$, or $x = 2$.   **(2-31)**

2. **(A)** Effective rate equals still water rate plus rate of current.
   Therefore, $21 = (5 + x)(3)$. $3x + 15 = 21$. $3x = 6$, or $x = 2$.   **(2-31)**

3. **(B)** In 4 hours, Bill does 1 job, and Joe does $\frac{4}{2}$, or 2 jobs. Together they do 3 jobs.   **(2-32)**

4. **(C)** The wind-assisted rate is $x + 100$. The wind-hindered rate is $x - 100$. Altogether $3400 = (x + 100)(5) + (x - 100)(3)$. $3400 = 5x + 500 + 3x - 300$. $x = 400$ miles per hour.   **(2-31, 2-22)**

5. **(C)** Let x be the time it takes. In x hours, Jane does $\frac{x}{2}$ part of the work, and Jill does $\frac{x}{5}$ part of the work. Together they do the complete job. $\frac{x}{2} + \frac{x}{5} = 1$. $5x + 2x = 10$. $x = \frac{10}{7} = 1\frac{3}{7}$.   **(2-31, 2-22)**

Instructional Material on Rate and Work

2-31 To do problems dealing with distance

1) Use this formula: Distance = Rate × Time.
2) If parts of the trip are at different rates (speeds), then to find the total distance, or the total time, you must separate the parts of the trip.

For example: If a boy flew from New York to Chicago, a distance of 1600 miles at the rate of 400 miles an hour, and then took a train home at the rate of 80 miles an hour, how long did the whole trip take?

We must use the formula Distance = Rate × Time, or Time = Distance ÷ Rate. First, Time going = 1600 ÷ 400 = 4 hours. Then, Time returning = 1600 ÷ 80 = 20 hours. The total trip took 20 + 4, or 24 hours.

If a wind or river current is helping a traveler, then his total speed is the normal speed (in windless conditions or still water) plus the speed of the wind or current. If the wind or current is hindering the traveler, then his speed is his normal speed minus the speed of the wind or river current.

For example: A man can row 2 miles an hour in still water. If he rows with the current helping him along, he can go 20 miles in 5 hours. How fast is the current? Let s be the speed of the current. Then $(s + 2)$ is his speed when the current is aiding him.

Distance = Rate × Time, so $20 = (s + 2)5$, or $20 = 5s + 10$, and $s = 2$ miles per hour.

Practice Exercises for 2-31

1. How long would a 1000-mile trip take if I were traveling at 50 miles per hour for the first 500 miles and at 60 miles an hour for the rest of the trip?

2. If a train travels at rate of r miles an hour and travels a distance of $2r$ miles, for how long does the train travel?

3. A boat can reach its destination in 3 hours. If it goes twice as fast, it can reach 10 miles more than its destination, in 2 hours. How fast does it originally go?

4. A pilot can fly a plane 500 miles in 4 hours. How much faster (rate) would he be flying if he traveled the same distance in 2 hours?

5. A man can drive a certain distance in 5 hours. If he increased his speed by 10 miles per hour, he could travel the same distance in $4\frac{1}{6}$ hours. What is the distance he travels?

2-32 To do work problems

Write an equation to tell how much of the work is done in one hour. Usually the unknown will be how long it takes two men working together to do a job, or how long it takes one man working alone to do the job.

The key is: If it takes x hours to do a job, $\dfrac{1}{x}$ of the job is done each hour.

For example: Bill can do a job alone in 5 hours. Bob can do it alone in 4 hours. If they work together, how long will it take?

Let x be the time it takes them to do the job together. Then $\dfrac{1}{x}$ is the part of the job they do in one hour. But Bill does $\dfrac{1}{5}$ of the work in one hour, and Bob can do $\dfrac{1}{4}$ of the work in one hour. Therefore, $\dfrac{1}{x} = \dfrac{1}{4} + \dfrac{1}{5}$. Multiplying by $20x$, we get $20 = 5x + 4x = 9x$. $x = \dfrac{20}{9}$ or $2\dfrac{2}{9}$ hours.

Another example: Jim and John can do a job together in 5 hours. It takes Jim twice as long to do the job alone as it takes John to do the job alone. How long will it take Jim to do the job alone?

Let x be the time it takes John to do the job alone. Then it takes $2x$ hours for Jim to do the job alone. In one hour, they do $\dfrac{1}{5}$ of the work. John does $\dfrac{1}{x}$ of the work and Jim does $\dfrac{1}{2x}$ of the work. Therefore, $\dfrac{1}{5} = \dfrac{1}{x} + \dfrac{1}{2x}$. Multiplying by $10x$, we get $2x = 10 + 5 = 15$. $x = 7\dfrac{1}{2}$. Since it takes $2x$ hours for Jim to do the job alone, it would take him 15 hours to complete the entire job.

Practice Exercises for 2-32

1. Harry can mow a lawn in 3 hours. Bill can mow the same lawn in 2 hours. If Harry and Bill work together, how long will it take to mow the lawn?

2. Paul and Mary can do a job in 2 hours. When Paul works alone, he can do 5 jobs in 15 hours. How many jobs can Mary do in 12 hours, alone?

3. John can complete a job in $\dfrac{1}{2}$ the time it takes Harry to complete the same job. If they both work together they can complete the job in 4 hours. How long does it take John to do the job alone?

4. Harry can do a job in 4 hours. Mary and Harry can do the job together in 3 hours. How long does it take Mary to do the job alone?

5. Sam can do a job in x hours. Denise can do the same job in $x + 2$ hours. How long will it take Sam and Denise to do the job together? (Express your answer in terms of x.)

2-33 Useful measurement information

The following table can be used to solve simple measurement problems:

Length	1 foot = 12 inches
	1 yard = 3 feet
	1 mile = 5280 feet
Time	1 minute = 60 seconds
	1 hour = 60 minutes
Volume	1 quart = 2 pints
	1 gallon = 4 quarts
Weight	1 pound = 16 ounces
	1 ton = 2000 pounds

Consider this problem: How many ounces are there in 4 pounds 3 ounces? 1 pound = 16 ounces, so 4 pounds = 4 × 16 = 64 ounces. Therefore, 4 pounds 3 ounces = 64 + 3 = 67 ounces.

Practice Exercises for 2-33

1. How many miles are 2000 yards and 20 feet?

2. How many pints are there in 2 gallons, 3 quarts, and 1 pint?

3. How many seconds are in 2 hours, 2 minutes?

4. How many pounds are there in 5.5 tons?

5. How many pints would I need to fill a 3-gallon container?

Averages

Diagnostic Test on Averages

1. What is the average of 3, 5, 7, 34, and 101?

   (A) 32 (D) 26
   (B) 30 (E) 38
   (C) 17

2. A basketball team scored a total of 7,865 points in a certain number of games. If they averaged 121 points per game, how many games did they play?

   (A) 55 (D) 73
   (B) 75 (E) 70
   (C) 65

3. If the average of 6, 9, and a is 10, find a.

   (A) 30 (D) 10
   (B) 21 (E) 15
   (C) 18

4. Find the average of m, $m + 1$, and $m + 2$.

   (A) m (D) $m + 3$
   (B) $m + 1$ (E) $3m + 3$
   (C) $m + 2$

5. If there are 9 boys and the average number of marbles per boy is 12, how many marbles do the boys have all together?

   (A) 19 (D) 108
   (B) 54 (E) 144
   (C) 72

Solutions for Diagnostic Test

1. **(B)** $\text{Average} = \dfrac{\text{Total}}{\text{Number}}$

   $\text{Average} = \dfrac{3+5+7+34+101}{5}$

   $\dfrac{150}{5} = 30$

   (2-24)

2. **(C)** $\text{Number} = \dfrac{\text{Total}}{\text{Average}}$

   $\text{Number of games} = \dfrac{7865}{121} = 65$

   (2-24)

3. **(E)** $\text{Average} = \dfrac{\text{Total}}{\text{Number}}$

   $10 = \dfrac{6+9+a}{3} = \dfrac{15+a}{3}$

   $a = 15$ **(2-24)**

4. **(B)** $\text{Average} = \dfrac{\text{Total}}{\text{Number}}$

   $\text{Average} = \dfrac{m+m+1+m+2}{3}$

   $= \dfrac{3m+3}{3} = m+1$

   (2-24)

5. **(D)** $\text{Total} = \text{Number} \times \text{Average}$

   Total number of marbles $= 9(12) = 108$

   (2-24)

Instructional Material on Averages

2-34 Description of an average

The average of a number of values is the sum of all the values divided by the number of values. The formula for finding the average of a list of values is

$$\text{Average} = \frac{\text{Total sum of the values}}{\text{Number of values}}$$

For example: Find the average of the following numbers: 10, 5, 110, 130, and 65.
To find the average of the numbers, first find the total sum.
Total sum = 10 + 5 + 110 + 130 + 65
= 320
Since there are five numbers, divide the total sum by 5.

$$\text{Average} = \frac{\text{Total sum of the values}}{\text{Number of values}} = \frac{320}{5} = 64$$

To solve problems involving averages:

All you have to remember is the formula for the average, and know how to apply the formula.
For example: The sum of a list of numbers is 486 and the average for the numbers is 40.5. How many numbers are there in the list?
The problem asks for how many numbers there are in the list. So, let n be the number of numbers in the list. Write the formula for the average.

$$\text{Average} = \frac{\text{Total sum of the values}}{\text{Number of values}}$$

From the problem, the total sum is 486 and the average is 40.5. Substitute the values into the formula.

$$40.5 = \frac{486}{n}$$

Solve the equation by multiplying both sides of the equation by n.

$$40.5\,n = 486$$

Divide both sides by 40.5.

$$n = 486 \div 40.5$$
$$n = 12$$

There are 12 numbers in the list.

Practice Exercises for 2-34

1. What is the average of 10, 25, 65, and 13?

2. John made $45.24 for the first week, $54.89 for the second week, and $47.29 for the third week. For the three weeks, what was his average income?

3. The sum of n numbers is q. What is the average of the n numbers in terms of n and q?

4. A man can run uphill a distance of 500 yards in 8 minutes. He can run downhill a distance of 500 yards in 4 minutes. What is his average speed for both the uphill and downhill trips?

5. The average of 8 numbers is $15\frac{1}{8}$. If 7 of the 8 numbers are all equal and the unequal number is 1 greater than the other equal numbers, what are the numbers?

6. John got the following scores on a test:

   55, 41, 43, 30, and 45

   What was his average score?

7. What score must I get on the fourth test in order to obtain an average of 80%, if my first three scores were 70%, 75%, and 95%?

8. How many more tests must I take in order to have a chance of scoring an average of 90% if I obtained 50% on my first test? (Hint: I must score 100% on my other tests.)

9. What is the average of 10.4, -3.6, and 7.4?

10. What is the average of 20.4, -17.6, and -2.8?

Combinations

Diagnostic Test on Combinations

1. A party has 12 boys and 15 girls. How many different dancing pairs can be formed?

   (A) 60   (D) 300

   (B) 180   (E) 250

   (C) 150

2. A combination lock has 12 numbers on the dial. If a combination of two numbers is needed to open the lock, how many possible combinations are there?

   (A) 24   (D) 144

   (B) 256   (E) 194

   (C) 96

3. There are 14 members in group I and 27 members in group II. If 5 people belong to both groups, how many people are there in the two groups altogether?

   (A) 30   (D) 36

   (B) 31   (E) 26

   (C) 29

4. With reference to Problem 3, how many members belong to group I only?

   (A) 9   (D) 16

   (B) 22   (E) 11

   (C) 19

5. Fifty people joined clubs. 30 joined club A and 25 joined club B. How many joined both clubs?

   (A) 15   (D) 3

   (B) 4   (E) 9

   (C) 5

Solutions for Diagnostic Test

1. **(B)** Each boy can form a pair with each of the 15 girls. 12(15), or 180, pairs can be formed.   **(2-35)**

2. **(D)** The total number of combinations is (12)(12) = 144.   **(2-35)**

3. **(D)** Number of people (total) = Number in I + Number in II − Number in both

   Total number = 14 + 27 − 5 = 36.   **(2-36)**

4. **(A)** Number in I only = Number in I − Number in both

   Number in I only = 14 − 5 = 9 **(2-36)**

5. **(C)** Since 30 joined A and 25 joined B, the number that joined both must be 30 + 25 − 50 = 5.   **(2-36)**

Instructional Material on Combinations

2-35 Number of ways of doing a job

Suppose that a job has 2 different parts. There are m different ways of doing the first part and n different ways of doing the second part. The problem is to find the number of ways of doing the entire job. For each way of doing the first part of the job, there are n ways of doing the second part. Since there are m ways of doing the first part, the total number of ways of doing the entire job is $m \times n$. The formula that can be used is

$$\text{Number of ways} = m \times n$$

For any problem that involves 2 actions or 2 objects, each with a number of choices, and asks for the number of combinations, the formula can be used. For example: A man wants a sandwich and a drink for lunch. If a restaurant has 4 choices of sandwiches and 3 choices of drinks, how many different ways can he order his lunch?

Since there are 4 choices of sandwiches and 3 choices of drinks, using the formula

$$\text{Number of ways} = 4(3)$$

$$= 12$$

Therefore, the man can order his lunch 12 different ways.

Practice Exercises for 2-35

1. A man has 4 different shirts and 6 different pairs of pants. How many different ways can the man dress with pants and shirts?

2. How many different 2-digit numbers (e.g., 10, 25, 76, 91) can be made?

3. Harry can buy a #2 pencil or a #4 pencil. Both pencils come in an orange or red color. How many different pencils can Harry buy?

4. How many different kinds of paper are there if paper comes in three sizes and each size comes in either a red, green or white color?

2-36 Number of members belonging to groups

Suppose there are two groups, each with a certain number of members. Some members of one group also belong to the other group. The problem is to find how many members there are in the two groups altogether. To find the numbers of members altogether, use the following formula:

Total number of members = Number of members in group I
+ Number of members in group II
− Number of members common to both groups

For example: In one class, 18 students received As for English and 10 students received As in math. If 5 students received As in both English and math, how many students received at least one A?

In this case, let the students who received As in English be in group I and let those who received As in math be in group II.

Using the formula:
Number of students who received at least one A

$$= \text{Number in group I} + \text{Number in group II} - \text{Number in both}$$
$$= 18 + 10 - 5 = 23$$

Therefore, there are 23 students who received at least one A.

> In combination problems such as those on the preceding page, the problems do not always ask for the total number. They may ask for any of the four numbers in the formula while the other three are given. In any case, to solve the problems, use the formula.

Practice Exercises for 2-36

1. 125 people joined clubs. 75 joined Club A, and 85 joined Club B. How many people joined both clubs?

2. 75 people joined Club A, and 50 people joined Club B. If 30 people joined both clubs, how many people joined clubs?

3. 65 people were members of group I. 40 people were members of group II. If one-half as many people belong to both groups, as the total number of members, how many people belong to both groups?

4. Twice as many people belong to group I as those who belong to group II. If 25 people belong to both groups and the total number of members is 200, how many members belong to group I? To group II?

Inequalities

Diagnostic Test on Inequalities

1. If $c > 0$, then

   (A) $3c > 2c$

   (B) $7c < 4c$

   (C) $-2c > 0$

   (D) $-c < -2c$

   (E) none of the above

2. If $a < 0$, then

   (A) $a + 1 > 0$ (D) $a > a^2$

   (B) $-a - 3 < 0$ (E) $4a < a$

   (C) $2a > 0$

3. If $a > b$ and $b > c$, then

   (A) $a > c$

   (B) $a - b > c$

   (C) $ab > bc$

   (D) $abc > 0$

   (E) none of the above

4. $x > y$. Then

   (A) $x^2 > y^2$

   (B) $xy > 0$

   (C) $x - y < 0$

   (D) $4 + 2x > 2y + 1$

   (E) $7x > 8y$

5. $2x + 1 > 0$. Then

   (A) $x > 0$ (D) $x < -2$

   (B) $x < 0$ (E) $x > -\dfrac{1}{2}$

   (C) $x > 2$

6. Arrange the following fractions in increasing order: $-\dfrac{2}{5}, -\dfrac{1}{2}, \dfrac{1}{5}$

   (A) $-\dfrac{2}{5}, -\dfrac{1}{2}, \dfrac{1}{5}$ (D) $\dfrac{1}{5}, -\dfrac{1}{2}, -\dfrac{2}{5}$

   (B) $-\dfrac{1}{2}, -\dfrac{2}{5}, \dfrac{1}{5}$ (E) $-\dfrac{1}{2}, \dfrac{1}{5}, -\dfrac{2}{5}$

   (C) $\dfrac{1}{5}, -\dfrac{2}{5}, -\dfrac{1}{2}$

7. $x^2 + x < 1$.   Which of the following is impossible?

   (A) $x > 1$ (D) $x > \dfrac{1}{2}$

   (B) $x > -1$ (E) $x > 0$

   (C) $x < 0$

8. If $x \neq y$ and $y \neq z$, then

   (A) $x \neq z$

   (B) $x > y$

   (C) $y > z$

   (D) $z > x$

   (E) none of the above is true

9. $x + 1 > 1 - 2x$. Then

   (A) $x > 0$ (D) $x < -3$

   (B) $x < 0$ (E) $x \neq 2$

   (C) $x > 3$

10. If $n > 0$, then $\dfrac{3}{n}$ is greater than which fraction?

    (A) $\dfrac{n}{3}$ (D) $\dfrac{5}{n}$

    (B) $\dfrac{2}{n-1}$ (E) $\dfrac{-1}{-4}$

    (C) $\dfrac{3}{n+1}$

Solutions for Diagnostic Test

1. **(A)** $3 > 2$. Since $c > 0$, we can multiply both sides by c to get $3c > 2c$. **(2-38)**

2. **(E)** $4 > 1$. Since $a < 0$, we multiply both sides by a, reversing the inequality. Therefore, $4a < a$. **(2-38)**

3. **(A)** If a is greater than b which is greater than c, a must be greater than c. **(2-37, 2-38)**

4. **(D)** $x > y$ means $2x > 2y$. Since $4 > 1$, we can add inequalities to get $4 + 2x > 2y + 1$. **(2-38)**

5. **(E)** $2x + 1 > 0$ means $2x > -1$, or $x > \frac{1}{2}$. **(2-38, 2-39)**

6. **(B)** Write the fractions as fractions with the same denominator. 10 is convenient.

$-\frac{2}{5} = \frac{-4}{10}$, $-\frac{1}{2} = \frac{-5}{10}$, $\frac{1}{5} = \frac{2}{10}$; since $-5 - 4 < 2$, the order is $-\frac{1}{2}, \frac{2}{5}, \frac{1}{5}$ **(2-40)**

7. **(A)** Assume $x > 1$. Since $x^2 > 0$, or $x^2 = 0$, we can add to get $x^2 + x > 1$, contradicting $x^2 + x < 1$. Therefore, choice A is impossible. **(2-38, 2-39)**

8. **(E)** Statements that two numbers are unequal do not tell the relative size of the numbers. Choice A is clearly false, so none of the listed choices must be true. **(2-37)**

9. **(A)** $x + 1 > 1 - 2x$. Adding $2x$ to both sides, $3x + 1 > 1$. Subtracting 1 from both sides, $3x > 0$, or $x > 0$. **(2-38)**

10. **(C)** Since both numerator and denominator of $\frac{3}{n}$ are known to be positive, increasing the denominator to $n + 1$ decreases the fraction. **(2-40)**

Instructional Material on Inequalities

2-37 Definition of an inequality

An inequality is a statement that one expression is greater than or less than another expression. Thus, $3 > 1$ is an inequality that says 3 is greater than 1. $3 < 5$ is an inequality that says 3 is less than 5. Also, if a number n is positive, we can write $n > 0$, and if n is negative, we can write $n < 0$.

The statements $a > b$ and $b < a$ mean the same thing. The symbol $>$ or $<$ always points to the lesser expression. The statement $x \neq y$ means x does not equal y (x may be greater than y or less than y). Note that $\geq$ means "greater than or equal to" and $\leq$ means "less than or equal to."

Practice Exercises for 2-37

Express the following with symbolic notation $(<, >, =, \neq, \text{etc.})$.

1. a is greater or equal to 0.

2. b is less than or equal to a.

3. c is positive or 0.

4. The sum of a and b is positive.

5. a is never equal to 0.

6. a is less than b and b is less than 0.

7. The sum of a and b is less than or equal to 0.

8. The square of a is greater than the square of b.

9. The product of x and y is positive.

10. x is a positive number less than 1.

2-38 To do problems involving inequalities, use the following rules

1) Inequalities can be added in this way: If $a > b$, and $c > d$, then $a + c > b + d$. Also, if $a > b$ and $c = d$, then $a + c > b + d$. The rules for $a < b$ follow similarly.

2) Inequalities can be multiplied in this way: If $a > b$, and if $c > 0$, then $ac > bc$. If $a > b$ and $c < 0$, then $ac < bc$. That is, multiplying by a negative number reverses the inequality.

For example: For what values of x is $3x > x + 2$ a true statement?

Just as in working with equations, we must get x alone on one side of the inequality, $3x > x + 2$. We can add $-x$ to both sides of the inequality. $3x + (-x) > x + 2 + (-x)$, or $2x > 2$. Now we multiply both sides by $\frac{1}{2}$ to get $x > 1$. Therefore $3x > x + 2$ is true whenever $x > 1$.

Another example: If $a > b$, then when is the inequality $ax^2 > bx^2$ true? If $x = 0$, then both sides are zero, and ax^2 is not greater than bx^2. But, if x is not equal to zero, then $x^2 > 0$, since any number multiplied by itself cannot be negative. Since $a > b$, and $x^2 > 0$, we can multiply by x^2 to get $ax^2 > bx^2$. Therefore, $ax^2 > bx^2$ is true unless $x = 0$.

Practice Exercises for 2-38

1. For what values of x is $2x > x + 1$?

2. If $1 > r > 0$, what is the relationship of r and r^2 (that is, is $r > r^2$, $r < r^2$, or $r = r^2$)?

3. If $r^2 > r > 0$, what is the relationship of r^2 and r^3?

4. If $(n)(n - 1) > 0$, what is the relationship of n and n^2?

5. If $3x > 2$ and $2y > 1$, what can be said about $3x + 2y$?

6. If $1 > r > 0$, what is the relationship of $-r$ and -1?

7. If $5x - 4 \geqq 3x$, what values can x have?

8. If $x^2 > y^2$, when is $ax^2 > ay^2$?

9. If $3x > 2y > 0$, when is $3xy > 2y^2$?

10. For what values of x is $3x - 4 > 2x + 8$?

2-39 Figuring out inequalities from certain statements

Some problems with inequalities give certain statements as true, and then ask which of several inequalities (or other statements) could not be true. To do these problems, you must be able to show that the reverse of one of the choices is always true.

For example: If $x + 2P = y$, and P is positive, which of the following statements could not be true?

(A) $x > y$ (B) $x + P > -y$ (C) $y = P$ (D) $y + x > 1$ (E) $y > x + 1$

Since P is positive, 2P is positive or 2P > 0. Multiplying this by -1, we get that $-2P < 0$ (reversing the inequality). Now we add $x + 2P = y$ and $-2P < 0$, to get $x + 2P + (-2P) < y + 0$, or $x < y$. Since $x < y$ is always true, $x > y$ can never be true. The correct choice is (A).

Practice Exercises for 2-39

1. If $2 > x$ and $2x + 4 > y$, which is not true?
   (i) $y > 8$
   (ii) y can be equal to 4
   (iii) $x + 2 > 4$

2. If $2x + y > 4$ and $x - y > 2$, then which could not be true?
   (i) $2 > x$
   (ii) $2 + y > x$
   (iii) $x - 2 > y > 4 - 2x$

3. If $-1 < r < +1$, which of the following is (are) always true?
   (i) $+1 > -r$
   (ii) $-r > -1$
   (iii) $r \neq 0$

4. If $1 > r$, which of the following is (are) always true?
   (i) $r > r^2$
   (ii) $r^2 > r^3$
   (iii) $r \neq 0$

5. If $x + y^2 = t$, which of the following could not be true?
   (i) $t > x$
   (ii) $x > t$
   (iii) $y > 0$
   (iv) $x = t$

2-40 To compare fractions

1) Change the given fractions to fractions with the same denominator (you can use one of the original denominators).
2) The greater fraction is the one with the greater numerator.

For example: Which fraction is greater, $\frac{1}{4}$ or $\frac{7}{27}$?

We can change $\dfrac{1}{4}$ to $\dfrac{\frac{1}{4} \times 27}{27} = \dfrac{6\frac{3}{4}}{27}$. Since $7 > 6\frac{3}{4}$, $\dfrac{7}{27} > \dfrac{1}{4}$.

> If a fraction has a positive numerator and denominator, then if the numerator increases, the fraction increases; if the denominator increases, the fraction decreases.

Here is *another* way to compare two fractions:

Example: Which fraction is greater?

$$\frac{1}{4} \text{ or } \frac{7}{27}$$

Multiply the *numerator of the first* with the *denominator of the second*:

$$1 \times 27 = 27$$

Now multiply the *denominator of the first* with the *numerator of the second*:

$$4 \times 7 = 28$$

Since

$$28 > 27,$$

the *second* fraction is *greater* than the *first*.

Another example: Which is greater?

$$\frac{3}{7} \text{ or } \frac{7}{17}$$

Solution:

Since 51 > 49,

$$\frac{3}{7} > \frac{7}{17}$$

Another example: Which is greater?

$$\frac{5}{8} \text{ or } \frac{11}{17}$$

Solution:

Since 85 < 88

$$\frac{5}{8} < \frac{11}{17}$$

Practice Exercises for 2-40

Which fraction is greater?

1. $\dfrac{3}{4}$ or $\dfrac{7}{8}$

2. $\dfrac{12}{13}$ or $\dfrac{11}{12}$

3. $\dfrac{6}{13}$ or $\dfrac{7}{12}$

4. $\dfrac{3}{7}$ or $\dfrac{9}{16}$

5. $\dfrac{22}{7}$ or $\dfrac{21}{8}$

6. $\dfrac{7}{15}$ or $\dfrac{7}{16}$

7. $\dfrac{3}{7}$ or $\dfrac{4}{7}$

8. $\dfrac{11}{10}$ or $\dfrac{10}{11}$

9. $\dfrac{11}{10}$ or $\dfrac{12}{11}$

10. $\dfrac{5}{6}$ or $\dfrac{7}{8}$

Answers to Practice Exercises in Algebra

(2-1 through 2-40)

2-1

1.	−4	5.	−16	9.	−1	13.	−2	17.	−25
2.	−1	6.	−1	10.	−10	14.	−2	18.	−8
3.	−3	7.	−3	11.	−2	15.	−2	19.	−3
4.	−9	8.	−6	12.	−1	16.	−17	20.	−25

2-2

1.	0	5.	7	9.	2	13.	0	17.	5
2.	−5	6.	−7	10.	0	14.	16	18.	16
3.	0	7.	8	11.	−11	15.	−6	19.	−10
4.	15	8.	−9	12.	0	16.	0	20.	11

2-3

1.	+6	5.	−8	9.	+15	13.	+56	17.	−36
2.	−12	6.	+24	10.	−15	14.	−24	18.	−12
3.	+21	7.	−15	11.	+15	15.	+26	19.	−12
4.	−8	8.	−15	12.	−56	16.	−26	20.	+12

2-4

1.	−5	5.	−6	9.	−3	13.	+3	17.	−3
2.	+5	6.	+5	10.	+3	14.	−3	18.	−5
3.	+5	7.	−5	11.	−3	15.	−3	19.	+5
4.	+3	8.	−3	12.	+3	16.	+3	20.	−5

2-5

1.	81	4.	−72	7.	−144	10.	4	13.	48
2.	16	5.	24	8.	24	11.	−8	14.	−240
3.	32	6.	−15	9.	1	12.	−24	15.	−1

2-6

1.	$A = s^2$	3.	$2x$	5.	$p = 4s$	7.	$\dfrac{x}{y}$	9.	$5x + 2$
2.	$A = \dfrac{1}{2}hb$	4.	$5 + x$	6.	$xy = yx$	8.	$x + 2x$ or $3x$	10.	$d = rt$

2-7

1. $+1$
2. $+y$
3. x^2
4. $x^2 - y$
5. $-4x^2$
6. $3x + y$
7. $2x + y$
8. $-2y$
9. $+4ab$
10. $-2b$
11. $2x^2 - 2y^2$
12. $-x^2 + y^2$
13. $-5y^2$
14. $5y$
15. $2x^2 + y^2$

2-8

1. $\dfrac{3y + 4x}{xy}$
2. $\dfrac{3y + 4x}{xy}$
3. $\dfrac{22x}{6x^2}$ or $\dfrac{22}{6x}$ or $\dfrac{11}{3x}$
4. $\dfrac{-14x}{6x^2}$ or $\dfrac{-14}{6x}$ or $\dfrac{-7}{3x}$
5. $\dfrac{ad + cb}{bd}$
6. $\dfrac{1}{y}$
7. $\dfrac{4a + 3b}{12}$
8. $\dfrac{ab + 16}{4b}$
9. $\dfrac{a^2 + 16}{4a}$
10. $\dfrac{4 - a^2}{2a}$
11. $\dfrac{2b - 2a}{ab}$
12. $\dfrac{4 - ab}{2a}$
13. $\dfrac{-a}{10}$
14. $\dfrac{x^2 + xy}{y^2}$
15. $\dfrac{x^2 - xy}{y^2}$

2-9

1. $6x^3$
2. $14x^4$
3. $6x^2$
4. $4x^2 + 2x$
5. $2x - 4x^2$
6. $(x + y)(x + y)$
7. $x^2 + 3x + 2$
8. $x^2 - x - 2$
9. $2x^2 - 2$
10. $9y^2 + 6y - 3$
11. $a^2 - b^2$
12. $-6x^3$
13. $4x^2 - 1$
14. $1 - y^2$
15. $y^4 - 2y^2 + 1$
16. $x^3 + 2x^2 + 2x + 4$
17. $x^2 - 8x + 15$
18. $x^2 - 2x - 15$
19. $x^2 + 8x + 15$
20. $x^2 + 2x - 15$

2-10

1. $5x^2y$
2. $3\dfrac{a}{b}$
3. $\dfrac{3a^2}{b} + \dfrac{b}{a}$
4. $3a^2 - 2a^3$
5. $(x + 3)(x - 2)$ or $x^2 + x - 6$
6. $4x^2 - 1$
7. $3y - 2$
8. $3xy^2z^3$
9. $36 - y$
10. $\dfrac{1}{y} - 1$ or $\dfrac{1 - y}{y}$
11. $\dfrac{1}{2ab}$
12. $\dfrac{1 - y}{1 - x}$
13. $4y^2 - 3\dfrac{x^2}{y}$
14. $8 - 2xy$
15. $x + y + z$

2-11

1. $6 + 3x$
2. $3 - 2x$
3. $3x - 5$
4. $\dfrac{1}{2} \times \dfrac{20}{100}x$ or $\dfrac{1}{10}x$
5. $6 + 2x$
6. $2(x + y)$ or $2x + 2y$
7. $\dfrac{1}{x}$
8. $5 - 4n$
9. $24 - 16n$
10. $2x + 3x = 5x$, or five times the original number

2-12

1. 1
2. $\dfrac{1}{2}$
3. 72
4. $\dfrac{10}{3}$ or $3\dfrac{1}{3}$
5. $\dfrac{75}{10}$ or $7\dfrac{1}{2}$ or 7.5
6. $-\dfrac{7}{3}$ or $-2\dfrac{1}{3}$
7. 162
8. $\dfrac{1}{2}$
9. 8
10. -8

2-13

1. $\dfrac{-49}{6}$ or $-8\dfrac{1}{6}$

2. -2

3. $-\dfrac{3}{4}$

4. 9

5. $2!(-1) = 7; (-1)!(2) = 1,$ so $2!(-1)$ is greater than $(-1)!(2)$

2-14

1. $x(x+1)$
2. $5(x+1)$
3. $a(a-b)$
4. $a(a+b)$
5. $5(x-1)$
6. $x(x-1)$
7. $ab(1+b)$
8. $3x(y-1)$
9. $x(2-x)$
10. $x(x-y^2)$

2-15

1. $x(x)(x-1)$
2. $x(x)(x+1)$
3. $x(1+y)$
4. $ab(a-b)$
5. $yx(1-y)$
6. $ab(a+b)$
7. $3xy(1-xy)$
8. $4(xy-1)$
9. $4x(y-1)$
10. $4xy(1-x)$

2-16

1. $(a+b)(a-b)$

2. $(2ab+xy)(2ab-xy)$

3. $(4x^2y^2+2)(4x^2y^2-2)$

4. $(100+1)(100-1)$ or $(101)(99)$

5. $[(x+a)+(x+b)]$
   $[(x+a)-(x+b)]$
   or
   $(2x+a+b)(a-b)$

6. $(4xy+4)(4xy-4)$

7. $(x^2+y^2)(x^2-y^2)$ or
   $(x^2+y^2)(x+y)(x-y)$

8. $(100+2)(100-2)$ or $(102)(98)$

9. $(3x+2y)(3x-2y)$

10. $(2xy+3x^2y^2)(2xy-3x^2y^2)$ or
    $x^2y^2(2+3xy)(2-3xy)$

2-17

1. $(x+2)(x+2)$
2. $(x+1)(x+1)$
3. $(x-4)(x-2)$
4. $(x+4)(x-2)$
5. $(x+4)(x+2)$
6. $(x+y)(x+y)$
7. $(x-y)(x-y)$
8. $(x-3)(x-2)$
9. $(x+3)(x+2)$
10. $(x+3)(x-2)$

2-18

1. $(2x+2)(x+1)$ or
   $2(x+1)(x+1)$
2. $(3x-1)(x+1)$
3. $(3x-1)(3x-1)$
4. $(2x+1)(2x-3)$
5. $(2x+1)(x+1)$
6. $(2x+1)(2x+1)$
7. $(2x+1)(x-1)$
8. $(2x-1)(x+1)$
9. $(9x+1)(x-1)$
10. $(9x-1)(x-1)$

2-19

1. $8(y + 2)(y - 2)$
2. $2(x + 1)(x - 3)$
3. $(x - 3)(x - 1)$
4. $4(y - 1)(y + 2)$
5. $4(x + 1)(x - 1)$
6. $3(x + y)(x + y)$
7. $3(x - y)(x - y)$
8. $25(y + 1)(y - 1)$
9. $(2x + 3)(2x + 1)$
10. $(2x + 3)(2x - 1)$

2-20

1. $10x = 20$
2. $10y + 2 = 18$
3. $y = 2$
4. $75x^2 + 45 = 90$
5. $x = 3$

2-21

1. 7
2. 6
3. 5
4. 9
5. $\frac{1}{2}$
6. 8
7. 0
8. 1
9. 0
10. 4

2-22

1. $x = 2$
2. $x = 3$
3. $x = 3$
4. $x = 1$
5. $x = 100$
6. $x = 3$
7. $x = 0$
8. $x = 1$
9. $x = -2$
10. $x = -\frac{1}{6}$

2-23

1. $x = 1$
2. $x = 2, x = 3$
3. $x = -2, x = +1$
4. $x = +6, x = -6$
5. $x = +2, x = -1$
6. $x = +7, x = -7$
7. $x = 3, x = 1$
8. $x = -3, x = -2$
9. $x = 4, x = -3$
10. $x = +5, x = -5$
11. $x = +13, x = -13$
12. $x + \frac{1}{2}, x = 1$
13. $x = -\frac{1}{2}$
14. $x = +\frac{1}{2}, x = -1$
15. $x = +\frac{1}{8}, x = -\frac{1}{8}$

2-24

1. $x = 2y$
2. $x = 3y$
3. $x = \frac{6 - y}{2}$
4. $x = -2y$
5. $x = \frac{-y}{2}$
6. $x = 2y$
7. $x = y$
8. $x = 1 - y$
9. $x = 2y - 1$
10. $x = y$

2-25

1. $y = \frac{1}{8}, x = 1$
2. $y = -7, x = 10$
3. $y = 3, x = 6$
4. $y = 1, x = 2$
5. $y = \frac{1}{2}, x = \frac{1}{2}$
6. $x = 2, y = 2$
7. $x = 2, y = 2$
8. $x = 8, y = 1$
9. $x = -2, y = -2$
10. $x = 1, y = 2$

2-26

1. $\frac{4}{7}$ 5. $\frac{3}{2}$ 9. $\frac{2}{1}$ 13. $2:3$ 17. $7:3$

2. $\frac{8}{3}$ 6. $\frac{2}{3}$ 10. $\frac{10}{11}$ 14. $1:2$ 18. $3:1$

3. $\frac{4}{9}$ 7. $\frac{1}{1}$ 11. $5:6$ 15. $2:1$ 19. $1:7$

4. $\frac{6}{5}$ 8. $\frac{1}{2}$ 12. $6:5$ 16. $5:3$ 20. $9:10$

2-27

1. The area is multiplied by 9.
2. The circumference is doubled.
3. y is halved.
4. y becomes $(n+1)(n) = n^2 + n$, and since the old y was $y = (n)(n-1) = n^2 - n$, y is increased by $2n$.
5. y is multiplied by 9.
6. y is increased by 2.
7. The volume is multiplied by 27.
8. The area is multiplied by 4.
9. The perimeter is doubled.
10. y is tripled.

2-28

1. $x = 2$ 3. \$1.25   5. 150   7. \$10.00   9. $x = 3\frac{1}{5}$

2. 5   4. 5   6. $\frac{10}{3}$ or $3\frac{1}{3}$ 8. \$7.65   10. 10

2-29

1. $1\frac{1}{3}$
2. 5
3. 4.5 square miles
4. 1500
5. 4

2-30

1. 50
2. 72
3. 14
4. 7920
5. $1\frac{3}{5}$

2-31

1. $18\frac{1}{3}$ hours, or 18 hours, 20 minutes
2. 2 hours
3. 10 miles per hour
4. Twice as fast, or 125 miles per hour more.
5. 250 miles

2-32

1. $\frac{6}{5}$ or $1\frac{1}{5}$ hours
2. 2
3. 6 hours
4. 12 hours
5. $\frac{(x)(x+2)}{2x+2}$ or $\frac{x^2+2x}{2x+2}$ hours

2-33

1. $\frac{6020}{5280} = 1\frac{37}{264}$ miles
2. 23 pints
3. 7320 seconds
4. 11,000 pounds
5. 24 pints

2-34

1. $28\frac{1}{4}$
2. $49.14
3. $\frac{q}{h}$
4. $83\frac{1}{3}$ yards per minute
5. Seven are 15, one is 16.

6. 42.8
7. 80%
8. 4
9. $4.73\frac{1}{3}$ or 4.7333...
10. 0

2-35

1. 24
2. 90
3. 6
4. 9

2-36

1. 35
2. 95
3. 35
4. 150; 75

2-37

1. $a \geqq 0$
2. $b \leqq a$
3. $c \geqq 0$
4. $a + b > 0$
5. $a \neq 0$

6. $0 > b > a$ or $(a < b < 0)$
7. $a + b \leqq 0$
8. $a^2 > b^2$
9. $xy > 0$
10. $1 > x > 0$

2-38

1. $x > 1$
2. $r > r^2$
3. $r^3 > r^2$
4. $n^2 > n$
5. $3x + 2y > 3$
6. $-1 < -r$
7. $x \geqq 2$
8. when $a > 0$
9. Always
10. $x > 12$

2-39

1. $8 > y$, so (i) is false.

   $4 > x+2$, so (iii) is false.

   $8 > y$, so (ii) can be true.

2. $x > 2$, so (i) is false.

   $x - y > 2$, so (ii) is false.

   $y > 4-2x$ and $y < x -2$, so (iii) is true.

3. (i) and (ii) are true.

   (iii) is not always true, since r can be 0.

4. (i) is not always true, since r can be negative.

   (ii) is not always true, since r can be 0.

   (iii) is not always true, since r can be 0.

5. (i) can be true.

   (ii) cannot be true because

   $$t - x = y^2 \geqq 0$$

   $$t - x \geqq 0$$

   $$t \geqq x.$$

   (iii) can be true.

   (iv) can be true if $y = 0$.

2-40

1. $\frac{7}{8}$
2. $\frac{12}{13}$
3. $\frac{7}{12}$
4. $\frac{9}{16}$
5. $\frac{22}{7}$
6. $\frac{7}{15}$
7. $\frac{4}{7}$
8. $\frac{11}{10}$
9. $\frac{11}{10}$
10. $\frac{7}{8}$

Plane Geometry

Angles

Diagnostic Test on Angles

Use the following diagram to answer Question 1.

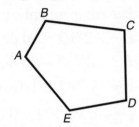

1. What is the vertex of ∠*ABC*?

    (A) *A*   (D) *D*

    (B) *B*   (E) *E*

    (C) *C*

Questions 2–5 refer to the following diagram.

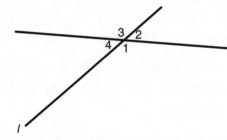

2. Which pair of angles is a pair of vertical angles?

    (A) ∠1,∠2   (D) ∠4,∠1

    (B) ∠2,∠3   (E) ∠1,∠3

    (C) ∠4,∠3

3. Which of the following is true?

    (A) ∠2 = ∠1   (D) ∠1 = ∠3

    (B) ∠2 = ∠3   (E) ∠1 = ∠4

    (C) ∠1 = ∠4

4. ∠1 and ∠2 together form a(n)

    (A) right angle   (D) acute angle

    (B) straight angle   (E) reflex angle

    (C) obtuse angle

5. What is the relation between ∠3 and ∠2?

    (A) They are complements.

    (B) They are supplements.

    (C) They are equal.

    (D) One is twice the other.

    (E) Their sum is 360 degrees.

6. If two angles are supplementary, then their sum is

    (A) 60 degrees   (D) 270 degrees

    (B) 90 degrees   (E) 360 degrees

    (C) 180 degrees

Questions 7–10 refer to the following diagram.

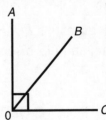

7. If ∠*AOC* is a right angle, then ∠*AOC* equals

    (A) 60 degrees   (D) 270 degrees

    (B) 90 degrees   (E) 360 degrees

    (C) 180 degrees

8. ∠AOB and ∠BOC are

(A) vertical angles

(B) straight angles

(C) corresponding angles

(D) adjacent angles

(E) obtuse angles

9. What is the relation between ∠AOB and ∠BOC?

(A) They are equal.

(B) They are complements.

(C) They are supplements.

(D) Their sum is 180 degrees.

(E) Their difference is 10 degrees.

10. If ∠AOB equals ∠BOC, then ∠AOB equals

(A) 45 degrees   (D) 30 degrees

(B) 60 degrees   (E) 75 degrees

(C) 90 degrees

Use the following diagram to answer Questions 11–13.

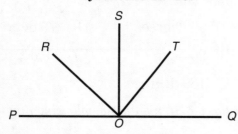

In the diagram, ∠POQ lies along a straight line, and OS bisects ∠POQ.

11. What is the measure of ∠SOQ?

(A) 45 degrees   (D) 180 degrees

(B) 90 degrees   (E) 360 degrees

(C) 135 degrees

12. If ∠ROQ is supplementary to ∠ROP and ∠TOQ, then

(A) ∠ROP = ∠TOQ

(B) ∠ROP is complementary to ∠TOQ

(C) ∠ROP + ∠TOQ = 90 degrees

(D) ∠ROP − ∠TOQ = 45 degrees

(E) ∠ROP + ∠TOQ = 120 degrees

13. If OS also bisects ∠ROT, then which of the following must be true?

(A) ∠ROS is complementary to ∠TOQ

(B) ∠SOT = ∠TOQ

(C) ∠ROS = ∠TOQ

(D) ∠ROS = ∠ROP

(E) ∠ROS = 45 degrees

14. If an angle measures one-sixtieth of a degree, then it measures

(A) .01 of a minute   (D) .6 second

(B) 1 minute   (E) .1 second

(C) 1 second

15. If two angles are complementary, and one angle is 75 degrees, then the other is

(A) 45 degrees   (D) 15 degrees

(B) 30 degrees   (E) 5 degrees

(C) 25 degrees

Solutions for Diagnostic Test

1. **(B)** The vertex of an angle is the point where its sides meet. **(3-1)**

2. **(E)** Vertical angles are angles opposite each other with a common vertex where two lines meet. **(3-1)**

3. **(D)** Vertical angles are equal. **(3-1)**

4. **(B)** ∠1 and ∠2 add up to an angle that lies along a line, that is, a straight angle. **(3-1)**

5. **(B)** Angles 3 and 2 form a straight angle, and are therefore supplements. **(3-1)**

6. **(C)** Supplementary angles add up to a straight angle, or 180 degrees. **(3-1)**

7. **(B)** Right angles measure 90 degrees.
(3-1)

8. **(D)** ∠*AOB* and ∠*BOC* share a side and a vertex and hence are adjacent angles.
(3-1)

9. **(B)** ∠*AOB* and ∠*BOC* add up to a right angle and are therefore complementary.
(3-1)

10. **(A)** ∠*AOB* + ∠*BOC* = 90 degrees. If ∠*AOB* = ∠*BOC*, then each is $\frac{90}{2}$, or 45 degrees.
(3-1)

11. **(B)** Since *OS* bisects a straight angle, ∠*SOQ* is half of the straight angle, or $\frac{1}{2}$ (180), or 90 degrees.
(3-1)

12. **(A)** Angles supplementary to the same angle are equal, and ∠*ROP* and ∠*TOQ* are supplementary to ∠*ROQ* and are therefore equal.
(3-1)

13. **(A)** ∠*SOT* and ∠*TOQ* are complementary. If *OS* bisects ∠*ROT*, then ∠*ROS* = ∠*SOT*, and ∠*ROS* is complementary to ∠*TOQ*.
(3-1)

14. **(B)** There are 60 minutes in one degree. Therefore there is 1 minute in one-sixtieth of a degree.
(3-1)

15. **(D)** x + 75 degrees = 90 degrees, or x = 15 degrees.
(3-1)

3-1 Instructional Material on Angles

1) An angle is formed by 2 lines meeting at a point. The point at which the lines meet is called the vertex of the angle, and the lines are called the sides of the angle. The symbol "∠" is used to indicate an angle.

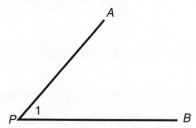

An angle can be named 3 different ways:
   (a) According to its vertex point (∠*P*)
   (b) According to the names of the endpoints of the lines forming the angle—the vertex is the middle term (∠*APB*, ∠*BPA*).
   (c) According to the number indicated inside an angle (∠1).

2) When two lines meet, they form four angles. Pairs of opposite angles are called vertical angles.

For example:

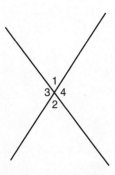

∠3 and ∠4 are vertical angles; ∠1 and ∠2 are vertical angles.

3)   Vertical angles are equal.
    In the example, $\angle 3 = \angle 4$ and $\angle 1 = \angle 2$.

4)   A straight angle is one whose sides lie on the same straight line.

For example:

$\angle AOB$ is a straight angle. A straight angle measures 180°.

5)   Two angles whose sum is 180° are supplementary angles.
    For example:

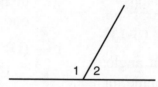

$\angle 1$ and $\angle 2$ are supplementary angles.

6)   Two angles supplementary to the same angle are equal.

7)   A right angle is half of a straight angle. The symbol ⌐ indicates a right angle.

For example:

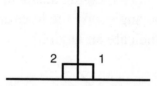

$\angle 1$ and $\angle 2$ are right angles. A right angle measures 90°.

8)   Two angles whose sum is 90° are complementary angles.

For example:

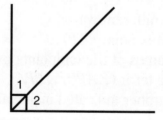

$\angle 1$ and $\angle 2$ are complementary angles.

9)   Two angles complementary to the same angle are equal.

10) Adjacent angles are two angles with the same vertex and a common side (one angle is not inside the other).

For example:

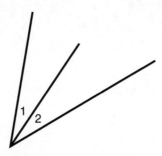

∠1 and ∠2 are adjacent angles.

11) An angle bisector of an angle is a line that cuts the original angle in half (*bisect* means to divide into two equal parts).

For example:

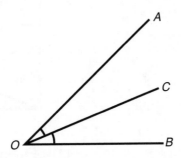

∠AOC = ∠COB, so OC is an angle bisector of ∠AOB.

Angle Measures

1° = 60′ (that is, 1 degree = 60 minutes)
1′ = 60″ (that is, 1 minute = 60 seconds)

Practice Exercises for 3-1*

1. Find the value of *x*:

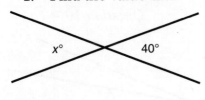

2. Which pairs of angles are equal?

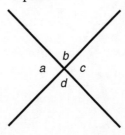

* Answers for Practice Exercises 3-1 through 3-6 begin on page 208.

3. Find the value of *y*:

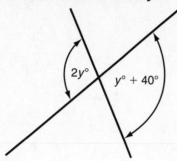

4. What is the number of degrees in $\angle 1 + \angle 2 - \angle 3 - \angle 4$?

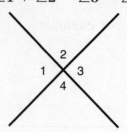

Questions 5–9

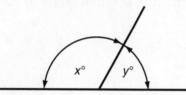

In the diagram above, find *x* if *y* =

5. 20

6. 40

7. 150

8. 90

9. 30

Questions 10–13

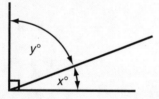

In the diagram above, find *x* if *y* =

10. 20

11. 40

12. 60

13. 90

Question 14

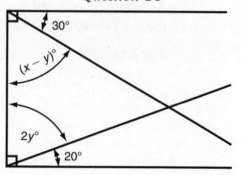

14. Find *x* and *y* in the above diagram.

Question 15

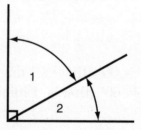

15. When is $\angle 1 = \angle 2$ in the above diagram?

Question 16

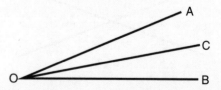

16. If CO is an angle bisector of $\angle AOB$, and $\angle AOB = 45°$, what is $\angle AOC$?

Question 17

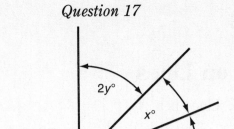

17. What is the value of $(x + y)$ in the above diagram?

Question 18

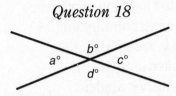

18. In the above diagram, what is the value of $a + b + c + d$?

Question 19

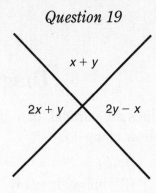

19. In the above diagram, what is the value of x and y?

Question 20

20. In the above diagram, what is the value of x?

Lines

Diagnostic Test on Lines

1. If two lines are parallel, then they intersect in how many points?

   (A) 0   (D) 4
   (B) 1   (E) infinitely many
   (C) 2

2. If two lines intersect at right angles, then

   (A) they are parallel
   (B) they are skew
   (C) they are perpendicular
   (D) they do not lie in a plane
   (E) none of the above is true

3. How many lines can be drawn passing through two distinct points?

   (A) 0   (D) 3
   (B) 1   (E) infinitely many
   (C) 2

4. All of the following are true *except*:

   (A) Two lines parallel to the same line are parallel.
   (B) A line ⊥ to one of two parallel lines is ⊥ to the other.
   (C) Two lines ⊥ to the same line are ⊥.
   (D) Two lines ⊥ to the same line are parallel.
   (E) A line parallel to one of two parallel lines is parallel to the other.

Use the following diagram to answer Questions 5–10.

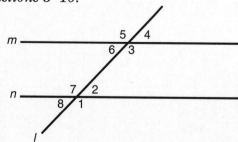

5. Line *l* is a

   (A) bisector   (D) half-line
   (B) perpendicular   (E) transversal
   (C) parallel

6. ∠1 and ∠3 are

   (A) alternate interior angles
   (B) corresponding angles
   (C) consecutive angles
   (D) base angles
   (E) exterior angles

7. ∠2 and ∠6 are

   (A) alternate interior angles
   (B) corresponding angles
   (C) consecutive angles
   (D) base angles
   (E) exterior angles

8. ∠2 and ∠3 are

   (A) alternate interior angles
   (B) corresponding angles
   (C) consecutive angles
   (D) base angles
   (E) exterior angles

9. If *m* and *n* are parallel, which of the following must be true?

   (A) $\angle 2 = \angle 7$ (D) $\angle 2 = \angle 6$
   (B) $\angle 2 = \angle 5$ (E) $\angle 1 = \angle 4$
   (C) $\angle 1 = \angle 6$

10. Which of the following is not sufficient to prove lines *m* and *n* parallel?

   (A) $\angle 2 = \angle 6$
   (B) $\angle 7 = \angle 5$
   (C) $\angle 1 = \angle 3$
   (D) ∠8 is supplementary to ∠5
   (E) ∠2 is supplementary to ∠4

Solutions for Diagnostic Test

1. **(A)** Parallel lines do not intersect.
   (3-2)

2. **(C)** Perpendicular lines intersect at right angles. **(3-2)**

3. **(B)** One and only one line can be drawn through two points. **(3-2)**

4. **(C)** Two lines ⊥ to the same line are parallel, not ⊥. **(3-2)**

5. **(E)** A line that cuts two other lines is called a transversal. **(3-2)**

6. **(B)** Corresponding angles are in the same relative position with respect to the lines cut by a transversal. **(3-2)**

7. **(A)** Angles on opposite sides of a transversal, like ∠2 and ∠6, are alternate interior angles. **(3-2)**

8. **(C)** Angles "inside" and on the same side of a transversal are consecutive angles. **(3-2)**

9. **(D)** Alternate interior angles are equal if lines are parallel. **(3-2)**

10. **(E)** ∠2 and ∠4 must be equal to ensure the lines are parallel. If the angles are supplementary, the lines need not be equal. **(3-2)**

3-2   Instructional Material on Lines

1) In a plane, two lines are parallel if they never meet.
2) Two lines are perpendicular if they meet at right angles.
   For example:

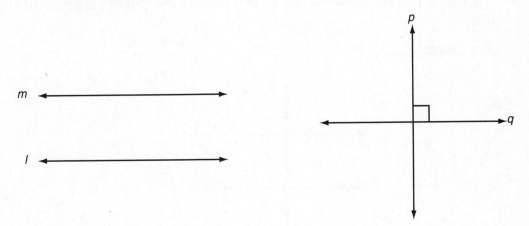

Lines *l* and *m* are parallel and the symbol for parallel is ||. (Line *l* || line *m*)
Line *p* and line *q* are perpendicular. The symbol for perpendicular is ⊥. (Line *p* ⊥ line *q*)

3) Two points determine a line. This can also be expressed as: Only one line can pass through any two points.

4) Two different lines can meet at no more than one point.

5) If two lines in a plane are perpendicular to the same line, they are parallel.

For example:

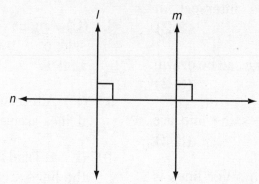

Line *l* and line *m* are perpendicular to line *n*. So, line *l* and line *m* are parallel.

6) If two lines are parallel to the same line, they are parallel.

For example:

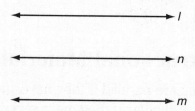

Line *l* and line *m* are parallel to line *n*. So, line *l* and line *m* are parallel.

7) If a line is perpendicular to one of two parallel lines, it is perpendicular to the other.

For example:

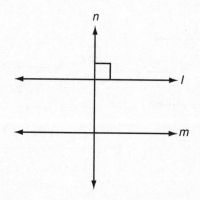

Line *l* and line *m* are parallel. Since line *n* is perpendicular to line *l*, it is also perpendicular to line *m*.

8) A line that cuts through two lines is a transversal line. (The transversal usually cuts parallel lines.)

9) If two lines are parallel, and are cut by a transversal line,
   a) the alternate interior angles are equal
   b) the corresponding angles are equal
   c) consecutive interior angles are supplementary.

For example: Line *l* and line *m* are parallel. Line *n* is a transversal line.

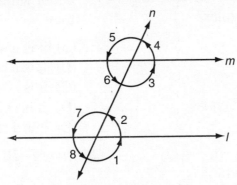

$\angle 2$ and $\angle 6$ are alternate interior angles, and so are $\angle 3$ and $\angle 7$. So, $\angle 2 = \angle 6$, and $\angle 3 = \angle 7$. $\angle 1$ and $\angle 3$ are a pair of corresponding angles, and so are $\angle 2$ and $\angle 4$, $\angle 6$ and $\angle 8$, and $\angle 5$ and $\angle 7$. So, $\angle 1 = \angle 3$, $\angle 2 = \angle 4$, $\angle 6 = \angle 8$, and $\angle 5 = \angle 7$. $\angle 2$ and $\angle 3$ are a pair of consecutive angles, and so are $\angle 6$ and $\angle 7$. So, $\angle 2$ is supplementary to $\angle 3$, and $\angle 6$ is supplementary to $\angle 7$.

10) If two lines are cut by a transversal and if either a) the alternate interior angles are equal, or b) the corresponding angles are equal, or c) the consecutive angles are supplementary, then the two lines are parallel.

Practice Exercises for 3-2

Questions 1–10

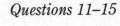

In the above, l_1 is parallel to l_2 and *n* is a transversal. Find the value of the following angles:

1. *x*
2. *y*
3. *z*
4. *a*
5. *b*
6. *c*
7. *d*
8. *e*
9. *f*
10. *g*

Questions 11–15

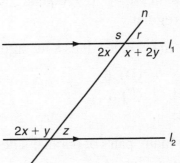

In the above, l_1 is parallel to l_2. *n* is a transversal.

11. Find the value of *x*.
12. Find the value of *y*.
13. Find the value of *z*.
14. Find the value of *r*.
15. Find the value of *s*.

Polygons

Diagnostic Test on Polygons

1. Which of the following is sufficient to show that a polygon is regular?

    (A) It has equal sides.
    (B) It has equal angles.
    (C) It has 3 sides.
    (D) It has equal sides and equal angles.
    (E) None of the above.

2. Two polygons are congruent if

    (A) they are both regular
    (B) they have the same number of sides
    (C) they have the same shape
    (D) their corresponding sides are equal
    (E) their corresponding sides and angles are equal

3. If two polygons have the same shape, they must be

    (A) congruent   (D) irregular
    (B) similar   (E) equiangular
    (C) regular

4. How many sides does a hexagon have?

    (A) 3   (D) 6
    (B) 4   (E) 7
    (C) 5

5. How many pairs of parallel sides does a trapezoid have?

    (A) 0   (D) 3
    (B) 1   (E) 4
    (C) 2

6. In a trapezoid, the line segment joining the midpoints of the legs is a(n)

    (A) transversal (D) side
    (B) diagonal   (E) altitude
    (C) median

7. If four sides of a quadrilateral are equal, then

    (A) it is a square
    (B) it is a rectangle
    (C) it is equiangular
    (D) it is regular
    (E) it is a rhombus

Questions 8–12 refer to the following:

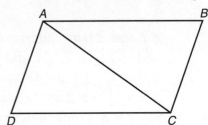

AB is parallel to *DC,* and *AD* is parallel to *BC*.

8. Polygon *ABCD* is a

    (A) square   (D) parallelogram
    (B) rectangle   (E) rhombus
    (C) trapezoid

9. Which pairs of line segments are equal?

    (A) *AD* and *AB*
    (B) *AD* and *AC*
    (C) *AB* and *DC*
    (D) *AC* and *BC*
    (E) *DC* and *AC*

10. *AC* is a(n)

    (A) side
    (B) diagonal
    (C) medium
    (D) altitude
    (E) angle bisector

11. Which two angles are equal?

   (A) $\angle ADC$ and $\angle ABC$
   (B) $\angle DAC$ and $\angle CAB$
   (C) $\angle DCA$ and $\angle BCA$
   (D) $\angle DAB$ and $\angle ADC$
   (E) $\angle DCB$ and $\angle ABC$

12. If $AD = AB$, then the quadrilateral is a

   (A) parallelogram   (D) rectangle
   (B) square   (E) trapezoid
   (C) rhombus

13. The sum of all interior angles of a pentagon is

   (A) 900°   (D) 480°
   (B) 180°   (E) 540°
   (C) 360°

14. How many interior angles are there in an eight-sided polygon?

   (A) 4   (D) 8
   (B) 12   (E) 6
   (C) 16

15. Each angle of a regular hexagon measures

   (A) 108°   (D) 100°
   (B) 120°   (E) 115°
   (C) 136°

Solutions for Diagnostic Test

1. **(D)** A regular polygon must have all of its sides equal and all of its angles equal. **(3-3)**

2. **(E)** Two polygons are congruent if their corresponding sides and angles are equal. **(3-3)**

3. **(B)** Two polygons are similar if they have the same shape. **(3-3)**

4. **(D)** A hexagon has 6 sides. **(3-3)**

5. **(B)** A trapezoid is a quadrilateral with exactly one pair of parallel sides. **(3-3)**

6. **(C)** The line segment joining the midpoints of the legs of a trapezoid is the median. **(3-3)**

7. **(E)** A quadrilateral with 4 equal sides must be a rhombus; it is not necessarily a square. **(3-3)**

8. **(D)** Since quadrilateral $ABCD$ has two pairs of parallel sides, it is a parallelogram. **(3-3)**

9. **(C)** The opposite sides of a parallelogram are equal. Since AB and DC are opposite sides of parallelogram $ABCD$, $AB = DC$. **(3-3)**

10. **(B)** AC joins two non-adjacent vertices of the parallelogram. So, it is a diagonal. **(3-3)**

11. **(A)** $\angle ADC = \angle ABC$, since the opposite angles of a parallelogram are equal. **(3–3)**

12. **(C)** If $AD = AB$, then $ABCD$ is a rhombus, since a parallelogram with two adjacent sides equal is a rhombus. **(3-3)**

13. **(E)** The sum of all interior angles of a polygon with n sides is $180(n - 2)$. Since a pentagon has 5 sides, the sum of all interior angles of a pentagon is $180(5 - 2)$ or 540°. **(3-3)**

14. **(D)** A polygon with n sides has n interior angles. **(3-3)**

15. **(B)** The sum of the interior angles of a hexagon (6 sides) is $180(6 - 2)$, or 720°. Since a regular hexagon has 6 equal angles, each angle measures $\frac{1}{6}$ of 720°, or 120°. **(3-3)**

3-3   Instructional Material on Polygons

1) A polygon is a plane figure that consists of a set of points and a set of line segments joining the points. Each point is called a vertex, and each segment is a side of the polygon. A polygon is named by giving its vertices in the order they are connected.

For example:

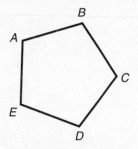 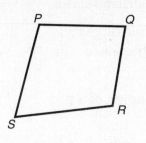 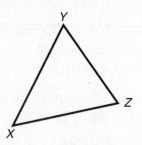

The polygons in the figure are *ABCDE*, *PQRS*, and *XYZ*. If a line were drawn from *A* to *C*, the line segment *AC* would be a diagonal of the polygon *ABCDE*, since it connects two non-adjacent vertices.

2) A regular polygon is a polygon in which all the sides are equal and all the angles are equal.

3) Two polygons are congruent if their corresponding sides and angles are equal. For example:

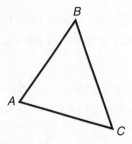 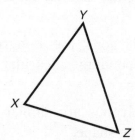

Polygons *ABC* and *XYZ* are congruent, since *AB* = *XY*, *AC* = *XZ*, ∠*A* = ∠*X*, ∠*B* = ∠*Y*, etc.

4) Two polygons are similar if their angles are equal and their corresponding sides are in proportion.

5) A triangle is a polygon with 3 sides.

6) A quadrilateral is a polygon with 4 sides.

7) A pentagon is a polygon with 5 sides.

8) A hexagon is a polygon with 6 sides.

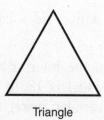

Triangle

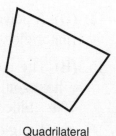

Quadrilateral

Pentagon

Hexagon

9)   A parallelogram is a quadrilateral with the 2 pairs of opposite sides parallel. The pairs of opposite sides are equal, and the pairs of opposite angles are also equal.

For example:

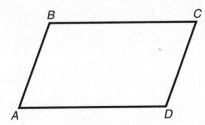

AB‖*CD, BC*‖*AD, AB = CD,* ∠*A* = ∠*C,* etc.

10)   A rhombus is a parallelogram with all sides equal.

11)   A rectangle is a parallelogram with 4 right angles.

12)   A square is a rectangle with 4 equal sides.

13)   A trapezoid is a quadrilateral with 1 pair of parallel sides. The two parallel sides are called bases; the other sides are called legs. The median of a trapezoid is the line segment connecting the midpoints of the legs.

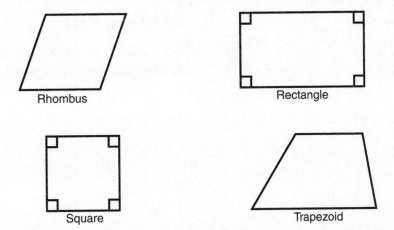

14)   The sum of the interior angles of a polygon with *n* sides is $180°(n - 2)$.

For example:

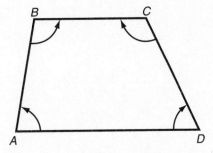

Since the figure has 4 sides, ∠*A* + ∠*B* + ∠*C* + ∠*D* = $180°(4 - 2)$, or 360°.

Practice Exercises for 3-3

Questions 1–5

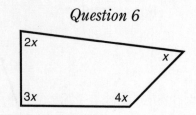

ABCD is a parallelogram.

1. Find the value of angle *a*.

2. Find the value of angle *x*.

3. Find the value of angle *y*.

4. Find the value of angle *z*.

5. How many degrees are there in
   $\angle A + \angle B + \angle C + \angle D$?

Question 6

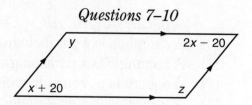

6. Find the value of *x*.

Questions 7–10

7. Find the value of *x*.

8. Find the value of *y*.

9. Find the value of *z*.

10. How many degrees are there in the
    smaller angles of the parallelogram?

Triangles

Diagnostic Test on Triangles

1. In triangle ABC, if $AB = AC$, then

    (A) $\angle A = \angle B$
    (B) $\angle B = \angle C$
    (C) $\angle A = \angle C$
    (D) $\angle A + \angle B = \angle C$
    (E) $\angle A + \angle B = 90°$

2. In any triangle ABC, $\angle A + \angle B + \angle C =$

    (A) $90°$ (D) $180°$
    (B) $135°$ (E) $360°$
    (C) $270°$

3. If triangle ABC is equilateral, then $\angle A =$

    (A) $60°$ (D) $90°$
    (B) $45°$ (E) $30°$
    (C) $75°$

4. In any right triangle, the acute angles are

    (A) complementary angles
    (B) supplementary angles
    (C) vertical angles
    (D) adjacent angles
    (E) equal

5. Given triangles ABC and $A'B'C'$. If $\angle A = \angle A'$, $\angle B = \angle B'$, and $\angle C = \angle C'$, then the triangles are

    (A) congruent   (D) equilateral
    (B) similar   (E) isosceles
    (C) regular

6. If two sides of a triangle are 5 and 6, then the third side cannot be

    (A) 2   (D) 10
    (B) 3   (E) 12
    (C) 7

7. In triangle MNP, if $\angle M$ is the largest angle, then

    (A) MP is the longest side
    (B) NP is the longest side
    (C) MN is the longest side
    (D) $\angle N$ is the smallest angle
    (E) $\angle P$ is the smallest angle

8. In triangle ABC, if $\angle A = 20°$ and $\angle B = 80°$, then

    (A) $\angle C = 100°$ (D) $AB = AC$
    (B) $\angle C = 60°$ (E) $AB = BC$
    (C) $\angle A = \angle C$

Questions 9–12 refer to the following diagram:

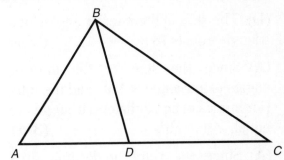

9. Which of the following relations is correct?

    (A) $\angle A = \angle BDC + \angle C$
    (B) $\angle ADB = \angle BDC$
    (C) $\angle BDC = \angle A + \angle ABD$
    (D) $\angle C + \angle A = \angle ABC$
    (E) $\angle BDC = \angle DBC + \angle C$

10. If $\angle ABD = \angle ACB$ and $\angle ADB = \angle ABC$, then which of the following is true?

    (A) Triangles ABD and ABC are similar.
    (B) Triangles ABD and BDC are similar.
    (C) Triangles BDC and ABC are similar.
    (D) Triangles ABD and BDC are congruent.
    (E) Triangles ABC and DBC are congruent.

11. If $AD = DC$, then BD is a(n)

    (A) angle bisector   (D) hypotenuse
    (B) altitude   (E) diagonal
    (C) median

12. If $\angle ADB = \angle DBC$, then BD is a(n)

    (A) angle bisector   (D) hypotenuse
    (B) altitude   (E) diagonal
    (C) median

13. For any triangle, if C is a right angle, then AB is a(n)

    (A) altitude   (D) median
    (B) hypotenuse   (E) base
    (C) leg

14. In right triangle XYZ with right angle Z, if $XZ = 5$ and $YZ = 12$, then $XY =$

    (A) 15   (D) 18
    (B) 16   (E) 21
    (C) 13

15. In right triangle MNP with right angle N, if $MP = 15$ and $NP = 9$, then $MN =$

    (A) $9\sqrt{2}$ (D) 9
    (B) 18   (E) 12
    (C) $\sqrt{314}$

Solutions for Diagnostic Test

1. **(B)** $\angle B = \angle C$ since in a triangle angles opposite equal sides are equal. **(3-4)**

2. **(D)** The sum of the interior angles of a triangle equals 180°. **(3-4)**

3. **(A)** Since the sum of the interior angles of a triangle is 180° and the interior angles of an equilateral triangle are equal, $\angle A = 60°$. **(3-4)**

4. **(A)** Since the right angle measures 90°, the sum of the two acute angles must be 180° − 90° or 90°. **(3-4)**

5. **(B)** Two triangles are similar if the corresponding angles are equal. **(3-4)**

6. **(E)** The third side cannot be 12, because the sum of any two sides of a triangle must be greater than the third side. **(3-4)**

7. **(B)** NP is the longest side, since in a triangle the longest side is opposite the largest angle. **(3-4)**

8. **(D)** If $\angle A = 20°$ and $\angle B = 80°$, then $\angle C = 180° − 20° − 80° = 80°$. So, $\angle B = \angle C$. Therefore, $AB = AC$, since sides opposite equal angles are equal. **(3-4)**

9. **(C)** Since $\angle A + \angle ABD + \angle ADB = 180°$ and $\angle BDC + \angle ADB = 180°$, $\angle BDC = \angle A + \angle ABD$. **(3-4)**

10. **(A)** If $\angle ABD = \angle ADB$ and $\angle ADB = \angle ABC$, triangles ABD and ABC are similar, since $\angle A = \angle A$. **(3-4)**

11. **(C)** Since BD joins vertex B and the midpoint D of the opposite side, BD is a median. **(3-4)**

12. **(A)** Since BD bisects angle ABC, BD is an angle bisector. **(3-1)**

13. **(B)** The side opposite the right angle of a triangle is the hypotenuse. **(3-4)**

14. **(C)** By the Pythagorean Theorem,

$$XZ^2 + YZ^2 = XY^2$$
$$5^2 + 12^2 = XY^2$$
$$XY = 13 \qquad \textbf{(3-4)}$$

15. **(E)** By the Pythagorean Theorem,

$$MP^2 = NP^2 + MN^2$$
$$15^2 = 9^2 + MN^2$$
$$MN = 12 \qquad \textbf{(3-4)}$$

3-4   Instructional Material on Triangles

1) An equilateral triangle is one with three equal sides.
2) An isosceles triangle is one with two equal sides.
3) A right triangle is one with a right angle.
4) The sum of the interior angles of a triangle is 180°.

Example: Find the value of x in the triangle below:

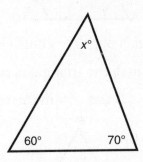

Since the sum of the interior angles of the triangle = 180°,

$$60 + 70 + x = 180$$
$$x = 180 - 130$$
$$x = 50$$

5) Each angle of an equilateral triangle measures 60°.
6) Two triangles are similar if the corresponding angles are equal.

For example:

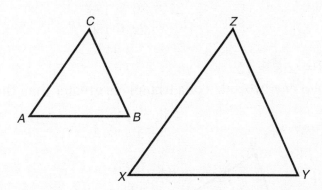

$\angle A = \angle X$, $\angle B = \angle Y$, and $\angle C = \angle Z$. So, triangle ABC is similar to triangle XYZ.

7) If two triangles are similar, then the corresponding sides are proportional. In the above figure,
$$\frac{AB}{XY} = \frac{BC}{YZ} = \frac{AC}{XZ}.$$

8) In any triangle, the sides opposite equal angles are equal.

For example: In triangle ABC, $\angle A = \angle C$. So, $AB = BC$.

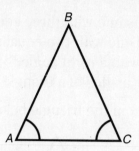

9)   In any triangle, the angles opposite equal sides are equal.

Note: If the two sides are equal, the triangle is *isosceles.*

Example: Find the value of $\angle B$ and $\angle C$ in the isosceles triangle below:

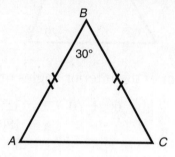

Since triangle ABC is isosceles, $\angle B = \angle C$.
Call $\angle B = \angle C = x$. The sum of the interior angles of a triangle is $180°$, so

$$x + x + 30 = 180$$
$$2x + 30 = 180$$
$$2x = 150$$
$$x = 75$$

Therefore $\angle B = \angle C = 75°$.

10)   The sum of any two sides of a triangle is greater than the third side.

For example:

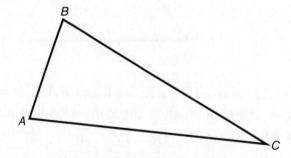

$AB + BC$ is greater than AC. $AC + BC$ is greater than AB. $AB + AC$ is greater than BC.

11)   In any triangle, the side opposite the largest angle is the longest, and the side opposite the smallest angle is the shortest.

For example:

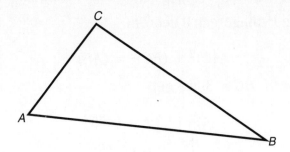

In triangle *ABC*, ∠*C* is the largest angle. So, *AB* is the longest side. ∠*B* is the smallest angle. So, *AC* is the shortest side.

12) A median of a triangle is a line segment joining a vertex and the midpoint of the opposite side.

13) An angle bisector of a triangle is a line segment bisecting an angle and joining the vertex of that angle and the opposite side.

For example:

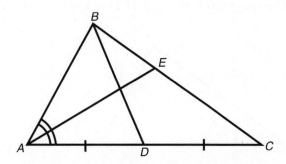

In triangle *ABC*, *AD* = *DC*. So, *BD* is a median. ∠*BAE* = ∠*CAE*. So, *AE* is an angle bisector.

14) In a right triangle, the side opposite the right angle is called the hypotenuse, and the other two sides are called the legs.

Pythagorean Theorem: In a right triangle, the sum of the squares of the two legs is equal to the square of the hypotenuse.

For example: In right triangle *ABC* below, $AC^2 + BC^2 = AB^2$.

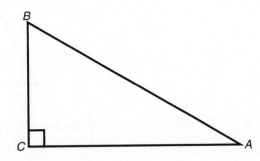

Example: In the preceding right triangle, $AC = 4$ and $BC = 3$. What is AB?

Solution: Use the Pythagorean Theorem.

$$(AC)^2 + (BC)^2 = (AB)^2$$

Substituting $AC = 4$, $BC = 3$, we get

$$(4)^2 + (3)^2 = (AB)^2$$

$$16 + 9 = (AB)^2$$

$$25 = (AB)^2$$

Take the square root of both sides of the above.

$$\sqrt{25} = \sqrt{(AB)^2} = AB$$

$$5 = AB$$

$$\text{Thus, } AB = 5$$

15) An exterior angle of a triangle is equal to the sum of the remote interior angles. That is, in the diagram below, $\angle ACD = \angle B + \angle A$.

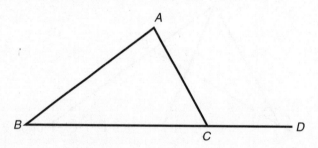

Example: In the above diagram, if $\angle ACD = 100°$ and $\angle A = 80°$, find $\angle B$. Since $100° = 80° + \angle B$, $\angle B$ must be $20°$.

Practice Exercises for 3-4

1.

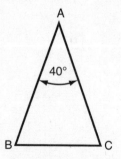

In the triangle above, $\angle A = 40°$. $\triangle ABC$ is isosceles. Find $\angle B$ and $\angle C$.

2.

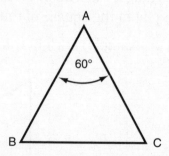

In triangle ABC, above, $\angle A = 60°$ and $AB = AC$. Find $\angle B$ and $\angle C$. If $AB = 3$, find BC.

3. The ratio of three angles of a triangle is $3 : 4 : 5$. Find the angles.

4. In an isosceles triangle, the vertex angle is one-half each base angle. Find the angles of the triangle.

5.

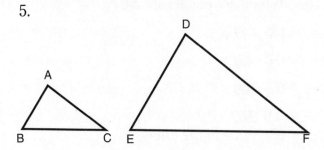

Triangles ABC and DEF are similar. If $AB = 3$, $BC = 5$, $DE = 7$, find EF.

Questions 6–10

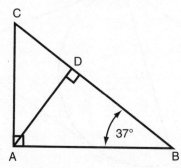

In triangle above, $CD = 4$, $DB = 9$, $\angle B = 37°$.

6. Find $\angle DAB$.

7. Find $\angle DAC$.

8. Is $\triangle ADC$ similar to $\triangle ABD$? Why or why not?

9. Find the length of AD.

10. What is the ratio of AC to AB?

Questions 11–13

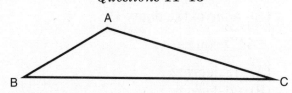

11. Which is greater: $BC - AC$ or AB?

12. If $AB = 5$, $AC = 9$, and $BC = 13$, which angle is greatest? Which angle is smallest?

13. If $\angle A = 80°$ and $\angle B = 40°$, which must be the largest side of the triangle ABC?

14. What is the hypotenuse of a right triangle whose sides are 6 and 8?

15. What is the remaining side of a right triangle whose hypotenuse is 17 and whose side is 8?

16. The ratio of two sides of a right triangle is $3 : 4$. What are the sides of the triangle if the hypotenuse of the triangle is 20?

17.

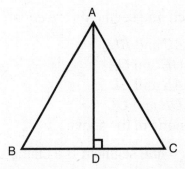

One side of the above equilateral triangle is 4. What is the length of the altitude AD?

Questions 18–20

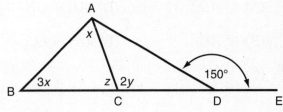

18. Find y.

19. Find x.

20. Find z.

Circles

Diagnostic Test on Circles

Use the following diagram to answer questions 1–5.

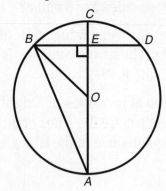

1. Which line segments are equal?

   (A) *AC* and *BD*
   (B) *OE* and *OA*
   (C) *AB* and *CD*
   (D) *OB* and *OC*
   (E) none of the above

2. Which line segment is a diameter?

   (A) *AB*   (D) *OE*
   (B) *AC*   (E) *AE*
   (C) *BD*

3. *BE* equals

   (A) $\frac{1}{2}AB$ (D) $AB - OB$

   (B) $\frac{1}{2}AC$ (E) $OB - EC$

   (C) $\frac{1}{2}BD$

4. Which angle is half of angle *BOC*?

   (A) $\angle CED$
   (B) $\angle OBA$
   (C) $\angle CAB$
   (D) $\angle EBO$
   (E) It cannot be determined.

5. Which arc equals arc *BC*?

   (A) $\overset{\frown}{CD}$

   (B) $\overset{\frown}{AB}$

   (C) $\overset{\frown}{AD}$

   (D) $\overset{\frown}{BD}$

   (E) none of the above

Use the following diagram to answer Questions 6–10.

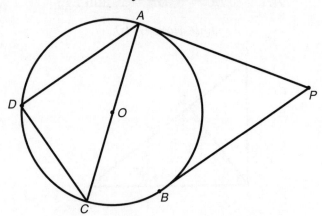

6. $\angle OAP$ equals

   (A) 45 degrees   (D) 180 degrees
   (B) 90 degrees   (E) $\angle ACD$
   (C) 135 degrees

7. Which line segments are equal?

   (A) *AD* and *AC*
   (B) *AD* and *BC*
   (C) *PA* and *PB*
   (D) *PO* and *AC*
   (E) none of the above

8. $\angle ACD$ equals

   (A) 45 degrees
   (B) 90 degrees
   (C) 135 degrees
   (D) 180 degrees
   (E) less than 45 degrees

9. $\overset{\frown}{ADC}$ equals

(A) $\angle ADC$ (D) $\overset{\frown}{AB}$
(B) 180 degrees   (E) $\angle ABP$
(C) $\angle APB$

10. $\angle ACD$ equals

(A) 45 degrees   (D) $\angle ADO$
(B) 90 degrees   (E) $\angle ABD$
(C) 135 degrees

Solutions for Diagnostic Test

1. **(D)** OB and OC are both radii. Radii of a circle are equal. **(3-5)**

2. **(B)** AC is a diameter because its endpoints are on the circle, and it passes through the center of the circle. **(3-5)**

3. **(C)** Since OE is perpendicular to BD and since it passes through the center of the circle, it bisects BD. Thus, $BE = \frac{1}{2}BD$. **(3-5)**

4. **(C)** For a given arc (in this case arc BC), the central angle is twice the inscribed angle. Therefore, angle CAB is half of angle BOC. **(3-5)**

5. **(A)** Since OB equals OD, triangle OBD is isosceles. Therefore, altitude OE is also an angle bisector. Since angle COB equals angle COD, their arcs are equal. $\overset{\frown}{BC} = \overset{\frown}{CD}$ **(3-5)**

6. **(B)** AP is tangent to the circle at A, and is therefore perpendicular to the radius drawn to that point. **(3-5)**

7. **(C)** PA equals PB, because tangents to a circle from the same point are equal. **(3-5)**

8. **(B)** Arc ADC is a semicircle, and angles inscribed in a semicircle have 90 degrees. Thus, $\angle ADC = 90$ degrees. **(3-5)**

9. **(B)** Arc ADC is a semicircle, and therefore contains $\frac{1}{2}(360)$, or 180 degrees. **(3-5)**

10. **(E)** Angles ACD and ABD are both inscribed in arc AD. Since both contain half as many degrees as their arc, they are equal to each other. **(3-5)**

3-5   Instructional Material on Circles

1) When there is only one circle with a given center, the circle is named by its center.

2) A radius of a circle is a line segment from the center to a point on the circle. (The plural of *radius* is *radii*.) All the radii of the same circle are equal.

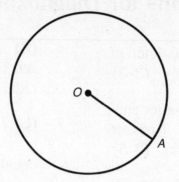

This circle is called circle *O*. *OA* is a radius of circle *O*.

3) A chord of a circle is a line segment whose endpoints are on the circle. A diameter is a chord that passes through the center. If a line passes through the center of a circle and is perpendicular to a chord, then it bisects the chord.

For example:

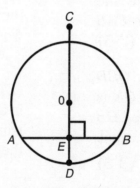

AB is a chord of circle *O*. Since *CD* passes through *O* and is perpendicular to *AB*, *AE = BE*.

4) An arc of a circle is any part of the circle. An arc of a circle is named by its endpoints; to identify the arc, the symbol ⌢ is written on top.

For example:

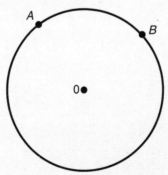

The indicated arc is $\overset{\frown}{AB}$. There are actually two arcs (the circumference of the circle has been divided into two parts). The smaller arc is usually meant by the symbol $\frown$.

5) A central angle is an angle whose vertex is the center of the circle.

An intercepted arc is the arc formed by the points where the sides of the angle meet the circle.

For example:

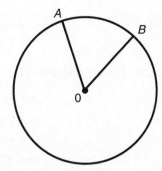

$\angle AOB$ is a central angle, and $\overset{\frown}{AB}$ is the intercepted arc for central angle $\angle AOB$.

6) An arc can be measured in degrees. The degree measure of an arc is the same as that of its central angle. In the diagram above, $\overset{\frown}{AB} = \angle AOB$.

7) An inscribed angle is an angle whose vertex is on the circle and whose sides are chords of the circle. An inscribed angle is one half of the central angle of its intercepted arc.
For example:

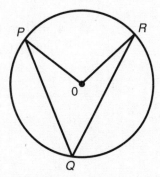

$\angle PQR$ is an inscribed angle, and therefore $\angle PQR = \frac{1}{2}\angle PQR = \frac{1}{2}\overset{\frown}{PR}$.
Specifically, an angle inscribed in a semicircle (half of a circle) is a right angle.

8) Concentric circles are circles with the same center.

9) A tangent to a circle is a line that touches the circle at only one point. From a point outside the circle, two tangents can be drawn to the circle. These tangents are equal. Also, the radius to the point where the tangent meets the circle is perpendicular to the tangent.

For example:

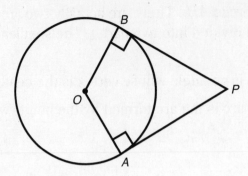

$PA = PB$, $OA \perp PA$, and $OB \perp PB$.

Practice Exercises for 3-5

Question 1

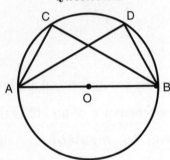

1. Triangles *ABC* and *ABD* are inscribed in a circle whose center is *O*. *AB* is the diameter of the circle. What can be said about angle *C* and angle *D*?

Question 2

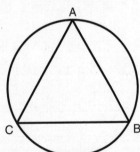

2. A triangle *ABC* is inscribed in a circle. If arc *AC* = 100° and arc *BC* = 120°, what is angle *C*?

Question 3

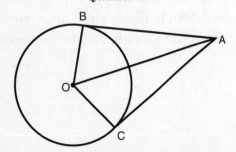

3. *AB* and *AC* are tangent to a circle whose center is at *O*. *OB* and *OC* are radii of the circle. If the radius of the circle is 5 and the tangent *AB* is 12, what is *AO*?

Question 4

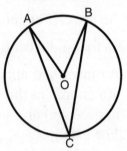

4. *O* is the center of the circle above. If ∠*AOB* = 60°, what is ∠*ACB*?

Question 5

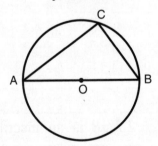

5. *AOB* is a diameter of the circle above. If the radius *AO* = 5, and $\overline{AC} = 8$, what is $\overline{CB}$?

Formulas

Diagnostic Test on Formulas

1. If the base and height of a triangle are 6 and 8 respectively, what is the area of the triangle?

   (A) 48   (D) 28
   (B) 36   (E) 24
   (C) 14

2. If the three sides of a triangle are 7, 8, and a, and if the perimeter is 28, what is a?

   (A) 14   (D) 13
   (B) 11   (E) 6
   (C) 9

3. If two sides of a rectangle are 11 and 13, the area of the rectangle is

   (A) 143   (D) $72\frac{1}{2}$
   (B) 48   (E) 66
   (C) 24

4. If the perimeter of a square is 56, the length of each side is

   (A) 10   (D) 8
   (B) 12   (E) not
   (C) 14   determinable

5. If each side of a square is 16, the area is

   (A) 128   (D) 64
   (B) 256   (E) 16
   (C) 300

6. If a triangle and a parallelogram have the same base and altitude, then which of the following is true?

   (A) The two areas are equal.
   (B) The area of the triangle is half that of the parallelogram.
   (C) The area of the triangle is twice the area of the parallelogram.
   (D) The area of the triangle is $\frac{1}{4}$ the area of the parallelogram.
   (E) None of the above is true.

7. The bases of a trapezoid are 4 and 10, and the height is 5. What is the area of the trapezoid?

   (A) 200   (D) 50
   (B) 400   (E) 150
   (C) 35

8. If the bases of a trapezoid are 4 and 10, then the median is

   (A) 14   (D) 7
   (B) 40   (E) 28
   (C) 20

9. The diameter of a circle is 10. Find its area.

   (A) 100   (D) 50π
   (B) 100π (E) 10π
   (C) 25π

10. If the radius of a circle is 12, its circumference is

    (A) 12π (D) 96π
    (B) 24π (E) 64π
    (C) 144π

Solutions for Diagnostic Test

1. **(E)** The area of a triangle is $\frac{1}{2}$ of base times height. So, area = $\frac{1}{2}(6)(8) = 24$. **(3-4, 3-6)**

2. **(D)** The perimeter of a triangle equals the sum of all its sides. So, $7 + 8 + a = 28$.

   $$a = 13 \qquad \textbf{(3-4, 3-6)}$$

3. **(A)** The area of a rectangle is length times height. So, area = $(11)(13) = 143$. **(3-6)**

4. **(C)** The perimeter of a square is 4 times the length of each side. If the perimeter is 56, then each side is $\frac{1}{4}(56) = 14$. **(3-3, 3-6)**

5. **(B)** The area of a square is the square of the length of each side. So, area = $16(16) = 256$. **(3-6)**

6. **(B)** If b is base and h is height, the area of the triangle is $\frac{1}{2}bh$ and the area of the parallelogram is bh. So, the area of the triangle is $\frac{1}{2}$ the area of the parallelogram. **(3-6)**

7. **(C)** The area of a trapezoid is $\frac{1}{2}$ the product of the height and the sum of the bases. So, area = $\frac{1}{2}(5)(4 + 10) = 35$. **(3-6)**

8. **(D)** The median of a trapezoid is the average of the lengths of its bases. So, median = $\frac{1}{2}(4 + 10) = 7$. **(3-3, 3-6)**

9. **(C)** The area of a circle is π times radius squared. Since the diameter is 10, radius is $\frac{1}{2}(10)$, or 5. So, the area = $\pi(5)(5) = 25\pi$. **(3-6)**

10. **(B)** The circumference of a circle is π times twice the radius. So, circumference = $\pi(2)(12) = 24\pi$. **(3–6)**

3-6 Instructional Material on Formulas

Triangle: Area = $\frac{1}{2}bh$ (b = base, h = height)

Perimeter = $a + b + c$ (a, b, and c are the 3 sides)

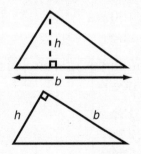

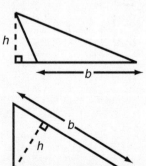

Area = $\frac{1}{2}bh$

The area of any triangle is $\frac{1}{2}bh$, where b is the length of *any* side and h is the length of the altitude (height) to that side. Note that the altitude is defined as the perpendicular distance from the vertex of the triangle to the opposite side.

Perimeter $= a + b + c$, where a, b, and c are the sides.

Rectangle: Area $= lw$ (l = length, w = width)
　　　　　Perimeter $= 2(l + w)$

Square: Area $= s^2$ (s = side of square)
　　　　Perimeter $= 4s$

Parallelogram: Area $= bh$ (b = base, h = height)
　　　　　　　Perimeter = sum of 4 sides

Trapezoid: Area $= \frac{1}{2}(a + b)h$

　　　　(a and b are the two bases, h = height)

　　　　Median $= \frac{1}{2}(a + b)$

Circle: $d = 2r$ (d = diameter, r = radius)
　　　Circumference $= 2\pi r = \pi d$ (π is about 3.14)
　　　Area $= \pi r^2$

Rectangular Box: Volume $= lwh$
　　　　　　　　(l = length, w = width, h = height)

Cube: Volume $= s^3$
　　　(s = side of cube)

Cylinder: Volume $= \pi r^2 h$
　　　　　(r = radius, h = height)

Practice Exercises for 3-6

1.

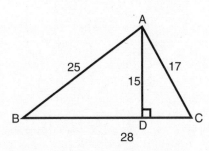

The sides of the triangle above are 17, 25, and 28. The altitude (height) to the base is 15. What is the area of the triangle? What is the perimeter?

2. The length of a rectangle is twice its width. If the perimeter of the rectangle is 60, what are the sides of the rectangle? What is its area?

3. The area of a square is equal to the area of a rectangle with sides 4 and 9. What is the length of a side of the square?

4. The sides of a parallelogram are 5 and 9, and the altitude to the base is 4. What are the parallelogram's perimeter and area?

5.

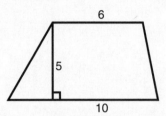

What is the area of the above parallelogram?

6.

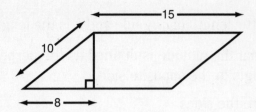

What is the area of the above trapezoid?

7. The area of a circle is equal to the circumference of the circle. What must be its radius?

8.

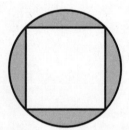

If 4 is the radius of the above circle, and a square is inscribed in the circle, then what is the area of the square? What is the area of the shaded region?

9.

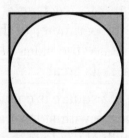

If 4 is the radius of the above circle inscribed in a square as shown, what is the area of the square? What is the area of the shaded region?

10. In descending order, which of the following figures has the greatest area?

I.

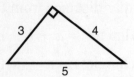

II.

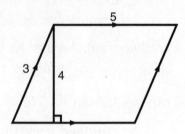

III.

IV.

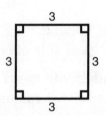

Geometry Tips

There is no general method for attacking geometry problems. If the problem requires that you make some statement about a figure, think about the theorems that apply to a statement of that kind. For example, if you want to show that two angles are equal, list the methods for showing that two angles are equal: vertical angles, angles of similar triangles, angles opposite equal sides in a triangle, angles formed by a bisector, etc. Then examine the given information to see which of these approaches might work. Examine the diagram carefully for clues. (Sometimes you will be told that the diagram is drawn to scale.) You might want to add some new line segments to the given diagram.

For problems that require a numerical answer, try breaking up the problem into parts. If you cannot find the answer directly, try to find the length of other line segments, or the measure of other angles, which might lead to the unknown quantity you are looking for. To find the area of a figure, divide the figure into parts whose area you can find (triangles, rectangles, etc.) and then add these to find the total area.

Answers to Practice Exercises in Plane Geometry

(3-1 through 3-6)*

3-1

1. $x = 40$ (3)
2. $a = c; b = d$ (3)
3. $y = 40$ (3)
4. 0 (3)
5. 160 (4)
6. 140 (4)
7. 30 (4)
8. 90 (4)
9. 150 (4)
10. 70 (7)
11. 50 (7)
12. 30 (7)
13. 0 (7)
14. $x = 95, y = 35$ (7)
15. When $\angle 1 = 45° = \angle 2$ (7)
16. $22\frac{1}{2}°$ (11)
17. $x + y = 45$ (7)
18. 360 (4)
19. $x = 20°, y = 60°$ (3 and 4)
20. $x = 20°$ (7)

3-2

1. 140° (9)
2. 40° (9)
3. 140° (9)
4. 140° (9)
5. 40° (9)
6. 140° (9)
7. 40° (9)
8. 90° (9)
9. 90° (9)
10. 90° (9)
11. 36° (9)
12. 36° (9)
13. 72° (9)
14. 72° (9)
15. 108° (9)

3-3

1. 50° (9)
2. 30° (9)
3. 100° (9)
4. 100° (9)
5. 360° (14)
6. $x = 36°$ (14)
7. $x = 40°$ (9)
8. $y = 120°$ (9)
9. $z = 120°$ (9)
10. 60° (9)

*The number in parentheses ( ) after the answer refers to the subdivision where the instructional material can be found relating to the question. For example, for the answer to the first question in 3-1, you will find

1. $x = 40$ (3)

The (3) means that you can find the instructional material needed to solve question 1 in section 3-1 (3).

3-4

1. $\angle B = \angle C = 70°$ (2, 4, 9)

2. $\angle B = \angle C = 60°$ (4 and 9), $BC = 3$ (8)

3. $45°, 60°, 75°$ (4)

4. $36°, 72°, 72°$ (2, 4, 9)

5. $11\dfrac{2}{3}$ (7)

6. $53°$ (4)

7. $37°$ (4)

8. Yes, $\angle CAD = \angle ABD = 37°$
   $\angle ADC = \angle ADB = 90°$ (6)

9. $\dfrac{AD}{DC} = \dfrac{DB}{AD}$ so $(AD)^2 = (DB)(DC)$

   $(AD)^2 = (9)(4)$

   $(AD)^2 = 36$

   $AD = \sqrt{36} = 6$

10. $\dfrac{AC}{AB} = \dfrac{AD}{DB} = \dfrac{6}{9} = \dfrac{2}{3}$ (7)

11. $AB + AC > BC$ so $AB > BC - AC$ (10)

12. $\angle C$ is smallest; $\angle A$ is largest (11)

13. BC (11)

14. 10 (14)

15. 15 (14)

16. 12 and 16 (14)

17. $2\sqrt{3}$ (14)

18. $y = 50°$ (15)

19. $x = 25°$ (15)

20. $z = 80°$ (4)

3-5

1. Since $\angle C$ and $\angle D$ are measured by $\dfrac{1}{2}$ the $\overset{\frown}{AB}$, they are equal.

   Furthermore, since the arc is $180°$ (AB cuts the circle in half), $\angle C = \dfrac{1}{2}$ $(180°) = 90° = \angle D$ (7)

2. $70°$ (7)

3. 13 (9)

4. $30°$ (7)

5. $\angle C$ is $90°$, so
   $\overline{AC}^2 + \overline{CB}^2 = \overline{AB}^2$, and $CB = 6$. (7)

3-6

1. Area $= \dfrac{1}{2}(28)(15) = 210$
   Perimeter $= 25 + 17 + 28 = 70$

2. Width $= 10$, Length $= 20$
   Area $= 200$

3. 6

4. Perimeter $= 28$; Area $= 36$

5. 90

6. 40

7. $2\pi r = \pi r^2$; $2r = r^2$; $2 = r$
   The radius is 2.

8. Area of square $= 32$
   Area of shaded region $= 16\pi - 32$

9. Area of square $= 64$
   Area of shaded region $= 64 - 16\pi$

10. II, III, IV, I

Analytic Geometry

Diagnostic Test on Analytic Geometry

1. For a point below the *x*-axis,

    (A) the *x*-coordinate is negative
    (B) the *y*-coordinate is negative
    (C) the sum of the coordinates
       is negative
    (D) the difference of the coordinates
       is negative
    (E) none of the above is correct

2. Points whose *x*-coordinates are positive
   are located

    (A) to the left of the *y*-axis
    (B) to the right of the *y*-axis
    (C) inside a unit circle
    (D) outside of a unit circle
    (E) under a diagonal line

3. If two points have the same
   x-coordinate, then they lie

    (A) inside the same unit circle
    (B) on the same side of the *x*-axis
    (C) on the same vertical line
    (D) on the same horizontal line
    (E) in no position described above

4. The two axes intersect at the point

    (A) (1,1)   (D) (1,−1)
    (B) (−1,−1)   (E) (−1,1)
    (C) (0,0)

5. The distance between (2,5) and (5,9) is

    (A) 1   (D) 4
    (B) 2   (E) 5
    (C) 3

6. The distance between (3,0) and *P* is 5.
   P could *not* be

    (A) (3,−5)   (D) (3,5)
    (B) (0,−8)   (E) (8,0)
    (C) (−2,0)

*Use the following graph to answer
Questions 7–10.*

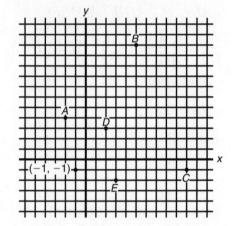

7. What point has coordinates (3,−2)?

    (A) *B*
    (B) *C*
    (C) *D*
    (D) *E*
    (E) none of the above

8. What are the coordinates of point *A*?

    (A) (4,2)   (D) (8,2)
    (B) (2,4)   (E) (5,−3)
    (C) (−2,4)

9. The distance between B and C is

(A) 5   (D) 13

(B) 8   (E) 17

(C) 12

10. The midpoint of the line segment connecting C and D is

(A) (3,4)   (D) (1,6)

(B) (4,3)   (E) $\left(3\frac{1}{2}, 3\frac{1}{2}\right)$

(C) (6,1)

Solutions for Diagnostic Test

1. **(B)** On the x-axis, the y-coordinate is 0. As we move down, the y-coordinate decreases, and therefore below the x-axis, the y-coordinate is negative. **(4-2)**

2. **(B)** On the y-axis, the x-coordinate is zero. As we move to the right, the x-coordinate increases, and becomes positive. **(4-2)**

3. **(C)** Points with the same x-coordinate lie on a vertical line. **(4-4)**

4. **(C)** The axes intersect at the origin, (0,0). **(4-2)**

5. **(E)** Using the distance formula,

$$d = \sqrt{(5-2)^2 + (9-5)^2}$$
$$= \sqrt{9+16}$$
$$= \sqrt{25} = 5 \qquad \textbf{(4-5)}$$

6. **(B)** If two points have one coordinate the same, the distance between them is the difference between the other coordinates. This applies to choices A, C, D, E. In each case the distance between them and (3,0) is 5. P could not be (0,−8). **(4-5)**

7. **(D)** Counting, we find that E is 3 units to the right, and 2 units below the point (0,0). **(4-3)**

8. **(C)** Counting, we find that A is 2 units to the left, and 4 above the point (0,0). **(4-3)**

9. **(D)** Counting, $B = (5,11)$ and $C = (10,-1)$.
Using the distance formula,

$$d = \sqrt{(5-10)^2 + (11-[-1])^2}$$
$$= \sqrt{5^2 + 12^2}$$
$$= \sqrt{169}$$
$$= 13$$

(4-5)

10. **(C)** $C = (10,-1)$. $D = (2,3)$. Using the midpoint formula,

$$M = \left(\frac{10+2}{2}, \frac{(-1)+3}{2}\right) = (6,1)$$

(4-6)

4-1 Number Lines

Numbers, positive and negative, can be represented as points on a straight line. Conversely, points on a line can also be represented by numbers. This is done by use of the number line.

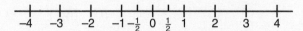

The diagram above is an example of a number line. On a number line, a point is chosen to represent the number zero. Then a point that is 1 unit to the right of 0 represents +1; a point that is $\frac{1}{2}$ unit to the right of 0 is $+\frac{1}{2}$; and a point that is 2 units to the right of 0 is +2, and so on. A point that is 1 unit to the left of 0 is −1; a point that is $\frac{1}{2}$ unit to the left of 0 is $-\frac{1}{2}$; and a point that is 2 units to the left of 0 is −2, and so on. As you can see, all points to the right of the 0 point represent positive numbers, and all those to the left of the 0 point represent negative numbers.

To find the distance between two points on the line:

1) Find the numbers that represent the points.
2) The distance is the smaller number subtracted from the larger.

For example: Find the distance between point *A* and point *B* on the number line.

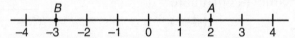

Point *A* is +2 on the number line and point *B* is −3. +2 is larger than −3. So the distance is +2 − (−3), or +2 + 3 = 5. You can also find the distance to be 5 by counting the number of units between *A* and *B*.

Practice Exercises for 4-1*

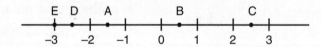

What is the approximate value of the following points?
1. A   3. C   5. E
2. B   4. D

* Answers for Practice Exercises 4-1 through 4-10 begin on page 223.

4-2 X-Axis and Y-Axis

To represent points on plane

Just as points can be represented as numbers on a number line, points can be represented as pairs of numbers on a plane. To represent points on a plane by pairs of numbers, two number lines are used. One number line is horizontal and is commonly called the x-axis. The other is vertical and is called the y-axis. The point where the two number lines (axes) meet is the 0 point for each line. This point is called the origin. On the x-axis, the points to the right of the origin represent positive numbers and those to the left represent negative numbers. On the y-axis, the points above the origin represent positive numbers, and those below it represent negative numbers. See the diagram below.

Practice Exercises for 4-2

Questions 1–5

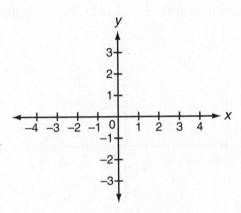

1. What number on the x-axis is represented by point A?

2. What number on the x-axis is represented by point B?

3. What number on the y-axis is represented by point C?

4. What number on the y-axis is represented by point D?

5. What number on the y-axis is represented by point E?

4-3 Ordered Pairs

To represent points on plane

1) Drop perpendiculars from the point to the *x*-axis and to the *y*-axis.
2) The point where the perpendicular meets the *x*-axis represents a number on the *x*-axis, since the *x*-axis is a number line. This number is called the *x*-coordinate of the point. The point where the perpendicular meets the *y*-axis represents a number on the *y*-axis. This number is the *y*-coordinate of the point.
3) To describe the point, write the *x*-coordinate first and then the *y*-coordinate after it, with a comma separating them and parentheses around them. This is called the ordered pair of the point.

For example: Describe points *A* and *B* in the diagram by their ordered pairs.

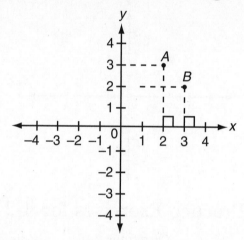

First describe point *A*.
Step 1: Drop perpendiculars from *A* to the *x*-axis and to the *y*-axis.
Step 2: Find the *x*-coordinate and *y*-coordinate of point *A*. Since the perpendicular meets the *x*-axis at $+2$, the *x*-coordinate of *A* is $+2$. Since the perpendicular meets the *y*-axis at $+3$, the *y*-coordinate of *A* is $+3$.
Step 3: Point *A* is represented by the ordered pair $(+2, +3)$.
Similarly, point *B* can be found to be represented by the ordered pair $(+3, +2)$.

Note that the two ordered pairs $(+2, +3)$ and $(+3, +2)$ represent different points. Therefore, the order in which the numbers are written is very important. It is for this reason that these pairs of numbers are called ordered pairs.

Practice Exercises for 4-3

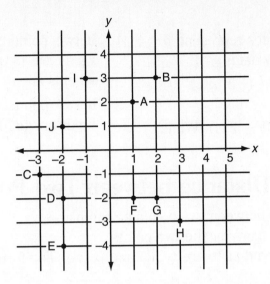

Represent points A, B, C, D, E, F, G, H, I, and J as ordered pairs (x,y).

4-4   Facts about Coordinates

The following facts will be helpful.

1) The ordered pair for the origin is (0,0).
2) For any point on the x-axis, the y-coordinate is always 0.
3) For any point on the y-axis, the x-coordinate is always 0.
4) All points that lie on the same line, parallel to the x-axis, have the same y-coordinate.
5) All points that lie on the same line, parallel to the y-axis, have the same x-coordinate.

Coordinates of Points on a Curve or a Line

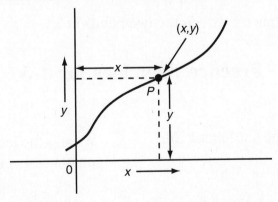

The coordinates of a point on a line or curve in a plane are denoted by (x,y) where x is the horizontal distance (x value) from the y-axis, and y is the vertical distance (y value) from the x-axis. (See figure above.)

Practice Exercises for 4-4

1. The origin has coordinates represented by (x,y). What is x, and what is y?

2. A point on the x-axis is $(-3, a + 2)$. What is a?

3. A point on the y-axis is $(b - 2, 4)$. What is b?

4. If two points on a line parallel to the x-axis are $(3, m + 2)$ and $(4, 2m - 6)$, what is m?

5. If two points on a line parallel to the y-axis are $(a,5)$ and $(2a,6)$, what is a?

4-5 Distance between Two Points

To find the distance between two points on the plane
1) Find the ordered pairs for the two points.
2) Suppose the ordered pairs are (x_1,y_1) and (x_2,y_2). The formula is:

$$\text{Distance} = \sqrt{(x_1 - x_2)^2 + (y_1 - y_2)^2}$$

For example: Find the distance between the two points that are represented by the ordered pairs $(-2,-2)$ and $(1,2)$.
Since the ordered pairs are known, let $(x_1,y_1) = (1,2)$ and $(x_2,y_2) = (-2,-2)$.

Substitute into the formula.

$$
\begin{aligned}
\text{Distance} &= \sqrt{(x_1 - x_2)^2 + (y_1 - y_2)^2} \\
&= \sqrt{(1-(-2))^2 + (2-(-2))^2} \\
&= \sqrt{3^2 + 4^2} \\
&= \sqrt{9+16} \\
&= \sqrt{25} \\
&= 5
\end{aligned}
$$

Therefore, the distance between the two points is 5.

Practice Exercises for 4-5

1. What is the length of the line joining the points $(0,0)$ and $(3,4)$?

2. What is the length of the line joining the points $(-1,-1)$ and $(3,2)$?

3.

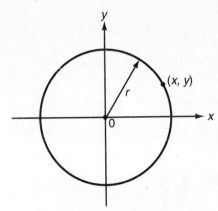

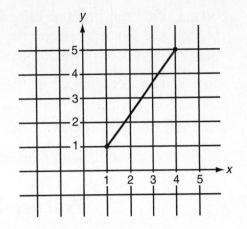

A circle of radius r has its center at $(0,0)$. What is the relationship between x and y for any point on the circle's circumference?

4. What is the unit distance of the slanted line drawn above?

5. What is the length of the line joining the points $(-1,-1)$ and $(+1,+1)$?

4-6 Midpoints

To find the midpoint of a line segment

1) Find the ordered pairs for the end points of the line segment.
2) The x-coordinate of the midpoint is the average of x-coordinates of the end points. The y-coordinate of the midpoint is the average of the y-coordinates of the end points.

If (x_1,y_1) and (x_2,y_2) are the ordered pairs for the end points, the ordered pair for the midpoint is

$$\left(\frac{x_1 + x_2}{2}, \frac{y_1 + y_2}{2} \right)$$

For example: Find the midpoint of segment AB.

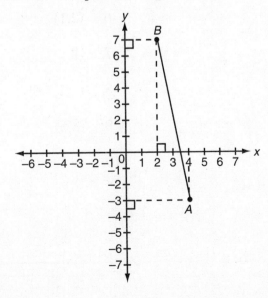

<u>Step 1:</u> Find the ordered pairs for the end points. The ordered pair for point A is $(4,-3)$, and the ordered pair for point B is $(2,7)$.

<u>Step 2:</u> The x-coordinate of the midpoint is the average of the x-coordinates of the end points. The x-coordinate of the midpoint is the average of 4 and 2, or $\dfrac{4+2}{2}=3$.

Similarly, the y-coordinate of the midpoint is the average of -3 and 7, or $\dfrac{-3+7}{2}=2$.

Therefore, the midpoint of the line segment is $(3,2)$.

Practice Exercises for 4-6

Find the midpoint of the line connecting the points

1. (1,2) and (3,5)

2. $(-1,-1)$ and (1,1)

3. (0,1) and (1,0)

4. (a,b) and $(-a,-b)$

5. (0,0) and (1,1)

4-7   Graphs Representing Functions or Equations

Suppose $y = x^2$.   Then every ordered pair (x,y) on the graph of $y = x^2$ is such that $y = x^2$.   In general, if $y = f(x)$, the graph of $y = f(x)$ requires that every point on the graph (x,y) be such that $y = f(x)$.

Practice Exercises for 4-7

Questions 1–5

Find s if a point on the graph $y = x^2$ is represented by

1. $(s,0)$

2. $(0,s)$

3. $(-1,s)$

4. $(1,s)$

5. $(s,4)$

Questions 6–10

Which points are *not* on the graph $y = 3x - 5$?

6. (2,1)

7. (3,4)

8. $(-1,-8)$

9. (2,5)

10. $(-1,-1)$

4-8 Straight Line Graph

The graph of a straight line is represented by $y = mx + b$, where m is the slope of the line and b is the y-coordinate where the graph intersects the y-axis.

Practice Exercises for 4-8

1. Which graphs have the same slopes?
   (i) $y = 2x + 4$, (ii) $y = 3x + 7$,
   (iii) $y = 2x - 6$

2. Which graphs have the same y intercepts?
   (i) $y = 2x + 4$, (ii) $y = -2x + 4$,
   (iii) $y = 2x + 8$

3. What is the slope of the graph $2y = x + 5$?

4. What is the y-coordinate of the point where the graph $2y = 3x + 4$ intercepts the y-axis?

4-9 Intersection of Two Lines or Graphs

Suppose we have a graph $y = 2x + 3$ and a graph $y = x + 4$. We wish to find out where they intersect.

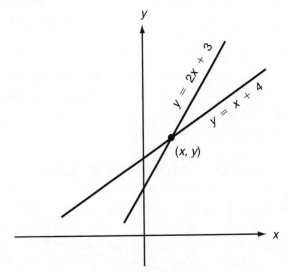

We set $y = 2x + 3 = y = x + 4$ and solve for x:

$$2x + 3 = x + 4$$
$$x = 1$$

Now we substitute $x = 1$ back in *either* equation for y. We use the simpler of the two equations:

$$y = x + 4 \text{ where } x = 1$$

Thus
$$y = 1 + 4 = 5$$

So, we have found that $x = 1$, and $y = 5$. These are the coordinates of the intersection point. Therefore we say that the graph $y = 2x + 3$ and the graph $y = x + 4$ intersect at the point whose coordinates are represented as (1,5), which means $x = 1$ and $y = 5$.

In general, if we want to find the coordinates of the intersection point of two graphs, we set y values equal, and thus get an equation for x. Then we solve for x and substitute back into one of the y-equations to obtain the value of y. These x and y values represent the coordinates of intersection, that is, (x,y).

Sometimes two lines never intersect.

Example: Where do the lines $y = x - 4$ and $y = x - 7$ intersect?

Solution: Set $y = x - 4 = y = x - 7$.
$$x - 4 = x - 7$$
$$-4 = -7, \text{ which is impossible.}$$
Therefore the lines cannot intersect.

Practice Exercises for 4-9

1. Where does the graph $y = 2x + 1$ touch the x-axis?

2. Where does the graph $y = 3x - 1$ touch the y-axis?

3. Where do the graphs $y = 2x + 6$ and $y = -x - 3$ intersect?

4. Where do the graphs $y = x + 3$ and $y = x + 4$ intersect?

5. A line is of the form $y = mx + b$. The line passes through the points (0,2) and (1,3). What is m and what is b?

4-10   Slope of a Line

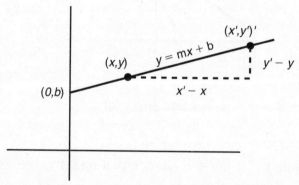

Suppose we have two points on the same line as in the above diagram. Then the *ratio* of the *difference* in y-coordinates to the *difference* in x-coordinates is the *slope* of the line and is constant no matter what points we choose on the line. According to the above diagram, this slope for the points (x',y') and (x,y) is

$$\frac{y' - y}{x' - x}$$

Thus, if we had another point (x'',y'') on the same line we must have

$$\frac{y'-y}{x'-x} = \frac{y''-y'}{x''-x'} = \frac{y''-y}{x''-x}$$

For example, the points (2,3), (4,5), and (6,7) all lie on the same line because

$$\frac{5-3}{4-2} = \frac{7-5}{6-4} = \frac{7-3}{6-2} = 1$$

which is the slope of the line. If the equation of the line is $y = mx + b$, the slope is

$$\frac{y'-y}{x'-x} = m$$

Another example: A line contains the following points:
$$(2,3), (-1,-4), (x,5), \text{ and } (-2,y)$$

Find the values of x and y.

Solution: The slope of the line is constant. That is, we equate the slopes of any two points:

$$\frac{-4-3}{-1-2} = \frac{5-(-4)}{x-(-1)}$$

We get

$$\text{SLOPE} = \frac{-7}{-3} = \frac{9}{x+1}$$
$$7x+7 = 27$$
$$7x = 20$$
$$x = 2\frac{6}{7}$$

Since the slope is $\frac{7}{3}$ (from before), we get

$$\frac{7}{3} = \frac{y-3}{-2-2}$$

because the slope of the points $(-2,y)$ and $(2,3)$ must be equal to $\frac{7}{3}$. Solving for y, we get

$$-28 = 3y-9$$
$$-19 = 3y$$
$$-6\frac{1}{3} = y$$

Therefore, $x = 2\frac{6}{7}$ and $y = -6\frac{1}{3}$

If two lines are perpendicular, the slope of one is the negative reciprocal of the other.

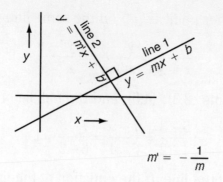

$$m' = -\frac{1}{m}$$

Example: What is the slope of a line perpendicular to the line $y = -3x + 4$?

Since the slope of the line $y = -3x + 4$ is -3, the slope of the line perpendicular to that line is the negative reciprocal, or $\frac{-1}{-3} = \frac{1}{3}$.

Practice Exercises for 4-10

1. Two points on a line are (2,4) and (3,5). If the point (x,8) is also on the line, what is x?

2. The points (3,4) and (4,5) lie on the same line. Which of the following points are also on the same line?

   (A) (6,5)

   (B) (6,7)

   (C) (8,8)

3. A line contains points (1,y), (4,5), (2,−1), and (x,3). What are x and y?

4. What is the slope of a line that passes through points (2,5) and (5,−9)?

5. Two lines, $y = mx + b$ and $y = m'x + b'$, intersect at right angles. What is the product of their slopes?

Answers to Practice Exercises in Analytic Geometry

(4-1 through 4-10)

4-1

1. $A = -1\frac{1}{2}$ 2. $B = +\frac{1}{2}$ 3. $C = +2\frac{1}{2}$ 4. $D = -2\frac{1}{2}$ 5. $E = -3$

4-2

1. 2   2. -2 3. -2 4. 1   5. $2\frac{1}{2}$

4-3

A = (1,2)   C = (−3,−1)   E = (−2,−4)   G = (2,−2)   I = (−1,3)
B = (2,3)   D = (−2,−2)   F = (1,−2)   H = (3,−3)   J = (−2,1)

4-4

1. $x = 0, y = 0$ 2. $a = -2$ 3. $b = 2$ 4. $m = 8$ 5. $a = 0$

4-5

1. 5   2. 5   3. $x^2 + y^2 = r^2$ 4. 5 units   5. $2\sqrt{2}$
(or $x = \pm \sqrt{r^2 \ y^2}$)

4-6

1. $(2,\frac{7}{2})$ or $(2,3\frac{1}{2})$ or $(2,3.5)$ 2. (0,0)   3. $(\frac{1}{2},\frac{1}{2})$ 4. (0,0)   5. $(\frac{1}{2},\frac{1}{2})$

4-7

1. 0
2. 0
3. +1
4. +1
5. ±2 (+2 or −2)
6. On graph, since $1 = 3(2) - 5$
7. On graph, since $4 = 3(3) - 5$
8. On graph, since $-8 = 3(-1) - 5$
9. Not on graph, since $5 \neq 3(2) - 5$
10. Not on graph, since $-1 \neq 3(-1) - 5$

4-8

1. (i) and (iii)   2. (i) and (ii)   3. $\frac{1}{2}$ 4. 2

4-9

1. $x = -\frac{1}{2}$ 3. (−3,0)   5. $m = 1, b = 2$, so the equation of the line is $y = x + 2$.
2. $y = -1$ 4. At no place; they are parallel.

4-10

1. $x = 6$ 2. (B) (6,7)   3. $x = 3\frac{1}{3}, y = -4$ 4. $-4\frac{2}{3}$ 5. -1

Tables, Charts, and Graphs

5-1   Charts and Graphs

Graphs and charts show the relationship of numbers and quantities in visual form. By looking at a graph, you can see at a glance the relationship between two or more sets of information. If such information were presented in written form, it would be hard to read and understand.

Here are some things to remember when doing problems based on graphs or charts:

1. Understand what you are being asked to do before you begin figuring.

2. Check the dates and types of information required. Be sure that you are looking in the proper columns, and on the proper lines, for the information you need.

3. Check the units required. Be sure that your answer is in thousands, millions, or whatever the question calls for.

4. In computing averages, be sure that you add the figures you need and no others, and that you divide by the correct number of years or other units.

5. Be careful in computing problems asking for percentages.

    (a) Remember that to convert a decimal into a percent you must multiply it by 100. For example, 0.04 is 4%.
    (b) Be sure that you can distinguish between such quantities as 1% (1 percent) and .01% (one one-hundredth of 1 percent), whether in numerals or in words.
    (c) Remember that if quantity x is greater than quantity y, and the question asks what percent quantity x is of quantity y, the answer must be greater than 100 percent.

5-2   Tables and Charts

A table or chart shows data in the form of a box of numbers or chart of numbers. Each line describes how the numbers are connected.

Test Score	Number of Students
90	2
85	1
80	1
60	3

Example: How many students took the test?

Solution: To find out the number of students that took the test, just add up the numbers in the column marked "Number of Students." That is, add $2 + 1 + 1 + 3 = 7$.

Example: What was the difference in score between the highest and the lowest score?

Solution: First look at the highest score: 90. Then look at the lowest score: 60. Now calculate the difference: $90 - 60 = 30$.

Example: What was the *median* score?

Solution: The median score means the score that is in the *middle* of all the scores. That is, there are just as many scores above the median as below it. So in this example, the scores are 90, 90 (there are two 90s), 85, 80, and 60, 60, 60 (there are three 60s). So we have:

90
90
85
80
60
60
60

80 is right in the middle. That is, there are three scores above it and three scores below it. So 80 is the median.

Example: What was the *mean* score?

Solution: The mean score is defined as the *average* score. That is, it is the

$$\frac{\text{sum of the scores}}{\text{total number of scores}}$$

The sum of the scores is $90 + 90 + 85 + 80 + 60 + 60 + 60 = 525$. The total number of scores is $2 + 1 + 1 + 3 = 7$, so divide 7 into 525 to get the average: 75.

5-3   Graphs

To read a graph, you must know what *scale* the graph has been drawn to. Somewhere on the face of the graph will be an explanation of what each division of the graph means. Sometimes the divisions will be labeled. At other times, this information will be given in a small box called a *scale* or *legend*. For instance, a map, which is a specialized kind of graph, will always carry a scale or legend on its face telling you such information as $1'' = 100$ miles or $\frac{1''}{4} = 2$ miles.

5-4 Bar Graphs

The bar graph shows how information is compared by using broad lines, called bars, of varying lengths. Sometimes single lines are used as well. Bar graphs are good for showing a quick comparison of the information involved; however, the bars are difficult to read accurately unless the end of the bar falls exactly on one of the divisions of the scale. If the end of the bar falls between divisions of the scale, it is not easy to arrive at the precise figure represented by the bar. In bar graphs, the bars can run either vertically or horizontally. The sample bar graph following is a horizontal graph.

EXPENDITURES PER PUPIL—2009

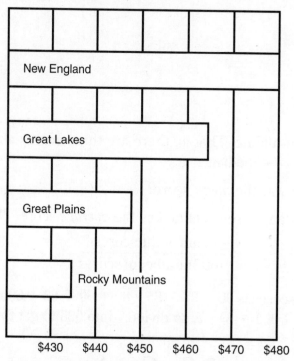

$430 $440 $450 $460 $470 $480

The individual bars in this kind of graph may carry a label within the bar, as in this example. The label may also appear alongside each bar. The scale used on the bars may appear along one axis, as in the example, or it may be noted somewhere on the face of the graph. Each numbered space on the *x*- (or horizontal) axis represents an expenditure of $10 per pupil. A wide variety of questions may be answered by a bar graph, such as:

(1) Which area of the country spends the least per pupil? Rocky Mountains.
(2) How much does the New England area spend per pupil? $480.
(3) How much less does the Great Plains spend per pupil than the Great Lakes? $464 − 447 = $17/pupil.
(4) How much more does New England spend on a pupil than the Rocky Mountain area? $480 − 433 = $47/pupil.

5-5 Circle Graphs

A circle graph (also called pie chart) shows how an entire quantity has been divided or apportioned. The circle represents 100 percent of the quantity; the different parts into which the whole has been divided are shown by sections, or wedges, of the circle. Circle graphs are good for showing how money is distributed or collected, and for this reason they are widely used in financial graphing. The information is usually presented on the face of each section, telling you exactly what the section stands for and the value of that section in comparison to the other parts of the graph.

SOURCES OF INCOME—PUBLIC COLLEGES OF U.S.

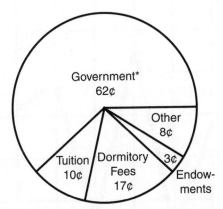

*Government refers to all levels of government—not exclusively the federal government.

The circle graph above indicates where the money originates that is used to maintain public colleges in the United States. The size of the sections tells you at a glance which source is most important (government) and which is least important (endowments). The sections total 100¢, or $1.00. This graph may be used to answer the following questions:

(1) What is the most important source of income to the public colleges? Government.

(2) What part of the revenue dollar comes from tuition? 10¢.

(3) Dormitory fees bring in how many times the money that endowments bring in?

$5\dfrac{2}{3}$ times $\left(\dfrac{17}{3} = 5\dfrac{2}{3}\right)$.

(4) What is the least important source of revenue to public colleges? Endowments.

5-6 Line Graphs

Graphs that have information running both across (horizontally) and up and down (vertically) can be considered to be laid out on a grid having a *y*-axis and an *x*-axis. One of the two quantities being compared will be placed along the *y*-axis, and the other quantity will be placed along the *x*-axis. When we are asked to compare two values, we subtract the smaller from the larger.

SHARES OF STOCK SOLD OF STOCK X
NEW YORK STOCK EXCHANGE DURING ONE SIX-MONTH PERIOD

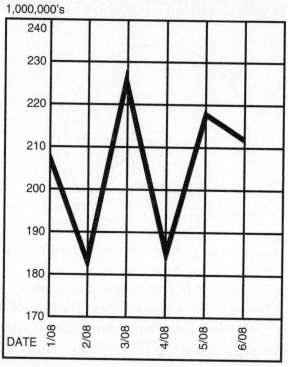

Our sample line graph represents the total shares of stock sold on the New York Stock Exchange between January and June. The months are placed along the *x*-axis, while the sales, in units of 1,000,000 shares, are placed along the *y*-axis.

(1) How many shares were sold in March? 225,000,000.
(2) What was the trend of stock sales between April and May? The volume of sales rose.
(3) Compare the share sales in January and February. 25,000,000 fewer shares were sold in February.
(4) During which months of the period was the increase in sales largest? February to March.

Practice Exercises for 5-1 through 5-6

TABLE CHART TEST

Questions 1–5 are based on this table chart.

The following chart is a record of the performance of a baseball team for the first seven weeks of the season.

	Games won	Games lost	Total no. of games played
First Week	5	3	8
Second Week	4	4	16
Third Week	5	2	23
Fourth Week	6	3	32
Fifth Week	4	2	38
Sixth Week	3	3	44
Seventh Week	2	4	50

1. How many games did the team win during the first seven weeks?

    (A) 32
    (B) 29
    (C) 25
    (D) 21
    (E) 50

2. What percent of the games did the team win?

    (A) 75%
    (B) 60%
    (C) 58%
    (D) 29%
    (E) 80%

3. According to the chart, which week was the worst for the team?

    (A) second week
    (B) fourth week
    (C) fifth week
    (D) sixth week
    (E) seventh week

4. Which week was the best week for the team?

    (A) first week
    (B) third week
    (C) fourth week
    (D) fifth week
    (E) sixth week

5. If there are fifty more games to play in the season, how many more games must the team win to end up winning 70% of the games?

    (A) 39
    (B) 35
    (C) 41
    (D) 34
    (E) 32

Solutions

1. Choice B is correct. To find the total number of games won, add the number of games won for all the weeks, $5 + 4 + 5 + 6 + 4 + 3 + 2 = 29$. **(5-2)**

2. Choice C is correct. The team won 29 out of 50 games, or 58%. **(5-2)**

3. Choice E is correct. The seventh week was the only week that the team lost more games than it won. **(5-2)**

4. Choice B is correct. During the third week the team won 5 games and lost 2, or it won about 70% of the games that week. Compared with the winning percentages for other weeks, the third week's was the highest. **(5-2)**

5. Choice C is correct. To win 70% of all the games, the team must win 70 out of 100. Since it won 29 games out of the first 50 games, it must win $70 - 29$, or 41 games out of the next 50 games. **(5-2)**

PIE CHART TEST

Questions 1–5 are based on this pie chart.

POPULATION BY REGION, 1964

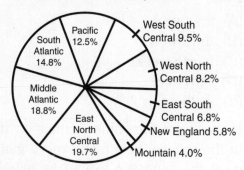

Total U.S. 191.3 million = 100%

1. Which region was the most populated region in 1964?

   (A) East North Central
   (B) Middle Atlantic
   (C) South Atlantic
   (D) Pacific
   (E) New England

2. What part of the entire population lived in the Mountain region?

   (A) $\dfrac{1}{10}$ (D) $\dfrac{1}{25}$

   (B) $\dfrac{1}{30}$ (E) $\dfrac{1}{8}$

   (C) $\dfrac{1}{50}$

3. What was the approximate population in the Pacific region?

   (A) 20 million
   (B) 24 million
   (C) 30 million
   (D) 28 million
   (E) 15 million

4. Approximately how many more people lived in the Middle Atlantic region than in the South Atlantic?

   (A) 4.0 million
   (B) 7.7 million
   (C) 5.2 million
   (D) 9.3 million
   (E) 8.5 million

5. What was the total population in all the regions combined?

   (A) 73.3 million
   (B) 100.0 million
   (C) 191.3 million
   (D) 126.8 million
   (E) 98.5 million

Solutions

1. Choice A is correct. East North Central, with 19.7% of the total population, had the largest population. **(5-5)**

2. Choice D is correct. The Mountain region had 4.0% of the population. 4.0% is $\dfrac{1}{25}$. **(5-5)**

3. Choice B is correct. Pacific had 12.5% of the population. 12.5% of 191.3 million is .125 × 191.3 or about 24 million. **(5-5)**

4. Choice B is correct. Middle Atlantic had 18.8%, and South Atlantic had 14.8% of the population. So, Middle Atlantic had 4.0% more. 4.0% of 191.3 million is .04 × 191.3, or about 7.7 million. **(5-5)**

5. Choice C is correct. All the regions combined had 100% of the population or 191.3 million. **(5-5)**

LINE GRAPH TEST

Questions 1–5 are based on this line graph.

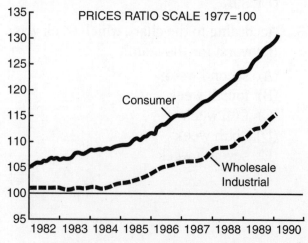

1. On the ratio scale, what were consumer prices recorded as of the end of 1985?

   (A) 95
   (B) 100
   (C) 105
   (D) 110
   (E) 115

2. During what year did consumer prices rise fastest?

   (A) 1983
   (B) 1985
   (C) 1987
   (D) 1988
   (E) 1989

3. When wholesale and industrial prices were recorded as 110, consumer prices were recorded as

   (A) between 125 and 120
   (B) between 120 and 115
   (C) between 115 and 110
   (D) between 110 and 105
   (E) between 105 and 100

4. For the 8 years 1982–1989 inclusive, the average increase in consumer prices was

   (A) 1 point
   (B) 2 points
   (C) 3 points
   (D) 4 points
   (E) 5 points

5. The percentage increase in wholesale and industrial prices between the beginning of 1982 and the end of 1989 was

   (A) 1 percent
   (B) 5 percent
   (C) 10 percent
   (D) 15 percent
   (E) less than 1 percent

Solutions

1. Choice D is correct. Drawing a vertical line at the end of 1985, we reach the consumer price graph at about the 110 level. **(5-6)**

2. Choice E is correct. The slope of the consumer graph is clearly steepest in 1989. **(5-6)**

3. Choice A is correct. Wholesale and industrial prices were about 110 at the beginning of 1989, when consumer prices were between 120 and 125. **(5-6)**

4. Choice C is correct. At the beginning of 1982 consumer prices were about 105; at the end of 1989 they were about 130. The average increase is $\dfrac{130-105}{8}=\dfrac{25}{8}$ or about 3. **(5-6)**

5. Choice D is correct. At the beginning of 1982 wholesale prices were about 100; at the end of 1989 they were about 115. The percent increase is about $\dfrac{115-100}{100}\times100\%$ or 15%. **(5-6)**

BAR GRAPH TEST

Questions 1–3 are based on this bar graph.

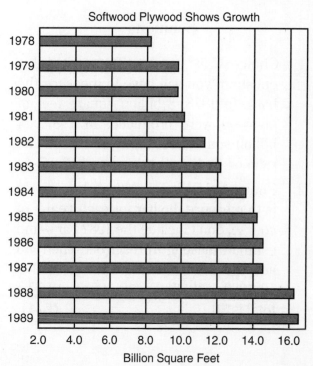

Softwood Plywood Shows Growth

1. What was the ratio of soft plywood produced in 1978 as compared with that produced in 1987?

   (A) 1 : 1
   (B) 2 : 3
   (C) 1 : 2
   (D) 3 : 4
   (E) 1 : 3

2. For the years 1978 through 1983, excluding 1982, how many billion square feet of plywood were produced altogether?

   (A) 23.2
   (B) 29.7
   (C) 34.1
   (D) 40.7
   (E) 50.5

3. Between which consecutive odd years and between which consecutive even years was the plywood production jump greatest?

   (A) 1985 and 1987; 1978 and 1980
   (B) 1983 and 1985; 1984 and 1986
   (C) 1979 and 1981; 1980 and 1982
   (D) 1981 and 1983; 1980 and 1982
   (E) 1983 and 1985; 1982 and 1984

Solutions

1. Choice C is correct. To answer this question, you will have to measure the bars. In 1978, 8 billion square feet of plywood were produced. In 1987, 14 billion square feet were produced. The ratio of 8 : 14 is the same as 4 : 7. **(5-4)**

2. Choice D is correct. All you have to do is to measure the bar for each year—of course, don't include the 1982 bar—and estimate the length of each bar. Then you add the five lengths. 1978 = 8, 1979 = 10, 1980 = 10, 1981 = 10, 1983 = 12. The total is 50. **(5-4)**

3. Choice E is correct. The jump from 1983 to 1985 was from 12 to 14 = 2 billion square feet. The jump from 1982 to 1984 was from 11 to 13.5 = 2.5 billion square feet. None of the other choices show such broad jumps. **(5-4)**

CUMULATIVE GRAPH TEST

Questions 1–5 are based on this cumulative graph.

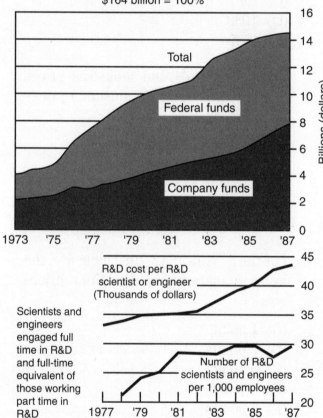

Spending for Research & Develpment
by Type of Research, 1987
$164 billion = 100%

1. About how much in government funds was spent for research and development in 1987?

   (A) $16 billion
   (B) $8 billion
   (C) $12 billion
   (D) $24 billion
   (E) $4 billion

2. In 1987, about what percent of the total spending in research and development were company funds?

(A) 40%
(B) 25%
(C) $33\frac{1}{3}$%
(D) 50%
(E) 20%

3. What was the change in the relative number of research and development scientists and engineers with respect to all employees from 1984 to 1985?

(A) 10%
(B) 5%
(C) 2%
(D) 3%
(E) 0%

4. What was the increase in company funds in research and development from 1973 to 1987?

(A) $12 billion
(B) $6 billion
(C) $8 billion
(D) $4 billion
(E) $14 billion

5. What was the percent of increase of the company funds spent in research and development from 1973 to 1987?

(A) 100%
(B) 50%
(C) 300%
(D) 400%
(E) 1,000%

Solutions

1. Choice B is correct. Total spending was about $16 billion, and company spending was $8 billion. So, government spending was about $8 billion. **(5-6)**

2. Choice D is correct. Company funds totalled $8 billion, and the total funds were $16 billion. So, company funds were $\frac{1}{2}$ of total funds, or 50%. **(5-6)**

3. Choice E is correct. The graph showing the relative employment of research and development scientists and engineers was horizontal between 1984 and 1985. This means no change. **(5-6)**

4. Choice B is correct. Company funds totalled $8 billion in 1987 and $2 billion in 1973. The increase was $6 billion. **(5-6)**

5. Choice C is correct. Company funds totalled $2 billion in 1973, and the increase from 1973 to 1987 was $6 billion, or 300% of $2 billion. **(5-6)**

Miscellaneous Problems

Including Averages, Properties of Integers, Approximations, Combinations, Probability, the Absolute Value Sign, and Functions

6-1   Averages, Medians, and Modes

Averages. The average of *n* numbers is merely their sum, divided by *n*.

Example: Find the average of: 20, 0, 80, and 12.

Solution: The average is the sum divided by the number of entries, or:

$$\frac{20+0+80+12}{4} = \frac{112}{4} = 28$$

A quick way of obtaining an average of a set of numbers that are close together is the following:

Step 1: Choose any number that will approximately equal the average.
Step 2: Subtract this approximate average from each of the numbers (this sum will give some positive and negative results). Add the results.
Step 3: Divide this sum by the number of entries.
Step 4: Add the result of Step 3 to the approximate average chosen in Step 1. This will be the true average.

Example: Find the average of 92, 93, 93, 96, and 97.

Solution: Choose 95 as an approximate average. Subtracting 95 from 92, 93, 93, 96, and 97 gives −3, −2, −2, 1, and 2. The sum is −4. Divide −4 by 5 (the number of entries) to obtain −0.8. Add −0.8 to the original approximation of 95 to get the true average, 95 − 0.8, or 94.2.

6-1a   *Medians.* The median of a set of numbers is the number that is in the middle of all the numbers.

Example: Find the median of 20, 0, 80, 12, and 30.

Solution: Arrange the numbers in increasing order:

$$0$$
$$12$$
$$20$$
$$30$$
$$80$$

The *middle* number is 20, so 20 is the *median*.

Note: If there is an *even* number of items, such as

0
12
20
24
30
80

there is no *middle* number.

So in this case we take the average of the two middle numbers, 20 and 24, to get 22, which is the *median*.

If there are numbers such as 20 and 22, the median would be 21 (just the average of 20 and 22).

6-1b   *Modes.* The mode of a set of numbers is the number that occurs most frequently. If we have numbers 0, 12, 20, 30, and 80, there is *no* mode, since no one number appears with the greatest frequency. But consider this:

Example: Find the mode of 0, 12, 12, 20, 30, 80.

Solution: 12 appears most frequently, so it is the mode.

Example: Find the mode of 0, 12, 12, 20, 30, 30, 80.

Solution: Here *both* 12 and 30 are modes.

6-2   Properties of Integers

Even-Odd. These are problems that deal with even and odd numbers. An even number is divisible by 2, and an odd number is not divisible by 2. All even numbers end in the digits 0, 2, 4, 6, or 8; odd numbers end in the digits 1, 3, 5, 7, or 9. For example, the numbers 358, 90, 18, 9,874, and 46 are even numbers. The numbers 67, 871, 475, and 89 are odd numbers.

6-3   Advanced Combinations (see also 2-35, 2-36)

Suppose that a job has 2 different parts. There are *m* different ways of doing the first part, and there are *n* different ways of doing the second part. The problem is to find the number of ways of doing the entire job. For each way of doing the first part of the job, there are *n* ways of doing the second part. Since there are *m* ways of doing the first part, the total number of ways of doing the entire job is $m \times n$. The formula that can be used is

$$\text{Number of ways} = m \times n$$

For any problem that involves 2 actions or 2 objects, each with a number of choices, and asks for the number of combinations, the formula can be used. For example: A man wants a sandwich and a drink for lunch. If a restaurant has 4 choices of sandwiches and 3 choices of drinks, how many different ways can he order his lunch?

Since there are 4 choices of sandwiches and 3 choices of drinks, use the formula

$$\text{Number of ways} = 4(3)$$
$$= 12$$

Therefore, the man can order his lunch 12 different ways.

If we have objects a, b, c, d, and want to arrange them two at a time—that is, like ab, bc, cd, etc.—we have four combinations taken two at a time. This is denoted as $_4C_2$. The rule is that $_4C_2 = \dfrac{(4)(3)}{(2)(1)}$. In general, n combinations taken r at a time is represented by the formula:

$$_nC_r = \frac{(n)(n-1)(n-2)...(n-r+1)}{(r)(r-1)(r-2)...(1)}$$

$$\text{Examples: } _3C_2 = \frac{3\times2}{2\times1}; _8C_3 = \frac{8\times7\times6}{3\times2\times1}$$

Suppose there are 24 people at a party and each person shakes another person's hand (only once). How many handshakes are there?

Solution: Represent the people at the party as a,b,c,d, etc.

The combinations of handshakes would be ab, ac, bc, bd, etc. or 24 combinations taken 2 at a time:

$$_{24}C_2. \text{ This is } \frac{24\times23}{2\times1} = 276.$$

Permutations:

Permutations are like combinations, except in permutations the order is important. As an example, if we want to find how many permutations there are of three objects taken 2 at a time, we would have for a, b, c, ab, ba, ac, ca, bc, cb. Thus as an example, ba would be one permutation and ab would be another. The permutations of 3 objects taken 2 at a time would be $_3P_2 = 3 \times 2$, and not $\dfrac{3\times2}{2\times1}$, as in combinations. The number of permutations of n objects taken r at a time would be $_nP_r = (n)(n-1)...(n-r+1)$.

Example: How many permutations of the digits 142 are there, where the digits are taken two at a time?

Solution: You have 14, 41, 12, 21, 42, 24. That is, $_3P_2 = 3 \times 2 = 6$.

Other combination problems:

Suppose there are two groups, each with a certain number of members. It is known that some members of one group also belong to the other group. The problem is to find how many members there are in the 2 groups altogether. To find the number of members altogether, use the following formula:

Total number of members = Number of members in group I
+ Number of members in group II
− Number of members common to both groups

For example: In one class, 18 students received As for English and 10 students received As in math. If 5 students received As in both English and math, how many students received at least one A?

In this case, let the students who received As in English be in group I and let those who received As in math be in group II.

Using the formula:

Number of students who received at least one A

= Number in group I + Number in group II − Number in both

= 18 + 10 − 5 = 23

Therefore, there are 23 students who received at least one A.

In combination problems such as these, the problems do not always ask for the total number. They may ask for any of the four numbers in the formula while the other three are given. In any case, to solve the problems, use the formula.

6-4   Probability

The probability that an event will occur equals the number of favorable ways divided by the total number of ways. If P is the probability, m is the number of favorable ways, and n is the total number of ways, then

$$P = \frac{m}{n}$$

For example: What is the probability that a head will turn up on a single throw of a penny?

The favorable number of ways is 1 (a head).

The total number of ways is 2 (a head and a tail). Thus, the probability is $\frac{1}{2}$.

If a and b are two mutually exclusive events, then the probability that a or b will occur is the sum of the individual probabilities.

Suppose P_a is the probability that an event a occurs. Suppose that P_b is the probability that a second independent event b occurs. Then the probability that the first event a occurs *and* the second event b occurs subsequently is $P_a \times P_b$.

6-5   The Absolute Value Sign

The symbol | | denotes absolute value. The absolute value of a number is the numerical value of the number without the plus or minus sign in front of it. Thus all absolute values are positive. For example, $|+3|$ is 3, and $|-2|$ is 2. Here's another example:

If x is positive and y is negative, $|x| + |y| = x - y$.

6-6   Functions

Suppose we have a function of x. This is denoted as $f(x)$ (or $g(y)$ or $h(z)$, etc.). As an example, if $f(x) = x$, then $f(3) = 3$. In this example, we substitute the value 3 wherever x appears in the function. Similarly, $f(-2) = -2$. Consider another example: If $f(y) = y^2 - y$, then $f(2) = 2^2 - 2 = 2$. $f(-2) = (-2)^2 - (-2) = 6$. $f(z) = z^2 - z$. $f(2z) = (2z)^2 - (2z) = 4z^2 - 2z$.

Let us consider still another example: Let $f(x) = x + 2$ and $g(y) = 2^y$. What is $f[g(-2)]$?

Now $g(-2) = 2^{-2} = \frac{1}{4}$. Thus $f[g(-2)] = f\left(\frac{1}{4}\right)$. Since $f(x) = x + 2, f\left(\frac{1}{4}\right) = \frac{1}{4} + 2 = 2\frac{1}{4}$.

Verbal Problems

Diagnostic Test on Verbal Problems

1. Jane is a receptionist and earns $50.50 per week. Her hospitalization insurance, which is deducted from her salary, is at the rate of 3%. What does Jane pay each week for hospitalization insurance?

    (A) $1.50

    (B) $2.50

    (C) $1.53

    (D) $1.76

    (E) none of the above

2. A private breakfast party was charged $3.20 per person for 16 people. However, only five of the people shared the expenses, which were equally divided among the five. How much did each of the five pay?

    (A) $3.20

    (B) $9.40

    (C) $10.24

    (D) $12.36

    (E) $11.52

3. Sally is three years younger than John. The sum of the ages of John and Sally is 35 years. What is John's age?

    (A) 16 years

    (B) 19 years

    (C) 21 years

    (D) 18 years

    (E) 17 years

4. An ocean liner was sailing from New York to London at 20 miles per hour. A slower ocean liner was also sailing from New York to London and left the same time as the first ocean liner. After sailing for 40 hours, the two ocean liners were a distance of 200 miles from each other. What was the slower ocean liner's speed?

    (A) 10 miles per hour

    (B) 12 miles per hour

    (C) 15 miles per hour

    (D) 18 miles per hour

    (E) 19 miles per hour

5. The two smallest angles of a triangle are in a ratio of 1 : 2. The largest angle of the triangle is equal to the sum of the first two smaller angles. The number of degrees in each angle is

    (A) 30°, 60°, 90°

    (B) 25°, 50°, 105°

    (C) 40°, 80°, 60°

    (D) 120°, 30°, 30°

    (E) none of the above

Solutions for Diagnostic Test

1. **(E)** Jane's weekly hospitalization insurance cost is found by multiplying her weekly earnings ($50.50) by her hospitalization insurance deduction rate (3%).

$$50.50 \times \frac{3}{100} = \frac{151.50}{100} = 1.515$$

(7-1, 1-22)

2. **(C)** The total cost for the private breakfast party is found by multiplying $3.20 (the cost per person) by 16 (the total number of people present). Thus the total cost is

$$\$3.20 \times 16 = \$51.20$$

However, it is mentioned that the expenses were shared by only five people and also that the expenses were equally divided among the five. Thus, we divide the total cost ($51.20) by 5 to find out how much each of the five people paid.

$$\$51.20 \div 5 = \$10.24 \qquad \textbf{(7-1)}$$

3. **(B)** Let S represent Sally's age, and J represent John's age. Sally is three years younger than John, so

$$S = J - 3$$

The sum of the ages of John and Sally is 35, so

$$J + S = 35$$

We now have the following two equations:

$$J + S = 35$$

and

$$S = J - 3$$

Subtracting the left-hand side of the second equation from the left-hand side of the first equation and setting this result equal to what we get by subtracting the right-hand side of the second equation from the right-hand side of the first equation, we obtain

$$J + S - S = 35 - (J - 3)$$
$$J = 35 - J + 3$$
$$J = 38 - J$$
$$2J = 38$$
$$J = 19$$

Thus John's age (which we represented by J) is 19 years. **(7-1, 2-11, 2-22, 2-25)**

4. **(C)** The distance the first ocean liner traveled after 40 hours is found by multiplying its speed (20 mph) by the time traveled (40 hours).

$$20 \times 40 = 800$$

Thus after 40 hours the first ocean liner traveled 800 miles.

We want to determine the slower ocean liner's speed. Call its speed x. Since it traveled for 40 hours, the distance it covered is represented by

$$x \times 40$$
(since rate×time = distance).

The ocean liners were 200 miles from each other after the 40 hours.
Therefore, the distance the faster ocean liner traveled minus the distance the slower ocean liner traveled must be equal to 200 miles.

Thus

$$800 - 40x = 200$$
$$800 - 200 = 40x$$
$$600 = 40x$$
$$15 = x$$

Therefore, the speed of the slower ocean liner is 15 miles per hour.

(7-1, 2-22, 2-31)

5. **(A)** Let the smallest angle of the triangle be denoted by x. Since the two smallest angles of the triangle are in a ratio of $1:2$, the second smallest angle of the triangle is $2x$, since $x:2x = 1:2$. The largest angle of the triangle is stated to be equal to the sum of the two smaller angles. Thus the largest angle of the triangle is given as $x + 2x = 3x$. So, the largest angle is given as $3x$. The three angles of the triangle are x, $2x$, and $3x$. Since the sum of the interior angles of a triangle must equal $180°$, we must have

$$x + 2x + 3x = 180$$
$$6x = 180$$
$$x = 30$$

since $x = 30$, $2x = 60$, and $3x = 90$. Thus, the angles of the triangle are $30°$, $60°$, and $90°$.   **(7-1, 2-22, 3-4)**

7-1   Instructional Material for Verbal Problems

Some problems are presented in verbal format. The verbal statement presents a sets of facts from which you have to draw conclusions. In drawing these conclusions, you must rely on some of your own mathematical background. You have already gotten some practice in this type of problem in Section 2-11 (converting words to algebraic expressions).

The way to approach the verbal problem is to look for *key* words that can be translated into mathematical terms. Here is an example of a verbal problem:

The sum of the measures of two angles of a triangle is one-half the measure of the third angle. What is the largest angle of the triangle?

In this problem, the key words are *sum, measures, angles, triangle, largest angle,* etc. We have to find what is given and then translate into mathematical terms. We are given:

"The *sum* of the *measures* of *two angles* of a *triangle* is *one-half* the *measure* of the *third angle.*"

Let us represent the *measure of the sum of the two angles* by x, and the *measure of the third angle* by y. The word *is* mathematically means *equals*, so we can translate what we are given into mathematical terms:

$$x = \frac{1}{2}y$$

Now we have to rely on some of our knowledge about the angles of triangles. We should be aware that the sum of the measure of all three angles of a triangle is $180°$. Since x represents the sum of the measures of two angles and y represents the measure of the third angle, in mathematical notation we have

$$x + y = 180$$

We now have at our disposal two equations:

(1) $\qquad x = \frac{1}{2}y$

(2) $\qquad x + y = 180$

We want to find the measure of the largest angle of the triangle, using these two equations. We proceed as follows:

Equals subtracted from equals are equal. Subtract the left-hand side of Equation (1) from the left-hand side of Equation (2) and set this result equal to the result obtained by subtracting the right-hand side of Equation (1) from the right-hand side of Equation (2). You should now have the equation

$$x + y - x = 180 - \frac{1}{2}y$$

Therefore,

$$y = 180 - \frac{1}{2}y$$

or $\qquad y + \frac{1}{2}y = \frac{3}{2}y = 180$

and $\qquad y = 120$

Thus the third angle, y, is 120°. But we are asked to find the *largest* angle of the triangle. Since the third angle is 120° and *each* of the other angles of the triangle must be *less than* 60° (because the sum of the three angles must be 180°), the largest angle must be 120° (the third angle). Let us consider another verbal problem:

A 212° Fahrenheit thermometer costs $10 a dozen. A 120° Fahrenheit thermometer costs $5 a dozen. What is the difference in cost between the greatest and least cost of 6 dozen Fahrenheit thermometers?

Here we are given that a 212° Fahrenheit thermometer costs $10 for 1 dozen, and that a 120° Fahrenheit thermometer costs $5 for 1 dozen. We would like to find the *difference* in cost between the *greatest* and *least* cost of 6 dozen thermometers.

First we must find the greatest cost of 6 dozen thermometers. Since the most expensive thermometers cost $10 a dozen, 6 dozen of these thermometers cost $10 × 6 = $60. Thus the greatest cost of 6 dozen thermometers is $60. The least expensive thermometers cost $5 a dozen, so 6 dozen of these thermometers cost $30. Thus the least cost of 6 dozen thermometers is $30. Now we can calculate the difference in cost between the greatest and least cost of 6 dozen thermometers. This is $60 (the greatest cost of 6 dozen) minus $30 (the least cost of 6 dozen). $60 − $30 = $30, so the difference in cost between the greatest and least cost of 6 dozen thermometers is $30.

In summary, the way to attack a verbal problem is to determine the key words, know what is given (translating into mathematical terms), understand what is being asked for, and use any knowledge that you already know and feel is applicable to the solution of the problem.

Practice Exercises for 7-1

1. Harry buys a dozen oranges for $1.20 and buys a can of tuna fish for $1.08. The tax on these items amounts to 14¢. How much change should Harry get back if he gives the cashier a $10 bill?

2. A woman bought 3 items, one weighing 3 pounds, 7 ounces; the second weighing 4 pounds, 5 ounces; and the third weighing 6 pounds, 10 ounces. What was the total weight of the items in pounds and ounces?

3. What is the minimum number of coins (from 25¢, 10¢, 5¢, and 1¢ pieces) that would make $2.77?

4. How many feet of fencing are necessary to fence completely a rectangular yard 20 × 30 feet?

5. If a 4-pint bucket weighs 2 pounds and a pint of a certain chemical liquid weighs 1 pound 3 ounces, what is the weight of the bucket when it is full of the chemical liquid?

6. Mr. Smith drove from point A to point B in 2 hours. He drove back from point B to point A in 3 hours. If the distance from point A to point B is 100 miles, what is Mr. Smith's average speed for the entire trip?

7. A box of pencils can contain 20 dozen to 30 dozen pencils. If the largest box of pencils (with the greatest amount of pencils) costs $10.80, how much does the smallest box cost?

8. John has $250 in his bank account. If he makes a withdrawal of $13.73 and a deposit of $25.53, how much will he have in his bank account?

9. If 560 people are equally divided into 8 groups, and each group is equally divided into 7 sections, how many people are there in each section?

10. If metal A weighs between 40 kilograms per cubic meter and 50 kilograms per cubic meter, what is the greatest variation in weight of 10 cubic meters of metal A?

Answers to Practice Exercises in Verbal Problems

7-1

1. $7.58

2. 14 pounds, 6 ounces

3. 13 (11 quarters, 2 pennies)

4. 100 feet

5. 6 pounds, 12 ounces

6. 40 miles per hour

7. $7.20

8. $261.80

9. 10

10. 100 kilograms $(500 - 400 = 100)$

Part V
Complete Time-Saving Strategies and Shortcuts

Using Critical Thinking Skills
to Score High on the SAT

General Strategies for Taking the SAT

Before studying the fourteen specific strategies for the math questions (p. 250), you will find it useful to review the following five general strategies for taking the Math SAT.

Strategy 1:

Don't rush into getting an answer without thinking. Be careful if your answer comes too easily, especially if the question is toward the end of the section.

Beware of Choice A If You Get the Answer Fast or Without Really Thinking.

Everybody panics when they take an exam like the SAT. And what happens is that they rush into getting answers. That's OK, except that you have to think carefully. If a problem looks too easy, beware! And, especially beware of the Choice A answer. It's usually a "lure" choice for those who rush into getting an answer without critically thinking about it. Here's an example:

Below is a picture of a digital clock. The clock shows that the time is 6:06. Consider all the times on the clock where the hour digit is the same as the minute digit like in the clock shown below. Another such "double" time would be 8:08 or 9:09. What is the smallest time period between any two such doubles?

(A) 61 minutes
(B) 60 minutes
(C) 58 minutes
(D) 50 minutes
(E) 49 minutes

6:06

Did you subtract 7:07 from 8:08 and get 1 hour and 1 minute (61 minutes)? If you did you probably chose Choice A: the *lure* choice. Think—do you really believe that the test maker would give you such an easy question? The fact that you figured it out so easily and saw that Choice A was your answer should make you think twice. The thing you have to realize is that there is another possibility: 12:12 to 1:01 gives 49 minutes, and so Choice E is correct.

So, in summary, if you get the answer fast and without doing much thinking, and it's a Choice A answer, think again. You may have fallen for the Choice A lure.

Note: Choice A is often a lure choice for those who quickly get an answer without doing any real thinking. However, you should certainly realize that Choice A answers can occur, especially if there is no lure choice.

Strategy 2:

Know and learn the directions to the question types before you take the actual test.

Never Spend Time Reading Directions During the Test or Doing Sample Questions That Don't Count.

All SATs are standardized. For example, all the regular math questions have the same directions from test to test, as do the math grid-in questions. So it's a good idea to learn these sets of directions and familiarize yourself with their types of questions early in the game before you take your actual SAT.

For an example of a set of grid-in directions, see p. 252.

If on your actual test you spend time reading these directions and/or answering the sample question, you will waste valuable time.

Strategy 3:

It may be wiser not to leave an answer blank.

The Penalty for Guessing Is Much Smaller Than You Might Expect.

On the SAT you lose a percentage of points if you guess and get the wrong answer. Of course, you should always try to eliminate choices. You'll find that, after going through this book, you'll have a better chance of eliminating wrong answers. However, if you cannot eliminate any choice in a question and have no idea of how to arrive at an answer, you might want to pick any answer and go on to the next question.

There are two reasons for this:

1. You don't want to risk mismarking a future answer by leaving a previous answer blank.
2. Even though there is a penalty for guessing, the penalty is much smaller than you might expect, and this way you have at least a chance of getting the question right. Suppose, for example, that you have a five-choice question:

From a probabilistic point of view, it is very likely that you would get one choice right and four wrong (you have a 1-in-5 chance of getting a five-choice question right) if you randomly guess at the answers. Since $\frac{1}{4}$ point is taken off for each wrong five-choice question, you've gotten $1 - \frac{1}{4} \times 4 = 0$ points, because you've gotten 1 question right and 4 wrong. Thus you break even. So the moral is: whether you randomly guess at questions you're not sure of at all or whether you leave those question answers blank, it doesn't make a difference in the long run!

Strategy 4:

Write as much as you want in your test booklet.

Test Booklets Aren't Graded—So Use Them As You Would Scrap Paper.

Many students are afraid to mark up their test booklets. But, the booklets are not graded! Make any marks you want. In fact, some of the strategies demand that you extend or draw lines in geometry questions or label diagrams, or circle incorrect answers, etc. That's why when I see computer programs that show only the questions on a screen and prevent the student from marking a diagram or circling an answer, I realize that such programs prevent the student from using many powerful strategies. *So write all you want on your test booklet—use your test paper as you would scrap paper.*

Strategy 5:

Use your own coding system to tell you which questions to return to.

If You Have Extra Time after Completing a Test Section, You'll Know Exactly Which Questions Need More Attention.

When you are sure that you have answered a question correctly, mark your question paper with ✓. For questions you are not sure of but for which you have eliminated some of the choices, use **?**. For questions that you're not sure of at all or for which you have not been able to eliminate any choices, use **??**. This will give you a bird's-eye view of what questions you should return to, if you have time left after completing a particular test section.

Using Easy-to-Learn Strategies

14 Math Strategies

Critical thinking is the ability to think clearly in order to solve problems and answer questions of all types—SAT questions, for example, both math and verbal!

Educators who are deeply involved in research on critical thinking skills tell us that such skills are straightforward, practical, teachable, and learnable.

The 14 Math Strategies in this section are critical thinking skills. These strategies have the potential to raise your SAT scores dramatically— a realistic estimate is anywhere from approximately 50 points to 300 points in the math part of the test. Since each correct SAT question gives you an additional 10 points on average, it is reasonable to assume that if you can learn and then use these valuable SAT Math strategies, you can boost your SAT math scores phenomenally!

BE SURE TO LEARN AND USE THE STRATEGIES THAT FOLLOW!

How to Learn the Strategies

1. For each strategy, look at the heading describing the strategy.

2. Try to answer the first example without looking at the EXPLANATORY ANSWER.

3. Then look at the EXPLANATORY ANSWER, and if you got the right answer, see if the method described would enable you to solve the question in a better way with a faster approach.

4. Then try each of the next EXAMPLES without looking at the EXPLANATORY ANSWERS.

5. Use the same procedure as in (3) for each of the EXAMPLES.

Important Note on the Allowed Use of Calculators on the SAT

Although the use of calculators on the SAT I will be allowed, using a calculator may be sometimes more tedious, when in fact you can use another problem-solving method or shortcut. So you must be selective on when and when not to use a calculator on the test.

Here's an example of when a calculator should *not* be used:

$$\frac{2}{5} \times \frac{5}{6} \times \frac{6}{7} \times \frac{7}{8} \times \frac{8}{9} \times \frac{9}{10} \times \frac{10}{11} =$$

(A) $\frac{9}{11}$ (B) $\frac{2}{11}$ (C) $\frac{11}{36}$

(D) $\frac{10}{21}$ (E) $\frac{244}{360}$

Here, the use of a calculator may take some time. However, if you use the strategy of cancelling numerators and denominators as shown:

Cancel numerators/denominators:

$$\frac{2}{\cancel{5}} \times \frac{\cancel{5}}{\cancel{6}} \times \frac{\cancel{6}}{7} \times \frac{7}{8} \times \frac{8}{9} \times \frac{9}{\cancel{10}} \times \frac{\cancel{10}}{11} = \frac{2}{11}$$

You can see that the answer comes easily as $\frac{2}{11}$.

Later I will show you an example of the *grid-type* question where using a calculator will take longer to solve a problem than without using the calculator. Here's an example where using a calculator may get you the solution *as fast as* using a strategy without the calculator:

25 percent of 16 is equivalent to $\frac{1}{2}$ of what number?

(A) 2   (B) 4   (C) 8   (D) 16   (E) 32

Using a calculator, you'd use Math Strategy VIII (page 276) (translating *of* to *times* and *is* to *equals*), first calculating 25 percent of 16 to get 4. Then you'd say 4 = half of what number and you'd find that number to be 8.

Without using a calculator, you'd still use Math Strategy VIII, but you could write 25 percent as $\frac{1}{4}$, so you'd figure out that $\frac{1}{4} \times 16$ was (4). Then you'd call the number

you want to find x, and say $4 = \frac{1}{2}(x)$. You'd find $x = 8$.

Note that both methods, with and without a calculator, are about equally efficient; however, the technique in the second method can be used for many more problems and hones more thinking skills.

Important Note on Math Questions on the SAT

There are two types of math questions on the SAT.

1. The Regular Math Question (total of 44 counted questions), which has five choices. The strategies for these start on page 257.

2. The Grid-Type Math Question (total of 10 counted questions) is described below.

   Note: The grid-type questions can be solved using the Regular Math Strategies.

The Grid-Type Math Question

There will be 10 questions on the SAT where you will have to "grid" in your answer rather than choose from a set of five choices. Here are the directions to the "grid-type" question. Make sure that you understand these directions completely before you answer any of the grid-type questions.

Directions: For Student-Produced Response questions 9–18, use the grids at the bottom of the answer sheet page on which you have answered questions 1–8.

Each of the remaining 10 questions requires you to solve the problem and enter your answer by marking the circles in the special grid, as shown in the examples below. You may use any available space for scratchwork.

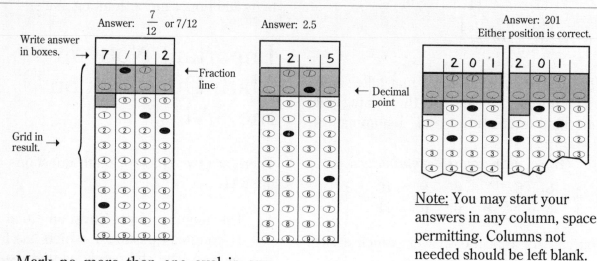

- Mark no more than one oval in any column.

- Because the answer sheet will be machine-scored, **you will receive credit only if the ovals are filled in correctly.**

- Although not required, it is suggested that you write your answer in the boxes at the top of the columns to help you fill in the ovals accurately.

- Some problems may have more than one correct answer. In such cases, grid only one answer.

- No question has a negative answer.

- **Mixed numbers** such as $2\frac{1}{2}$ must be gridded as 2.5 or 5/2. (If ⊡ is gridded, it will be interpreted as $\frac{21}{2}$, not $2\frac{1}{2}$.)

- *Decimal Accuracy:* If you obtain a decimal answer, **enter the most accurate value the grid will accommodate.** For example, if you obtain an answer such as 0.6666… , you should record the result as .666 or .667. **Less accurate values such as .66 or .67 are not acceptable.**

Acceptable ways to grid $\frac{2}{3}$ = .6666…

Practice with Grids

According to the directions on the previous page, grid the following values in the grids 1–15:

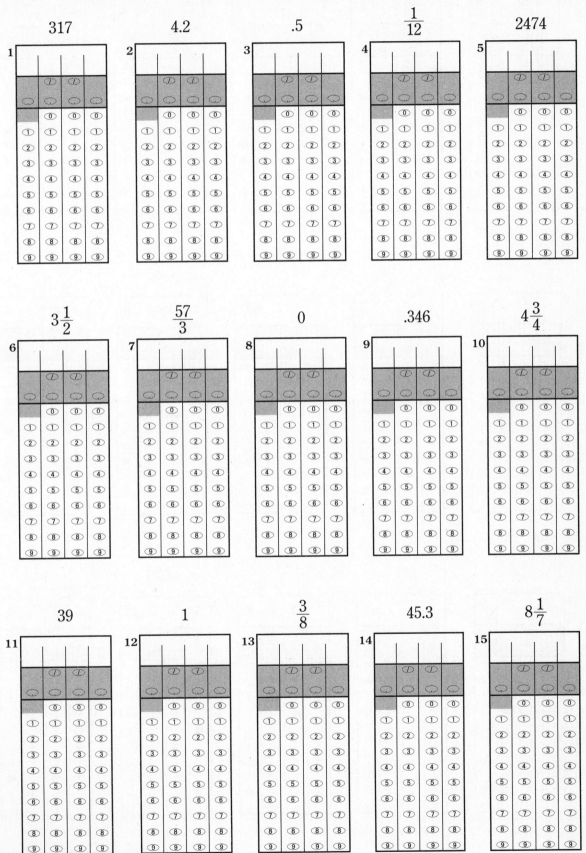

Answers

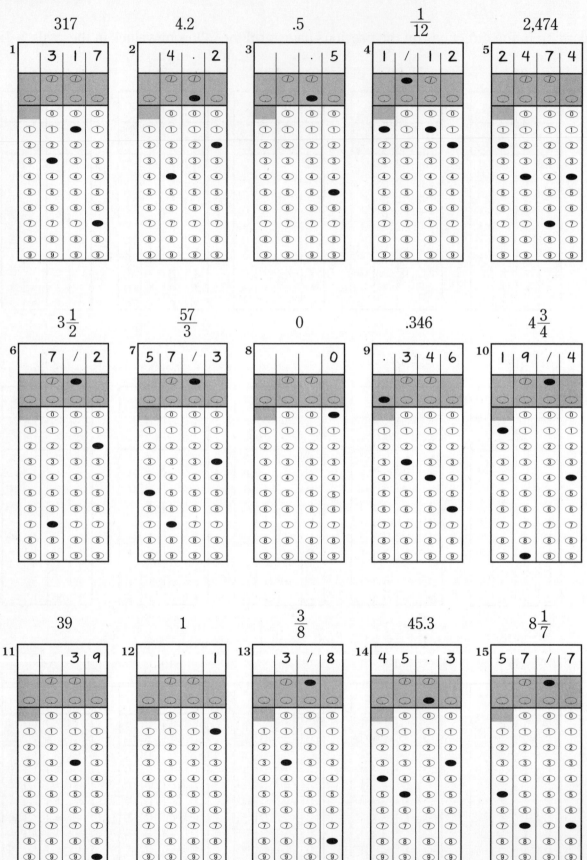

Use of a Calculator in the Grid-Type Question

In the following example, you can either use a calculator or not. However, the use of a calculator will require a different gridding.

Example:

If $\frac{2}{7} < x < \frac{3}{7}$, find one value of x.

Solution *without* a calculator:

Get some value between $\frac{2}{7}$ and $\frac{3}{7}$. Write

$\frac{2}{7} = \frac{4}{14}$ and $\frac{3}{7} = \frac{6}{14}$.

So we have $\frac{4}{14} < x < \frac{6}{14}$ and x can be $\frac{5}{14}$.

The grid will look like:

Solution *with* a calculator:

Calculate on calculator:

$$\frac{3}{7} = .4285714\ldots$$

$$\frac{2}{7} = .2857142\ldots$$

So $.2857142 < x < .4285714$.

You could have the grid as follows:

all the way to:

14 Time-Saving Strategies and Shortcuts for Answering the Math Questions on the SAT

What follows are 14 key strategies and approaches for solving math questions on the SAT. These approaches are necessary for short-cutting almost all of the questions on the SAT. It is very important that you understand how to use the methods described here, and understand how they are used in the examples presented, so that you may use these powerful techniques and shortcuts in the questions that you encounter on your SAT. You will probably find that the time it takes you to correctly solve the math problems (after you have worked on this section) may well be cut by a factor of 12.

Note: We have chosen some hard problems here so that you will be equipped to tackle the hardest SAT problems as well as the easiest.

IMPORTANT: It is wise for you to try to solve each example yourself, first. Then compare (after each example tried) your solution to the solution given below the example. When trying the example yourself, cover up the solution given in the book. Even though you might get the right answer or feel that you did the problem the right way, it will be useful for you to compare your solution with that in the book, as you may have missed important strategies and techniques that will facilitate solutions of many more problems.

I. Anticipating What Will Be Asked, and How to Set Up a Problem Rapidly, in Mathematical Terms

In most cases, you should be able to anticipate what is going to be asked in the problem.

EXAMPLE: $\frac{3}{4}$ of all the men at a meeting are married. There are 6 more married men than there are single men. How many men are there at the meeting?

(A) 6   (B) 8   (C) 10   (D) 12   (E) 14

SOLUTION: Here's the attack: In reading the first sentence, $\frac{3}{4}$ *of all the men at a meeting are married*, one should realize that a question will be asked relating to the number of men at the meeting (or relating to the number of married or single men at the meeting). Let's use the letter M for the total number of men, and the letter m for the number of married men. Then, the first sentence translates mathematically to

$$(1) \quad \frac{3}{4}M = m$$

Now we translate the second sentence into mathematical terms: *There are 6 more married men than there are single men*. Since $\frac{3}{4}$ of the total number of men are married, $\frac{1}{4}$ of the total must be single. Therefore the second sentence of the question translates mathematically as:

$$(2) \quad 6 + \frac{1}{4}M = m \text{ (since } \frac{1}{4}M = \text{number of single men)}$$

Reading the last sentence, we are asked to find the number of men, so we have to find the value of M.

Use equations (1) and (2) above:

$$(1) \quad \frac{3}{4}M = m \quad \text{and} \quad (2) \quad 6 + \frac{1}{4}M = m$$

Subtract to eliminate m and retain M:

$$\frac{3}{4}M = m$$
$$-\left(6 + \frac{1}{4}M = m\right)$$
$$\overline{\frac{3}{4}M - 6 - \frac{1}{4}M = m - m = 0}$$

or

$$\frac{2}{4}M - 6 = 0$$

$$\frac{2}{4}M = 6$$

$$2M = 24$$

$$M = 12.$$

Thus the correct answer is Choice D.

See Strategy VIII for a more detailed description of the Translation Strategy and for more problems relating to the Translation Strategy Technique (page 276).

In some problems, the question may look rather complicated to solve. However, there is usually a direct, rapid way to set up the solution to the problem.

EXAMPLE:

> There are 10 vacant seats on a train and all passengers are seated. The train stops at a place where the number of boarding passengers is 25% of those passengers on the train, and those boarding fill all the vacant seats. How many passenger seats are on the train?
> (A) 49   (B) 50   (C) 52   (D) 55   (E) 56

SOLUTION: Do not spend time trying to gather a lot of information from the first sentence of the question. Look at the second sentence: *the number of boarding passengers is 25% of those passengers on the train and those boarding fill all the vacant seats.* If the number boarding fill all the vacant seats, and there were 10 vacant seats to begin with, *there must be 10 boarding.* Now the number boarding (10) is given as 25% of those on the train. Calling the number of those previously on the train as x, we get

$$10 = 25\% \, x$$
$$10 = \frac{25}{100} x$$
$$10 = \frac{1}{4} x$$
$$40 = x$$

The number seated originally was 40 and since there were 10 vacant seats, the total number of seats on the train is $40 + 10 = 50$. Thus the correct answer is Choice B.

II. Spotting Key Words

Many examples require you to be aware of "key words" such as *average, maximum, minimum,* etc.

EXAMPLE:

> What is the average speed of a car traveling 70 miles per hour for the first two hours and 40 miles per hour for the next hour?
> (A) 30 mph   (B) 40 mph   (C) 50 mph
> (D) 60 mph   (E) 70 mph

SOLUTION: Here's the attack: Spot the keyword: AVERAGE. Now you had better know what the word *average* means. It means the *sum total divided by* the *sum of the entities*. For example, the average of 2 and 4 is 3 because:

$$2 + 4 = sum\ total\ (6)$$

and the *number of entities* is 2 (there are only *2* numbers, namely 2 and 4). Thus the *average* of 2 and 4 is

$$\text{Sum total} \rightarrow \frac{2+4}{2} = 3 \leftarrow \text{average}$$
$$\text{Number of entities}$$

Now let's get back to the original question. You should know that

$$\text{SPEED} = \frac{\text{DISTANCE}}{\text{TIME}}$$

so that *average speed* must be

$$\frac{\text{TOTAL DISTANCE}}{\text{TOTAL TIME}}$$

The car traveled 70 miles per hour in 2 hours, at first. So it went a distance of $70 \times 2 = 140$ miles. It then traveled 40 miles per hour in 1 hour, so it went a distance of $40 \times 1 = 40$ miles. The *total distance* traveled was then

$$140 + 40 = 180\ \text{miles}$$

The *total time* that the car traveled was
2 hours (at first) + 1 hour (next) = 3 hours (total)

Therefore, the *average speed* is

$$\frac{\text{TOTAL DISTANCE}}{\text{TOTAL TIME}} = \frac{180\ \text{miles}}{3\ \text{hours}} = 60\ \text{mph}$$

Thus Choice D is correct.

EXAMPLE:

> A plane travels at a rate of 70 miles per hour and flies 50 miles. It returns the same distance at a rate of 210 miles per hour. What is the average speed in miles per hour for the complete trip?
> (A) 140 (B) 280 (C) 105 (D) 115
> (E) It cannot be determined.

SOLUTION: Remember that the average rate means, from the previous problem:

$$\text{AVERAGE SPEED} = \frac{\text{TOTAL DISTANCE}}{\text{TOTAL TIME}}$$

First, let's find what the *total distance* is and what the *total time* is for the trip. The total distance is 50 miles going and 50 miles returning (50 + 50). Thus the total distance is *100 miles*. Now the total time is just the sum of the time going (call it t_G) and the time returning (call it t_R). So the total time is given as $t_G + t_R$. The average speed is then

$$\text{AVERAGE SPEED} = \frac{100}{t_G + t_R}$$

Now we'll proceed to find what t_G and t_R are.

Use RATE × TIME = DISTANCE for the trip going:

$$\text{Rate} = 70$$
$$\text{Time} = t_G$$
$$\text{Distance} = 50$$

So,

$$70 \times t_G = 50 \text{ and thus } t_G = \frac{50}{70}$$

Similarly for the return trip where rate × time = distance, we get

$$210 \times t_R = 50 \text{ and thus, } t_R = \frac{50}{210}$$

$$\text{Thus the total time} = t_G + t_R = \frac{50}{70} \quad \frac{50}{210}$$

The total distance = 50 + 50 = 100

So the average speed =

$$\frac{100}{\dfrac{50}{70}+\dfrac{50}{210}}=\frac{100}{\dfrac{150}{210}+\dfrac{50}{210}}=\frac{100}{\dfrac{200}{210}}=100\times\frac{210}{200}$$

$$=\frac{210}{2}=105$$

Thus Choice C is correct.

III. Making the Approach to a Problem as Simple as Possible

Sometimes there are many approaches to solving a problem. Obviously, on your exam, you will want to solve the problem in the simplest way because of the time factor involved.

EXAMPLE:

> An equilateral triangle is inscribed in a circle. Another circle is inscribed in the equilateral triangle. What is the ratio of the radius of the larger circle to the radius of the smaller circle?
> (A) 2 : 1   (B) 3 : 1   (C) 4 : 1   (D) $2\sqrt{2}$: 1
> (E) It cannot be determined.

SOLUTION: Here's the attack:

1.   Draw the diagram as close to scale as possible:

2.   Now draw the radii of the two circles. Be very careful, though. Since the equilateral triangle determines the relative size of the two circles, you must somehow link the radius of each circle to the equilateral triangle. That is, you should relate the radius of each circle to the equilateral triangle. Draw the radius as follows (R_2 is the larger radius and R_1 is the smaller radius): Each radius should touch some part of the equilateral triangle.

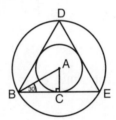

3. Since we have drawn the diagram pretty much to scale, you can get a good idea of the angles and symmetries involved. For example, in the diagram below, you can see that line *AB* bisects angle *DBE*, and since angle *DBE* = 60° (triangle *DBE* is an equilateral triangle with all angles 60°), angle *ABC* = 30°. Now angle *BCA* pretty much looks like a right angle (90°), which it is. Thus the remaining angle of the triangle *ABC* must be 60°, since the sum of the interior angles of any triangle is 180°. You should be familiar with the fact that in a 30°-60°-90° triangle, the longest side is twice the shortest side. Therefore *AB* = 2*AC*, and the ratio of the large radius to that of the small radius is 2 : 1. Choice A is therefore correct.

EXAMPLE: What is the least integral value of *y* for which

$$\left|\frac{y}{3} - \frac{3}{8}\right| = \frac{y}{3} - \frac{3}{8}?$$

(A) 0
(B) 1
(C) 2
(D) 3
(E) 4

SOLUTION: The first thing to notice is that the value in the quantity on the left side of the equation must be greater or equal to 0 because of the absolute value sign.

Thus

$$\left|\frac{y}{3}-\frac{3}{8}\right|=\frac{y}{3}-\frac{3}{8}\geqq 0$$

So

$$\frac{y}{3}-\frac{3}{8}\geqq 0$$

Adding $\frac{3}{8}$ to both sides of the inequality, we get

$$\frac{y}{3}\geqq\frac{3}{8}$$

Multiplying both sides of the inequality by 3, we get

$$y\geqq\frac{9}{8}$$

So the least integral value of y is 2.

EXAMPLE:

> Given: $c > d$, $a > b$, $e > c$, $b > c$, $a > e$. For which two quantities can one *not* establish a relationship?
> (A) a and d (B) a and c (C) e and d (D) b and d
> (E) e and b

SOLUTION: First write the inequalities in a vertical line:

$c > d$
$a > b$
$e > c$
$b > c$
$a > e$

Now consolidate them as follows:

$c > d$
$a > b\ (> c)$ Make sure that you now cross
$e > c$ out $b > c$, since you consolidated
$\widebar{b > c}$ it into $a > b > c$.
$a > e$

We can further consolidate:

$c > d$ Make sure that you cross out
$a > b > c$ $a > e$, since you consolidated it
$(a > e) > c$ into $a > e > c$.
$a > e$

Thus we are left with:

$c > d$
$a > b > c$
$a > e > c$

We can now consolidate further:

Since $c > d$, we get:
$a > b > c > d$
$a > e > c > d$

We can see from this that b is between a and c, and e is between a and c. But we have no way of telling whether b is greater than e, whether b is less than e, or whether b is equal to e. Thus there is no relationship between b and e. Choice E is correct.

IV. Problems Necessitating Shortcuts

Sometimes you are given a question that you think will take you a long time to solve. The chances are that there is a shortcut that you can employ for the solution of the problem.

EXAMPLE:

> The product of four consecutive integers is given by $n^4 + 6n^3 + 11n^2 + 6n$, where n is denoted as the first integer. Find the product of 201, 202, 203, and 204.
> (A) 1,681,410,024 (B) 1,681,410,025 (C) 1,681,400,200
> (D) 1,681,410,020 (E) 1,681,410,029

SOLUTION:
It would certainly be foolish to multiply $201 \times 202 \times 203 \times 204$ even with a calculator. It would also be equally foolish to substitute $n = 201$ in the formula given: $n^4 + 6n^3 + 11n^2 + 6n$. You should realize that there must be a shorter way of doing this problem. Just multiply the units digits of 201, 202, 203, 204 to get $1 \times 2 \times 3 \times 4 = 24$. Thus the last digit in our answer is 4. The only choice that satisfies this is Choice A.

<u>Another method:</u> You should be aware that a number that is the product of *four* consecutive integers must be exactly divisible by both 2 and 3, since one of the integers must be a multiple of three and another integer must be a multiple of two. Now look at the choices. Choice B

must be incorrect, since the number is not evenly divisible by 2: it has a 5 at the end of it. Choices C and D are incorrect because a number ending in 0 cannot be divisible by 3. Choice E is incorrect because a number ending in 9 cannot be evenly divisible by 2. The only remaining choice is Choice A. Therefore Choice A must be the right one.

EXAMPLE:

Which is true, assuming that $a > 0$, $b > 0$, $c > 0$, and $a > b$?

(A) $\dfrac{a+c}{b+c} = \dfrac{a}{b}$

(B) $\dfrac{a+c}{b+c} < \dfrac{a}{b}$

(C) $\dfrac{a+c}{b+c} > \dfrac{a}{b}$

(D) $\dfrac{a+c}{b+c} = 1$

(E) Depending on the value of c,

$$\dfrac{a+c}{b+c} > \dfrac{a}{b} \text{ or } \dfrac{a+c}{b+c} < \dfrac{a}{b}$$

SOLUTION:

You might try to substitute numbers for a, b, and c in the above example. There is, however, an easier and more general approach that should be used. Let's first review the shortcut for comparing two fractions.

Suppose you wanted to compare (find out which is greater of) the fractions.

$$\dfrac{3}{7} \text{ with } \dfrac{7}{16}$$

You'd cross multiply the 16 with the 3 and put the answer (48) below the first fraction $\left(\dfrac{3}{7}\right)$:

Multiply

$$\dfrac{3}{7} \xleftarrow{\quad} \dfrac{7}{16}$$

48

Then you'd cross multiply the 7 with the 7 and put the answer (49) under the second fraction $\left(\dfrac{7}{16}\right)$:

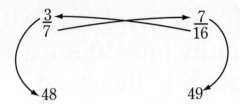

Now for whichever number is greater (48 or 49), the fraction above that number is greater. Thus

$$\frac{7}{16} > \frac{3}{7}$$

Now let's look at our example. We are really trying to compare

$$\frac{a+c}{b+c} \text{ with } \frac{a}{b}$$

We follow the above shortcut procedure. After all, we are still comparing two fractions.

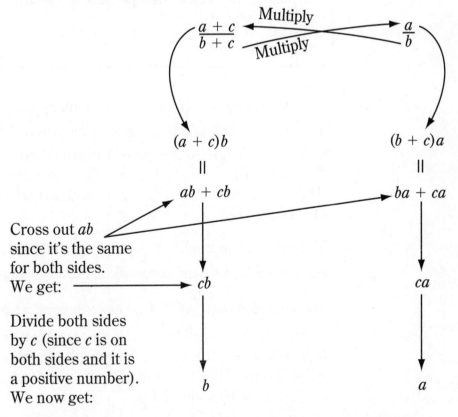

Cross out ab since it's the same for both sides. We get:

Divide both sides by c (since c is on both sides and it is a positive number). We now get:

Now remember we were given that $a > b$, so that the quantity *vertically above* a *must be greater than the quantity vertically above* b from the shortcut method of comparing fractions. Therefore,

$$\frac{a}{b} > \frac{a+c}{b+c}$$

And so Choice B is correct.

V. Problems Involving an Unknown Quantity but Where a Definite Solution Is Required

Many problems test whether you know how to obtain a definite answer if you are given an unknown quantity.

EXAMPLE:

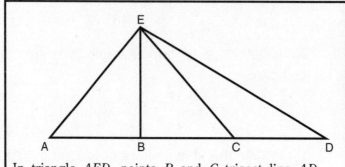

In triangle *AED*, points *B* and *C* trisect line *AD*. The ratio of the area of triangle *AEB* to the area of triangle *AED* is

(A) 3:4 (B) 2:3 (C) 1:3 (D) 1:2
(E) indeterminable

SOLUTION: As soon as you see the word *area*, remember what *area* is. The area of a triangle is given as $\frac{1}{2}bh$, where *b* is the base and *h* is the height to that base. You are asked to determine the ratio of the area of triangle *AEB* to the area of triangle *AED*. So we must find the area of triangle *AEB* and the area of triangle *AED*.

The area of triangle $AEB = \frac{1}{2}$ base × height, where the *base* is *AB* and the *height* is the perpendicular distance from *E* to *AD*.

The area of triangle $AED = \frac{1}{2}$ base × height, where the base = *AD* (which is equal to 3 × *AB*, since *AD* is trisected). The height, *h*, is also the same perpendicular distance from *E* to *AD* as before. Thus the ratio of the area of the triangle *AEB* to the area of triangle *AED* =

$$\frac{\frac{1}{2}(AB)h}{\frac{1}{2}(AB)h} = \frac{1}{3}$$

Notice that the $\frac{1}{2}$s cancel, the *AB*s cancel, and the *h*es cancel, and we are left with $\left(\frac{1}{3}\right)$, which can be represented as 1:3 (Choice C).

Though h and AB were unknown quantities, both of these quantities canceled in the final answer.

EXAMPLE:

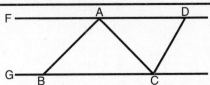

In the diagram above, the lines F and G are parallel, the area of triangle ABC = 10, and the area of triangle ADC = 8. What is the value of $\dfrac{\text{length } AD}{\text{length } BC}$?

(A) $\dfrac{4}{5}$ (B) $\dfrac{5}{4}$ (C) $\dfrac{8}{9}$ (C) $\dfrac{9}{8}$

(E) It cannot be determined.

SOLUTION: Let us relate the area of the triangles (given) to the lengths of the sides AD and BC. Now, what is the area of any triangle? Remember, it's $\dfrac{1}{2}$ the product of the side and the altitude to that side. That is, where s is the side and h is the altitude to that side, the area of the triangle is $A = \dfrac{1}{2}sh$. Let's draw the altitudes to the sides in question, AD and BC:

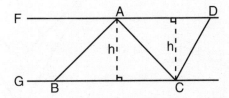

Notice that the altitude, h, is the same for both triangles, because the lines F and G are parallel (a rectangle is formed). Thus the area of triangle $ABC = \dfrac{1}{2}hBC$ and the area of triangle $ACD = \dfrac{1}{2}hAD$. Since we were given that these areas respectively are 10 and 8, we get:

$$\text{Area of triangle } ACD \;=\; 8 = \frac{1}{2}hAD$$

$$\text{Area of triangle } ABC = 10 = \frac{1}{2}hBC$$

Dividing (equals divided by equals are equal):

$$\frac{\text{Area of triangle } ACD}{\text{Area of triangle } ABC} = \frac{8}{10} = \frac{\dfrac{1}{2}hAD}{\dfrac{1}{2}hBC}$$

Cancelling the *h*es and the $\frac{1}{2}$s from the right side, we get

$$\frac{8}{10} = \frac{AD}{BC}$$

$$\frac{8}{10} = \frac{4}{5}$$

$\dfrac{AD}{BC} = \dfrac{4}{5}$, and thus Choice A is correct. Notice that we didn't

have to know what the value of *h* was.

VI. Problems Involving the Completion of a Diagram or Drawing of Additional Lines

There is a group of problems that must be solved by completing a diagram or drawing something in a given diagram that will enable you to readily solve the problem.

EXAMPLE:

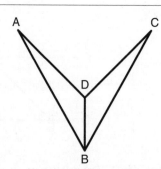

Two triangles above are connected by line *DB*. *AB = BC* = 10. Angle *ABD* = angle *DBC* = 30°, and angle *ADC* = 90°. Side *DC* is equal to

(A) $\sqrt{50}$　(B) 10　(C) 5　(D) 8　(E) $\dfrac{5}{\sqrt{2}}$

SOLUTION:　Connect *A* and *C* by a line.

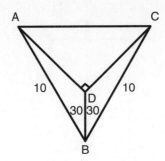

Now, because triangles *ABD* and *BDC* are congruent, angle *A* = angle *C*. Since angle *B* = 60° (because 30° + 30° = 60°), angle *A* = angle *C* = 60° (the sum of the interior angles of a triangle is 180°). Now, since all angles of the triangle are 60°, we have an equilateral triangle (all sides of the triangle being equal). Therefore, *AB* = *CB* = *AC* = 10.

Now, since we want to find *DC*, call *DC* = *x*. We want to relate *x* with *AC*. Since angle *ADC* = 90°, by the Pythagorean Theorem, $x^2 + (AD)^2 = (AC)^2$. But it is obvious that *AD* = *x*, and since *AC* = 10, we get $x^2 + x^2 = 10^2$. Or $2x^2 = 10^2$ and

$$x^2 = \frac{10^2}{2} = \frac{100}{2} = 50$$

Thus $x = \sqrt{50}$, and Choice A is correct.

EXAMPLE: The flat lawn described below is to be mowed. How many square feet of lawn must be mowed for the lawn to be completely mowed?
(A) 4000   (B) 4500   (C) 5000   (D) 5500
(E) This cannot be determined unless the value of *x* is given.

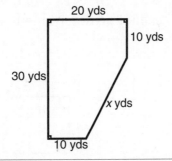

SOLUTION: First convert yards to feet by multiplying yards by 3. Then divide the plot of land given into 3 rectangles and 1 triangle. Now, since rectangles have opposite equal sides, the following is true:

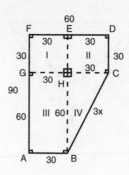

Since $AB = 30$, $FE = 30$.

Now, since $FE = 30$, and $FD = 60$, ED must be 30.

Therefore, because $EDCH$ is a rectangle and $ED = 30$, $HC = 30$.

Since $DC = 30$, $FG = 30$, because $FDCG$ is a rectangle.

Since $FA = 90$, and $FG = 30$, GA must be 60.

Since $GA = 60$, $HB = 60$, because $GHBA$ is a rectangle.

The area of the whole lawn is the sum of the areas of the figures I, II, III, and IV.

The area of I (rectangle) $= 30 \times 30 = 900$.

The area of II (rectangle) $= 30 \times 30 = 900$.

The area of III (rectangle) $= 60 \times 30 = 1800$.

The area of IV (triangle) $= \frac{1}{2}(30)(60) = 900$.

The sum of all the areas $= 4500$, so the correct answer is Choice B.

EXAMPLE:

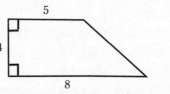

In the diagram above, the perimeter of the quadrilateral
(A) is 21   (B) is 22   (C) is 23   (D) is 24
(E) cannot be determined

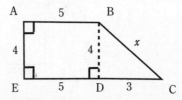

In order to find the perimeter, we must find all the sides. So *drop* a perpendicular line from B to side EC, as shown above and then *label sides* with $BC = x$.

Notice that you have thus created a parallelogram, *ABDE*.

Thus $ED = AB = 5$. Since $EC = 8$ (given), and $ED = 5$, *DC must be 3*. Now $AE = BD$ (because *ABDE* is a parallelogram), so $AE = 4 = BD$. Triangle *BDC* is a right triangle with sides 3 and 4. Call side $BC = x$.

Then
$3^2 + 4^2 = x^2$ (Pythagorean Theorem)
$$25 = x^2$$
$$5 = x$$

Thus the perimeter is
$4 + 5 + 8 + 5 = 22$
Choice B is correct.

VII. Problems Where Solutions for All Unknowns Are Not Necessary

Sometimes you are presented with a problem that involves more than one unknown. And it may seem that in order to solve the problem, you have to solve for *both* unknowns. However, it is not always necessary to do so.

EXAMPLE:

If $\dfrac{xy}{x-y} = 10$ and $\dfrac{x+y}{xy} = \dfrac{1}{20}$, find the value of

$$\frac{\dfrac{1}{x}+\dfrac{1}{y}}{\dfrac{1}{x}-\dfrac{1}{y}}$$

(A) $+\dfrac{1}{2}$ (B) $-\dfrac{1}{2}$ (C) $+\dfrac{1}{4}$ (D) $-\dfrac{1}{4}$ (E) $+1$

SOLUTION: There is no need to find what x is and what y is to evaluate the quantity above. First we add the numerator of the quantity:

$$\frac{1}{x} - \frac{1}{y} = \frac{y+x}{xy}$$

See Section 2-8 in Part IV to determine the steps to this shortcut method for adding fractions.

Now we add the denominator:

$$\frac{1}{x} - \frac{1}{y} = \frac{y-x}{xy}$$

Therefore,

$$\frac{\dfrac{1}{x} + \dfrac{1}{y}}{\dfrac{1}{x} - \dfrac{1}{y}} = \frac{\dfrac{y+x}{xy}}{\dfrac{y-x}{xy}} = \frac{\dfrac{1}{20}}{-\dfrac{1}{10}}$$

$$= \frac{-10}{20} = -\frac{1}{2}$$

$$\left[\text{Note that } \frac{y-x}{xy} = -\left(\frac{x-y}{xy}\right) \right]$$

Therefore Choice B is correct.

EXAMPLE:

> If $x^2 + xy + y^2 = p$ and $x^2 - xy + y^2 = q$, find $(x-y)^2$ in terms of p and q.
>
> (A) $\dfrac{p-3q}{2}$ (B) $\dfrac{p-q}{2}$ (C) $2-3p$
>
> (D) $\dfrac{3q-p}{2}$ (E) $p-q$

SOLUTION: First write $(x-y)^2 = x^2 - 2xy + y^2$. (Remember that relation?)

Now we have two equations to work with:

$$(1)\ x^2 + xy + y^2 = p$$

and

$$(2)\ x^2 - xy + y^2 = q$$

Since $(x-y)^2 = x^2 - 2xy + y^2$, you should realize from equations (1) and (2) above that by some manipulation we can find what $x^2 + y^2$ is and what $2xy$ is, which then will enable us to evaluate $(x-y)^2$.

Let's first simply *add* equations (1) and (2).

$$
\begin{array}{rl}
(1) & x^2 + xy + y^2 = p \\
(2) & +(x^2 - xy + y^2 = q) \\
\hline
& 2x^2 + 0 + 2y^2 = p + q
\end{array}
$$

We can do this because equals added to equals are always equal. Therefore we find that

$$2x^2 + 2y^2 = p + q$$

and from this we can get (by dividing both sides by 2):

$$(3)\ x^2 + y^2 = \frac{p+q}{2}$$

Now let's *subtract* equations (1) and (2):

$$(1) \quad x^2 + xy + y^2 = p$$
$$(2)\ -(x^2 - xy + y^2 = q)$$
$$x^2 + xy + y^2 - x^2 - (-xy) - y^2 = p - q$$
$$= xy + xy = 2xy = p - q$$

Thus we find that

$$(4)\ 2xy = p - q$$

Using equations (3) and (4) we have:

$$(x - y)^2 = x^2 - 2xy + y^2 = x^2 + y^2 - 2xy$$
$$= \frac{p+q}{2} - (p - q)$$
$$= \frac{p+q}{2} - \frac{2(p-q)}{2}$$
$$= \frac{p + q - 2p + 2q}{2}$$
$$= \frac{3q - p}{2}$$

Choice D is the correct answer.

EXAMPLE:

If $(a + b)^2 = 20$ and $ab = -3$, then $a^2 + b^2 =$

(A) 14   (B) 20   (C) 26   (D) 32   (E) 38

SOLUTION:

Use $(a + b)^2 = a^2 + 2ab + b^2 = 20$ (equation (2))

$ab = -3$

So, $2ab = -6$

Substitute $2ab = -6$ in:
$a^2 + 2ab + b^2 = 20$
We get:

$$a^2 - 6 + b^2 = 20$$
$$a^2 + b^2 = 26$$

Choice C is correct.

VIII. Problems That Require You to Carefully Translate Words into Mathematical Terms

USE THE "TRANSLATION TECHNIQUE" ON VERBAL PROBLEMS TO TURN WORDS INTO MATH SYMBOLS.

A verbal problem is simply a question in which you must translate words into mathematical terms. Many students have difficulty with such problems. Here's a way to make them quite simple and direct. If you master this technique, you should be able to do more verbal problems almost mechanically, with very little anxiety and brain-racking. We call this the **Translation Technique.**

Many people have difficulty with verbal or word problems, like the upcoming one. It is always best to *translate* what is stated verbally to math symbols.

What percent of 3 is 15?

Here's the rule for translating:

What becomes x
percent becomes $\dfrac{}{100}$
of becomes   (times)
is becomes   (equals)

Pictorially,

What   percent   of   3   is   15?

x $\overline{100}$ $\times$ 3 $=$ 15

We get:

$$\frac{x}{100} \times 3 = 15$$

Multiplying by 100, we get

$$x \times 3 = 15 \times 100 = 1500$$

Simplifying,

$$x = \frac{1500}{3} = 500$$

And so we obtain $x = 500$, and our answer is 500%.

Here's another example like the last one:

5 is what percent of 20?

Remember,

> *is* becomes = (equals)
> *of* becomes × (times)
> *what* becomes x
> *percent* becomes $\overline{100}$

Pictorially,

5   is   what   percent   of   20?
↓   ↓   ↓   ↓   ↓   ↓
5   = x $\overline{100}$ ×   20

We get:

$$5 = \frac{x}{100} \times 20$$

Multiplying by 100, we get

$$5 = x \times \frac{20}{100} = x \times \frac{1}{5}$$

And so we obtain $x = 25$, and our answer is then 25%.

You will find that by always translating *is* to =, *what* to *x*, *of* to *times* (×), etc., you will be able to solve many more verbal (word) math problems faster, and without exhaustive thinking.

Here's another problem:

John is three times as old as Paul, and Paul is two years older than Sam. If Sam is y years old, find an expression for the age of John:

(A) $6 - 3y$ (B) $6 + 3y$ (C) $3y + 2$ (D) $3y - 2$ (E) $3y - 6$

SOLUTION:

The key thing to remember about verbal problems is to translate the *key words*:

> *is* becomes $=$ (equals)
> *of* becomes $\times$ (times)
> *more than, older than,* etc. become $+$ (plus)
> *less than, younger than,* etc. become $-$ (minus)
> *percent* becomes $\overline{100}$
> *what* becomes x, y, etc.

So let's look at the first part of the question:

"John is three times as old as Paul…"

This translates (with John $= J$, and $P =$ Paul) as

1. $J = 3 \times P$

The next part, "and Paul is two years older than Sam…" is translated as (Let $S =$ Sam or Sam's age):

2. $P = 2 + S$

Now look at the second sentence: "If Sam is y years old, find an expression for the age of John." We translate this as:

$S = y$

Now substitute $S = y$ into Equation 2 above:

We get: $P = 2 + y$. Now substitute $P = 2 + y$ into Equation 1. We get:

$$J = 3 \times P = 3 \times (2 + y) = 3 \times 2 + 3 \times y$$

$$= 6 + 3y$$

Thus, Choice B is correct.

Here's another typical and very tricky problem of this kind:

Bill bought 4 times as many apples as Harry and 3 times as many apples as Martin. If Bill, Harry, and Martin purchased less than a total of 190 apples, what is the greatest number of apples that Bill could have purchased?
(A) 168 (B) 120 (C) 119 (D) 108 (E) 90

SOLUTION:

Translate: The number of apples that Bill bought = B
The number of apples that Harry bought = H
The number of apples that Martin bought = M

The phrase "Bill bought 4 times as many apples as Harry" is translated to:

1. $B = 4 \times H$

The phrase "...and three times as many apples as Martin" is translated to:

2. $B = 3 \times M$

The phrase "If Bill, Harry, and Martin purchased less than a total of 190 apples..." is translated to:

3. $B + H + M < 190$

Now, the question asks for the greatest number of apples that Bill could have purchased. Translated, it asks for the *maximum value of the variable* B. So let's just get some equation involving B and get rid of the H and the M. We can do this by substituting what H is in terms of B and what M is in terms of B in Equation 3.

That is, from Equation 1 we have: $B = 4H$ or $\dfrac{B}{4} = H$, and from Equation 2 we have $B = 3M$ or $\dfrac{B}{3} = M$.

Now look at Equation 3: $B + H + M < 190$. Substitute $\dfrac{B}{4} = H$ and $\dfrac{B}{3} = M$.

$$B + \frac{B}{4} + \frac{B}{3} < 190$$

Factor: $B\left(1 + \dfrac{1}{4} + \dfrac{1}{3}\right) < 190$

or $B\left(\dfrac{12}{12} + \dfrac{3}{12} + \dfrac{4}{12}\right) < 190$

$$B\left(\frac{19}{12}\right) < 190$$

Get the B alone (multiply both sides of the inequality by 12 and divide by 19):

$$B < 190 \times \frac{12}{19}; \text{ so } B < 120$$

You might think the answer is Choice C: 119. But $\frac{B}{4} = H$ and $\frac{B}{3} = M$, so $B \neq 119$, since $\frac{B}{4}$ and $\frac{B}{3}$ must be integers. So B must be exactly divisible by 12, and thus the greatest value of $B = 12 \times 9 = 108$ (Choice D).

Thus, the answer is Choice D.

Remember, many word problems are easy if you can immediately translate the words into mathematical symbols and then work directly with the symbols.

Here's a difficult example that's easier if you use the strategy:

The retail price of a certain item is 50% greater than the wholesale price. The wholesale price is 20% greater than the manufacturer's cost. What percentage of the retail price is the manufacturer's cost?

(A) 54%   (B) 46%   (C) $55\frac{5}{9}$%   (D) $44\frac{4}{9}$%   (E) 45%

SOLUTION: First translate into mathematical terms what the first sentence means: *The retail price of a certain item is 50% greater than the wholesale price.*

Call the retail price R.
Call the wholesale price W.

50% greater than the wholesale price means 50% of the wholesale price + the wholesale price. Mathematically, this translates to

$$50\% \; W + W$$

The word *is* in the first sentence means *equals,* so we get

$$50\% \; W + W = R$$

$50\% = \dfrac{50}{100}$; therefore, $50\%W$ must mean $\dfrac{50}{100} \times W$

Thus the first sentence is translated mathematically into

$$(1) \quad R = \frac{50}{100}W + W$$

Now let's translate the second sentence of the question into mathematical terms: *The wholesale price is 20% greater than the manufacturer's cost.*

Call M the manufacturer's cost.

Then using the same reasoning as before, we get

$$W = 20\% \, M + M$$

$$(2) \quad W = \frac{20}{100}M + M$$

Now let's translate the third sentence into mathematical terms. *What percentage of the retail price is the manufacturer's cost?*

This means what is the value of

$$\frac{M}{R} \times 100?$$

Let's first simplify equation (1):

$$R = \frac{50}{100}W + W = \frac{1}{2}W + W = \frac{3}{2}W; \text{ so } R = \frac{3}{2}W$$

Let's simplify equation (2):

$$W = \frac{20}{100}M + M = \frac{1}{5}M + M = \frac{6}{5}M; \text{ so } W = \frac{6}{3}M$$

Now we have two simplified equations:

$$(1) \quad R = \frac{3}{2}W \quad \text{and} \quad (2) \quad W = \frac{6}{5}M$$

Let's get rid of the W, since we want to find the value of $\dfrac{M}{R}$.

We can do this by substituting $W = \dfrac{6}{5}M$ into the equation $R = \dfrac{3}{2}W$:

$$R = \frac{3}{2}\left(\frac{6}{5}M\right)$$

Therefore

$$R = \frac{18}{10}M$$

and

$$\frac{M}{R} = \frac{10}{18}$$

Thus

$$\frac{M}{R} \times 100 = \frac{5}{9} \times 100$$

Now let's look at the choices. Since $\dfrac{5}{9}$ is greater than $\dfrac{1}{2}$, Choices B, D, and E are incorrect since all those choices represent numbers less than $\dfrac{1}{2}$ (less than 50%). Choice A cannot be correct, because it doesn't look like $\dfrac{5}{9} \times 100$ is an even or whole number. Thus by elimination, Choice C must be correct. Of course, you could have multiplied 5×100 and divided by 9 to get the exact answer, $55\dfrac{5}{9}$, but this would have taken longer.

EXAMPLE:

> For a three-year period, the cost of living rose 25%, while in that same period Mr. Jenkins' wages increased 30%. What was the percent of increase in Mr. Jenkins' wages, relative to the new cost of living?
>
> (A) 5%   (B) 7%   C) 4%   (D) $7\dfrac{1}{2}$%   (E) $2\dfrac{1}{2}$%

SOLUTION: This is a tricky question. The first thing to do is to assign a particular *original salary* to Mr. Jenkins. Let's make it a simple $10,000. Therefore, if Mr. Jenkins' wages increased 30%, his final wages are given by

$$10,000 + 30\% \times 10,000 = 10,000 + \frac{30}{100} \times 10,000$$
$$= 10,000 \quad 3,000$$
$$= 13,000 \,(\text{dollars})$$

But since the cost of living increased 25%, the amount that his original $10,000 could buy *before* the three-year period is what

$$10,000 + 25\% \times 10,000 \,(\text{dollars})$$

could buy *after* the three-year period. This amount comes to

$$10,000 + \frac{25}{100} \times 10,000 = 10,000 + 2,500$$
$$= 12,500 \,(\text{dollars})$$

And this ($12,500) is the *new cost of living*. Now the question asks what is the *percent of increase in Mr. Jenkins' wages, relative to the new cost of living*.

First we calculate Mr. Jenkins' *increase in wages, relative to the new cost of living*:

$13,000 (final wages) − $12,500 (new cost of living)

This comes out to $500 (13,000 − 12,500).

The *percent* increase in wages *relative to the new cost of living* is translated mathematically to

$$\frac{\text{Increase}}{\text{New Cost of Living}} \frac{\$500}{\$12,500} \times 100 = \frac{1}{25} \times 100 = 4\%$$

Thus the correct answer is Choice C.

IX. Problems That Require You to Draw Mathematical Diagrams Representing What Is Being Presented

Many problems require you to represent what is being given in the form of a diagram, as in Strategy III.

EXAMPLE:

A satellite is traveling in a circle about the earth, at all times, at a height h from the surface of the earth. What is the total circular distance that the satellite travels in one revolution, if the circumference of the earth is C? (Assume the earth to be perfectly round.)

(A) $2\pi h$ (B) C (C) $C + 2\pi h$ (D) $C - 2\pi h$
(E) $2\pi hC + C$

SOLUTION:

Here we must draw two circles, one for the earth and one for the satellite:

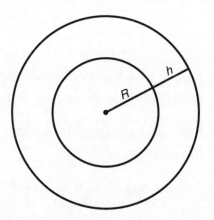

Call the radius of the earth R. The height of the satellite from the surface of the earth can be denoted by h. Note that the radius of the larger circle is now $R + h$. Now the problem requires us to find the *circumference* of the larger circle. Call it X. Therefore relating circumference to radius, we get

$$C = 2\pi R$$

for the small circle (the earth), and

$$X = 2\pi (R + h)$$

for the larger circle.

Expanding $X = 2\pi(R + h)$, we get

$$X = 2\pi R + 2\pi h$$

Since $C = 2\pi R$, we can see that

$$X = C + 2\pi h$$

and Choice C is correct.

EXAMPLE:

> A rectangular lawn is 20 feet by 30 feet. A rectangular plot (call it A) can be used for a play area in the lawn, where one side of the plot is exactly the *width* of the lawn. Another rectangular plot (call it B) can also be used as a play area, where one side of that plot is exactly the *length* of the lawn. What is the difference in perimeters (in feet) of the two plots if the area of plot A = area of plot B $= \dfrac{2}{3}$ the area of the lawn?
>
> (A) 5   (B) $6\dfrac{1}{3}$ (C) $3\dfrac{1}{2}$ (D) $6\dfrac{1}{4}$ (E) $6\dfrac{2}{3}$

SOLUTION: Here we draw two diagrams, one for Plot A and the other for Plot B. For Plot A, one side of the plot is exactly the *width* of the original lawn, so we can draw the plot as follows. (Here we call the length of plot A, *L*, and the width is 20, since that is the width of the lawn.)

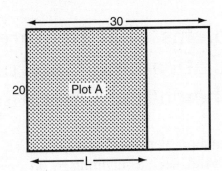

For Plot B, one side is exactly the *length* of the original lawn, so we can draw Plot B as follows. (Call the width of plot B *W*, and the length is 30, since that is the length of the lawn.)

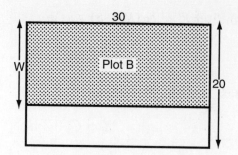

Since the area of both plots A and B are equal, and equal to $\frac{2}{3}$ the area of the original lawn, we get:

$$\text{Area of A} = 20 \times L = \text{Area of B} = W \times 30$$

$$\frac{2}{3}(20)(30)$$

Thus,

$$20L = 30W = 400$$

Solving for L, we get: $L = \dfrac{400}{20} = 20$, and solving for W, we get, $W = \dfrac{400}{30} = 13\frac{1}{3}$. The perimeter of A $= 20 + 20 + 20 + 20 = 80$ and the perimeter of B $= 30 + 30 + 13\frac{1}{3} + 13\frac{1}{3} = 86\frac{2}{3}$.

Therefore the difference in perimeters is $86\frac{2}{3} - 80 = 6\frac{2}{3}$. Choice E is correct.

X. Problems That Require You to Be Critical and Careful with the Mathematical Operations You Perform

Many times in a problem, you may perform a mathematical operation that is not always valid, such as dividing by 0.

EXAMPLE:

If $2x^2y = 2xy^2$, then which is true for all values of x and y?

(A) $x = y$ (B) $x = 2y$ (C) $y = 2x$ (D) $x = 0, y = 0$
(E) none of the above

SOLUTION: First we divide both sides of the equality by 2. We obtain:

$$x^2 y = xy^2$$

Next we divide both sides of the equation by common variables, x and y.

$$\frac{x^2 y}{xy} = \frac{xy^2}{xy}$$

Thus we obtain:

$$x = y$$

At this point you may be tempted to choose Choice A. This would be incorrect, however. When we divided by x and by y, we could have only done this if x and y were not 0. So now we have to consider the case where $x = 0$. We note that if $x = 0$, according to the equality $2x^2 y = 2xy^2$, y can be any number, since any number multiplied by 0 is 0. Thus Choice E is correct.

EXAMPLE:

> How many positive integers are there (excluding 1 and 135) such that each of the integers is a divisor of 135?
>
> (A) 3 (B) 4 (C) 5 (D) 6 (E) 7

SOLUTION: Let's factor 135 into the simplest divisors: First divide 135 by the most obvious divisor, 5. We find that 135 divided by 5 is 27. So we have divisors of 135 to be 5 and 27. Now let's break 27 into simpler divisors. You can divide 27 by 3 evenly, and get 9. So now we have the divisors of 135 as 5, 3, and 9. But 9 can be divided by 3 to get 3. So the divisors (now the simplest ones) of 135 are

$$5, 3, 3, \text{ and } 3$$

We of course check to make sure that $5 \times 3 \times 3 \times 3 = 135$. Now we have to be careful to obtain all integer divisors of 135 (excluding 1 and 135). So, from the integers (the simplest divisors of 135), 5, 3, 3, and 3, we must get *all the combinations*. Let's take *two at a time*, first.

What I mean by taking two at a time from the integers 5, 3, 3, and 3 is taking combinations: 5×3 and 3×3. Note these are the only *different* integer combinations (two at a time) that can be taken from 5, 3, 3, and 3. Now let's take (from 5, 3, 3, and 3) combinations, three at a time. We get:

$$5 \times 3 \times 3 \text{ and } 3 \times 3 \times 3$$

Again, these are the only *different* integer combinations taken from 5, 3, 3, and 3, three at a time. Now, are there any more combinations? What about 5, 3, 3, and 3 taken 4 at a time? That would be $5 \times 3 \times 3 \times 3$. But that number would be 135, which we are excluding from our divisors. Thus the only combinations (integral divisors of 135) are:

The simple ones: 5 and 3
Combinations taken 2 at a time:
5×3 and 3×3
Combinations taken 3 at a time:
$5 \times 3 \times 3$ and $3 \times 3 \times 3$

Thus the total number of divisors (excluding 1 and 135) are 5, 3, 5×3, 3×3, $5 \times 3 \times 3$, $3 \times 3 \times 3$, or a total of 6 divisors. Thus, Choice D is correct.

XI. Problems That Are More Easily Solved by Putting the Problem or Variables in a More Obvious or Revealing Form

For many questions, you may be able to represent a problem or the variables or equations in a more apparent or revealing form.

EXAMPLE:

If n is a positive integer, what can be said about the value of $n^3 - n$?

(A) It is always exactly divisible by 12.
(B) It is always exactly divisible by 6.
(C) It is sometimes a prime number.
(D) It is always exactly divisible by n^2.
(E) None of the above

SOLUTION: Here we must put the quantity $n^3 - n$ in a more revealing form. Let's factor $n^3 - n$. We get

$$n^3 - n = n(n^2 - 1)$$

We can further factor this last quantity:

$$n(n^2 - 1) = n(n + 1)(n - 1)$$

Thus

$$n^3 - n = n(n + 1)(n - 1)$$

Notice that $n(n + 1)(n - 1)$ represents the product of three consecutive integers, such as 3, 4, 5 or 4, 5, 6, where $(n - 1)$ is the first integer, n is the second, and $n + 1$ is the third. You should now realize that of three consecutive integers, one of the integers must be a *multiple of 3*. Thus the product of three consecutive integers must be a multiple of three. Therefore, the product of three consecutive integers is *exactly divisible by three*. Now, since at least one of these consecutive three integers must be even (divisible by 2 exactly), the product of the three consecutive integers must be exactly divisible by $2 \times 3 = 6$. Thus Choice B is correct. Note that Choice A is incorrect because the consecutive integers may be 1, 2, and 3, of which the product is not divisible exactly by 12. Choice C is incorrect because the product of the consecutive integers is *always* exactly divisible by a number other than 1 and itself. Choice D is incorrect because as an example, where $n = 2$, $n(n + 1)(n - 1) = 2 \times 3 \times 1 = 6$, and 6 is not exactly divisible by n^2, which is 4.

EXAMPLE:

What is y if $\dfrac{(y - x)^z - (y - z)^z}{z - x} = y - z$? Assume $x \neq z$.

(A) z (B) x (C) xz (D) $xz - z$ (E) $x^2 + z^2 - xz$

SOLUTION: You should recognize that $(y - x)^2 - (y - z)^2$ is like the familiar form, $a^2 - b^2$, which is equal to $(a + b)(a - b)$. Here a is represented by $y - x$, and b is represented by $y - z$.

Therefore let $y - x = a$ and $y - z = b$, so we can write the numerator of the left side of the equation,

$$\frac{(y-x)^2 - (y-z)^2}{z-x} (= y - z)$$

as

$$\frac{a^2 - b^2}{z-x} (= y - z)$$

Since

$$(1) \quad y - x = a$$

and

$$(2) \quad y - z = b,$$

the denominator of the left side of the equation, $z - x$ becomes

$$z - x = a - b$$

subtracting the sides of equation (2) from equation (1). Thus our original equation

$$\frac{(y-x)^2 - (y-z)^2}{z-x} = y - z$$

becomes:

$$\frac{a^2 - b^2}{a - b} = y - z \ (= b, \text{ since } y - z = b)$$

Thus we get

$$\frac{(a+b)(a-b)}{a-b} = b$$

Cancelling $a - b$ (since it is not 0, because $a - b = z - x \neq 0$), we get

$$a + b = b, \text{ or } a = 0.$$

Since $a = y - x$ and $a = 0$, $y - x = 0$ and $y = x$. Therefore Choice B is correct.

Note that we didn't have to make these substitutions, and could have solved the problem the "longer" way. But if you can get used to methods like this one, you will be able to solve many more problems of this type, and much faster.

XII. In Problems Containing Unfamiliar Symbols, Use Simple Substitution

From my experience, many students have problems with questions containing unfamiliar symbols. For example, here's a problem containing an unfamiliar symbol: a small square. This is not a standard math symbol at all. It is an arbitrary symbol invented by the test-maker to express a particular relationship between the quantities A and B. However, symbols like these can be "translated" and used fairly easily:

If for all real numbers, $A \square B = A^2 + B^2 - AB$, then what is the value of $(2 \square 3) \square 3$?

(A) 6   (B) 18   (C) 37   (D) 64   (E) 108

All that $A \square B$ means is that every time you see a quantity on the left of the box (an A quantity) and a quantity on the right (a B quantity) you write the following:

$$A \square B = A^2 + B^2 - AB$$

Now the question asks what is $(2 \square 3) \square 3$?

Calculate what $(2 \square 3)$ is first, since this is inside the parentheses.

It is

$$(2 \square 3) = 2^2 + 3^2 - (2)(3) = 4 + 9 - 6 = 7$$

Now we are asked to find what $(2 \square 3) \square 3$ is. We know that $(2 \square 3) = 7$, so $(2 \square 3) \square 3 = 7 \square 3$. But $7 \square 3 = 7^2 + 3^2 - (7)(3) = 49 + 9 - 21 = 37$.

Choice C is then correct.

Here's another SAT example of the same type. In this problem, the arbitrary symbol is Ø.

If x, y, z, m, n, q are all positive numbers, and if $xyz \varnothing mnq = \dfrac{xyz}{mnq} + \dfrac{mnq}{xyz}$, then $xxy \varnothing xyz =$

(A) $\dfrac{zx}{mn}$ (B) $\dfrac{zx}{x^2 + y^2}$ (C) $\dfrac{zx}{x^2 + z^2}$ (D) $\dfrac{x^2 + z^2}{zx}$ (E) none of these

---

Now remember to substitute as shown in the diagram:

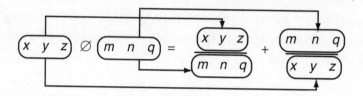

So

$$(x\ x\ y) \varnothing (x\ y\ z) = \dfrac{(x\ x\ y)}{(x\ y\ z)} + \dfrac{(x\ y\ z)}{(x\ x\ y)}$$

Now cancel like terms:

$$\dfrac{\cancel{x} x \cancel{y}}{\cancel{x} \cancel{y} z} + \dfrac{\cancel{x} \cancel{y} z}{\cancel{x} x \cancel{y}} = \dfrac{x}{z} + \dfrac{z}{x}$$

But, what? There is no answer in the choice with the form $\dfrac{x}{z} + \dfrac{z}{x}$!

You may at this point be tempted to choose Choice E (none of these), but what I'd do first is to *add*:

$$\dfrac{x}{z} + \dfrac{z}{x}$$

Remember the shortcut way?

$$\overset{\text{multiply}}{\underset{\text{multiply}}{\dfrac{x \quad z}{z \quad x}}} = \dfrac{x^2 + z^2}{zx}$$

So, $\dfrac{x}{z} + \dfrac{z}{x} = \dfrac{x^2 + z^2}{zx}$, which is just Choice D.

XIII. If You Must Test *All* Choices, Work From Choice E Backwards

Many questions ask you to work through many of the choices before coming to the correct one. And many students would start with Choice A first. Is that the best approach? Here's an example:

Which fraction is less than $\dfrac{2}{3}$?

(A) $\dfrac{3}{4}$ (B) $\dfrac{13}{19}$ (C) $\dfrac{15}{22}$ (D) $\dfrac{9}{13}$ (E) $\dfrac{7}{11}$

In this question, where you essentially have to *look through* the choices and cannot necessarily zero in on the correct choice, the test-maker will expect you to work through Choices A, B, C, etc. in that order. And the chances are that if you're careless, you'll make a mistake before you get to the right choice. That's how the text-maker makes up the choices. So, in cases such as this, *start with Choice E and work backwards* with Choice D, C, etc., in that order. The chances are that Choice E or D is the correct answer! So in the above question, let's compare $\dfrac{2}{3}$ with $\dfrac{7}{11}$ in Choice E. Remember our shortcut way?

Multiply

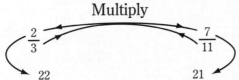

Since 22 is greater than 21, $\dfrac{2}{3}$ is greater than $\dfrac{7}{11}$; and so Choice E is in fact the correct answer.

Here's another SAT-type question that involves the same strategy:

If p is an even integer and q is an odd integer, which of the following could be an even integer?

(A) $q - p$ (B) $q + p$ (C) $\dfrac{p+q}{2}$ (D) $\dfrac{p}{2} - q$ (E) $\dfrac{p}{2} + q$

Note the words *could be* in the question. So, we just have to find one set of numbers that makes the choice an even number. Again, *work with Choice E first.* Since p is **even,** let $p = 2$ (for example). Since q is **odd,** let $q = 3$ (for example). Then Choice E, which is $\dfrac{p}{2} + q$, becomes $\dfrac{2}{2} + 3 = 1 + 3 = 4$. So we see that Choice E *could be even,* and so it is the correct answer.

So remember, when you have to work with all the choices or have to substitute numbers in the choices (that is, when you cannot just arrive at a correct answer without looking through all the choices), *work with Choice E first,* then Choice D, etc., in that order. Chances are that Choice E or Choice D is correct.

XIV. Know How to Find Unknown Expressions by Adding, Subtracting, Multiplying, or Dividing Equations or Expressions

When you want to calculate composite quantities such as $x + 3y$ or $m - n$, often you can do it by adding, subtracting, multiplying, or dividing the right equations or expressions.

Note: We have included many examples because there are many variations to this strategy.

EXAMPLE 1

If $4x + 5y = 10$ and $x + 3y = 8$,

then $\dfrac{5x + 8y}{3} =$

(A) 18
(B) 15
(C) 12
(D) 9
(E) 6

Choice E is correct. Don't solve for x, then for y.

Try to get the quantity $\dfrac{5x + 8y}{3}$ by adding or subtracting the equations. In this case, *add* equations.

$$
\begin{array}{r}
4x + 5y = 10 \\
+\ x + 3y = 8 \\
\hline
5x + 8y = 18
\end{array}
$$

Now divide by 3:

$$40.5 = \frac{486}{n}$$

EXAMPLE 2

If $25x + 8y = 149$ and $16x + 3y = 89$, then

$$\frac{9x + 5y}{5} =$$

(A) 12
(B) 15
(C) 30
(D) 45
(E) 60

Choice A is correct. We are told

$$25x + 8y = 149 \qquad \boxed{1}$$
$$16x + 3y = 89 \qquad \boxed{2}$$

The long way to do this problem is to solve $\boxed{1}$ and $\boxed{2}$ for x and y, and then substitute these values into $\dfrac{9x + 5y}{5}$. The fast way to do this problem is to *subtract* $\boxed{2}$ from $\boxed{1}$ and get

$$9x + 5y = 60 \qquad \boxed{3}$$

Now all we have to do is to divide $\boxed{3}$ by 5:

$$\frac{9x + 5y}{5} = 12 \quad (\textit{Answer})$$

EXAMPLE 3

If $21x + 39y = 18$, then $7x + 13y =$

(A) 3
(B) 6
(C) 7
(D) 9
(E) It cannot be determined from the information given.

Choice B is correct. We are given

$$21x + 39y = 18 \qquad \boxed{1}$$

Divide $\boxed{1}$ by 3:

$$7x + 13y = 6 \quad (Answer)$$

EXAMPLE 4

If $x + 2y = 4$, then $5x + 10y - 8 =$

(A)　10
(B)　12
(C)　−10
(D)　−12
(E)　0

Choice B is correct.

Multiply $x + 2y = 4$ by 5 to get:

$$5x + 10y = 20$$

Now subtract 8:

$$5x + 10y - 8 = 20 - 8$$
$$= 12$$

EXAMPLE 5

If $6x^5 = y^2$ and $x = \dfrac{1}{y}$, then $y =$

(A) x^6

(B) $\dfrac{x^5}{5}$

(C) $6x^6$

(D) $\dfrac{6x^5}{5}$

(E) $\dfrac{x^5}{6}$

Choice C is correct.

Multiply $6x^5 = y^2$ by $x = \dfrac{1}{y}$ to get:

$$6x^6 = y^2 \times \dfrac{1}{y} = y$$

EXAMPLE 6

If $\dfrac{m}{n} = \dfrac{3}{8}$ and $\dfrac{m}{q} = \dfrac{4}{7}$, then $\dfrac{n}{q} =$

(A) $\dfrac{12}{15}$

(B) $\dfrac{12}{56}$

(C) $\dfrac{56}{12}$

(D) $\dfrac{32}{21}$

(E) $\dfrac{21}{32}$

Choice D is correct.

First get rid of fractions!

Cross-multiply $\dfrac{m}{n} \times \dfrac{3}{8}$ to get $8m = 3n$. $\boxed{1}$

Now cross-multiply $\dfrac{m}{q} \times \dfrac{4}{7}$ to get $7m = 4q$. $\boxed{2}$

Now divide equations $\boxed{1}$ and $\boxed{2}$:

$$\frac{8m}{7m} = \frac{3n}{4q} \qquad \boxed{3}$$

The ms cancel and we get:

$$\frac{8}{7} = \frac{3n}{4q} \qquad \boxed{4}$$

Multiply equation $\boxed{4}$ by 4 and divide by 3 to get

$$\frac{8 \times 4}{7 \times 3} = \frac{n}{q}$$

Thus $\qquad \dfrac{n}{q} = \dfrac{32}{21}.$

EXAMPLE 7

If $\dfrac{a+b+c+d}{4} = 20$

And $\dfrac{b+c+d}{3} = 10$

Then $a =$

(A) 50
(B) 60
(C) 70
(D) 80
(E) 90

Choice A is correct.

We have

$$\frac{a+b+c+d}{4} = 20 \qquad \boxed{1}$$

$$\frac{b+c+d}{3} = 10 \qquad \boxed{2}$$

Multiply equation $\boxed{1}$ by 4:

We get: $a + b + c + d = 80$ $\boxed{3}$

Now *multiply* equation $\boxed{2}$ by 3:

We get: $b + c + d = 30$ $\boxed{4}$

Now *subtract* equation $\boxed{4}$ from equation $\boxed{3}$:

$$
\begin{array}{ll}
a + b + c + d = 80 & \boxed{3} \\
-(b + c + d = 30) & \boxed{4} \\
\hline
\end{array}
$$

We get $a = 50$.

EXAMPLE 8

If $a - b = 4$ and $a + b = 7$, then $a^2 - b^2 =$

(A) $5\frac{1}{2}$
(B) 11
(C) 28
(D) 29
(E) 56

Choice C is correct.

Multiply: $(a - b)(a + b) = a^2 - b^2$ $\boxed{1}$

$$
\begin{array}{c}
a - b = 4 \\
a + b = 7 \\
(a - b)(a + b) = 28 = a^2 - b^2
\end{array}
$$

EXAMPLE 9

If $y^8 = 4$ and $y^7 = \dfrac{3}{x}$,

what is the value of y in terms of x?

(A) $\dfrac{4x}{3}$

(B) $\dfrac{3x}{4}$

(C) $\dfrac{4}{x}$

(D) $\dfrac{x}{4}$

(E) $\dfrac{12}{x}$

Choice A is correct.

Don't solve for the *value* of y first, by finding

$y = 4^{\frac{1}{8}}$

Just divide the two equations:

(Step 1) $y^8 = 4$

(Step 2) $y^7 = \dfrac{3}{x}$

(Step 3) $\dfrac{y^8}{y^7} = \dfrac{4}{\dfrac{3}{x}}$

(Step 4) $y = 4 \times \dfrac{x}{3}$

(Step 5) $y = \dfrac{4x}{3}$ (*Answer*)

EXAMPLE 10

If $\dfrac{p+1}{r+1} = 1$ and p, r are nonzero, and p is not equal to -1, and r *is* not equal to -1, then

(A) $2 > \dfrac{p}{r} > 1$ always

(B) $\dfrac{p}{r} < 1$ always

(C) $\dfrac{p}{r} = 1$ always

(D) $\dfrac{p}{r}$ can be greater than 2

(E) $\dfrac{p}{r} = 2$ always

Choice C is correct.

Get rid of the fraction. *Multiply* both sides of the equation

$$\frac{p+1}{r+1} = 1 \text{ by } r+1$$

$$\left(\frac{p+1}{\cancel{r+1}}\right)\cancel{r+1} = r+1$$

$$p+1 = r+1$$

Cancel the 1s:

$$p = r$$

So:

$$\frac{p}{r} = 1$$

10 Additional Questions Involving a Shortcut or Strategy

(Try these and look at the explanatory answers after the questions.)

1. If $2x + 3y = 9$ and $x + y = 6$, then $x + 2y =$
   - (A) 1
   - (B) 2
   - (C) 3
   - (D) 4
   - (E) 6

2.

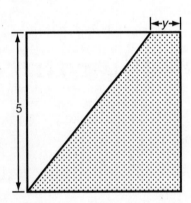

In the figure of the square of side 5 above, what is the area of the shaded region divided by the area of the unshaded region?

   - (A) $\dfrac{y-5}{5+y}$
   - (B) $\dfrac{y+5}{5-y}$
   - (C) $25 - (5 + y)$
   - (D) $25 - (5 - y)$
   - (E) $\dfrac{5-y}{y+5}$

3. If $(m + n)^2 = 15$ and $mn = 3$, then $m^2 + n^2 =$
   - (A) 9
   - (B) 25
   - (C) 21
   - (D) 12
   - (E) 18

4. If $p°$ and $(p + 20)°$ are the measures of two angles of a right triangle, what are the possible values of p?
   - (A) 30 and 60
   - (B) 20 and 80
   - (C) 35 and 70
   - (D) p can have any value between 0 and 90, inclusive.
   - (E) none of the above

5.

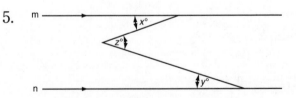

In the figure above, lines m and n are parallel. $z =$
   - (A) $x - y$
   - (B) $y - x$
   - (C) $x + y$
   - (D) $x + 2y - 90$
   - (E) none of the above

6. A typist increased her speed from 60 words per minute to 80 words per minute. What percent did her speed increase?

   (A) $33\frac{1}{3}\%$

   (B) 25%

   (C) 40%

   (D) 20%

   (E) 75%

7. There is a ratio of 2 to 5 men to women at a particular conference. If 3 more men attended the conference, the ratio of men to women would be 3 to 5. How many women are there at the conference?

   (A) 10

   (B) 12

   (C) 6

   (D) 18

   (E) 15

8. A circle of radius 5 has two points, A and B, on its circumference. What is the distance between points A and B?

   (A) 5

   (B) 5π

   (C) 25π

   (D) $\dfrac{5}{\pi}$

   (E) This cannot be determined.

9. If $\dfrac{y}{2} - \dfrac{y}{4} + \dfrac{y}{6} - \dfrac{y}{8} = 1 - \dfrac{1}{2} + \dfrac{1}{3} - \dfrac{1}{4}$ then $y =$

   (A) 0

   (B) 1

   (C) 2

   (D) $1\frac{1}{3}$

   (E) $2\frac{2}{3}$

10. If $x + y = m$ and $x - y = \dfrac{1}{m}$, then $x^2 - 1 =$

   (A) y^2

   (B) y

   (C) $m^2 - y^2$

   (D) m^2

   (E) $my - y^2$

Explanatory Answers Describing Shortcuts and Strategies

1. **(C)** Many students would try to solve for x and then for y, and then plug in the values of x and y to find the value of $x + 2y$. Since the question does not ask you to find x alone or y alone, but $x + 2y$, you should look for a solution that would give you $x + 2y$ directly from the two equations. This can be done by subtracting the second equation from the first equation:

$$\begin{aligned} 2x+3y &= 9 \\ \underline{(x+y \ \ = 6)} \\ x+2y &= 3 \end{aligned}$$

$x + 2y = 3$, and so our answer is Choice C.

2. **(B)** Let us first figure out what the shorter leg of the unshaded triangle is. Since the side of the square is 5, we get the following figure:

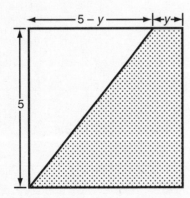

The area of the shaded region looks like it may be complicated, so let's simplify it. The area of the shaded region is the area of the square *minus* the area of the unshaded region. The area of the square is just $5 \times 5 = 25$. The area of the unshaded region is just the area of a right triangle, which in this case is $5 \times (5 - y)$ divided by 2. Thus the area of the *shaded region* is

$$25 - \frac{5(5-y)}{2}$$

Since the area of the *unshaded region* was found to be

$$\frac{5(5-y)}{2}$$

the area of the shaded region divided by the area of the unshaded region is

$$\frac{25 - \dfrac{5(5-y)}{2}}{\dfrac{5(5-y)}{2}} = \frac{50 - 5(5-y)}{5(5-y)}$$

$$\frac{50 - 25 + 5y}{25 - 5y} = \frac{25 + 5y}{25 - 5y}$$

Dividing both numerator and denominator by 5, we get:

$$\frac{5+y}{5-y}$$

which is Choice B.

3. **(A)** Multiply out $(m + n)^2$. We get $(m + n)^2 = m^2 + 2mn + n^2$. Now since $mn = 3$, and $(m + n)^2 = 15$, we get

$$(m + n)^2 = 15 = m^2 + 2mn + n^2 = m^2 + 2(3) + n^2 = m^2 + n^2 + 6$$

So we find that

$$15 = m^2 + n^2 + 6$$

and we obtain
$$15 - 6 = m^2 + n^2$$
Thus $m^2 + n^2 = 9$, and Choice A is correct.

Note that there was no need to solve for m and n and then find the value of $m^2 + n^2$.

4. **(C)** The two angles $p°$ and $(p + 20)°$ can either be two acute angles (which must add up to 90°) in a right triangle or one acute angle and one right angle. If the angles are acute angles then we get

$p + p + 20 = 90$ (two acute angles
  must add up to 90°)

Thus
$$2p + 20 = 90$$
$$2p = 70$$
$$p = 35$$

Thus p may be 35.

Now if one of the angles is a right angle, it must be $(p + 20)°$, *not* $p°$, since the right angle is the greatest angle of the triangle and $p + 20$ is greater than p. Therefore

$p + 20 = 90$ (the right angle)
$p = 70$

Thus the other possibility of p is $p = 70$, and so Choice C is correct.

5. **(C)** It may first look like there is no relation between z and x and y. Let's add a parallel line as shown below:

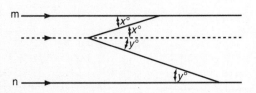

Now you can see that because the alternate interior angles are equal, $x + y = z$. Thus Choice C is correct.

6. **(A)** This can easily be done if you know exactly how to translate the verbal message into a mathematical one. Look at the word *increased*. You are asked to find *what percent the speed increased*. So let's first find out what the increase in speed was. It is $80 - 60 = 20$ (words per minute). Now the percent increase means the increase as compared with the *original* typing speed. So the percent increase would be

$$\frac{20}{60} \times 100 = \frac{1}{3} \times 100 = 33\frac{1}{3}\%$$

Therefore Choice A is correct.

7. **(E)** This is another example for knowing how to translate a verbal message into mathematical terms. Let's denote the women by w and the men by m. Since the ratio of men to women is given as 2 to 5, we get:

$$\frac{m}{w} = \frac{2}{5}$$

Cross-multiplying, we get

$$(1)\ 5m = 2w$$

Now look at the second sentence of the question. If *three more men* attended the conference, the *ratio of men to women* would be *3 to 5*. Since the women remain in the same number, this second sentence translates to

$$\frac{m+3}{w} = \frac{3}{5}$$

Cross multiplying, we get

$$(2) \; 5m + 15 = 3w$$

Now from equation (1) above, since $5m = 2w$, let's substitute $2w$ for $5m$ in equation (2):

$$5m + 15 = 3w$$

Since $5m = 2w$, we get:

$$2w + 15 = 3w$$
$$15 = w$$

Therefore $w = 15$, and this tells us that there are 15 women at the conference. So Choice E is correct.

8. **(E)** Even though the radius is specified, don't let that mislead you. Points A and B can be at opposite ends of the circle or they can be extremely close together. Therefore Choice E is correct.

9. **(C)** Whatever you do, don't add $\dfrac{y}{2} - \dfrac{y}{4} +$ etc.! Note 2, 4, 6, 8 in the denominators of the left side of the equation. Also notice that y is in all the numerators on that side. So let's factor the y, and also we can factor $\dfrac{1}{2}$ from the string of terms on the left side of the equation.

$$\frac{y}{2} - \frac{y}{4} + \frac{y}{6} - \frac{y}{8} = \frac{y}{2}\left(1 - \frac{1}{2} + \frac{1}{3} - \frac{1}{4}\right)$$

Now, doesn't that look like something on the right side of the original equation?

Therefore we get

$$\frac{y}{2} - \frac{y}{4} + \frac{y}{6} - \frac{y}{8} = \frac{y}{2}\left(1 - \frac{1}{2} + \frac{1}{3} - \frac{1}{4}\right) =$$
$$1 - \frac{1}{2} + \frac{1}{3} - \frac{1}{4}$$

So the $\left(1 - \dfrac{1}{2} + \dfrac{1}{3} - \dfrac{1}{4}\right)$ *cancels* and we are left with:

$$\frac{y}{2} = 1$$

which gives us $y = 2$. Therefore Choice C is correct.

10. **(A)** As soon as you see a term like $x + y$ and a term like $x - y$ and an x^2 term, you should multiply the $x + y$ with the $x - y$ to give you

$$(x + y)(x - y) = x^2 - y^2$$

So we get:

$$(x + y)(x - y) = m\left(\frac{1}{m}\right)$$
$$x^2 - y^2 = m\left(\frac{1}{m}\right) = 1$$

Therefore,

$$x^2 - y^2 = 1 \text{ and so, } x^2 - 1 = y^2$$

Thus the correct answer is Choice A.

Math Shortcuts You Ought to Know

Comparing Fractions

Which fraction do you think is greater?

$$\frac{3}{7} \quad \text{or} \quad \frac{7}{16}$$

You would try to obtain the *common denominator* by multiplying the 7 by the 16. What a long way! Here's how to do this the "shortcut" way:

As shown in the following diagram, multiply the 16 by the 3 and put that number directly below the $\frac{3}{7}$. Now multiply the 7 by the 7 and put that number directly below the $\frac{7}{16}$:

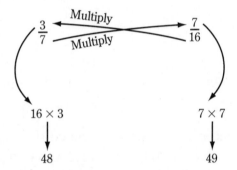

Since 48 is less than 49 (and the 48 is directly below the $\frac{3}{7}$ and the 49 is directly below the $\frac{7}{16}$), $\frac{3}{7}$ is less than $\frac{7}{16}$. This works for any two fractions. More on this method later when we consider GRE-type questions.

How to Quickly Add Fractions

Suppose that you want to add the fractions $\frac{3}{7} + \frac{9}{10}$.

As shown in the following diagram, multiply the 3 by the 10. You get 30. Now multiply the 7 by the 9. You get 63. Now add 30 + 63 = 93. This is the *numerator* of our answer. Now multiply the denominators, 7 and 10, to get 70. This is the *denominator* of our answer. So the answer is:

$$\frac{\text{numerator}}{\text{denominator}} = \frac{93}{70} = 1\frac{23}{70}$$

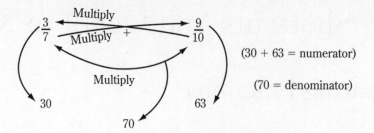

$(30 + 63 = \text{numerator})$

$(70 = \text{denominator})$

You can add any two fractions by this method.

Simplifying Fractions or Numbers

Example: What is the value of $\dfrac{900}{25}$?

Do not divide the 25 into 900 for this example. It will take too long. *Simplify the denominator first.* That is, multiply both the numerator and denominator by 4 to get:

$$\frac{900}{25} \times \frac{4}{4} = \frac{900 \times 4}{100}$$

The result becomes 3600 divided by the simple denominator, 100. And that result is the number 36. We have simplified the original fraction, $\dfrac{900}{25}$, by making the denominator a simple "100." Since the denominators are the parts of fractions that give the most trouble, we change the fraction to an *equivalent one with a simpler denominator.* This is because it is easiest to divide by simple numbers.

Percent Word Problems I

How would you go about solving this problem: *What is the selling price of an article that lists for $200 and is discounted 20%?* You might multiply 20% by $200 and then subtract that number from $200. That's *not* the fastest approach! Subtract the 20% from *100% first.* You get 80%. Now multiply the 80% by $200 to get

$$\frac{80}{1\cancel{0}\cancel{0}} \times 2\cancel{0}\,\cancel{0} = 160$$

And so, $160 is the answer. You can do all discount problems this way, by first subtracting the % of the discount from 100% and then multiplying the result by the list price of the item.

Percent Word Problems II

Some numbers lend themselves to easy manipulation. For example, suppose you are working with the number 15. Here's the problem: *If my restaurant bill comes to a total of $36.00, and I wish to give the waiter a 15% tip, how much money should I leave as the tip?*

You might consider multiplying 15% by $36.00. But you'd probably have to do that on paper, longhand. There's a simpler way.

1. Take 10% of $36.00 (You get $3.60)
2. Take half of $3.60 (You get $1.80)
3. Add $3.60 to $1.80 (You get $5.40)

And so $5.40 is your tip.

Part VI
Two SAT Math
Practice Tests

Four Important Reasons for Taking These Practice Tests

Each of the two Practice SATs in the final part of this book is modeled very closely after the actual SAT.

There are four important reasons for taking each of these Practice Math SATs:

1. To find out in which areas of the SAT you are still weak.

2. To know just where to concentrate your efforts to eliminate these weaknesses.

3. To reinforce the Critical Thinking Skills—14 Math Strategies that you learned in Part V of this book, "Complete Time-Saving Strategies and Shortcuts." As we advised you at the beginning of Part V, diligent study of these strategies will result in a sharp rise in your SAT math scores.

4. To strengthen your basic math skills that might still be a bit rusty. We hope that Part III, "Mini Math Refresher," and Part IV, "Diagnostic Tests and Instructional Material," substantially helped you to scrape off some of this rust.

These four reasons for taking the two Practice Tests in this section of the book tie up closely with a very important educational principle:

WE LEARN BY DOING!

10 Tips for Taking the Practice Tests

1. Observe the time limits exactly as given.

2. Allow no interruptions.

3. Permit no talking by anyone in the "test area."

4. Use the answer sheets provided at the beginning of each Practice Test. Don't make extra marks. Two answers for one question constitute an omitted question.

5. Use scratch paper to figure things out. (On your actual SAT, you are permitted to use the test book for scratchwork.)

6. Omit a question when you start "struggling" with it. Go back to that question later if you have time to do so.

7. Don't get upset if you can't answer several of the questions. You can still get a high score on the test. Even if only 40 to 60 percent of the questions you answer are correct, you will get an average or above-average score.

8. You get the same credit for answering an easy question correctly as you do for answering a tough question correctly.

9. It is advisable to guess if you are sure that at least one of the answer choices is wrong. If you are not sure whether one or more of the answer choices are wrong, statistically it will not make a difference to your total score if you guess or leave the answer blank.

10. *Your SAT score increases by approximately 10 points for every answer you get correct.*

To See How You'd Do on a Math SAT and What You Should Do to Improve

This SAT Math Test is very much like the actual math SAT. It follows the genuine SAT very closely. Taking this test is like taking the actual SAT. Following is the purpose of taking this test:

1.   to find out what you are *weak* in and what you are *strong* in;

2.   to know where to concentrate your efforts in order to be fully prepared for the actual test.

Taking this test will prove to be a very valuable TIME SAVER for you. Why waste time studying what you already know? Spend your time profitably by studying what you *don't* know. That is what this test will tell you.

In this book, we do not waste precious pages. We get right down to the business of helping you to increase your SAT scores.

Other SAT preparation books place their emphasis on drill, drill, drill. We do not believe that drill work is of primary importance in preparing for the SAT exam. Drill has its place. In fact, this book contains a great variety of drill material—questions, practically all of which have explanatory answers. But drill work must be coordinated with learning Critical Thinking Skills. These skills will help you to think clearly and critically so that you will be able to answer many more SAT questions correctly.

After you finish the test, make sure you read Part V of this book—"Complete Time-Saving Strategies and Shortcuts," beginning on page 245.

Ready? Start taking the test. It's just like the real thing.

SAT Math
Practice Test 1

Practice Test 1   Answer Sheet

Start with number 1 for each new section. If a section has fewer questions than answer spaces, leave the extra answer spaces blank. Be sure to erase any errors or stray marks completely.

SECTION 1

1 A B C D E	11 A B C D E	21 A B C D E	31 A B C D E
2 A B C D E	12 A B C D E	22 A B C D E	32 A B C D E
3 A B C D E	13 A B C D E	23 A B C D E	33 A B C D E
4 A B C D E	14 A B C D E	24 A B C D E	34 A B C D E
5 A B C D E	15 A B C D E	25 A B C D E	35 A B C D E
6 A B C D E	16 A B C D E	26 A B C D E	36 A B C D E
7 A B C D E	17 A B C D E	27 A B C D E	37 A B C D E
8 A B C D E	18 A B C D E	28 A B C D E	38 A B C D E
9 A B C D E	19 A B C D E	29 A B C D E	39 A B C D E
10 A B C D E	20 A B C D E	30 A B C D E	40 A B C D E

SECTION 2

1 A B C D E	11 A B C D E	21 A B C D E	31 A B C D E
2 A B C D E	12 A B C D E	22 A B C D E	32 A B C D E
3 A B C D E	13 A B C D E	23 A B C D E	33 A B C D E
4 A B C D E	14 A B C D E	24 A B C D E	34 A B C D E
5 A B C D E	15 A B C D E	25 A B C D E	35 A B C D E
6 A B C D E	16 A B C D E	26 A B C D E	36 A B C D E
7 A B C D E	17 A B C D E	27 A B C D E	37 A B C D E
8 A B C D E	18 A B C D E	28 A B C D E	38 A B C D E
9 A B C D E	19 A B C D E	29 A B C D E	39 A B C D E
10 A B C D E	20 A B C D E	30 A B C D E	40 A B C D E

CAUTION   Use the answer spaces in the grids below for Section 2.

Student-Produced Responses   ONLY ANSWERS ENTERED IN THE CIRCLES IN EACH GRID WILL BE SCORED. YOU WILL NOT RECEIVE CREDIT FOR ANYTHING WRITTEN IN THE BOXES ABOVE THE CIRCLES.

9   10   11   12   13

14   15   16   17   18

Start with number 1 for each new section. If a section has fewer questions than answer spaces, leave the extra answer spaces blank. Be sure to erase any errors or stray marks completely.

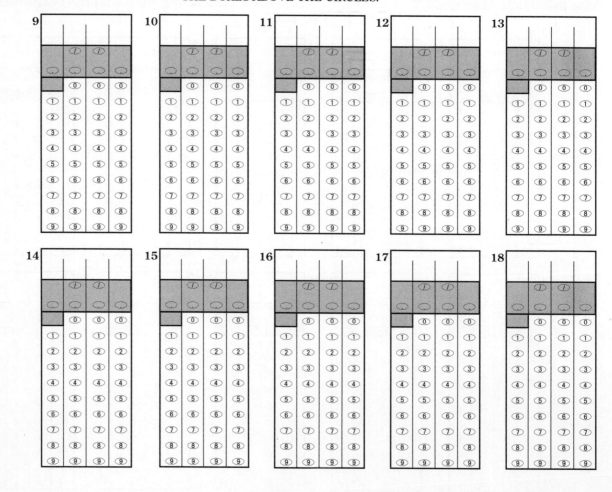

SECTION
3

SECTION
4

CAUTION Use the answer spaces in the grids below for Section 3.

Student-Produced Responses ONLY ANSWERS ENTERED IN THE CIRCLES IN EACH GRID WILL BE SCORED. YOU WILL NOT RECEIVE CREDIT FOR ANYTHING WRITTEN IN THE BOXES ABOVE THE CIRCLES.

Section 1

Time: 25 Minutes—Turn to Section 1 (page 313) of your answer sheet to answer the questions in this section.
   20 Questions

Directions: For this section, solve each problem and decide which is the best of the choices given. Fill in the corresponding circle on the answer sheet. You may use any available space for scratchwork.

Notes:

1. The use of a calculator is permitted.
2. All numbers used are real numbers.
3. Figures that accompany problems in this test are intended to provide information useful in solving the problems. They are drawn as accurately as possible EXCEPT when it is stated in a specific problem that the figure is not drawn to scale. All figures lie in a plane unless otherwise indicated.
4. Unless otherwise specified, the domain of any function f is assumed to be the set of all real numbers x for which $f(x)$ is a real number.

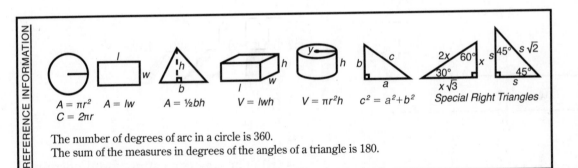

REFERENCE INFORMATION

$A = \pi r^2$ $A = lw$ $A = \frac{1}{2}bh$ $V = lwh$ $V = \pi r^2h$ $c^2 = a^2 + b^2$ *Special Right Triangles*
$C = 2\pi r$

The number of degrees of arc in a circle is 360.
The sum of the measures in degrees of the angles of a triangle is 180.

1. What is another expression for 8 less than the quotient of x and 3?

   (A) $\dfrac{x-8}{3}$

   (B) $\dfrac{x}{3} - 8$

   (C) $8 - 3x$

   (D) $3x - 8$

   (E) $3(8 - x)$

2. Each of Phil's buckets has a capacity of 11 gallons. Each of Mark's buckets can hold 8 gallons. How much more water, in gallons, can 7 of Phil's buckets hold than 7 of Mark's buckets?

   (A) 3
   (B) 7
   (C) 21
   (D) 24
   (E) 56

3. Which of the following is equal to $\dfrac{|x|}{|y|}$ for all real numbers x and y?

(A) $\dfrac{x}{y}$

(B) $\dfrac{|x|}{y}$

(C) $\dfrac{x}{|y|}$

(D) $\left|\dfrac{x}{y}\right|$

(E) $-\left|\dfrac{x}{y}\right|$

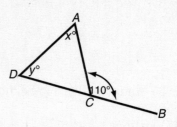

5. In the figure above, $m \angle ACB = 110°$ and $AC = CD$. What is the value of $2y$?

(A) 45
(B) 70
(C) 90
(D) 110
(E) 140

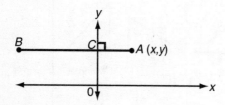

4. If $3AC = BC$ in the figure above, what are the coordinates of B?

(A) $(x, 3y)$

(B) $(-x, 3y)$

(C) $(3x, y)$

(D) $(-3x, y)$

(E) $(-3x, 3y)$

6. If $(x + y)^2 = 9$, what is $x + y$?

(A) 0
(B) 3
(C) 9
(D) 27
(E) The answer cannot be determined from the information given.

GO ON TO THE NEXT PAGE

7. The average (arithmetic mean) of five numbers is 34. If three of the numbers are 28, 30, and 32, what is the sum of the other two?

(A) 40
(B) 50
(C) 60
(D) 70
(E) 80

9. For any positive integer, x, $ⓧ = \dfrac{x^2}{3}$ and $\boxed{x} = \dfrac{9}{x}$. What is an expression for $ⓧ \times \boxed{x}$?

(A) $3x$
(B) x
(C) 1
(D) $\dfrac{x^3}{64}$
(E) $27x^3$

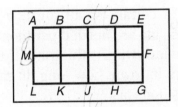

8. In the figure above, rectangle *AEGL* has been divided into 8 congruent squares. If the perimeter of one of these squares is 16, what is the value of $AE + MF + LG + AL + BK + CJ + DH + EG$?

(A) 32
(B) 44
(C) 88
(D) 128
(E) 176

10. If each of the 3 distinct points, *A, B,* and *C* are the same distance from point *D*, which of the following could be true?

  I. *A, B, C,* and *D* are the four vertices of a square.
  II. *A, B, C,* and *D* lie on the circumference of a circle.
  III. *A, B,* and *C,* lie on the circumference of the circle whose center is *D*.

(A) I only
(B) II only
(C) III only
(D) II and III only
(E) I, II, and III

GO ON TO THE NEXT PAGE

11. Of the following four diagrams below, which diagram describes the dark region as the set of elements that belongs to all of the sets A, B, and C?

(A)

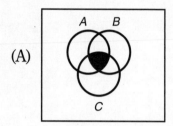

(B)

(C)

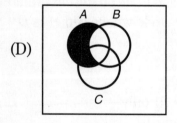

(D)

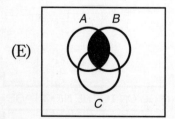

(E)

12. If the points (1,3), (3,5), and (6,y) all lie on the same line, the value of y is

(A) 8
(B) 7
(C) 6
(D) 5
(E) 4

13. At a certain small town, p gallons of gasoline are needed per month for each car in town. At this rate, if there are r cars in town, how long, in months, will q gallons last?

(A) $\dfrac{pq}{r}$

(B) $\dfrac{qr}{p}$

(C) $\dfrac{r}{pq}$

(D) $\dfrac{q}{pr}$

(E) pqr

GO ON TO THE NEXT PAGE

Questions 14–15

The next two questions refer to the following definition:

The *l*-length of the segment from point A to point B is $B-A$.

14. What is the *l*-length from -3 to 3?

(A) -6
(B) -3
(C) 0
(D) 3
(E) 6

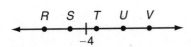

15. Of all segments beginning at -4 and ending at one of the integers indicated above on the number line, which segment has the *l*-length?

           least

(A) R
(B) S
(C) T
(D) U
(E) V

16. If the sum of 5 consecutive positive integers is w, in terms of w, which of the following represents the sum of the next 5 consecutive positive integers?

(A) $w+5$
(B) $5w+5$
(C) $5w+25$
(D) $w+25$
(E) w^2+25

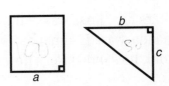

17. If the area of the square is twice the area of the triangle, and $bc = 100$, then find a^2.

(A) 400
(B) 200
(C) 100
(D) 50
(E) 25

GO ON TO THE NEXT PAGE

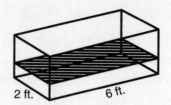

2 ft.   6 ft.

Note: Figure is not drawn to scale.

18. In the figure above, $\overline{AB}$ and $\overline{CD}$ are diameters of the circle whose center is O. If the radius of the circle is 2 inches and the sum of the lengths of arcs $\overarc{AD}$ and $\overarc{BC}$ is 3π inches, then $y =$

   (A) 45
   (B) 60
   (C) 75
   (D) 90
   (E) 120

20. The figure above shows water in a tank whose base is 2 feet by 6 feet. If a rectangular solid whose dimensions are 1 foot by 1 foot by 2 feet is totally immersed in the water, how many *inches* will the water rise?

   (A) $\dfrac{1}{6}$
   (B) 1
   (C) 2
   (D) 3
   (E) 12

19. Five years ago, Ross was N times as old as Amanda was. If Amanda is now 19 years old, how old is Ross now in terms of N?

   (A) $14N - 5$
   (B) $14N + 5$
   (C) $19N + 5$
   (D) $15N + 5$
   (E) $19N - 5$

STOP

If you finish before time is called, you may check your work on this section only.
Do not turn to any other section in the test.

Take a 5-minute break

before starting section 2

The following Section 2
is not scored, but it would
be wise to attempt this anyway.

Section 2

Time: 25 Minutes—Turn to Section 2 (page 313) of your answer sheet to answer the questions in this section.
18 Questions

Directions: This section contains two types of questions. You have 25 minutes to complete both types. For questions 1–8, solve each problem and decide which is the best of the choices given. Fill in the corresponding circle on the answer sheet. You may use any available space for scratchwork.

Notes:

1. The use of a calculator is permitted.
2. All numbers used are real numbers.
3. Figures that accompany problems in this test are intended to provide information useful in solving the problems. They are drawn as accurately as possible EXCEPT when it is stated in a specific problem that the figure is not drawn to scale. All figures lie in a plane unless otherwise indicated.
4. Unless otherwise specified, the domain of any function f is assumed to be the set of all real numbers x for which $f(x)$ is a real number.

REFERENCE INFORMATION

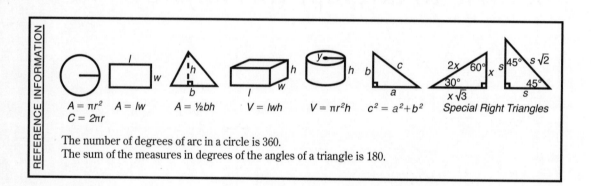

$A = \pi r^2$ $A = lw$ $A = \frac{1}{2}bh$ $V = lwh$ $V = \pi r^2 h$ $c^2 = a^2 + b^2$ *Special Right Triangles*
$C = 2\pi r$

The number of degrees of arc in a circle is 360.
The sum of the measures in degrees of the angles of a triangle is 180.

1. If $x + by = 3x + y = 5$ and $y = 2$, then $b =$
   (A) 0
   (B) 1
   (C) 2
   (D) 3
   (E) 4

2. There are 2 boys and 3 girls in the class. The ratio of boys to girls in the class is equal to all of the following *except*
   (A) 4 : 6
   (B) 9 : 12
   (C) 6 : 9
   (D) 12 : 18
   (E) 18 : 27

GO ON TO THE NEXT PAGE

3. What fraction of 1 week is 24 min?

(A) $\frac{1}{60}$

(B) $\frac{1}{168}$

(C) $\frac{1}{420}$

(D) $\frac{1}{1440}$

(E) $\frac{1}{10080}$

5. Johnny spent $\frac{2}{5}$ of his allowance on candy and $\frac{5}{6}$ of the remainder on ice cream. If his allowance is \$30, how much money did he have left after buying the candy and ice cream?

(A) \$1
(B) \$2
(C) \$3
(D) \$5
(E) \$10

4. $2 \times 10^{-5} \times 8 \times 10^2 \times 5 \times 10^2 =$

(A) .00008
(B) .008
(C) .08
(D) 8
(E) 800

Questions 6–7 refer to the following diagram:

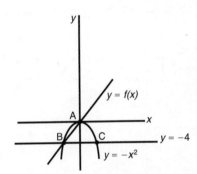

6. The x-coordinate of point B is

(A) -2
(B) -3
(C) -4
(D) -5
(E) -6

GO ON TO THE NEXT PAGE

7. The graph of the equation $y = f(x)$ is of the form $y = mx + b$, where b is

(A) 0
(B) 1
(C) 2
(D) 3
(E) 4

8. At how many points does the graph of the equation $y = x^4 + x^3$ intersect the x-axis?

(A) 0
(B) 1
(C) 2
(D) 3
(E) 4

GO ON TO THE NEXT PAGE

Directions: For Student-Produced Response questions 9–18, use the grids at the bottom of the answer sheet page on which you have answered questions 1–8.

Each of the remaining 10 questions requires you to solve the problem and enter your answer by marking the circles in the special grid, as shown in the examples below. You may use any available space for scratchwork.

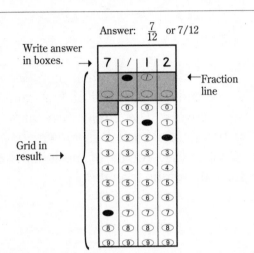

Answer: $\frac{7}{12}$ or 7/12

Write answer in boxes. →

← Fraction line

Grid in result. →

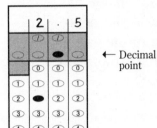

Answer: 2.5

← Decimal point

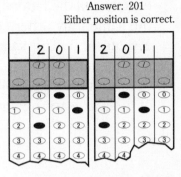

Answer: 201
Either position is correct.

Note: You may start your answers in any column, space permitting. Columns not needed should be left blank.

- Mark no more than one oval in any column.

- Because the answer sheet will be machine-scored, **you will receive credit only if the ovals are filled in correctly.**

- Although not required, it is suggested that you write your answer in the boxes at the top of the columns to help you fill in the ovals accurately.

- Some problems may have more than one correct answer. In such cases, grid only one answer.

- No question has a negative answer.

- **Mixed numbers** such as $2\frac{1}{2}$ must be gridded as 2.5 or 5/2. (If [2 1 / 2] is gridded, it will be interpreted as $\frac{21}{2}$, not $2\frac{1}{2}$.)

- *Decimal Accuracy:* If you obtain a decimal answer, **enter the most accurate value the grid will accommodate.** For example, if you obtain an answer such as 0.6666… , you should record the result as .666 or .667. **Less accurate values such as .66 or .67 are not acceptable.**

Acceptable ways to grid $\frac{2}{3}$ = .6666…:

---

9. If $\frac{5}{8}$ of x is 40, then find the value of $\frac{3}{8}$ of x.

10. A piece of wire is bent to form a circle of radius 3 feet. How many pieces of wire, each 2 feet long, can be made from the wire?

11. Dick spent \$7 in order to buy baseballs and tennis balls. If baseballs are 70¢ each and tennis balls are 60¢ each, what is the greatest possible number of tennis balls that Dick could have bought?

12. Let $f(x)$ be defined for all x by the equation $f(x) = 12x + 8$. Thus, $f(2) = 32$. If $f(x) \div f(0) = 2x$, then find the value of x.

GO ON TO THE NEXT PAGE →

ABA	BBB	CBA	BBA
ACC	CBC	CCC	ACA
BAC	ABC	BCA	CAB
CBB	BCA	AAB	ACC

13. In the triple arrangement of letters above, a triple has a value of 1 if exactly 2 of the letters in the triple are the same. Any other combination has a value of 0. The value of the entire arrangement is the sum of the values of each of the triples. What is the value of the above arrangement?

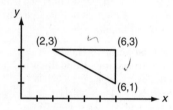

14. In the figure above, what is the area of the triangle?

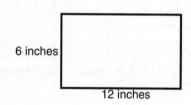

15. How many squares 2 inches on an edge can be placed, without overlapping, into the rectangle shown above?

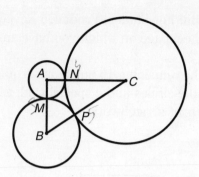

16. The circles having their centers at A, B, and C have radii of 1, 2, and 3, respectively. The circles are tangent at points M, N, and P as shown above. What is the product of the lengths of the sides of the triangle?

17. If the average (arithmetic mean) of 4 numbers is 8000 and the average (arithmetic mean) of 3 of the 4 numbers is 7500, then what must the fourth number be?

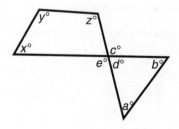

18. Five line segments intersect to form the figure above. What is the value of $x + y + z$ if $c = 100$?

STOP

If you finish before time is called, you may check your work on this section only.
Do not turn to any other section in the test.

Section 3

Notes:

1. The use of a calculator is permitted.
2. All numbers used are real numbers.
3. Figures that accompany problems in this test are intended to provide information useful in solving the problems. They are drawn as accurately as possible EXCEPT when it is stated in a specific problem that the figure is not drawn to scale. All figures lie in a plane unless otherwise indicated.
4. Unless otherwise specified, the domain of any function f is assumed to be the set of all real numbers x for which $f(x)$ is a real number.

REFERENCE INFORMATION

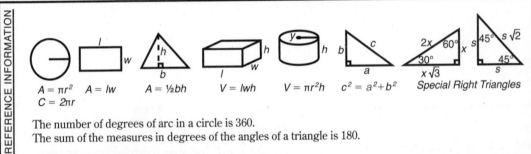

$A = \pi r^2$ $A = lw$ $A = \frac{1}{2}bh$ $V = lwh$ $V = \pi r^2 h$ $c^2 = a^2 + b^2$ *Special Right Triangles*
$C = 2\pi r$

The number of degrees of arc in a circle is 360.
The sum of the measures in degrees of the angles of a triangle is 180.

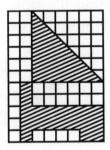

1. If each square in the grid above has a side of length 1, find the sum of the areas of the shaded regions.

    (A) 55
    (B) 46
    (C) 37
    (D) 30
    (E) 24

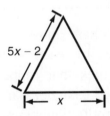

2. The figure above is an equilateral triangle. What is its perimeter?

    (A) $\dfrac{1}{4}$

    (B) $\dfrac{1}{2}$

    (C) $1\dfrac{1}{2}$

    (D) $3\dfrac{1}{2}$

    (E) The answer cannot be determined from the information given.

GO ON TO THE NEXT PAGE

3. If *w* waves pass through a certain point in *s* seconds, how many waves would pass through that point in *t* seconds?

(A) *wst*

(B) $\dfrac{t}{s}$

(C) $\dfrac{ws}{t}$

(D) $\dfrac{ts}{w}$

(E) $\dfrac{tw}{s}$

5. A box contains exactly 24 coins—nickels, dimes, and quarters. The probability of selecting a nickel by reaching into the box without looking is $\dfrac{3}{8}$. The probability of selecting a dime by reaching into the box without looking is $\dfrac{1}{8}$. How many quarters are in the box?

(A) 6

(B) 8

(C) 12

(D) 14

(E) 16

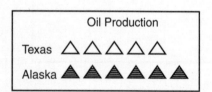

Oil Production

Texas △△△△△

Alaska ▲▲▲▲▲▲

4. In the chart above, the amount represented by each shaded triangle is three times that represented by each unshaded triangle. What fraction of the total production represented by the chart was produced in Alaska?

(A) $\dfrac{6}{11}$

(B) $\dfrac{18}{5}$

(C) $\dfrac{18}{23}$

(D) $\dfrac{12}{17}$

(E) $\dfrac{23}{17}$

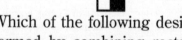

6. Which of the following designs can be formed by combining rectangles with size and shading the same as that shown above, if overlap is not permitted?

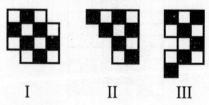

I   II   III

(A) I only

(B) II only

(C) III only

(D) I and II only

(E) II and III only

GO ON TO THE NEXT PAGE
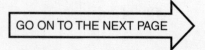

7. If x is a real number for which $f(x) = (x-1)^2 + (x-2)^2 + (x-3)^2$, $f(x+2) =$

(A) $3x^2 + 4x + 2$

(B) $3x$

(C) $(x+2)^2 + x^2 + (x-2)^2$

(D) $3x^2 + 2$

(E) $4x^2 + 4$

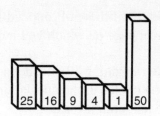

8. Six containers, whose capacities in cubic centimeters are shown, appear in the figure above. The 25-cubic-centimeter container is filled with flour, and the rest are empty. The contents of the 25-cubic-centimeter container are used to fill the 16-cubic centimeter container, and the excess is dumped into the 50-cubic-centimeter container. Then the 16-cubic-centimeter container is used to fill the 9-cubic-centimeter container, and the excess is dumped into the 50-cubic-centimeter container. The process is repeated until all containers, except the 1-cubic-centimeter and the 50-cubic-centimeter containers, are empty. What percent of the 50-cubic-centimeter container is *empty*?

(A) 24%

(B) 48%

(C) 50%

(D) 52%

(E) 76%

GO ON TO THE NEXT PAGE

Directions: For Student-Produced Response questions 9–18, use the grids at the bottom of the answer sheet page on which you have answered questions 1–8.

Each of the remaining 10 questions requires you to solve the problem and enter your answer by marking the circles in the special grid, as shown in the examples below. You may use any available space for scratchwork.

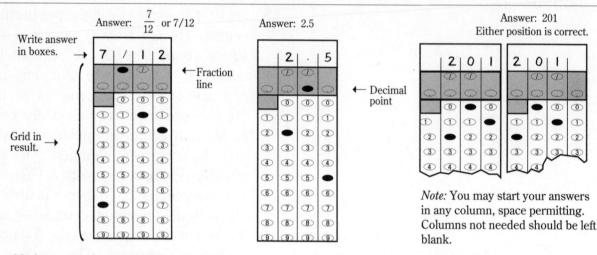

- Mark no more than one oval in any column.

- Because the answer sheet will be machine-scored, **you will receive credit only if the ovals are filled in correctly.**

- Although not required, it is suggested that you write your answer in the boxes at the top of the columns to help you fill in the ovals accurately.

- Some problems may have more than one correct answer. In such cases, grid only one answer.

- No question has a negative answer.

- **Mixed numbers** such as $2\frac{1}{2}$ must be gridded as 2.5 or 5/2. (If $\boxed{2\ |\ 1\ /\ 2}$ is gridded, it will be interpreted as $\frac{21}{2}$, not $2\frac{1}{2}$.)

- *Decimal Accuracy:* If you obtain a decimal answer, **enter the most accurate value the grid will accommodate.** For example, if you obtain an answer such as 0.6666... , you should record the result as .666 or .667. **Less accurate values such as .66 or .67 are not acceptable.**

Acceptable ways to grid $\frac{2}{3}$ = .6666...:

9. If $ab = 40$, $\dfrac{a}{b} = \dfrac{5}{2}$, and a and b are positive numbers, find the value of a.

10. Stephanie earned \$$x$ while working 10 hours. Evelyn earned \$$y$ while working 20 hours. If they both earn the same hourly wage and $x + y = 60$, how many dollars did Stephanie earn?

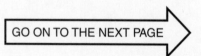
GO ON TO THE NEXT PAGE

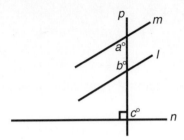

11. In the figure above, m is parallel to l and p is perpendicular to n. Find the value of $a + b + c$.

12. The difference of the areas of two circles is 21π. If their radii are $r + 3$ and r, find the radius of the *larger* circle.

	FIRST PLACE	SECOND PLACE	THIRD PLACE
	(8 points)	(4 points)	(2 points)
EVENT ①	TEAM A	TEAM B	TEAM C
EVENT ②	TEAM B	TEAM A	TEAM C

13. The results of two games involving 3 teams are shown above. Thus, we have the following standings: A and B both have 12 points, and C has 4 points. Assuming no ties, what is the least number of additional games that Team C will have to play in order to have the highest total score?

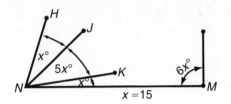

Note: Figure is not drawn to scale.

14. If the figure above were drawn to scale and all line segments were extended indefinitely in *both directions*, how many intersection points would there be in addition to N and M?

15. If a is 10 percent greater than b, and ac is 32 percent greater than bd, then c is what percent greater than d?

16. Since one gross = 12 dozen, what fraction of a gross of eggs is 3 eggs?

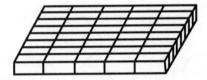

17. This figure above represents a layer of bricks, where each brick has a volume of 40 cubic inches. If all bricks are stacked in layers as shown, and the final pile of bricks occupies 8,000 cubic inches, how many layers are there in the final pile of bricks?

18. Let x be the smallest possible 3-digit number greater than or equal to 100 in which no digit is repeated. If y is the largest positive 3-digit number that can be made using all of the digits of x, what is the value of $y - x$?

STOP

If you finish before time is called, you may check your work on this section only.

Do not turn to any other section in the test.

Take a 5-minute break

before starting section 4

Section 4

Time: 20 Minutes—Turn to Section 4 (page 314) of your answer sheet to answer the questions in this section.
   16 Questions

Directions: For this section, solve each problem and decide which is the best of the choices given. Fill in the corresponding circle on the answer sheet. You may use any available space for scratchwork.

Notes:

1.   The use of a calculator is permitted.
2.   All numbers used are real numbers.
3.   Figures that accompany problems in this test are intended to provide information useful in solving the problems. They are drawn as accurately as possible EXCEPT when it is stated in a specific problem that the figure is not drawn to scale. All figures lie in a plane unless otherwise indicated.
4.   Unless otherwise specified, the domain of any function f is assumed to be the set of all real numbers x for which $f(x)$ is a real number.

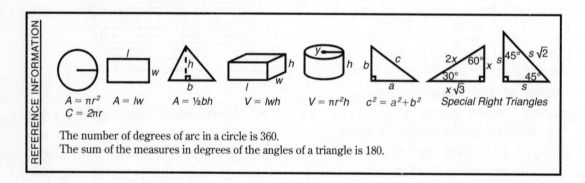

REFERENCE INFORMATION

$A = \pi r^2$ $A = lw$ $A = \frac{1}{2}bh$ $V = lwh$ $V = \pi r^2 h$ $c^2 = a^2 + b^2$ *Special Right Triangles*
$C = 2\pi r$

The number of degrees of arc in a circle is 360.
The sum of the measures in degrees of the angles of a triangle is 180.

---

1.   If $5x = 3$, then $(5x + 3)^2 =$

   (A) 0
   (B) 9
   (C) 25
   (D) 36
   (E) 64

2.   The ratio of girls to boys in a class is 8 : 7. The number of students in the class could be any of the following *except*

   (A) 15
   (B) 45
   (C) 50
   (D) 60
   (E) 90

GO ON TO THE NEXT PAGE

3. The above figure is an equilateral triangle divided into four congruent, smaller, equilateral triangles. If the perimeter of a smaller triangle is 1, then the perimeter of the whole large triangle is

(A) 2
(B) 4
(C) 6
(D) 8
(E) 16

4. Dick has $15.25 and spent $7.50 at the sporting goods store. How much money does he have left?

(A) $0.25
(B) $1.75
(C) $6.75
(D) $7.75
(E) $8.25

5. Given $\dfrac{4^3 + 4^3 + 4^3 + 4^3}{4^y} = 4$, find y.

(A) 3
(B) 4
(C) 8
(D) 12
(E) 64

6. If $\dfrac{2x^2 + x - 5}{x^3 + 4x^2} = \dfrac{1}{2}$
then which of the following is true?

(A) $x^3 - 2x = 10$
(B) $x^3 + 2x = 10$
(C) $x^3 - 2x = -10$
(D) $x^3 + 2x = -10$
(E) $x^3 + 2x + 2x^2 = 10$

GO ON TO THE NEXT PAGE

7. A population that starts at 100 and doubles after eight years can be expressed as the following, where t stands for the number of years that have elapsed from the start:

(A) 100×2^t

(B) $100 \times 2^{\frac{t}{7}}$

(C) $100 \times 2^{t-8}$

(D) $100 \times 2^{\frac{t}{8}}$

(E) 100×2^{16t}

8. Find the solution set in positive integers of $2x + 5 < 5$.

(A) $\{1, 2, 3, 4\}$

(B) $\{1, 2\}$

(C) $\{0\}$

(D) $\varnothing$

(E) infinity

9. If $a^b = x$ and $x^b = y$, then

(A) $a^{2b} = y$

(B) $a^{b^2} = y$

(C) $b^a = y$

(D) $(ax)^b = y$

(E) $(ax)^b = x$

10. Two lines in a plane are represented by $y = x - 1$ and $2x + 5y = 9$. The coordinates of the point at which the lines intersect are

(A) $(2,1)$

(B) $(1,2)$

(C) $(2,5)$

(D) $(5,2)$

(E) $(3,3)$

GO ON TO THE NEXT PAGE

$$C = md + t$$

11. The cost, C, of a business trip is represented by the equation above, where m is a constant, d is the number of days of the complete trip, and t is the cost of transportation, which does not change. If the business trip was increased by 5 days, how much more did the business trip cost than the original planned trip?

(A) $5d$

(B) $5m$

(C) $5t$

(D) $d(m - 3)$

(E) $m(d - 3)$

$$4x - 3y = 9$$
$$8x + ky = 19$$

13. For which value of k will the system of equations above have *no* solution?

(A) $+6$

(B) $+3$

(C) 0

(D) -3

(E) -6

12. Which of the following represents x on a number line if $(x - 3) \leq 0$?

(A)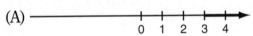

(B)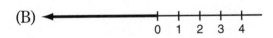

(C)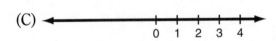

(D)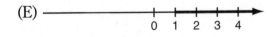

(E)

14. Given that $r \neq 0$ and $r = 5w = 7a$, find the value of $r - w$ in terms of a.

(A) $\frac{1a}{7}$

(B) $\frac{7a}{5}$

(C) $3a$

(D) $\frac{28a}{5}$

(E) $28a$

GO ON TO THE NEXT PAGE

15. The figure above consists of equal semi-circles each touching the other at the ends of their diameters. If the radius of each circle is 2, what is the *total enclosed* area?

(A) $\dfrac{\sqrt{3}}{4}+\pi$

(B) $\sqrt{3}+2\pi$

(C) $4\sqrt{3}+6\pi$

(D) 6π

(E) $\dfrac{\sqrt{2}}{4}+4\pi$

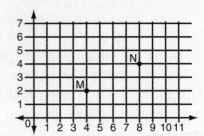

16. Which of the following points, when plotted on the grid above, will be three times as far from M (4,2) as from N (8,4)?

(A) (2,1)

(B) (4,4)

(C) (6,3)

(D) (7,1)

(E) (10,5)

STOP

If you finish before time is called, you may check your work on this section only.

Do not turn to any other section in the test.

How Did You Do on This Test?

Step 1.   Go to the Answer Key on page 338.

Step 2.   Calculate your "raw score" using the directions on page 339.

Step 3.   Get your "scaled score" for the test by referring to the SAT Math Score Conversion Table on page 340.

THERE'S ALWAYS ROOM FOR IMPROVEMENT!

Answer Key for the SAT Math Practice Test 1

Section 1		Section 2		Section 3		Section 4	
Correct Answer		Correct Answer		Correct Answer		Correct Answer	
1	B	1	C	1	C	1	D
2	C	2	B	2	C	2	C
3	D	3	C	3	E	3	A
4	D	4	D	4	C	4	D
5	D	5	C	5	C	5	A
6	E	6	A	6	C	6	C
7	E	7	A	7	D	7	D
8	C	8	C	8	D	8	D
9	A					9	B
10	C					10	A
11	A	Number correct		Number correct		11	B
12	A					12	D
13	D					13	E
14	E	Number incorrect		Number incorrect		14	D
15	A					15	C
16	D					16	E
17	C	**Student-Produced Response Questions**		**Student-Produced Response Questions**			
18	A					Number correct	
19	B	9	24	9	10		
20	C	10	9	10	20		
		11	7	11	270	Number incorrect	
Number correct		12	2	12	5		
		13	8	13	2		
		14	4	14	2		
Number incorrect		15	18	15	20		
		16	60	16	1/48		
		17	9500	17	5		
		18	280	18	108		
		Number correct		Number correct			
		Number incorrect		Number incorrect			

Scoring the Math SAT Practice Test 1

Check your responses with the correct answers on the previous pages. Fill in the blanks below and do the calculations to get your math, raw scores. Use the table to find your math, scaled score.

Get Your Math Score

How many math questions did you get **right?**

Section 1: Questions 1–20		_____	
Section 3: Questions 1–18	+	_____	
Section 4: Questions 1–16	+	_____	
Total	=	_____	**(A)**

How many multiple-choice math questions did you get **wrong?**

Section 1: Questions 1–20		_____	
Section 3: Questions 1–18	+	_____	
Section 4: Questions 1–16	+	_____	
Total	=	_____	**(B)**
$\times\ 0.25$	=	_____	
A – B	=	_____	

Math Raw Score

Round math raw score to the nearest whole number.

_____

Use the Score Conversion Table to find your math scaled score.

_____

SAT Math Score Conversion Table

Raw Score	Math Scaled Score	Raw Score	Math Scaled Score
		31	550
		30	540
		29	530
		28	520
		27	520
		26	510
		25	500
		24	490
		23	480
		22	480
		21	470
		20	460
		19	450
54	800	18	450
53	790	17	440
52	760	16	430
51	740	15	420
50	720	14	410
49	710	13	410
48	700	12	400
47	680	11	390
46	670	10	380
45	660	9	370
44	650	8	360
43	640	7	350
42	630	6	340
41	630	5	330
40	620	4	320
39	610	3	310
38	600	2	290
37	590	1	280
36	580	0	260
35	580	−1	240
34	570	−2	220
33	560	−3	200
32	550	−4	200
		and below	

This table is for use only with the test in this book.

CHART FOR SELF-APPRAISAL BASED ON THE PRACTICE TEST YOU HAVE JUST TAKEN

The Self-Appraisal Chart below tells you quickly where your SAT strengths and weaknesses lie.

	Math Questions*
EXCELLENT	44–54
GOOD	32–43
FAIR	27–31
POOR	16–26
VERY POOR	0–15

* Sections 1, 3, 4 only.

Note: In our tests, we have chosen to have Section 2 as the experimental section. Note that on the actual SAT you will take, the order of the sections can vary, and you will not know which one is experimental, so it is wise to answer all sections and not to leave any section out.

SAT VERBAL AND MATH SCORE/PERCENTILE CONVERSION TABLE

Math

SAT scaled math score	Percentile rank
800	99.5+
770–790	99.5
720–760	99
670–710	97
640–660	94
610–630	89
590–600	84
560–580	77
530–550	68
510–520	59
480–500	48
450–470	37
430–440	26
390–420	16
350–380	8
310–340	2
210–300	0.5
200	0

Explanatory Answers for Math Practice Test 1

Section 1

As you read these solutions, do the following if you answered the math question incorrectly:

When a specific Strategy is referred to in the solution, study that strategy, which you will find in "Math Strategies" (beginning on page 257).

1. Choice B is correct. **(Use Strategy: Translate from words to algebra.)**

The quotient of x and 3

$$\frac{x}{3}$$

$$\left.\frac{x}{3} - 8\right\} = 8 \text{ less than the quotient}$$

and is the required answer.

2. Choice C is correct. **(Use Strategy: Translate from words to algebra.)**

7 of Phil's buckets $-$ 7 of Mark's
buckets $=$
7×11 gallons $- 7 \times 8$ gallons $=$
77 gallons $-$ 56 gallons $=$
21 gallons

3. Choice D is correct. It is easily seen that

$$\frac{|x|}{|y|} = \left|\frac{x}{y}\right|$$

For example: $\dfrac{|-2|}{|4|} = \left|\dfrac{-2}{4}\right| = \dfrac{1}{2}; \dfrac{|-3|}{|-6|} = \left|\dfrac{-3}{-6}\right| = \dfrac{1}{2}$

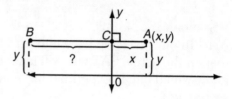

4. Choice D is correct.

As shown in the diagram above, the y-coordinates of A and B must be the same because they both lie along the same horizontal line. Since B lies to the left of the y-axis, its x-coordinate must be negative. Since $3AC = BC$, then the x-coordinate of B is

$$-3x$$

and we already know that the y-coordinate is y.

Thus, $(-3x,y)$ is the answer.

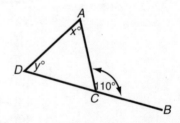

5. Choice D is correct. **(Use Strategy: Remember isosceles triangle facts.)**

Since $AC = CD$, we know that

$$x = y$$

1

We also know that

$$m\angle ACB = m\angle D + m\angle A \qquad \boxed{2}$$

Substituting the given into $\boxed{2}$, we have

$$110 = y + x \qquad \boxed{3}$$

Substituting $\boxed{1}$ into $\boxed{3}$, we get

$$110 = y + y$$
$$110 = 2y$$

6. Choice E is correct. **(Use Strategy: The obvious may be tricky!)**

Given: $(x + y)^2 = 9$
So that $x + y = 3$ or -3

From the information given, we cannot determine whether $x + y$ equals 3 or -3.

7. Choice E is correct.

$\left(\textbf{Use Strategy:}\right.$

$$\left. \textbf{Average} = \frac{\textbf{sum of values}}{\textbf{total number of values}} \right)$$

Let x, y = two unknown numbers.

Thus, $28 + 30 + 32 + x + y = 34 \qquad \boxed{1}$

Multiplying $\boxed{1}$ by 5,

$$28 + 30 + 32 + x + y = 170$$

or $90 + x + y = 170$

or $x + y = 80$

8. Choice C is correct. **(Use Strategy: Translate from words to algebra.)**

Let x = side of one of the eight squares.

Thus, we are given

$4x = 16$

or $x = 4 \qquad \boxed{1}$

From what we are told in the problem, we conclude that

$AE = MF = LG = 4x \qquad \boxed{2}$

and $AL = BK = CJ = DH = EG = 2x \qquad \boxed{3}$

(Use Strategy: The whole equals the sum of its parts.)

Thus,
$AE + MF + LG + AL + BK + CJ + DH + EG$
$= 4x + 4x + 4x + 2x + 2x + 2x + 2x + 2x$
$= 22x = 88$

using $\boxed{1}$, $\boxed{2}$, and $\boxed{3}$.

9. Choice A is correct. **(Use Strategy: Use new definitions carefully.)**

Given: $\;\textcircled{x} = \dfrac{x^2}{3}$ and $\boxed{x} = \dfrac{9}{x}$

$$\textcircled{x} \times \boxed{x} = \frac{x^2}{3} \times \frac{9}{x} = 3x$$

10. Choice C is correct. **(Use Strategy: Use the given information effectively.)**

For I, we have:

Clearly $DB > DA$. So I could not be true.

Clearly D can be the same distance from 2 points (A and B), but not from 3, so II does not apply.

Only Choice C, III only, is now possible.

Choice III is demonstrated below, although it was not necessary for us to examine it.

By definition, all points on the circle are the same distance from the center. So $DA = DB = DC$.

11. Choice A is correct. It can be seen that the dark region in Choice A is common to sets A, B, and C. Thus the diagram in Choice A describes the dark region as the set of elements that belongs to all of the sets A, B, and C.

12. Choice A is correct. Since the slope of a line is constant, the *ratio* of the *difference* in y-coordinates to the *difference* in x-coordinates must be constant for any two points on the line. For points $(1,3)$ and $(3,5)$, this ratio is

$$\frac{5 - 3}{3 - 1} = 1$$

Thus, for points $(6,y)$ and $(3,5)$, we must have

$$\frac{y - 5}{6 - 3} = 1$$

Therefore,

$$y - 5 = 3$$

and $y = 8$.

13. Choice D is correct. (**Use Strategy: Know how to use units.**)

$$\left(\frac{p \text{ gallons}}{\text{car}}\right) \times (r \text{ cars}) = pr \text{ gallons for each month}$$

$$\frac{q \text{ gallons}}{pr \dfrac{\text{gallons}}{\text{months}}} = \frac{q}{pr} \text{ months}$$

14. Choice E is correct. (**Use Strategy: Use new definitions carefully.**)

By definition, the l-length from -3 to $3 =$

$$3 - (-3) =$$
$$3 + 3 = 6$$

15. Choice A is correct.

By definition, the l-length from -4 to each of the other points follow:

$$R - (-4) = R + 4 \qquad \boxed{1}$$
$$S - (-4) = S + 4 \qquad \boxed{2}$$
$$T - (-4) = T + 4 \qquad \boxed{3}$$
$$U - (-4) = U + 4 \qquad \boxed{4}$$
$$V - (-4) = V + 4 \qquad \boxed{5}$$

From their position on the number line we know that:

$$R < S < T < U < V \qquad \boxed{6}$$

(**Use Strategy: Know how to manipulate inequalities.**)

Adding 4 to each term of $\boxed{6}$, we get

$$R + 4 < S + 4 < T + 4 < U + 4 < V + 4 \quad \boxed{7}$$

It is obvious from $\boxed{7}$ that $R + 4$ is smallest.

Thus, $\boxed{1}$ above, point R, has the least l-length from -4.

16. Choice D is correct. (**Use Strategy: Translate from words to algebra.**)

Let $x, x + 1, x + 2, x + 3, x + 4$ represent the 5 consecutive integers.

Then, $x + x + 1 + x + 2 + x + 3 + x + 4 = w$

$$5x + 10 = w \qquad \boxed{1}$$

The next 5 consecutive positive integers will be:

$$x + 5, x + 6, x + 7, x + 8, x + 9$$

Their sum will be:

$$x + 5 + x + 6 + x + 7 + x + 8 + x + 9 =$$

$$5x + 35 \qquad \boxed{2}$$

We can write $\boxed{2}$ as $5x + 35$

$$= 5x + 10 + 25 \quad \boxed{3}$$

Substituting $\boxed{1}$ and $\boxed{3}$, we get

$$5x + 10 + 25 = w + 25$$

17. Choice C is correct. **(Use Strategy: Translate from words to algebra.)**

We are told that the area of the square is twice the area of triangle. This translates to:

$$a^2 = 2\left(\frac{1}{2} \times bc\right) \qquad \boxed{1}$$
$$a^2 = bc \qquad \boxed{2}$$

We are given that $bc = 100$

Substituting $\boxed{2}$ into $\boxed{1}$, we get

$$a^2 = 100$$

18. Choice A is correct.

Given that the radius of the circle $= 2$, we have circumference $= 2\pi(\text{radius}) = 2\pi(2) = 4\pi$ inches $\qquad \boxed{1}$

We are given that

$$\overgroup{AD} + \overgroup{BC} = 3\pi \text{ inches} \qquad \boxed{2}$$

(Use Strategy: The whole equals the sum of its parts.)

We know that

$$\overgroup{AD} + \overgroup{BC} + \overgroup{AC} + \overgroup{DB} = \text{circumference}$$

of circle $\qquad \boxed{3}$

Substituting $\boxed{1}$ and $\boxed{2}$ into $\boxed{3}$, we have

$$3\pi \text{ inches} + \overgroup{AC} + \overgroup{DB} = 4\pi \text{ inches}$$
$$\overgroup{AC} + \overgroup{DB} = \pi \text{ inches} \qquad \boxed{4}$$

We know that the measure of an arc can be found by:

measure of arc

$$= \left(\frac{\text{length of arc}}{\substack{\text{circumference} \\ \text{of circle}}}\right) \times 360 \qquad \boxed{5}$$

Substituting $\boxed{1}$ and $\boxed{4}$ into $\boxed{5}$, we get
measure of $AC + DB$

$$= \left(\frac{\pi \text{ inches}}{4\pi \text{ inches}}\right) \times 360 = 90 \qquad \boxed{6}$$

(Use Strategy: Factor and reduce.)

From the diagram $m\angle AOC = m\angle DOB = y$

Therefore, $m\,\overgroup{AC} = m\,\overgroup{DB} = y.$ $\qquad \boxed{7}$
Substituting $\boxed{7}$ into $\boxed{6}$, we get
$$y + y = 90, \text{ or } 2y = 90$$
$$\text{or } y = 45$$

19. Choice B is correct. **(Use Strategy: Translate from words to algebra.)**

Let $r =$ Ross's age now.
$19 =$ Amanda's age now.
Thus, $r - 5 =$ Ross's age five
years ago. $\qquad \boxed{1}$
$19 - 5 = 14 =$ Amanda's age five
years ago. $\qquad \boxed{2}$

We are given: Five years ago, Ross was N times as old as Amanda was. $\boxed{3}$

Substituting $\boxed{1}$ and $\boxed{2}$ into $\boxed{3}$, we have

$$r - 5 = N(14)$$
$$r = 14N + 5$$

20. Choice C is correct.

The volume of the rectangular solid to be immersed is:

$$V = (1 \text{ ft})(1 \text{ ft})(2 \text{ ft}) = 2 \text{ ft}^3 \qquad \boxed{1}$$

When the solid is immersed, the volume of the displaced water will be:

$$(2 \text{ ft})(6 \text{ ft})(x \text{ ft}) = 12x \text{ ft}^3 \qquad \boxed{2}$$

where x represents the height of the displaced water. $\boxed{1}$ and $\boxed{2}$ must be equal. So

$$2 \text{ ft}^3 = 12x \text{ ft}^3$$
$$\frac{1}{6} \text{ ft} = x$$

(Use Strategy: Know how to use units.)

$$\left(\frac{1}{6}\text{ ft}\right)\left(\frac{12 \text{ inches}}{\text{foot}}\right) = \frac{12}{6} = 2 \text{ inches}$$

that the displaced water will rise.

Explanatory Answers for Math Practice Test 1 (continued)

Section 2

As you read these solutions, do the following if you answered the math question incorrectly:

When a specific Strategy is referred to in the solution, study that strategy, which you will find in "Math Strategies" (beginning on page 257).

1. Choice C is correct. **(Use Strategy: Use the given information effectively.)**

   Given:
   $$x + by = 5 \qquad \boxed{1}$$
   $$3x + y = 5 \qquad \boxed{2}$$
   $$y = 2 \qquad \boxed{3}$$

   We want to find b.

   Substituting $\boxed{3}$ into $\boxed{2}$, we get
   $$3x + 2 = 5$$
   or $\qquad x = 1 \qquad \boxed{4}$

   Substituting $\boxed{3}$ and $\boxed{4}$ into $\boxed{1}$, we have
   $$1 + 2b = 5$$
   or $\qquad 2b = 4$
   or $\qquad b = 2$

2. Choice B is correct.

   The ratio of boys to girls in the class is 2:3. Choice C is the answer, because $9:12 = 3:4$, which does not equal 2:3.

3. Choice C is correct. **(Use Strategy: Know how to use units.)**

   Since 7 days = 1 week, 24 hours = 1 day, and 60 minutes = 1 hour, then

   $$1\,\text{week} = (1\,\cancel{\text{week}})\left(\frac{7\,\text{days}}{\cancel{\text{week}}}\right)\left(\frac{24\,\text{hours}}{\cancel{\text{day}}}\right)\left(\frac{60\,\text{minutes}}{\cancel{\text{hour}}}\right)$$
   $$= (7)(24)(60)\,\text{minutes}$$

   Thus,

   $$\frac{24\,\text{minutes}}{1\,\text{week}} = \frac{24\,\cancel{\text{minutes}}}{(7)(24)(60)\,\cancel{\text{minutes}}} = \frac{1}{420}$$

4. Choice D is correct.

   (Use Strategy: Use the given information effectively.)

   $$2 \times 10^{-5} \times 8 \times 10^2 \times 5 \times 10^2$$
   $$= 2 \times 8 \times 5 \times 10^{-5} \times 10^2 \times 10^2$$
   $$= 8 \times 10^0$$
   $$= 8 \times 1$$
   $$= 8$$

5. Choice C is correct.

   (Use Strategy: Translate from words to algebra.)

   $$\text{Allowance} = \$30$$
   $$\text{Amount spent on candy} = \frac{2}{5} \times \$30 = \$12$$
   Amount left after
   Johnny bought candy $= \$30 - \$12 = \$18$

Amount spent on ice

$$\text{cream} = \frac{5}{6} \times \$18 = \$15$$

Amount left after buying

$$\text{candy and ice cream} = \$18 - \$15$$
$$= \$3$$

6. Choice A is correct. $y = -x^2 = -4$. $x = 2$ or $x = -2$. Since point B lies on the left side of the y-axis, $x = -2$.

7. Choice A is correct. It is seen from the graph of $y = f(x)$ that when $x = 0$, $y = 0$. Thus $0 = m(0) + b$ and $b = 0$.

8. Choice C is correct. When the graph intersects the x-axis, $y = 0$. Thus we set $y = 0 = x^4 + x^3$.

   We can write this as
   $$x^3(x + 1) = 0$$
   Thus $x = 0$ and $x = -1$.

   The graph therefore intersects the x-axis at two points.

9. 24 (Use Strategy: Translate from words to algebra.)

   Given:
   $$\frac{5}{8} \text{ of } x \text{ is } 40$$
   $$\downarrow \downarrow \downarrow \downarrow \downarrow$$
   $$\frac{5}{8} \times x = 40 \quad \boxed{1}$$

   (Use Strategy: Find unknowns by multiplication.)

   Fast Method: Multiply $\boxed{1}$ by $\frac{3}{5}$ to get

   $$\frac{3}{\cancel{5}}\left(\frac{\cancel{5}}{8}x\right) = \frac{3}{5}(40)$$
   $$\frac{3}{8}x = \frac{3}{\cancel{5}} \times \cancel{5} \times 8$$
   $$\frac{3}{8}x = 24$$

   Slow Method: Solve $\boxed{1}$ for x by multiplying $\boxed{1}$ by $\frac{8}{5}$:

   $$x = 64 \qquad \boxed{2}$$

   Now substitute $\boxed{2}$ into the unknown expression:

   $$\frac{3}{8}x = \frac{3}{8}(64)$$
   $$= \frac{3}{\cancel{8}} \times \cancel{8} \times 8$$
   $$= 24$$

10. 9 (Use Strategy: Translate from words to algebra.) We are given that the wire is bent to form a circle of radius 3 feet. This means that its length is equal to the circumference of the circle.

    Thus, length of wire $= 2\pi r = 2\pi(3)$ feet
    $$= 6\pi \text{ feet}$$
    $$\approx 6(3.14) \text{ feet}$$
    Length of wire ≈ 18.84 feet $\quad \boxed{1}$

    (Use Strategy: Know how to find unknown quantities.)

    $$\frac{\text{Number of pieces}}{\text{2 feet long}} = \frac{\text{Total length}}{\text{2 feet}} \quad \boxed{2}$$

    Substituting $\boxed{1}$ into $\boxed{2}$, we have

    Number of pieces 2 feet long $\approx \dfrac{18.84 \text{ feet}}{2 \text{ feet}}$
    $$\approx 9.42$$
    $$= 9 \text{ complete pieces}$$

11. 7 (Use Strategy: Translate from words to algebra.)

    Let $b =$ number of baseballs that Dick bought
    $t =$ number of tennis balls that Dick bought
    $.70b =$ amount spent on baseballs
    $.60t =$ amount spent on tennis balls

Thus, we are told

$$.70b + .60t = 7.00 \quad \boxed{1}$$

Multiply $\boxed{1}$ by 10:

$$7b + 6t = 70 \quad \boxed{2}$$

Solve $\boxed{2}$ for t:

$$t = \frac{70 - 7b}{6} \quad \boxed{3}$$

(Use Strategy: Use the given information effectively.) From $\boxed{3}$, we see that the maximum value of t occurs at the minimum value of b. Since b and t are numbers of balls, b and t must be non-negative integers. Thus, the minimum value of b is 0. When $b = 0$, $t = \frac{70}{6}$, which is not integral. For t to be an integer, $\boxed{3}$ tells us that $(10 - b)$ is a multiple of 6. The smallest value of b that makes $(10 - b)$ a multiple of 6 is $b = 4$. Thus, $t = 7$ is the maximum value of t, and 7 is the answer.

12. 2 (Use Strategy: Use new definitions carefully.)

Given:

$$f(x) = 12x + 8 \quad \boxed{1}$$

and $f(x) \div f(0) = 2x \quad \boxed{2}$

Calculate $f(0)$:

$$f(0) = 12(0) + 8 = 8 \quad \boxed{3}$$

Substitute $\boxed{1}$ and $\boxed{3}$ into $\boxed{2}$:

$$\frac{12x + 8}{8} = 2x \quad \boxed{4}$$

Multiply both sides of $\boxed{4}$ by 8:

$$12x + 8 = 16x$$
or $\quad 8 = 4x$
or $\quad x = 2$

13. 8 (Use Strategy: Use new definitions carefully.)

In the given letter columns, only 8 triples have the property that exactly 2 of the letters in the triple are the same. Thus, 8 triples have a value of 1, and all the other triples have a value of 0. Hence, the value of the entire group of letter columns is 8.

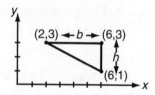

14. 4 (Use Strategy: Use the given information effectively.)

It is clear from the diagram above that the triangle is a right triangle whose area is

$$A = \frac{1}{2}bh \quad \boxed{1}$$

From the given coordinates, we can also say that

$$b = 6 - 2 = 4 \quad \boxed{2}$$
$$h = 3 - 1 = 2 \quad \boxed{3}$$

Substituting $\boxed{2}$ and $\boxed{3}$ into $\boxed{1}$,

$$A = \frac{1}{2}(4)(2)$$
$$A = 4$$

15. 18 (Use Strategy: Use the given information effectively.)

The area of a rectangle is length × width. The number of squares that can be packed into the rectangle

$$= \frac{\text{Area of entire rectangle}}{\text{Area of each square}}$$

$$= \frac{6 \times 12}{2 \times 2}$$

$$= \frac{72}{4}$$

$$= \frac{\cancel{4} \times 18}{\cancel{4}}$$

$$= 18$$

16. 60 Since we are given the radii of the circles, we have

$$AN = AM = 1 \qquad \boxed{1}$$
$$BM = BP = 2 \qquad \boxed{2}$$
$$CN = CP = 3 \qquad \boxed{3}$$

We want to find

$$(AB)(BC)(AC) \qquad \boxed{4}$$

(Use Strategy: The whole equals the sum of its parts.) From the diagram, we see that

$$AB = AM + BM \qquad \boxed{5}$$
$$BC = BP + CP \qquad \boxed{6}$$
$$AC = AN + CN \qquad \boxed{7}$$

Substituting $\boxed{1}$, $\boxed{2}$, $\boxed{3}$ into $\boxed{5}$, $\boxed{6}$, $\boxed{7}$ we have

$$AB = 3$$
$$BC = 5$$
$$AC = 4$$

Thus,

$$(AB)(BC)(AC) = (3)(5)(4)$$
$$= 60$$

17. 9,500

$$\left(\text{Use Strategy:} \right.$$

$$\left. \textbf{Average} = \frac{\textbf{Sum of values}}{\textbf{Total number of values}} \right)$$

We are given:

$$\frac{x + y + z + w}{4} = 8,000 \qquad \boxed{1}$$

(Use Strategy: Find unknowns by multiplication.) Multiplying $\boxed{1}$ by 4, we get

$$x + y + z + w = 32,000 \qquad \boxed{2}$$

We are given that any 3 have an average of 7,500, so using x, y and z as the 3, we get

$$\frac{x + y + z}{3} = 7,500 \qquad \boxed{3}$$

Multiplying $\boxed{3}$ by 3, we get

$$x + y + z = 22,500 \qquad \boxed{4}$$

Substituting $\boxed{4}$ into $\boxed{2}$, we get

$$22,500 + w = 32,000$$

or $\qquad w = 9,500$

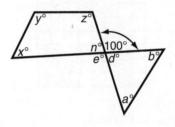

18. 280

(Use Strategy: Use the given information effectively.)

From the diagram, $n = d$ (vertical angles) $\qquad \boxed{1}$

We know $x + y + z + n = 360 \qquad \boxed{2}$

Substituting $\boxed{1}$ into $\boxed{2}$, we get

$$x + y + z + d = 360 \qquad \boxed{3}$$

Subtracting d from $\boxed{3}$, we have

$$x + y + z = 360 - d \qquad \boxed{4}$$

We know that $100 + d = 180$ from the diagram.

So, $d = 180 - 100 = 80 \qquad \boxed{5}$

Substituting $\boxed{5}$ into $\boxed{4}$, we get

$$x + y + z = 360 - 80$$
$$x + y + z = 280$$

Explanatory Answers for Math Practice Test 1 (continued)

Section 3

As you read these solutions, do the following if you answered the math question incorrectly:

When a specific Strategy is referred to in the solution, study that strategy, which you will find in "Math Strategies" (beginning on page 257).

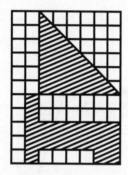

1. Choice C is correct.

Given: length of side of square = 1. $\boxed{1}$
Using $\boxed{1}$, we get $AB = 6$, $BC = 6$ $\boxed{2}$

We know that
Area of triangle = $\frac{1}{2}$ (base)(height) $\boxed{3}$
Substituting $\boxed{2}$ into $\boxed{3}$, we get

Area of shaded triangle

$$ABC = \frac{1}{2}(6)(6) = 18 \qquad \boxed{4}$$

We know that
Area of square = (side)^2 $\boxed{5}$
Substituting $\boxed{1}$ into $\boxed{5}$, we have

Area of each square = $(1)^2 = 1$ $\boxed{6}$

Counting the number of squares in the other shaded figure (*BDEFGHIJKL*), we find 19. $\boxed{7}$

Multiplying $\boxed{6}$ by $\boxed{7}$, we have

Area of *BDEFGHIJKL*
$$= 19 \times 1 = 19 \qquad \boxed{8}$$

(Use Strategy: The whole equals the sum of its parts.)

We know: Total shaded area
$$= \text{Area of } ABC +$$
$$\text{Area of } BDEFGHIJKL \qquad \boxed{9}$$

Substituting $\boxed{4}$ and $\boxed{8}$ into $\boxed{9}$, we get

Total shaded area = 18 + 19
$$= 37$$

2. Choice C is correct. **(Use Strategy: Use the given information effectively.)**

Since the triangle is equilateral, all of its sides are equal. Thus,

$$5x - 2 = x$$
$$4x = 2$$
$$x = \frac{1}{2}$$

Perimeter = Sum of 3 sides = $\frac{1}{2} + \frac{1}{2} + \frac{1}{2}$
$$= 1\frac{1}{2}$$

3. Choice E is correct. **(Use Strategy: Know how to use units of time, distance, area.)**

The number of waves that pass through a certain point in t seconds

$$= \frac{w \text{ waves}}{s \text{ seconds}} (t \text{ seconds})$$

$$= \frac{wt}{s} \text{ waves}$$

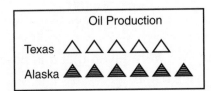

4. Choice C is correct. **(Use Strategy: Translate from words to algebra.)**

We are told $\blacktriangle = 3\triangle$

(Use Strategy: Use the given information effectively.)

Texas total $= 5$

Alaska total $= 3(6) = 18$

(Use Strategy: Know how to find unknown quantities from known quantities.)

$$\frac{\text{Alaska production}}{\text{Total production}} = \frac{18}{5+18} =$$

$$\frac{18}{23} = \text{required ratio}$$

5. Choice C is correct. Probability is defined as

$$\frac{\text{number of favorable ways (coins)}}{\text{total number of ways (coins)}} \quad \frac{F}{N}.$$

If the probability of selecting a nickel is $\frac{3}{8}$, then for nickels, $\frac{F}{N} = \frac{3}{8}$. But N [the total number of ways (or coins)] is 24.

So $\frac{F}{N} = \frac{3}{8} = \frac{F}{24}$; F = 9 (nickels)

The probability of selecting a dime is $\frac{1}{8}$, so for a dime, $\frac{F}{N} = \frac{1}{8} = \frac{F}{24}$;

F = 3 (dimes)

Since there are 24 coins, and there are 9 nickels and 3 dimes, $24 - 3 - 9 = 12$ quarters. **(Use Strategy: Subtract whole from parts.)**

6. Choice C is correct. **(Use Strategy: Use the given information effectively.)**

Given: ▢▉　　　　　　　▢1

In order for a given figure to have been formed from ▢1, it must have the same number of shaded and unshaded squares.

Choice I has 8 unshaded and 6 shaded squares. Thus, it could *not* be formed from ▢1.

Choice II has 5 unshaded and 6 shaded squares. Thus, it could *not* be formed from ▢1.

Looking at Choices A through E, we see that the correct choice must be Choice C: III only.

7. Choice D is correct. $f(x+2) = (x+2-1)^2 + (x+2-2)^2 + (x+2-3)^2 = (x+1)^2 + x^2 + (x-1)^2 = x^2 + 2x + 1 + x^2 + x^2 - 2x + 1 = 3x^2 + 2.$

8. Choice D is correct. The procedure, as described, can be summarized in the following table:

Given Container	–	Receiving Container	=	Excess to 50cc Container
25cc	–	16cc	=	9cc
16cc	–	9cc	=	7cc
9cc	–	4cc	=	5cc
4cc	–	1cc	=	3cc
		Total	=	24cc

(Use Strategy: Remember the definition of percent.)

Thus, $\dfrac{24\text{cc}}{50\text{cc}} \times 100 = 48\%$ of the 50cc container is full.

(Use Strategy: The whole equals the sum of its parts.)

So, $100\% - 48\% = 52\%$ of the 50cc container is empty.

9. 10

Given:
$$ab = 40 \qquad \boxed{1}$$
$$\frac{a}{b} = \frac{5}{2} \qquad \boxed{2}$$

(Use Strategy: Find unknowns by multiplication.)

Multiplying $\boxed{2}$ by $2b$, we get

$$2b\left(\frac{a}{b}\right) = \left(\frac{5}{2}\right)2b$$

$$2a = 5b$$

$$\frac{2a}{5} = b \qquad \boxed{3}$$

Substitute $\boxed{3}$ into $\boxed{1}$. We have

$$ab = 40$$

$$a\left(\frac{2a}{5}\right) = 40$$

$$\frac{2a^2}{5} = 40 \qquad \boxed{4}$$

Multiplying $\boxed{1}$ by $\dfrac{5}{2}$, we get

$$\frac{5}{2}\left(\frac{2a^2}{5}\right) = (40)\frac{5}{2}$$

$$a^2 = 100$$

$$\sqrt{a^2} = \sqrt{100}$$

$$a = \pm 10$$

Since we were given that a is positive, we have $a = 10$.

10. 20

(Use Strategy: Translate from words to algebra.)

Given: Stephanie's earnings = \$x $\qquad \boxed{1}$
Stephanie's time $\quad$ = 10 hours $\quad \boxed{2}$
Evelyn's earnings $\quad$ = \$y $\qquad \boxed{3}$
Evelyn's time $\qquad$ = 20 hours $\quad \boxed{4}$
$x + y \qquad\qquad$ = 60 $\qquad\quad \boxed{5}$

We know that hourly wage = $\dfrac{\text{Total Earnings}}{\text{Total Hours}}$
$\boxed{6}$

Substituting $\boxed{1}$ and $\boxed{2}$ into $\boxed{6}$, we get

Stephanie's hourly wage = $\dfrac{\$x}{10\,\text{hours}} \quad \boxed{7}$

Substituting $\boxed{3}$ and $\boxed{4}$ into $\boxed{6}$, we get

Evelyn's hourly wage = $\dfrac{\$y}{20\,\text{hours}} \quad \boxed{8}$

We are told that they have the same hourly wage. Using $\boxed{7}$ and $\boxed{8}$, we have

$$\frac{\$x}{10\,\text{hours}} = \frac{\$y}{20\,\text{hours}}$$

$$\frac{x}{10} = \frac{y}{20} \qquad \boxed{9}$$

$$\overset{2}{\cancel{20}}\left(\frac{x}{\cancel{10}}\right)=\left(\frac{y}{\cancel{20}}\right)\cancel{20}$$
$$2x=y \qquad \boxed{10}$$

Substituting $\boxed{10}$ into $\boxed{5}$, we get
$$x+2x=60$$
$$3x=60$$
$$x=20$$

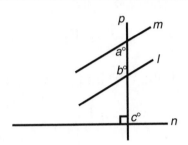

11. 270

Given: $m\parallel l$ $\qquad\qquad$ $\boxed{1}$

$\qquad\quad$ $p\perp n$ $\qquad\qquad$ $\boxed{2}$

From $\boxed{1}$ we get that $a+b=180$, $\qquad$ $\boxed{3}$ because when two lines are parallel, the interior angles on the same side of the transversal are supplementary.

From $\boxed{2}$ we get that $c=90$, $\qquad$ $\boxed{4}$ because perpendicular lines form right angles.

(Use Strategy: Find unknowns by addition.)

Add $\boxed{3}$ and $\boxed{4}$. We have
$$a+b+c=180+90$$
$$=270$$

12. 5

We know Area of circle $=\pi(\text{radius})^2$ $\quad$ $\boxed{1}$
Given: radius of larger
$\qquad$ circle $=r+3$ $\qquad\qquad\qquad$ $\boxed{2}$
radius of small circle $=r$ $\qquad\qquad$ $\boxed{3}$

Substitute $\boxed{2}$ into $\boxed{1}$. We have
$\qquad$ Area of larger circle $=\pi(r+3)^2$ $\quad$ $\boxed{4}$

(Use Strategy: Remember classic expressions.)

$$(r+3)^2=r^2+6r+9 \quad \boxed{5}$$

Substitute $\boxed{5}$ into $\boxed{4}$. We have
$\qquad$ Area of larger circle $=\pi(r^2+6r+9)$ $\quad$ $\boxed{6}$

Substituting $\boxed{3}$ into $\boxed{1}$, we get
$\qquad$ Area of small circle $=\pi r^2$ $\qquad\qquad$ $\boxed{7}$

(Use Strategy: Find unknowns by subtraction.)

Subtract $\boxed{7}$ from $\boxed{6}$. We have difference of areas
$$=\pi(r^2+6r+9)-\pi r^2 \quad \boxed{8}$$

Given: Difference of areas $=21\pi$ $\quad$ $\boxed{9}$

Substitute $\boxed{9}$ into $\boxed{8}$. We have
$$21\pi=\pi(r^2+6r+9)-\pi r^2 \quad \boxed{10}$$

(Use Strategy: Find unknowns by division.)

$$\frac{21\cancel{\pi}}{\cancel{\pi}}=\frac{\cancel{\pi}(r^2+6r+9)}{\cancel{\pi}}-\frac{\cancel{\pi}r^2}{\cancel{\pi}}$$
$$21=\cancel{r^2}+6r+9-\cancel{r^2}$$
$$21=6r+9$$
$$12=6r$$
$$2=r \qquad\qquad\qquad \boxed{11}$$

Substitute $\boxed{11}$ into $\boxed{2}$. We get

radius of larger circle $=2+3=5$

13. 2

(Use Strategy: Use the given information effectively.)

Team C has a total of $4+8+8=20$ points after 2 more games. Team A has $12+4+2=18$ points. Team B has $12+2+4=18$ points. Thus, Team C will have to play at least 2 more games.

14. 2

(Use Strategy: Use the given information effectively.)

Since $x = 15$, then

$$m\angle LMN = 90$$
$$m\angle JNK = 75$$
$$m\angle KNM = 15$$
$$m\angle JNM = 90$$

Thus, the figure, with dashed line extensions, follows:

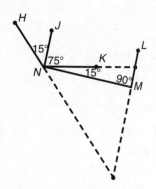

Clearly $\overleftrightarrow{JN} \parallel \overleftrightarrow{ML}$ and $\overleftrightarrow{JN}$ will not intersect $\overleftrightarrow{ML}$. $\overleftrightarrow{NK}$ and $\overleftrightarrow{NH}$ will each intersect $\overleftrightarrow{ML}$ exactly once. Thus, there will be exactly 2 more additional points of intersection.

15. 20

(Use Strategy: Translate from words to algebra.)

We are told that

$$a = b + \frac{10}{100}b = \frac{11}{10}b \qquad \boxed{1}$$

$$ac = bd + \frac{32}{100}bd = \frac{33}{25}bd \qquad \boxed{2}$$

(Use Strategy: Find unknowns by division.)

We divide $\boxed{2}$ by a

$$c = \frac{33}{25}\left(\frac{b}{a}\right)d \qquad \boxed{3}$$

(Use Strategy: Find unknowns by multiplication.)

Multiply $\boxed{1}$ by $\frac{1}{b}$, giving

$$\frac{a}{b} = \frac{11}{10}$$

or

$$\frac{b}{a} = \frac{10}{11} \qquad \boxed{4}$$

Substituting $\boxed{4}$ into $\boxed{3}$, we get

$$c = \frac{6}{5}d$$

or

$$c = d + \frac{1}{5}d$$

or

$$c = d + \frac{20}{100}d$$

Thus, c is 20 percent greater than d.

Alternate method:

(Use Strategy: Use numerics.) Let $b = 100$, $d = 10$. **(Use Strategy: Translate words to algebra.)**

Then $a = \frac{10}{100}(100) + 100 = 110$

$$ac = \frac{32}{100}bd + bd = \frac{32}{100}(100)d + 100d$$

$$110c = 32d + 100d = 132d \qquad \boxed{1}$$

$$c = \frac{x}{100}d = d = \frac{xd + 100d}{100} = \frac{(x+100)d}{100} \qquad \boxed{2}$$

Divide $\boxed{1}$ by 110:

$$c = \frac{132}{110}d \qquad \boxed{3}$$

Compare ③ with ②:

$$\frac{132}{110} = \frac{x+100}{100}$$

$$\frac{13200}{110} = x+100$$

$$120 = x+100$$

$$20 = x$$

16. $\dfrac{1}{48}$

(Use Strategy: Translate from words to algebra.)

Given: We know that

1 gross = 12 dozen

1 dozen = 12 (eggs)

Thus,

1 gross of eggs

$= (12 \text{ dozens})(12 \text{ eggs}/\text{dozen})$

$= 144 \text{ eggs}$

3 eggs, expressed as a fraction of a gross, $= \dfrac{3}{144} = \dfrac{1}{48}$

17. 5

We are given that

Volume of 1 brick = 40 cubic inches   ①

Volume of the final pile of bricks = 8000 cubic inches ②

(Use Strategy: The whole equals the sum of its parts.) Logically, we know the number of layers in the final pile of bricks =

$$\frac{\text{Volume of the final pile of bricks}}{\text{Volume of each layer of bricks}} \quad ③$$

From the diagram in the question, we see that

1 layer of bricks = 40 bricks   ④

Thus, by using ① and ④, we know that the volume of each layer of bricks

$=$ volume of 1 brick
  $\times$ number of bricks in 1 layer
$= 40$ cubic inches $\times 40$
$= 1600$ cubic inches   ⑤

Substituting ② and ⑤ into ③, the number of layers in the final pile of bricks =

$$\frac{8000 \text{ cubic inches}}{1600 \text{ cubic inches}}$$

(Use Strategy: Factor and reduce.)

$$= \frac{8 \times 1000}{16 \times 100}$$

$$= \frac{\cancel{8} \times 10 \times \cancel{100}}{\cancel{8} \times 2 \times \cancel{100}}$$

$$= \frac{10}{2} = 5$$

18. 108

(Use Strategy: Use new definitions carefully.)

The first few 3-digit numbers are 100, 101, 102, 103, 104, etc.

Clearly, the smallest possible 3-digit number in which no digit is repeated is $x = 102$.

From the definition of y, y must be $y = 210$.

Thus, $y - x = 210 - 102 = 108$

Explanatory Answers for Math Practice Test 1 (continued)

Section 4

> As you read these solutions, do the following if you answered the math question incorrectly:
>
> When a specific Strategy is referred to in the solution, study that strategy, which you will find in "Math Strategies" (beginning on page 257).

1. Choice D is correct.

Given:

$$5x = 3 \qquad \boxed{1}$$

(Use Strategy: Try not to make tedious calculations.)

Method 1: Add 3 to both sides of $\boxed{1}$

$$5x + 3 = 6 \qquad \boxed{2}$$

(Use Strategy: Find unknown expressions by multiplication.)

Square both sides of $\boxed{2}$

$$(5x + 3)^2 = 36 \qquad \boxed{3}$$

This method involves simpler arithmetic (no fractions) than the next method.

Method 2: This method is a bit slower. Solve $\boxed{1}$ for x to get

$$x = \frac{3}{5} \qquad \boxed{4}$$

Using $\boxed{4}$, calculate the unknown expression.

$$(5x + 3)^2 =$$

$$\left[5\left(\frac{3}{5}\right) + 3 \right]^2 =$$

$$(3 + 3)^2 =$$
$$6^2 = 36$$

2. Choice C is correct. **(Use Strategy: Translate from words to algebra.)**

$$\text{Let } 8n = \text{number of boys} \qquad \boxed{1}$$
$$7n = \text{number of girls} \qquad \boxed{2}$$

The ratio of $\dfrac{\text{boys}}{\text{girls}} = \dfrac{8n}{7n} = \dfrac{8}{7}$, and the given condition is satisfied.

(Use Strategy: The whole equals the sum of its parts.)

Total number of students = boys plus girls $\qquad \boxed{3}$

Substitute $\boxed{1}$ and $\boxed{2}$ into $\boxed{3}$, we get

Total number of students $= 8n + 7n = 15n$
$$\boxed{4}$$

$\boxed{4}$ is a multiple of 15

Choices A, B, D, and E are multiples of 15:

   Ⓐ $15 = 15 \times 1$

   Ⓑ $45 = 15 \times 3$

   Ⓓ $60 = 15 \times 4$

   Ⓔ $90 = 15 \times 6$

Only Choice C, 50, is *not* a multiple of 15.

3. Choice A is correct. **(Use Strategy: Translate from words to algebra.)**

Let x = side of smaller triangles

Thus, $3x$ = perimeter of each smaller triangle

$6x$ = perimeter of largest triangle

We are told

$$3x = 1$$
$$x = \frac{1}{3} \qquad \boxed{1}$$

(Use Strategy: Find unknowns by multiplication.)

Multiplying $\boxed{1}$ by 6, we get

$6x = 2$ = perimeter of largest triangle

4. Choice D is correct. **(Use Strategy: The whole equals the sum of its parts.)**

Amount left = original amount − amount spent

$$= \$15.25 - \$7.50$$
$$= \$7.75$$

5. Choice A is correct. **(Use Strategy: Use the given information effectively.)**

Given: $\dfrac{4^3 + 4^3 + 4^3 + 4^3}{4^y} = 4$

$$\frac{4(4^3)}{4^y} = 4$$
$$\frac{4^4}{4^y} = 4$$
$$4^{4+y} = 4^1 \qquad \boxed{1}$$

In $\boxed{1}$ each expression has base 4. Since the expressions are equal, the exponents must also be equal. Thus,

$$4 - y = 1$$
$$-y = -3$$
$$y = 3$$

6. Choice C is correct. Cross multiply:

$$2(2x^2 + x - 5) = x^3 + 4x^2$$
$$4x^2 + 2x - 10 = x^3 + 4x^2$$

Use Strategy:

Cancel $4x^2$ from both sides:

$2x - 10 = x^3$, and so $x^3 - 2x = -10$.

7. Choice D is correct. Perhaps the best way to answer this type of question is to write a description of what occurs:

starting point 100	$t = 0$
after 8 yrs	200	$t = 8$
after 8×2 yrs	400	$t = 16$
after 8×3 yrs	800	$t = 24$

You can see that this is represented as population $= 100 \times 2^{t/8}$

8. Choice D is correct. $2x + 5 < 5$

Subtracting 5 from both sides: $2x < 0$.

Dividing both sides by 2: $x < 0$.

Since x must be positive integer, i.e., x is greater than 0, the solution set is the empty set, or $\varnothing$.

9. Choice B is correct.

$$(a^b)^b = x^b = y. \ (a^b)^b = a^{b^2} = y.$$

10. Choice A is correct. To find the coordinates of the intersection point, we must first solve the equations $y = x - 1$ and $2x + 5y = 9$. In the equation $2x + 5y = 9$, we substitute $y = x - 1$. We obtain

$$2x + 5(x - 1) = 9$$

Thus

$$2x + 5x - 5 = 9$$

and

$$7x = 14$$
$$x = 2$$

From the first equation, $y = x - 1$, so $y = 2 - 1 = 1$. Thus $x = 2$ and $y = 1$ so the coordinates of the point are (2,1).

11. Choice B is correct. Using $C = md + t$, if the business trip were increased by 5 days, $C' = m(d + 5) + t$. Subtracting equations, $C' - C = m(d + 5) + t - (md + t) = md + 5m + t - md - t = 5m$.

12. Choice D is correct. Since $x - 3 \leqq 0$, $x \leqq 3$. Choice D represents x on the number line.

13. Choice E is correct. If we multiply the first equation by 2, we get: $8x - 6y = 18$. Subtract this equation from the second equation in the question:

$$8x + ky = 19$$
$$\underline{-[(8x - 6y) = 18]}$$
$$ky + 6y = 1$$

If $k = -6$, we would have: $-6y + 6y = 0 = 1$, which is not true. Thus if $k = -6$, there will be no solution to the equations.

14. Choice D is correct.

Given: $r = 7a$ $\boxed{1}$

$5w = 7a$ $\boxed{2}$

From $\boxed{2}$ we get $w = \dfrac{7a}{5}$ $\boxed{3}$

(Use Strategy: Find unknowns by subtracting.)

Subtract $\boxed{3}$ from $\boxed{1}$. We get

$$r - w = 7a - \frac{7a}{5}$$
$$= \frac{35a}{5} - \frac{7a}{5}$$
$$r - w = \frac{28a}{5}$$

15. Choice C is correct. **(Use Strategy: The whole equals the sum of its parts.)**

Total area = Area of triangle + 3(area of semicircle) $\boxed{1}$

Given: Radius of each semicircle $= 2$ $\boxed{2}$

From $\boxed{2}$ we know each diameter $= 4$

Thus, the triangle has three equal sides of length 4 and is equilateral. $\boxed{3}$

We know:

Area of equilateral trianlge $= \dfrac{S^2 \sqrt{3}}{4}$ $\boxed{4}$

Area of semicircle $= \dfrac{\pi r^2}{2}$ $\boxed{5}$

Substituting $\boxed{4}$ and $\boxed{5}$ into $\boxed{1}$, we get

Total area $= \dfrac{S^2 \sqrt{3}}{4} + 3\left(\dfrac{\pi r^2}{2}\right)$ $\boxed{6}$

Substituting $\boxed{2}$ and $\boxed{3}$ into $\boxed{6}$, we get

Total area $= \dfrac{4^2\sqrt{3}}{4} + 3\left(\dfrac{\pi(2)^2}{2}\right)$

$= \dfrac{16\sqrt{3}}{4} = 3\left(\dfrac{4\pi}{2}\right)$

Total area $= 4\sqrt{3} + 6\pi$

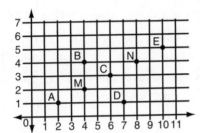

16. Choice E is correct. **(Use Strategy: When all choices must be tested, start with E and work backward.)**

In the diagram at left, we have plotted each of the points given in the choices. From the diagram, it is clear that

$$MC = CN = NE$$

Thus, since $ME = MC + CN + NE$, then

$$3NE = ME$$

as required, so that point E is the answer.

What You Must Do Now to Raise Your SAT Score

1. a) Follow the directions on p. 339 to determine your scaled score for the Math SAT test you've just taken. These results will give you a good idea about whether or not you ought to study hard in order to achieve a certain score on the actual Math SAT.

b) Using your test correct answer count as a basis, indicate for yourself your areas of strength and weakness as revealed by the "Self-Appraisal Chart" on page 341.

2. Eliminate your weaknesses in each of the SAT areas (as revealed in the "Self-Appraisal Chart") by taking the following Giant Steps toward SAT success:

Giant Step 1

Make good use of the Math Strategies that begin on page 257. Read again the solutions for each math question that you answered incorrectly. Refer to the Math Strategy that applies to each of your incorrect answers. Learn each of these Math Strategies thoroughly. We repeat that these strategies are crucial if you want to raise your SAT math score substantially.

Giant Step 2

You may want to take "The 101 Most Important Math Questions You Need to Know How to Solve" test on page 21 and follow the directions after the test for a basic math skills diagnosis.

3. After you have done some of the tasks you have been advised to do in the suggestions above, proceed to Practice Test 2, beginning on page 361.

After taking practice Test 2, concentrate on the weaknesses that still remain.

If you do the job *right* and follow the steps listed above, you are likely to raise your SAT score on the math parts of the test 150 points—maybe 200 points—and even more.

I am the master of my fate;
I am the captain of my soul.

—From the poem "Invictus"
by William Ernest Henley

SAT Math
Practice Test 2

Practice Test 2 Answer Sheet

Start with number 1 for each new section. If a section has fewer questions than answer spaces, leave the extra answer spaces blank. Be sure to erase any errors or stray marks completely.

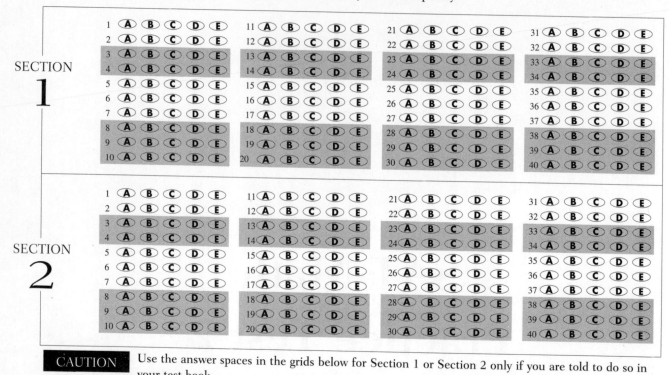

CAUTION Use the answer spaces in the grids below for Section 1 or Section 2 only if you are told to do so in your test book.

Student-Produced Responses ONLY ANSWERS ENTERED IN THE CIRCLES IN EACH GRID WILL BE SCORED. YOU WILL NOT RECEIVE CREDIT FOR ANYTHING WRITTEN IN THE BOXES ABOVE THE CIRCLES.

Start with number 1 for each new section. If a section has fewer questions than answer spaces, leave the extra answer spaces blank. Be sure to erase any errors or stray marks completely.

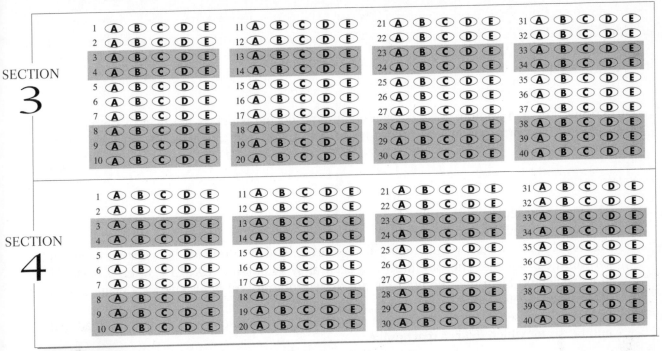

SECTION
3

SECTION
4

CAUTION   Use the answer spaces in the grids below for Section 3.

Student-Produced Responses

ONLY ANSWERS ENTERED IN THE CIRCLES IN EACH GRID WILL BE SCORED. YOU WILL NOT RECEIVE CREDIT FOR ANYTHING WRITTEN IN THE BOXES ABOVE THE CIRCLES.

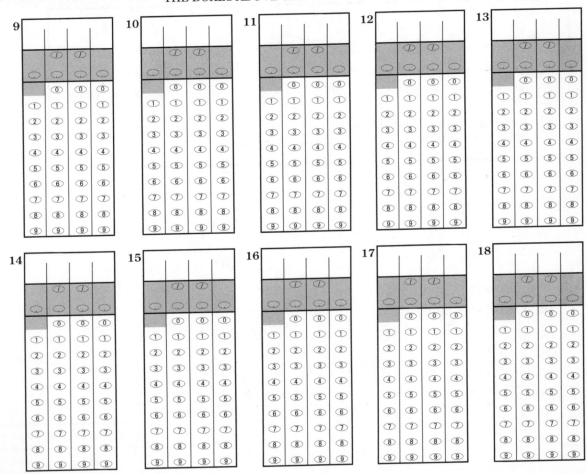

Section 1

Time: 25 Minutes—Turn to Section 1 (page 362) of your answer sheet to answer the questions in this section.
20 Questions

Directions: For this section, solve each problem and decide which is the best of the choices given. Fill in the corresponding circle on the answer sheet. You may use any available space for scratchwork.

Notes:

1. The use of a calculator is permitted.
2. All numbers used are real numbers.
3. Figures that accompany problems in this test are intended to provide information useful in solving the problems. They are drawn as accurately as possible EXCEPT when it is stated in a specific problem that the figure is not drawn to scale. All figures lie in a plane unless otherwise indicated.
4. Unless otherwise specified, the domain of any function f is assumed to be the set of all real numbers x for which $f(x)$ is a real number.

REFERENCE INFORMATION

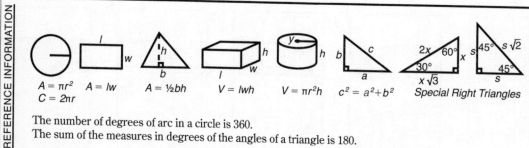

$A = \pi r^2$ $A = lw$ $A = \frac{1}{2}bh$ $V = lwh$ $V = \pi r^2 h$ $c^2 = a^2 + b^2$ *Special Right Triangles*
$C = 2\pi r$

The number of degrees of arc in a circle is 360.
The sum of the measures in degrees of the angles of a triangle is 180.

$$\begin{array}{r} 59\triangle \\ -293 \\ \hline \square 97 \end{array}$$

1. In the subtraction problem above, what digit is represented by the $\square$?

(A) 0
(B) 1
(C) 2
(D) 3
(E) 4

2. If $\dfrac{a-b}{b} = \dfrac{1}{2}$, find $\dfrac{a}{b}$.

(A) $\dfrac{9}{2}$

(B) $\dfrac{7}{2}$

(C) $\dfrac{5}{2}$

(D) $\dfrac{1}{2}$

(E) $\dfrac{3}{2}$

GO ON TO THE NEXT PAGE

Number of pounds of force	Height object is raised
3	6 feet
6	12 feet
9	18 feet

3. In a certain pulley system, the height an object is raised is equal to a constant c times the number of pounds of force exerted. The table above shows some pounds of force and the corresponding height raised. If a particular object is raised 15 feet, how many pounds of force were exerted?

(A) $3\frac{3}{4}$

(B) 7

(C) $7\frac{1}{2}$

(D) 8

(E) 11

4. If $\frac{y}{3}, \frac{y}{4}$, and $\frac{y}{7}$ represent integers, then y could be

(A) 42

(B) 56

(C) 70

(D) 84

(E) 126

5. The above line is marked with 12 points. The distance between any 2 adjacent points is 3 units. Find the total number of points that are more than 19 units away from point P.

(A) 2

(B) 3

(C) 4

(D) 5

(E) 6

6. Given $(a + 2, a - 2) = [a]$ for all integers a, $(6,2) =$

(A) [3]

(B) [4]

(C) [5]

(D) [6]

(E) [8]

GO ON TO THE NEXT PAGE

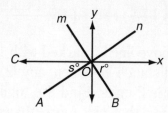

Note: Figure is not drawn to scale.

7. If $m \perp n$ in the figure above and COx is a straight line, find the value of $r + s$.
(A) 180
(B) 135
(C) 110
(D) 90
(E) The answer cannot be determined from the information given.

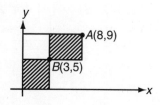

8. Points A and B have coordinates as shown in the figure above. Find the combined area of the two shaded rectangles.
(A) 20
(B) 26
(C) 32
(D) 35
(E) 87

9. One out of 4 students at Ridge High School studies German. If there are 2,800 students at the school, how many students do *not* study German?
(A) 2,500
(B) 2,100
(C) 1,800
(D) 1,000
(E) 700

10. The cost of a drive-in movie is $\$y$ per vehicle. A group of friends in a van shared the admission cost by paying $\$0.40$ each. If 6 more friends had gone along, everyone would have paid only $\$0.25$ each. What is the value of $\$y$?
(A) $4
(B) $6
(C) $8
(D) $10
(E) $12

GO ON TO THE NEXT PAGE

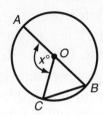

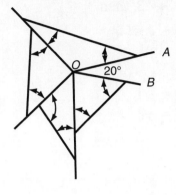

11. If AB is a diameter of circle O in the figure above, and $CB = OB$, then $\dfrac{x}{6}$ =

(A) 60
(B) 30
(C) 20
(D) 10
(E) 5

13. If $\angle AOB = 20°$ in the figure above and O is a common vertex of the four triangles, find the sum of the measures of the marked angles in the triangles.

(A) 380
(B) 560
(C) 740
(D) 760
(E) 920

12. A certain store is selling an $80 radio for $64. If a different radio had a list price of $200 and was discounted at $1\frac{1}{2}$ times the percent discount on the $80 model, what would its selling price be?

(A) $90
(B) $105
(C) $120
(D) $140
(E) $160

14. Some integers in set X are odd.

If the statement above is true, which of the following must also be true?

(A) If an integer is odd, it is in set X.
(B) If an integer is even, it is in set X.
(C) All integers in set X are odd.
(D) All integers in set X are even.
(E) Not all integers in set X are even.

GO ON TO THE NEXT PAGE

15. If $|y+3| < 3$, then

    (A) $0 > y > -6$

    (B) $y > 3$

    (C) $3 > y > 0$

    (D) $y = -1$

    (E) $y = -2$

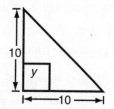

16. In the figure above, the area of the square is equal to $\frac{1}{5}$ the area of the triangle. Find the value of y, the side of the square.

    (A) 2

    (B) 4

    (C) 5

    (D) $2\sqrt{5}$

    (E) $\sqrt{10}$

17. A certain printer can print at the rate of 80 characters per second, and there is an average (arithmetic mean) of 2,400 characters per page. If the printer continued to print at this rate, how many *minutes* would it take to print an *M*-page report?

    (A) $\dfrac{M}{30}$

    (B) $\dfrac{M}{60}$

    (C) $\dfrac{M}{2}$

    (D) $\dfrac{2}{M}$

    (E) $\dfrac{60}{M}$

18. A certain satellite passed over Washington, D.C., at midnight on Friday. If the satellite completes an orbit every 5 hours, when is the next day that it will pass over Washington, D.C., at midnight?

    (A) Monday

    (B) Wednesday

    (C) Friday

    (D) Saturday

    (E) Sunday

GO ON TO THE NEXT PAGE

19. The price of a car is reduced by 30 percent. The resulting price is reduced 40 percent. The two reductions are equal to one reduction of

(A) 28%
(B) 42%
(C) 50%
(D) 58%
(E) 70%

20. In the figure above, the circle is inscribed in the equilateral triangle. If the diameter of the circle is 2, what is the sum of the shaded area?

(A) $3\sqrt{3} - \pi$

(B) $3\sqrt{3} - 4\pi$

(C) $3\sqrt{3} - \dfrac{3\pi}{2}$

(D) $6\sqrt{3} - \dfrac{3\pi}{2}$

(E) $108 - \pi$

STOP
If you finish before time is called, you may check your work on this section only.
Do not turn to any other section in the test.

Take a 5-minute break
before starting section 2

The following Section 2 is not
scored, but it would be wise
to attempt this anyway.

Section 2

Time: 25 Minutes—Turn to Section 2 (page 362) of your answer sheet to answer the questions in this section.
   20 Questions

Directions: For this section, solve each problem and decide which is the best of the choices given. Fill in the corresponding circle on the answer sheet. You may use any available space for scratchwork.

Notes:

1. The use of a calculator is permitted.
2. All numbers used are real numbers.
3. Figures that accompany problems in this test are intended to provide information useful in solving the problems. They are drawn as accurately as possible EXCEPT when it is stated in a specific problem that the figure is not drawn to scale. All figures lie in a plane unless otherwise indicated.
4. Unless otherwise specified, the domain of any function f is assumed to be the set of all real numbers x for which $f(x)$ is a real number.

REFERENCE INFORMATION

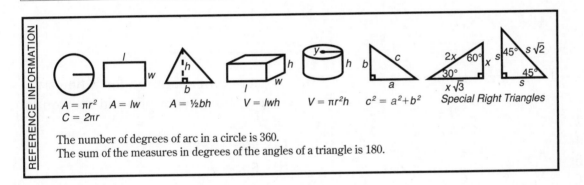

$A = \pi r^2$ $A = lw$ $A = \frac{1}{2}bh$ $V = lwh$ $V = \pi r^2 h$ $c^2 = a^2 + b^2$ *Special Right Triangles*
$C = 2\pi r$

The number of degrees of arc in a circle is 360.
The sum of the measures in degrees of the angles of a triangle is 180.

1. After giving $5 to Greg, David has $25. Greg now has $\frac{1}{5}$ as much as David does. How much did Greg start with?

    (A) $0
    (B) $5
    (C) $7
    (D) $10
    (E) $15

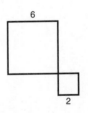

2. The figure above shows two squares with sides as shown. What is the ratio of the perimeter of the larger square to that of the smaller?

    (A) 3 : 2
    (B) 2 : 1
    (C) 3 : 1
    (D) 6 : 1
    (E) 9 : 1

GO ON TO THE NEXT PAGE

3. A car travels 1,056 feet in 12 seconds. In feet per second, what is the average speed of the car?

(A) 98.0
(B) 78.8
(C) 85.8
(D) 84.0
(E) 88.0

5. $2(w)(x)(-y) - 2(-w)(-x)(y) =$

(A) 0
(B) $-4wxy$
(C) $4wxy$
(D) $-4w^2x^2y^2$
(E) $2w^2x^2y^2$

4. If $2z + 1 + 2 + 2z + 3 + 2z = 3 + 1 + 2$, then $z + 4 =$

(A) 1
(B) 4
(C) 5
(D) 6
(E) 10

6. What is an expression for 5 times the sum of the square of x and the square of y?

(A) $5(x^2 + y^2)$
(B) $5x^2 + y^2$
(C) $5(x + y)^2$
(D) $5x^2 + y$
(E) $5(2x + 2y)$

GO ON TO THE NEXT PAGE

7. If p and q are positive integers, x and y are negative integers, and if $p > q$ and $x > y$, which of the following must be less than zero?

   I. $q - p$

  II. qy

 III. $p + x$

  (A) I only

  (B) III only

  (C) I and II only

  (D) II and III only

  (E) I, II, and III

9. If $y = 28j$, where j is any integer, then $\dfrac{y}{2}$ will always be

  (A) even

  (B) odd

  (C) positive

  (D) negative

  (E) less than $\dfrac{y}{3}$

8. If $a = 1$, $b = -2$ and $c = -2$, find the value of $\dfrac{b^2 c}{(a-c)^2}$.

  (A) $-\dfrac{8}{9}$

  (B) $-\dfrac{2}{3}$

  (C) $\dfrac{8}{9}$

  (D) 8

  (E) 9

10. If $3a + 4b = 4a - 4b = 21$, find the value of a.

  (A) 3

  (B) 6

  (C) 21

  (D) 42

  (E) The answer cannot be determined from the information given.

GO ON TO THE NEXT PAGE

11. If N is a positive integer, which of the following does *not* have to be a divisor of the sum of N, $6N$, and $9N$?

(A) 1
(B) 2
(C) 4
(D) 9
(E) 16

12. If $x = 3a - 18$ and $5y = 3a + 7$, then find $5y - x$.

(A) -11
(B) 11
(C) 18
(D) 25
(E) $6a - 11$

13. If $p + pq$ is 4 times $p - pq$, which of the following has exactly one value? $(pq \neq 0)$

(A) p
(B) q
(C) pq
(D) $p + pq$
(E) $p - pq$

14. If $2 + \dfrac{1}{z} = 0$, then what is the value of $9 + 9z$?

(A) $-\dfrac{9}{2}$

(B) $-\dfrac{1}{2}$

(C) 0

(D) $\dfrac{9}{2}$

(E) The answer cannot be determined from the information given.

GO ON TO THE NEXT PAGE

15. How many times does the graph of $y = x^2$ intersect the graph of $y = x$?

(A) 0
(B) 1
(C) 2
(D) 3
(E) 4

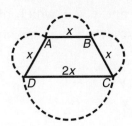

17. The quadrilateral $ABCD$ is a trapezoid with $x = 4$. The diameter of each semi-circle is a side of the trapezoid. What is the sum of the lengths of the 4 dotted semicircles?

(A) 8π
(B) 10π
(C) 12π
(D) 14π
(E) 20π

16. Let $wx = y$, where $wxy \neq 0$.

If both x and y are multiplied by 6, then w is

(A) multiplied by $\frac{1}{36}$

(B) multiplied by $\frac{1}{6}$

(C) multiplied by 1

(D) multiplied by 6

(E) multiplied by 36

18. $\dfrac{7x}{144}$ yards and $\dfrac{5y}{12}$ feet together equal how many inches?

(A) $\dfrac{7x}{12} + \dfrac{5y}{4}$

(B) $\dfrac{7x}{12} + 5y$

(C) $\dfrac{7x}{4} + 5y$

(D) $\dfrac{7x}{4} + 60y$

(E) $7x + \dfrac{5}{4}y$

GO ON TO THE NEXT PAGE

19. If $x < 0$ and $y < 0$, which of the following must always be positive?

   I. $x \times y$
  II. $x + y$
 III. $x - y$

(A) I only
(B) I and II only
(C) I and III only
(D) II and III only
(E) I, II, and III

20. Given that $a + 3b = 11$ and a and b are positive integers. What is the largest possible value of a?

(A) 4
(B) 6
(C) 7
(D) 8
(E) 10

STOP

If you finish before time is called, you may check your work on this section only.
Do not turn to any other section in the test.

Section 3

Time: 25 Minutes—Turn to Section 3 (page 363) of your answer sheet to answer the questions in this section.
   20 Questions

Directions: This section contains two types of questions. You have 25 minutes to complete both types. For questions 1–8, solve each problem and decide which is the best of the choices given. Fill in the corresponding circle on the answer sheet. You may use any available space for scratchwork.

Notes:

1. The use of a calculator is permitted.
2. All numbers used are real numbers.
3. Figures that accompany problems in this test are intended to provide information useful in solving the problems. They are drawn as accurately as possible EXCEPT when it is stated in a specific problem that the figure is not drawn to scale. All figures lie in a plane unless otherwise indicated.
4. Unless otherwise specified, the domain of any function *f* is assumed to be the set of all real numbers *x* for which *f(x)* is a real number.

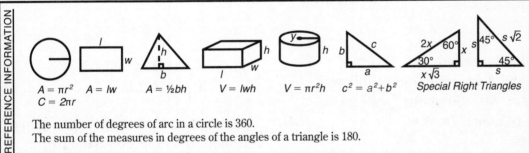

$A = \pi r^2$ $A = lw$ $A = \frac{1}{2}bh$ $V = lwh$ $V = \pi r^2 h$ $c^2 = a^2 + b^2$ *Special Right Triangles*
$C = 2\pi r$

The number of degrees of arc in a circle is 360.
The sum of the measures in degrees of the angles of a triangle is 180.

1. In the equation $5\sqrt{x} + 14 = 20$, the value of x is

    (A) $\sqrt{\dfrac{6}{5}}$

    (B) $\dfrac{34^2}{25^2}$

    (C) $6 - \sqrt{5}$

    (D) $\dfrac{6}{5}$

    (E) $\dfrac{36}{25}$

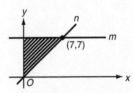

2. In the figure above, m is parallel to the x-axis. All of the following points lie in the shaded area EXCEPT

    (A) (4,3)
    (B) (1,2)
    (C) (5,6)
    (D) (4,5)
    (E) (2,5)

GO ON TO THE NEXT PAGE

3. At Lincoln County High School, 36 students are taking either calculus or physics or both, and 10 students are taking both calculus and physics. If there are 31 students in the calculus class, how many students are in the physics class?

(A) 14
(B) 15
(C) 16
(D) 17
(E) 18

5. Which of the following is always true for real numbers a, b, and c?

I. $\sqrt{a+b} = \sqrt{a} + \sqrt{b}$
II. $a^2 + b^2 = (a+b)^2$
III. $a^b + a^c = a^{(b+c)}$

(A) I only
(B) II only
(C) III only
(D) I, II, III
(E) neither I, II or III

4. Mr. Simmons stated that if $a^2 > b^2$ where a and b are real, then it follows that $a > b$. Mr. Simmons' statement would be refuted if $(a, b) =$

(A) (2,3)
(B) (3,2)
(C) (4,−2)
(D) (−4,−2)
(E) (−2,−3)

$$R = \{x : 1 \geqq x \geqq -1\}$$
$$S = \{x : x \geqq 1\}$$

6. The number of elements that is (are) common to both R and S is (are)

(A) 0
(B) 1
(C) 2
(D) 3
(E) infinite

GO ON TO THE NEXT PAGE

7. Two lines in a plane are represented by $y = x - 1$ and $2x + 5y = 9$. The coordinates of the point at which the lines intersect are

(A) (2,1)
(B) (1,2)
(C) (2,5)
(D) (5,2)
(E) (3,5)

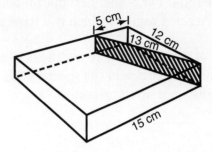

8. The rectangular box above has a rectangular dividing wall inside, as shown. The dividing wall has an area of 39 cm². What is the volume of the larger compartment?

(A) 90 cm³
(B) 180 cm³
(C) 360 cm³
(D) 450 cm³
(E) 540 cm³

GO ON TO THE NEXT PAGE

Directions: For Student-Produced Response questions 9–18, use the grids at the bottom of the answer sheet page on which you have answered questions 1–8.

Each of the remaining 10 questions requires you to solve the problem and enter your answer by marking the circles in the special grid, as shown in the examples below. You may use any available space for scratchwork.

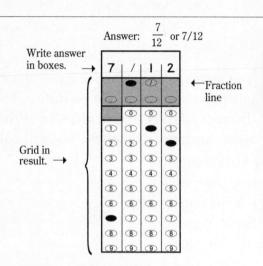

Answer: $\frac{7}{12}$ or 7/12

Answer: 2.5

Answer: 201
Either position is correct.

Write answer in boxes. →

←Fraction line

← Decimal point

Grid in result. →

Note: You may start your answers in any column, space permitting. Columns not needed should be left blank.

- Mark no more than one oval in any column.

- Because the answer sheet will be machine-scored, **you will receive credit only if the ovals are filled in correctly.**

- Although not required, it is suggested that you write your answer in the boxes at the top of the columns to help you fill in the ovals accurately.

- Some problems may have more than one correct answer. In such cases, grid only one answer.

- No question has a negative answer.

- **Mixed numbers** such as $2\frac{1}{2}$ must be gridded as 2.5 or 5/2. (If [2 1 / 2] is gridded, it will be interpreted as $\frac{21}{2}$, not $2\frac{1}{2}$.)

- *Decimal Accuracy:* If you obtain a decimal answer, **enter the most accurate value the grid will accommodate.** For example, if you obtain an answer such as 0.6666… , you should record the result as .666 or .667. **Less accurate values such as .66 or .67 are not acceptable.**

Acceptable ways to grid $\frac{2}{3}$ = .6666…

9. $\left(\dfrac{1}{2} - \dfrac{1}{3}\right) + \left(\dfrac{1}{3} - \dfrac{1}{4}\right) + \left(\dfrac{1}{4} - \dfrac{1}{5}\right) +$

$\left(\dfrac{1}{5} - \dfrac{1}{6}\right) + \left(\dfrac{1}{6} - \dfrac{1}{7}\right) + \left(\dfrac{1}{7} - \dfrac{1}{8}\right) +$

$\left(\dfrac{1}{8} - \dfrac{1}{9}\right)$ is equal to what value?

10. If the first two elements of a number series are 1 and 2, and if each succeeding term is found by multiplying the two terms immediately preceding it, what is the fifth element of the series?

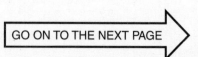

GO ON TO THE NEXT PAGE

11. If p is $\dfrac{3}{5}$ of m and if q is $\dfrac{9}{10}$ of m, then, when $q \neq 0$, the ratio $\dfrac{p}{q}$ is equal to what value?

12. If the average (arithmetic mean) of 40, 40, 40, and z is 45, then find the value of z.

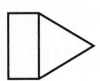

13. In the figure above, the perimeter of the equilateral triangle is 39 and the area of the rectangle is 65. What is the perimeter of the rectangle?

Game		Darrin	Tom
1		69	43
2		59	60
3		72	55
4		70	68
5		78	73
Totals		348	299

14. Darrin and Tom played five games of darts. The table above lists the scores for each of the games. By how many points was Tom behind Darrin at the end of the first four games?

15. A box contains 17 slips of paper. Each is labeled with a different integer from 1 to 17 inclusive. If 5 even-numbered slips of paper are removed, what fraction of the remaining slips of paper is even numbered?

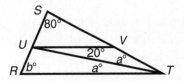

Note: Figure is not drawn to scale.

16. In $\triangle RST$, above, $UV \parallel RT$. Find b.

17. Rose has earned $44 in 8 days. If she continues to earn at the same daily rate, in how many *more* days will her total earnings be $99?

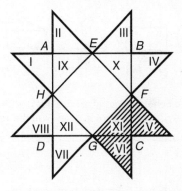

18. The areas of triangles I, II, III, IV, V, VI, VII, VIII, IX, X, XI, XII are the same. If the region outlined by the heavy line has area = 256 and the area of square $ABCD$ is 128, determine the shaded area.

STOP

If you finish before time is called, you may check your work on this section only.
Do not turn to any other section in the test.

Take a 5-minute break

before starting section 4

Section 4

Time: 20 Minutes—Turn to Section 4 (page 363) of your answer sheet to answer the questions in this section.
   16 Questions

Directions: For this section, solve each problem and decide which is the best of the choices given. Fill in the corresponding circle on the answer sheet. You may use any available space for scratchwork.

Notes:

1. The use of a calculator is permitted.
2. All numbers used are real numbers.
3. Figures that accompany problems in this test are intended to provide information useful in solving the problems. They are drawn as accurately as possible EXCEPT when it is stated in a specific problem that the figure is not drawn to scale. All figures lie in a plane unless otherwise indicated.
4. Unless otherwise specified, the domain of any function f is assumed to be the set of all real numbers x for which $f(x)$ is a real number.

REFERENCE INFORMATION

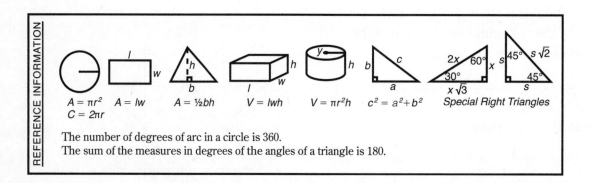

$A = \pi r^2$ $A = lw$ $A = \frac{1}{2}bh$ $V = lwh$ $V = \pi r^2 h$ $c^2 = a^2 + b^2$ *Special Right Triangles*
$C = 2\pi r$

The number of degrees of arc in a circle is 360.
The sum of the measures in degrees of the angles of a triangle is 180.

1. Johnny buys a frying pan and two coffee mugs for $27. Joanna buys the same-priced frying pan and one of the same-priced coffee mugs for $23. How much does one of those frying pans cost?

   (A) $4
   (B) $7
   (C) $19
   (D) $20
   (E) $21

2. A rectangular floor 8 feet long and 6 feet wide is to be completely covered with tiles. Each tile is a square with a perimeter of 2 feet. What is the least number of such tiles necessary to cover the floor?

   (A) 7
   (B) 12
   (C) 24
   (D) 48
   (E) 192

GO ON TO THE NEXT PAGE

3. If 9 and 12 each divide Q without remainder, which of the following must Q divide without remainder?

(A) 1
(B) 3
(C) 36
(D) 72
(E) The answer cannot be determined from the given information.

5. Given three segments of length x, $11 - x$, and $x - 4$, respectively, which of the following indicates the set of all numbers x such that the 3 segments could be the lengths of the sides of a triangle?

(A) $x > 4$
(B) $x < 11$
(C) $0 < x < 7$
(D) $5 < x < 15$
(E) $5 < x < 7$

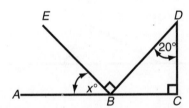

4. In the figure above, $DC \perp AC$, $EB \perp DB$, and AC is a line segment. What is the value of x?

(A) 15
(B) 20
(C) 30
(D) 80
(E) 160

6. Given three integers a, b, and 4, if their average (arithmetic mean) is 6, which of the following could *not* be the value of the product ab?

(A) 13
(B) 14
(C) 40
(D) 48
(E) 49

GO ON TO THE NEXT PAGE

7. If $mn \neq 0$, then $\dfrac{1}{n^2}\left(\dfrac{m^5 n^3}{m^3}\right)^2 =$

(A) mn^4
(B) $m^4 n^2$
(C) $m^4 n^3$
(D) $m^4 n^4$
(E) $m^4 n^5$

Question 9 refers to the figure above, where W, X, Y, and Z are four distinct digits from 0 to 9, inclusive, and $W + X + Y = 5Z$.

9. Under the given conditions, all of the following could be values of Z EXCEPT

(A) 1
(B) 2
(C) 3
(D) 4
(E) 5

8. From a party attended by 3 females and 3 males, 3 people at random enter a previously empty room. What is the probability that there are exactly 2 males in the room?

(A) $\dfrac{1}{4}$

(B) $\dfrac{3}{8}$

(C) $\dfrac{9}{20}$

(D) $\dfrac{2}{3}$

(E) $\dfrac{5}{6}$

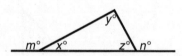

10. In the figure above, $m + n =$

(A) 90
(B) 180
(C) $180 + y$
(D) $90 + x + y + z$
(E) $2(x + y + z)$

GO ON TO THE NEXT PAGE

11. The volume of a cube is less than 25, and the length of one of its edges is a positive integer. What is the largest possible value for the total area of the six faces?

(A) 1
(B) 6
(C) 24
(D) 54
(E) 150

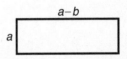

A B C D E F G

13. *AG* is divided into six equal segments in the figure above. A circle, not visible, with center *F* and radius $\frac{1}{5}$ the length of *AG*, will intersect *AG* between

(A) *F* and *G*
(B) *E* and *F*
(C) *D* and *E*
(D) *C* and *D*
(E) *A* and *B*

12. The ratio of females to males on a particular flight was 2 : 3. Females represented five more than $\frac{1}{3}$ of all the people aboard. How many people were on that flight?

(A) 15
(B) 25
(C) 30
(D) 45
(E) 75

a−b

a

14. The figure above is a rectangle having width *a* and length *a − b*. Find its perimeter in terms of *a* and *b*.

(A) $a^2 - ab$
(B) $4a - 2b$
(C) $4a - b$
(D) $2a - 2b$
(E) $2a - b$

GO ON TO THE NEXT PAGE

$$AB$$
$$\underline{+BA}$$
$$CDC$$

15. If each of the four letters in the sum above represents a *different* digit, which of the following *cannot* be a value of *A*?

(A) 6
(B) 5
(C) 4
(D) 3
(E) 2

16. If for real x, y, $f(x) = x^2 + x$ and $g(y) = y^2$, then $f[g(-1)] =$

(A) 2
(B) -2
(C) 4
(D) -4
(E) -8

STOP

If you finish before time is called, you may check your work on this section only.

Do not turn to any other section in the test.

How Did You Do on This Test?

Step 1. Go to the Answer Key on page 388.

Step 2. Calculate your "raw score" using the directions on page 389.

Step 3. Get your "scaled score" for the test by referring to the SAT Math Score Conversion Table on page 390.

THERE'S ALWAYS ROOM FOR IMPROVEMENT!

Answer Key for the SAT Math Practice Test 2

Section 1		Section 2		Section 3		Section 4	
Correct Answer		Correct Answer		Correct Answer		Correct Answer	
1	C	1	A	1	E	1	C
2	E	2	C	2	A	2	E
3	C	3	E	3	B	3	E
4	D	4	B	4	D	4	B
5	D	5	B	5	E	5	E
6	B	6	A	6	B	6	B
7	D	7	C	7	A	7	D
8	D	8	A	8	D	8	C
9	B	9	A			9	E
10	A	10	B			10	C
11	C	11	D			11	C
12	D	12	D			12	E
13	A	13	B			13	C
14	E	14	D			14	B
15	A	15	C			15	E
16	E	16	C			16	A
17	C	17	B				
18	B	18	C				
19	D	19	A				
20	A	20	D				

Section 3 — Number correct

Section 3 — Number incorrect

Student-Produced Response Questions

9	7/18 or .388 or .389
10	8
11	2/3 or .667 or .666
12	60
13	36
14	44
15	1/4 or .25
16	60
17	10
18	48

Section 1 — Number correct

Section 1 — Number incorrect

Section 2 — Number correct

Section 2 — Number incorrect

Section 4 — Number correct

Section 4 — Number incorrect

Student-Produced — Number correct

Student-Produced — Number incorrect

Scoring the Math SAT Practice Test 2

Check your responses with the correct answers on the previous pages. Fill in the blanks below and do the calculations to get your math raw score. Use the table to find your math scaled score.

Get Your Math Score

How many math questions did you get **right?**

Section 1: Questions 1–20   _____

Section 3: Questions 1–18 +   _____

Section 4: Questions 1–16 +   _____

          Total   = _____ **(A)**

How many multiple-choice math questions did you get **wrong?**

Section 1: Questions 1–20   _____

Section 3: Questions 1–8 +   _____

Section 4: Questions 1–16 +   _____

          Total   = _____ **(B)**

          $\times 0.25$ = _____

          A − B = _____

          Math Raw Score

Round math raw score to the nearest whole number.

_____

Use the Score Conversion Table to find your math scaled score.

_____

SAT Math Score Conversion Table

Raw Score	Math Scaled Score	Raw Score	Math Scaled Score
		31	550
		30	540
		29	530
		28	520
		27	520
		26	510
		25	500
		24	490
		23	480
		22	480
		21	470
		20	460
		19	450
54	800	18	450
53	790	17	440
52	760	16	430
51	740	15	420
50	720	14	410
49	710	13	410
48	700	12	400
47	680	11	390
46	670	10	380
45	660	9	370
44	650	8	360
43	640	7	350
42	630	6	340
41	630	5	330
40	620	4	320
39	610	3	310
38	600	2	290
37	590	1	280
36	580	0	260
35	580	−1	240
34	570	−2	220
33	560	−3	200
32	550	−4	200
		and below	

This table is for use only witht the test in this book.

CHART FOR SELF-APPRAISAL BASED ON THE PRACTICE TEST YOU HAVE JUST TAKEN

The Self-Appraisal Chart below tells you quickly where your SAT strengths and weaknesses lie.

	Math Questions*
EXCELLENT	44–54
GOOD	32–43
FAIR	27–31
POOR	16–26
VERY POOR	0–15

* Sections 1, 3, 4 only.

Note: In our tests, we have chosen to have Section 2 as the experimental section. Note that on the actual SAT you will take, the order of the sections can vary and you will not know which one is experimental, so it is wise to answer all sections and not to leave any section out.

SAT VERBAL AND MATH SCORE/PERCENTILE CONVERSION TABLE

Math

SAT scaled math score	Percentile rank
800	99.5+
770–790	99.5
720–760	99
670–710	97
640–660	94
610–630	89
590–600	84
560–580	77
530–550	68
510–520	59
480–500	48
450–470	37
430–440	26
390–420	16
350–380	8
310–340	2
210–300	0.5
200	0

Explanatory Answers
for Math Practice Test 2

Section 1

As you read these solutions, you are advised to do the following if you answered the math question incorrectly:

When a specific Strategy is referred to in the solution, study that strategy, which you will find in "Math Strategies" (beginning on page 257).

1. Choice C is correct.

Given:
$$\begin{array}{r} 59\Delta \\ -\,293 \\ \hline \square 97 \end{array} \quad \boxed{1}$$

(Use Strategy: Use the given information effectively.)

From $\boxed{1}$ we see that $\Delta - 3 = 7$ $\boxed{2}$

From $\boxed{2}$ we get $\Delta = 10$ $\boxed{3}$

From $\boxed{1}$ and $\boxed{3}$ we get $\Delta = 0$ in $\boxed{1}$ and we had to borrow to get 10. Thus, we have

$$\begin{array}{r} 8 \\ 5\cancel{9}0 \\ -\,293 \\ \hline \square 97 \end{array} \quad \boxed{4}$$

Calculating $\boxed{4}$, we get

$$\begin{array}{r} 8 \\ 5\cancel{9}0 \\ -\,293 \\ \hline \square 97 \end{array}$$

We see that the digit represented by the $\square$ is 2.

2. Choice E is correct.

Given: $\dfrac{a-b}{b} = \dfrac{1}{2}$ $\boxed{1}$

(Use Strategy: Find unknowns by multiplication.)

Multiply $\boxed{1}$ by $2b$. We have

$$2\cancel{b}\left(\frac{a-b}{\cancel{b}}\right) = \left(\frac{1}{\cancel{2}}\right)2\cancel{b}$$

$$2(a-b) = b$$

$$2a - 2b = b$$

$$2a = 3b \quad \boxed{2}$$

(Use Strategy: Find unknowns by division.)

Dividing $\boxed{2}$ by $2b$, we get

$$\frac{\cancel{2}a}{\cancel{2}b} = \frac{3\cancel{b}}{2\cancel{b}}$$

$$\frac{a}{b} = \frac{3}{2}$$

3. Choice C is correct.

☐1

Number of pounds of force	Height object is raised
3	6 feet
6	12 feet
9	18 feet

(Use Strategy: Translate from words to algebra.)

We are given that:

height raised = c (force exerted) ☐2

Substituting ☐1 into ☐1, we get

$$6 = c(3)$$
$$2 = c \qquad ☐3$$

Given: Height object is raised = 15 feet

☐4

Substituting ☐3 and ☐4 into ☐2, we have

$$15 = 2 \text{ (force exerted)}$$
$$7\frac{1}{2} = \text{force exerted}$$

4. Choice D is correct.

Given: $\dfrac{y}{3}, \dfrac{y}{4}, \dfrac{y}{7}$ are integers. ☐1

(Use Strategy: Use the given information effectively.)

If all items in ☐1 are integers, then 3, 4, and 7 divide y evenly (zero remainder). y must be a common multiple of 3, 4, and 7. Multiplying 3, 4, and 7, we get 84.

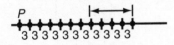

5. Choice D is correct. **(Use Strategy: Use new definitions carefully.)**

We are told that the points are each 3 units apart, as indicated above. We are looking for all those points that are more than 19 units away from point P. By checking the diagram we find 5 such points (marked with arrow in diagram).

6. Choice B is correct.

Given: ☐1
$(a + 2, a - 2) = [a]$ for all integers a.
We need to find $(6,2)$. ☐2

(Use Strategy: Use new definitions carefully.) Using ☐1 and ☐2 we have

$$a + 2 = 6 \quad \text{and} \quad a - 2 = 2$$
$$a = 4 \qquad\qquad a = 4 \quad ☐3$$

Using ☐1, ☐2, and ☐3, we get

$$(6,2) = [4]$$

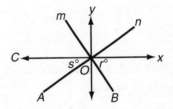

7. Choice D is correct.

Given: $m \perp n$ ☐1

From ☐1 we know that $\angle AOB$ is a right angle.

Thus $\angle AOB = 90°$ ☐2

From the diagram, we see that $\angle COx$ is a straight angle.

Thus $\angle COx = 180°$ ☐3

(Use Strategy: The whole equals the sum of its parts.)

We know that $\angle COA + \angle AOB + \angle BOx = \angle COx$ ☐4

Given: $\angle COA = s°$ ☐5
$\angle BOx = r°$ ☐6

Substituting ☐2, ☐3, ☐5, and ☐6 into ☐4, we get

$$s + 90 + r = 180$$
$$s + r = 90$$
$$r + s = 90$$

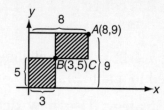

8. Choice D is correct. **(Use Strategy: Use the given information effectively.)**

From the given coordinates, we can find certain distances, as marked above.

Using these distances we find:

$$BC = 8 - 3 = 5 \quad \boxed{1}$$
$$AC = 9 - 5 = 4 \quad \boxed{2}$$

We know that area of a rectangle
= length × width $\quad \boxed{3}$

Using the diagram and $\boxed{3}$ we have

Area of lower rectangle
$$= 5 \times 3 = 15 \quad \boxed{4}$$

Substituting $\boxed{1}$ and $\boxed{2}$ into $\boxed{3}$, we get

Area of upper rectangle
$$= 5 \times 4 = 20 \quad \boxed{5}$$

(Use Strategy: Find unknowns by addition.)

Adding $\boxed{4}$ and $\boxed{5}$ together, we get

Total area = 15 + 20 = 35

9. Choice B is correct.

Given: Total number of students = 2,800 $\quad \boxed{1}$

(Use Strategy: Translate from words to algebra.)

Number of German students $= \dfrac{1}{4} \times 2,800$

$$= \dfrac{2,800}{4}$$

$$= 700 \quad \boxed{2}$$

(Use Strategy: Find unknown by subtraction.)

Subtracting $\boxed{2}$ from $\boxed{1}$ we get

Number of students
not studying German =
$$2,800 - 700 = 2,100$$

10. Choice A is correct. **(Use Strategy: Translate from words to algebra.)**

Given: cost per vehicle = y $\quad \boxed{1}$

Let x = number of students
paying $0.40 $\quad \boxed{2}$

Then $x + 6$ = number of students
paying $0.25 $\quad \boxed{3}$

Using $\boxed{1}$, $\boxed{2}$, and $\boxed{3}$,

We are told that: $x(\$0.40) = \$y$ $\quad \boxed{4}$

$(x + 6)(\$0.25) = \$y$ $\quad \boxed{5}$

From $\boxed{4}$ and $\boxed{5}$ we get

$$x(\$0.40) = (x + 6)(\$0.25)$$

$$.40x = .25x + 1.50$$

$$.15x = 1.50$$

$$x = 10 \quad \boxed{6}$$

Substitute $\boxed{6}$ into $\boxed{4}$. We have

$$10(\$0.40) = \$y$$

$$\$4.00 = y$$

$$\$4 = y$$

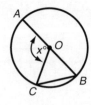

11. Choice C is correct.

Given: AB is a diameter. $\quad \boxed{1}$

O is the center of the circle. $\quad \boxed{2}$

$CB = OB$ $\quad \boxed{3}$

Using $\boxed{2}$, we know that OB and OC are radii. $\boxed{4}$

From $\boxed{4}$ we get that $OB = OC$. $\boxed{5}$

Using $\boxed{3}$ and $\boxed{5}$ together, we have

$$OB = OC = CB \qquad \boxed{6}$$

(Use Strategy: Remember the equilateral triangle.)

From $\boxed{6}$, we have $\triangle OBC$ is equilateral. $\boxed{7}$

From $\boxed{7}$, we get that $\angle B = \angle C = \angle COB = 60°$. $\boxed{8}$

From $\boxed{1}$, we get $\angle AOB$ is straight angle. $\boxed{9}$

From $\boxed{9}$, we have $\angle AOB = 180°$ $\boxed{10}$

(Use Strategy: The whole equals the sum of its parts.)

From the diagram we see that

$$\angle AOC + \angle COB = \angle AOB \qquad \boxed{11}$$

Given: $\angle AOC = x°$ $\boxed{12}$

Substituting $\boxed{8}$, $\boxed{10}$, and $\boxed{12}$ into $\boxed{11}$, we get

$$x + 60 = 180$$
$$x = 120 \qquad \boxed{13}$$

(Use Strategy: Find unknowns by division.)

Divide $\boxed{13}$ by 6. We have

$$\frac{x}{6} = \frac{120}{6}$$
$$\frac{x}{6} = 20$$

12. Choice D is correct.

Given: Selling price of radio = $64 $\boxed{1}$

Regular price of radio = $80 $\boxed{2}$

(Use Strategy: Remember how to find percent discount.)

$$\text{Percent discount} = \frac{\text{Amount off}}{\text{original price}} \times 100 \quad \boxed{3}$$

Subtracting $\boxed{1}$ from $\boxed{2}$, we get

Amount off = $80 − $64 = $16 $\boxed{4}$

Substituting $\boxed{2}$ and $\boxed{4}$ into $\boxed{3}$, we have

$$\text{Percent discount} = \frac{\$16}{\$80} \times 100$$
$$= \frac{\$16 \times 100}{\$80} \quad \boxed{5}$$

(Use Strategy: Factor and reduce.)

$$\text{Percent discount} = \frac{\cancel{\$16} \times \cancel{5} \times 20}{\cancel{\$16} \times \cancel{5}}$$

$$\text{Percent discount} = 20 \qquad \boxed{6}$$

Given: Regular price of different radio = $200 $\boxed{7}$

New percent discount
$$= 1\frac{1}{2} \times \text{Other radio's percent discount} \qquad \boxed{8}$$

Using $\boxed{6}$ and $\boxed{8}$, we have

New percent discount $= 1\frac{1}{2} \times 20 =$
$$= \frac{3}{2} \times 20$$
$$= 30 \qquad \boxed{9}$$

(Use Strategy: Remember how to find percent of a number.)

We know percent of a number = percent × number. $\boxed{10}$

Substituting $\boxed{7}$ and $\boxed{9}$ into $\boxed{10}$, we have

$$\text{Amount of discount} = 30\% \times \$200$$
$$= \frac{30}{100} \times \$200$$

Amount of discount = $60 $\boxed{11}$

(Use Strategy: Find unknowns by subtraction.)

Subtracting 11 from 7, we have

Selling price of different radio

= $200 − $60

= $140

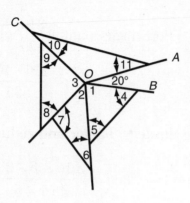

13. Choice A is correct.

Given: $\angle AOB = 20°$ 1

(Use Strategy: The whole equals the sum of its parts.)

We know that the sum of the angles
of a triangle = 180°   2

For each of the four triangles, applying
2 yields:

$\angle 8 + \angle 9 + \angle 3 = 180$ 3

$\angle 6 + \angle 7 + \angle 2 = 180$ 4

$\angle 4 + \angle 5 + \angle 1 = 180$ 5

$\angle 10 + \angle 11 + \angle COA = 180$ 6

We know that the sum of all the angles
about a point = 360°   7

Applying 7 to point O, we have

$\angle 1 + \angle 2 + \angle 3 + \angle COA + \angle AOB$
$= 360°$ 8

Substituting 1 into 8, we get

$\angle 1 + \angle 2 + \angle 3 + \angle COA + 20 = 360$

$\angle 1 + \angle 2 + \angle 3 + \angle COA = 340$ 9

(Use Strategy: Find unknowns by addition.)

Adding 3, 4, 5, and 6, we have

$\angle 4 + \angle 5 + \angle 6 + \angle 7 + \angle 8 + \angle 9$
$+ \angle 10 + \angle 11 + \angle 1 + \angle 2 + \angle 3 +$
$\angle COA = 720°$ 10

(Use Strategy: Find unknowns by subtraction.)

Subtracting 9 from 10, we get

$\angle 4 + \angle 5 + \angle 6 + \angle 7 + \angle 8 +$
$\angle 9 + \angle 10 + \angle 11 = 380°$ 11

Thus, the sum of the marked angles = 380°

14. Choice E is correct. **(Use Strategy: When all choices must be tested, start with choice E.)** If some of the integers in the set are odd, then not all are even. Note that the other choices are not correct. For (D), all integers cannot be even, since some are odd. For (C), since *some* integers are odd, we cannot imply that all integers are odd. For (B), if an integer is even, it may not be in set X. Similarly for (A) if an integer is odd, it may not be in set X.

15. Choice A is correct. Since the absolute value of $y + 3$ must be less than 3, y must be less than 0 but greater than −6.

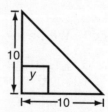

16. Choice E is correct.

We know that area of a triangle

$= \dfrac{1}{2} \times$ base $\times$ height   1

Use the diagram, and substituting into $\boxed{1}$, we get

Area of triangle $= \dfrac{1}{2} \times 10 \times 10$

$$= 50 \qquad \boxed{2}$$

(Use Strategy: Translate from words to algebra.)

We are told:

Area of square $= \dfrac{1}{5} \times$ area of triangle $\qquad \boxed{3}$

We know that

Area of a square $=$ (side)^2 $\qquad \boxed{4}$

Using the diagram, and substituting into $\boxed{4}$, we get

Area of square $= y^2$ $\qquad \boxed{5}$

Substituting $\boxed{2}$ and $\boxed{5}$ into $\boxed{3}$, we have

$$y^2 = \dfrac{1}{5} \times 50$$

$$y^2 = 10 \qquad \boxed{6}$$

Take the square root of both sides of $\boxed{6}$. We get

$$y = \sqrt{10}$$

17. Choice C is correct.

Given: Print rate $= \dfrac{80 \text{ characters}}{\text{second}}$ $\qquad \boxed{1}$

$\dfrac{\text{Number of characters}}{\text{Page}} = 2400$ $\qquad \boxed{2}$

(Use Strategy: Find unknowns by division.)

Dividing $\boxed{2}$ by $\boxed{1}$, we have

$$\dfrac{2,400 \text{ characters}}{\text{page}} \div \dfrac{80 \text{ characters}}{\text{second}} =$$

$$\dfrac{2,400 \text{ characters}}{\text{page}} \times \dfrac{\text{second}}{80 \text{ characters}} =$$

$$\dfrac{2,400 \text{ second}}{80 \text{ page}}$$

$$= \dfrac{30 \text{ seconds}}{\text{page}} \qquad \boxed{3}$$

The time for an M-page report will be

$\dfrac{30 \text{ seconds}}{\text{page}} = M \text{ pages} =$

Time for M-page report $= 30\,M$ seconds $\boxed{4}$

(Use Strategy: Know how to use units.)

To change time from seconds to minutes

we multiply by $\dfrac{1 \text{ minute}}{60 \text{ seconds}}$. $\qquad \boxed{5}$

Applying $\boxed{5}$ to $\boxed{4}$, we get

Time for M-page report, in minutes $= 30M$ seconds $\times \dfrac{1 \text{ minute}}{60 \text{ seconds}}$

$$= \dfrac{30\,M \text{ minutes}}{60}$$

$$= \dfrac{M}{2} \text{ minutes}$$

18. Choice B is correct.

Given: On Friday, the satellite passed over Washington, D.C., at midnight $\boxed{1}$

Complete orbit $= 5$ hours $\qquad \boxed{2}$

(Use Strategy: Use the given information effectively.)

Using $\boxed{2}$, we see that five complete orbits $= 5 \times 5 = 25$ hours $= 1$ day $+$ 1 hour $\qquad \boxed{3}$

From $\boxed{1}$ and $\boxed{2}$ we know that

DAY	TIME PASSING OVER D.C.	
Friday	7:00 P.M., midnight	$\boxed{4}$

Applying $\boxed{3}$ to $\boxed{4}$, and continuing this chart, we have

Saturday	8:00 P.M., 1:00 A.M.
Sunday	9:00 P.M., 2:00 A.M.
Monday	10:00 P.M., 3:00 A.M.
Tuesday	11:00 P.M., 4:00 A.M.
Wednesday	midnight, 5:00 A.M.

19. Choice D is correct. **(Use Strategy: Know how to find percent of a number.)**

Let x = price of car $\boxed{1}$

Given: 1st reduction = 30% $\boxed{2}$

2nd reduction = 40% $\boxed{3}$

We know amount of discount
$$= \text{percent} \times \text{price} \quad \boxed{4}$$

Using $\boxed{1}$, $\boxed{2}$, and $\boxed{4}$, we get

Amount of 1st discount = 30% $\times x$

$$= .30x \quad \boxed{5}$$

(Use Strategy: Find unknowns by subtraction.) Subtracting $\boxed{5}$ from $\boxed{1}$, we have

Reduced price = $x - .30x$

$$= .70x \quad \boxed{6}$$

Using $\boxed{3}$, $\boxed{6}$, and $\boxed{4}$, we get

Amount of 2nd discount = 40% $\times .70x$

$$= .40 \times .70x$$

$$= .28x \quad \boxed{7}$$

Subtracting $\boxed{7}$ from $\boxed{6}$, we have

Price after 2nd reduction = $.70x - .28x$

$$= .42x \quad \boxed{8}$$

(Use Strategy: The obvious may be tricky!)

Since $\boxed{8}$ = $.42x$, it is 42% of the original price of x. This is *not* the answer to the question.

Since $\boxed{8}$ is 42% of the original, it is the result of a 58% discount.

The answer is 58%.

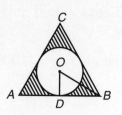

20. Choice A is correct.

(Use Strategy: Know how to find unknown quantities from known quantities.)

The total shaded area = area of triangle ABC − area of the circle.

Given: Diameter of circle = 2 $\boxed{1}$

The radius, r, of the circle = 1. Thus the area of the circle is $\pi r^2 = \pi(1) = \pi$. $\boxed{2}$

Now we have to find the area of the equilateral triangle.

(Use Strategy: Draw lines to help find the answer.)

Draw radius OD, with D the point of tangency and OB as shown above. $\boxed{3}$

(Use Strategy: Remember the equilateral triangle.)

Given: Triangle ACB is equilateral. $\boxed{4}$

From $\boxed{3}$ we get $OD \perp AB$, since radius $\perp$ tangent at point of tangency. $\boxed{5}$

From $\boxed{5}$, we get $\angle ODB = 90°$. $\boxed{6}$

From $\boxed{4}$, we get $\angle ABC = 60°$. $\boxed{7}$

From the geometry of regular polygons, we know that OB bisects $\angle ABC$. $\boxed{8}$

From $\boxed{7}$ and $\boxed{8}$ we get $\angle DBO = 30°$. $\boxed{9}$

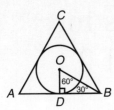

From $\boxed{6}$ and $\boxed{9}$ we have:

$\triangle ODB$ is a 30–60–90 triangle

From $\boxed{1}$, we get $OD = 1$. $\qquad \boxed{10}$

(Use Strategy: Remember the special right triangles.)

Using $\boxed{10}$ and the properties of the 30–60–90 right triangle, we get $OB = 2$, $DB = 1\sqrt{3} = \sqrt{3}$ $\qquad \boxed{11}$

We know $AB = 2 \times DB$ $\qquad \boxed{12}$

Substituting $\boxed{11}$ into $\boxed{12}$, we have

$$AB = 2\sqrt{3} \qquad \boxed{13}$$

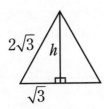

Where h is the altitude of the triangle, the area is:

$$= \frac{h \times 2\sqrt{3}}{2}$$
$$= h\sqrt{3}$$

By the Pythagorean Theorem,

$(2\sqrt{3})^2 - (\sqrt{3})^2 = h^2$

$(4 \times 3) - 3 = h^2$

$9 = h^2$

$3 = h$

So the area of the triangle

$$= \frac{h \times 2\sqrt{3}}{2} = 3\sqrt{3} \qquad \boxed{14}$$

From $\boxed{1}$, we know the area of the circle $= \pi$ $\qquad \boxed{15}$

(Use Strategy: Find unknowns by subtraction.)

Subtracting $\boxed{15}$ from $\boxed{14}$, we get

Shaded area $= 3\sqrt{3} - \pi$

Explanatory Answers for Math Practice Test 2 (continued)

Section 2

> As you read these solutions, do the following if you answered the math question incorrectly:
>
> When a specific Strategy is referred to in the solution, study that strategy, which you will find in "Math Strategies" (beginning on page 257).

1. Choice A is correct. **(Use Strategy: Translate from words to algebra.)**

Let x = Amount that Greg had to start.

Then $x + 5$ = Amount that Greg has after receiving $5 from David. $\boxed{1}$

$$\$25 = \text{Amount David has.} \quad \boxed{2}$$

We are told that Greg now has $\frac{1}{5}$ as much as David does.

This translates to:

$$\text{Greg} = \frac{1}{5}(\text{David}) \quad \boxed{3}$$

Substituting $\boxed{1}$ and $\boxed{2}$ into $\boxed{3}$, we get

$$x + 5 = \frac{1}{5}(25)$$
$$x + 5 = \frac{1}{5} \times 5 \times 5$$
$$x + 5 = 5$$
$$x = 0$$

2. Choice C is correct.

The ratio of the perimeter of the larger square to that of the smaller is

$$\frac{6+6+6+6}{2+2+2+2} = \frac{24}{8} = \frac{3}{1} \text{ or } 3{:}1$$

One can arrive at this result directly if one remembers that the ratio of the perimeters of two squares is the same as the ratio of the lengths of the sides of the two squares.

3. Choice E is correct. **(Use Strategy: Remember the rate, time, and distance relationship.)**

Remember that rate $\times$ time = distance

$$\text{or} \quad \text{average rate} = \frac{\text{total distance}}{\text{total time}}$$

$$\text{or} \quad \text{average rate} = \frac{1056 \text{ feet}}{12 \text{ seconds}}$$

$$= 88 \text{ feet/second}$$

4. Choice B is correct.

Given: $2z + 1 + 2 + 2z + 3 + 2z = 3 + 1 + 2$

(Use Strategy: Cancel numbers from both sides of an equation.)

We can immediately cancel the $+ 1$, $+ 2$, and $+ 3$ from each side.

We get $2z + 2z + 2z = 0$

$$6z = 0$$

$$z = 0$$

Thus, $z + 4 = 0 + 4 = 4$

5. Choice B is correct.

$$2(w)(x)(-y) - 2(-w)(-x)(y) =$$

$$-2wxy - 2wxy = -4wxy$$

6. Choice A is correct. **(Use Strategy: Translate from words to algebra.)**

The sum of the $\underbrace{\text{square of } x}$ and the $\underbrace{\text{square of } y}$

$$\quad x^2 \quad + \quad y^2$$

So, five times that quantity is

$$5(x^2 + y^2)$$

7. Choice C is correct. **(Use Strategy: Translate from words to algebra.)**
We are given

$$p > 0 \qquad \boxed{1}$$

$$q > 0 \qquad \boxed{2}$$

$$x < 0 \qquad \boxed{3}$$

$$y < 0 \qquad \boxed{4}$$

(Use Strategy: Know how to manipulate inequalities.)

$$p > q \text{ or } q < p \qquad \boxed{5}$$

$$x > y \text{ or } y < x \qquad \boxed{6}$$

For I: Add $-p$ to both sides of inequality $\boxed{5}$

$$q - p < 0$$

Thus, I is less than zero.

For II: From inequalities 2 and 4, $qy < 0$, and II is less than zero.

For III: The value of p and x depends on specific values of p and x:

(Use Strategy: Use numerics to help decide the answer.)

EXAMPLE 1

$$p = 3 \text{ and } x = -5$$

Thus, $\qquad p + x < 0$

EXAMPLE 2

$$p = 5 \text{ and } x = -3$$

Thus, $\qquad p + x > 0$

Thus, III is not always less than zero. Choice C is correct.

8. Choice A is correct.

Given: $\qquad a = 1, b = -2, c = -2 \qquad \boxed{1}$

$$\frac{b^2 c}{(a - c)^2} \qquad \boxed{2}$$

Substitute $\boxed{1}$ into $\boxed{2}$. We get

$$\frac{(-2)^2(-2)}{(1 - (-2))^2}$$

$$= \frac{4(-2)}{(3)^2}$$

$$= \frac{-8}{9}$$

9. Choice A is correct.

Given: $\qquad y = 28j \qquad \boxed{1}$

$$j \text{ is any integer} \qquad \boxed{2}$$

(Use Strategy: Find unknowns by division.)

Divide $\boxed{1}$ by 2. We have

$$\frac{y}{2} = \frac{28j}{2}$$

$$\frac{y}{2} = 14j \qquad \boxed{3}$$

(Use Strategy: Factor.)

Factor the 14 in $\boxed{3}$. We get

$$\frac{y}{2} = (2)(7)(j) \qquad \boxed{4}$$

Using $\boxed{2}$ and $\boxed{4}$ we see that $\frac{y}{2}$ is an integer with a factor of 2.

Thus, $\frac{y}{2}$ is even.

10. Choice B is correct.

Given: $3a + 4b = 4a - 4b = 21 \qquad \boxed{1}$

From $\boxed{1}$, we get

$$3a + 4b = 21 \qquad \boxed{2}$$
$$4a - 4b = 21 \qquad \boxed{3}$$

(Use Strategy: Find unknowns by addition.)

Add $\boxed{2}$ and $\boxed{3}$ together. We get

$$3a - \cancel{4b} = 21$$
$$\underline{+4a - \cancel{4b} = 21}$$
$$7a \quad\;\; = 42$$
$$a \quad\;\; = 6$$

11. Choice D is correct. **(Use Strategy: Translate from words to algebra.)**

$$N + 6N + 9N = 16N$$

Any divisor of 16 or of N will divide $16N$.

(Use Strategy: When all choices must be tested, start with Choice E and work backward.) Starting with Choice E, we see that 16 divides $16N$ evenly. Choice D, however, does *not* divide $16N$ evenly. Thus we have found the answer.

12. Choice D is correct.

We are given: $x = 3a - 18 \qquad \boxed{1}$
$$5y = 3a + 7 \qquad \boxed{2}$$

We need $5y - x$. $\qquad \boxed{3}$

(Use Strategy: Find unknown expressions by subtracting equations.) Subtracting $\boxed{1}$ from $\boxed{2}$, we get

$$5y - x = 3a + 7 - (3a - 18)$$
$$= 3a + 7 - 3a + 18$$
$$5y - x = 25$$

13. Choice B is correct. **(Use Strategy: Translate from words to algebra.)**

Given:

$$p + pq = 4(p - pq) \qquad \boxed{1}$$

(Use Strategy: Find unknown expressions by division.) Since $pq \neq 0$, divide 1 by p.

$$1 + q = 4(1 - q) \qquad \boxed{2}$$
$$\text{or} \quad 1 + q = 4 - 4q$$
$$\text{or} \quad\;\; 5q = 3$$
$$\text{or} \quad\;\; q = \frac{3}{5}$$

Thus, q has exactly one value.

Since p cannot be determined from equation $\boxed{1}$, none of the other choices is correct.

14. Choice D is correct. **(Use Strategy: Use the given information effectively.)**

Since $2 + \frac{1}{z} = 0$, we have

$$\frac{1}{z} = -2$$
$$z = -\frac{1}{2} \qquad \boxed{1}$$

We need $9 + 9z$ $\qquad \boxed{2}$

Substituting $\boxed{1}$ into $\boxed{2}$, we get

$$9 + 9\left(-\frac{1}{2}\right) = 9 - 4\frac{1}{2} = 4\frac{1}{2} = \frac{9}{2}$$

15. Choice C is correct. We set $y = x^2 = x$.

$x = 1$ or $x = 0$

Thus they intersect twice.

16. Choice C is correct.

We are given: $wx = y$ $\qquad \boxed{1}$

or $w = \dfrac{y}{x}$ $\qquad \boxed{2}$

(Use Strategy: Translate from words to algebra.) If x and y are multiplied by 6, in $\boxed{1}$, we have

$$w(6)(x) = (6)(y)$$
$$wx = y$$
$$w = \frac{y}{x} \qquad \boxed{3}$$

$\boxed{2}$ and $\boxed{3}$ are the same.

Therefore $\dfrac{y}{x} = 1\left(\dfrac{y}{x}\right)$

The answer is now clear.

17. Choice B is correct. **(Use Strategy: The whole equals the sum of its parts.)** The path is made up of 4 semicircles, three of diameter 4 and one of diameter 8.

[Remember circumference is $2\pi r$. Thus, $\dfrac{1}{2}$ circumference $= \dfrac{1}{2}(2\pi r)$.]

Therefore, the length of the path is

$$-\frac{1}{2}(2\pi)\left(\frac{4}{2}\right) + \frac{1}{2}(2\pi)\left(\frac{4}{2}\right) + \frac{1}{2}(2\pi)\left(\frac{4}{2}\right)$$
$$+ \frac{1}{2}(2\pi)\left(\frac{8}{2}\right)$$
$$= 10\pi$$

18. Choice C is correct. **(Use Strategy: Know how to use units.)**

$$\frac{7x}{144}\text{ yards} = \left(\frac{7x}{144}\text{ yards}\right)\left(\frac{36\text{ inches}}{\text{yards}}\right)$$

(Use Strategy: Factor and reduce.)

$$= \frac{7x}{\cancel{12} \times 12} \times \cancel{12} \times 3\text{ inches}$$
$$= \frac{7x}{\cancel{3} \times 4} \times \cancel{3}\text{ inches}$$
$$\frac{7x}{144}\text{ yards} = \frac{7x}{4}\text{ inches} \qquad \boxed{1}$$

$$\frac{5y}{12}\text{ feet} = \left(\frac{5y}{\cancel{12}}\text{ feet}\right)\left(\cancel{12}\frac{\text{inches}}{\text{foot}}\right) =$$
$$\frac{5y}{12}\text{ feet} = 5y\text{ inches} \qquad \boxed{2}$$

(Use Strategy: Find unknown expressions by addition of equations.) Adding $\boxed{1}$ and $\boxed{2}$, we have

$$\frac{7x}{144}\text{ yards} + \frac{5y}{12}\text{ feet} = \left(\frac{7x}{4} + 5y\right)\text{inches}$$

19. Choice A is correct.

Given: $x < 0$ $\qquad \boxed{1}$

$y < 0$ $\qquad \boxed{2}$

(Use Strategy: Know how to manipulate inequalities.)

Multiplying $\boxed{1}$ by $\boxed{2}$, we get

$$x \cdot y > 0 \qquad \boxed{3}$$

Thus I is always positive.

Adding $\boxed{1}$ and $\boxed{2}$, we get

$$x + y < 0 \qquad \boxed{4}$$

Thus II is not positive.

(Use Strategy: Use numerics to help find the answer.)

Let $x = -2, y = -3$

III becomes $x - y = -2 - (-3)$

$$= -2 + 3$$
$$= 1 \qquad \boxed{5}$$

Now let $x = -3, y = -2$

III becomes $x - y = -3 - (-2)$

$$= -3 + 2$$
$$= -1 \qquad \boxed{6}$$

From $\boxed{5}$ and $\boxed{6}$, we see that III is not always positive.

Using $\boxed{3}$, $\boxed{4}$, and $\boxed{6}$, we find that only Choice A, I only, is correct.

20. Choice D is correct.

Given: $a + 3b = 11 \qquad \boxed{1}$

a and b are positive integers $\boxed{2}$

(Use Strategy: Use the given information effectively.)

From $\boxed{1}$, we get

$$a = 11 - 3b \qquad \boxed{3}$$

From $\boxed{3}$, we see that a will be largest when b is smallest. Using $\boxed{2}$, we get

$$b = 1 \text{ is its smallest value.} \qquad \boxed{4}$$

Substituting $\boxed{4}$ into $\boxed{3}$, we have

$$a = 11 - 3(1)$$
$$a = 11 - 3$$
$$a = 8$$

Explanatory Answers for Math Practice Test 2 (continued)

Section 3

As you read these solutions, do the following if you answered the math question incorrectly:

When a specific Strategy is referred to in the solution, study that strategy, which you will find in "Math Strategies" (beginning on page 257).

1. Choice E is correct. Subtract 14 from both sides of the equation:

$$5\sqrt{x} + 14 = 20$$

$$5\sqrt{x} = 6$$

Divide by 5:

$$\sqrt{x} = \frac{6}{5}$$

Square both sides:

$$x = \frac{36}{25}$$

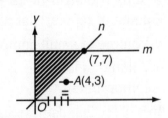

2. Choice A is correct. **(Use Strategy: Use the given information effectively.)** Since n goes through point O, the origin, whose coordinates are $(0,0)$, and through $(7,7)$, all of the points on n have the same x and y coordinates. Choice A, $(4,3)$, is 4 units to the right of O but only 3 units up. It is below n and not in the shaded area.

3. Choice B is correct. **(Use Strategy: Translate from words to algebra.)** This problem tests the concepts of set union and set intersection. We can solve these types of problems with a diagram. Let

$$c = \text{set of all calculus students}$$
$$p = \text{set of all physics students}$$

Thus, draw the diagram:

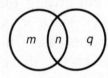

Where

m = number of students taking *only* calculus

q = number of students taking *only* physics

n = number of students taking *both* calculus and physics

Thus,

$m + n$ = number of students in calculus class

$n + q$ = number of students in physics class

$m + n + q$ = number of students taking either calculus or physics or both

We are given that

$$m + n + q = 36 \qquad \boxed{1}$$

$$n = 10 \qquad \boxed{2}$$

$$m + n = 31 \qquad \boxed{3}$$

We want to find

$$n + q \qquad \boxed{4}$$

(Use Strategy: Find unknowns by subtracting equations.) Subtract equation $\boxed{2}$ from equation $\boxed{3}$ to get

$$m = 21 \qquad \boxed{5}$$

Now subtract equation $\boxed{5}$ from equation $\boxed{1}$ to get

$$n + q = 15$$

4. Choice D is correct. In order to show a counterexample to refute Mr. Simmons' argument, we must come up with two numbers a and b such that $a^2 > b^2$ but that a is not greater than b. Choice A is incorrect, since it is not true that $a^2 > b^2$ in this case. Choice B is incorrect, since it is true that $a^2 > b^2$ and that $a > b$. Choice C is incorrect because $a^2 > b^2$ and $a > b$. Choice D is correct: a^2 is greater than b^2, since $(-4)^2 > (-2)^2$. But it is not true that $a > b$ since -4 is *not* greater than -2.

5. Choice E is correct. **(Use Strategy: Use specific numerical examples to prove or disprove your guess.)**

$$\sqrt{2+2} \neq \sqrt{2} + \sqrt{2}$$

$$2^2 + 2^2 \neq (2+2)^2$$

$$2^1 + 2^2 \neq 2^{1+2}$$

Therefore, neither (I) nor (II) nor (III) is generally true.

6. Choice B is correct. The only element common to R and S is $x = 1$.

7. Choice A is correct. To find the coordinates of the intersection point, we must first solve the equations $y = x - 1$ and $2x + 5y = 9$. In the equation $2x + 5y = 9$, we substitute $y = x - 1$. We obtain

$$2x + 5(x - 1) = 9$$

Thus

$$2x + 5x - 5 = 9$$

and

$$7x = 14$$

$$x = 2$$

From the first equation, $y = x - 1$, so $y = 2 - 1 = 1$. Thus $x = 2$ and $y = 1$ so the coordinates of the point are $(2,1)$.

8. Choice D is correct. **(Use Strategy: The whole equals the sum of its parts.)**

Volume of rectangular solid

= Volume of small compartment

+ Volume of larger compartment $\qquad \boxed{1}$

Area of rectangular dividing wall

= $l \times h$, where h is the height of the rectangular solid

$$39 \text{ cm}^2 = 13 \text{ cm} \times h \qquad \boxed{2}$$

$$3 \text{ cm} = h$$

$\boxed{2}$ is the height of the rectangular solid as well.

Volume of rectangular solid $= l \times w \times h$

$$= 15 \text{ cm} \times 12 \text{ cm} \times h \boxed{3}$$

Substituting $\boxed{2}$ into $\boxed{3}$, we get

Volume of rectangular solid =

$15 \text{ cm} \times 12 \text{ cm} \times 3 \text{ cm}$

Volume of rectangular solid $= 540 \text{ cm}^3 \boxed{4}$

Volume of small compartment

$\qquad = \text{Area of base} \times \text{height}$

$$= \frac{1}{2} \times 12 \text{ cm} \times 5 \text{ cm} \times 3 \text{ cm} \boxed{5}$$

Volume of small compartment $= 90 \text{ cm}^3$

Substitute $\boxed{4}$ and $\boxed{5}$ into $\boxed{1}$. We get

$540 \text{ cm}^3 = 90 \text{ cm}^3 + \text{volume of larger compartment}$

$450 \text{ cm}^3 = \text{Volume of larger compartment}$

9. $\dfrac{7}{18}$ **or .388 or .389**

(Use Strategy: Simplify by cancelling.)

$$\left(\frac{1}{2} - \frac{1}{3}\right) + \left(\frac{1}{3} - \frac{1}{4}\right) + \left(\frac{1}{4} - \frac{1}{5}\right) +$$

$$\left(\frac{1}{5} - \frac{1}{6}\right) + \left(\frac{1}{6} - \frac{1}{7}\right) + \left(\frac{1}{7} - \frac{1}{8}\right) +$$

$$\left(\frac{1}{8} - \frac{1}{9}\right) =$$

$$\frac{1}{2} + \left(-\frac{1}{3} + \frac{1}{3}\right) + \left(-\frac{1}{4} + \frac{1}{4}\right) +$$

$$\left(-\frac{1}{5} + \frac{1}{5}\right) + \left(-\frac{1}{6} + \frac{1}{6}\right) + \left(-\frac{1}{7} + \frac{1}{7}\right) +$$

$$\left(-\frac{1}{8} + \frac{1}{8}\right) - \frac{1}{9} =$$

$$\frac{1}{2} + 0 + 0 + 0 + 0 + 0 + 0 - \frac{1}{9} =$$

$$\frac{1}{2} - \frac{1}{9} =$$

$$\frac{9}{18} - \frac{2}{18} =$$

$$\frac{7}{18}$$

10. 8

(Use Strategy: Use new definitions carefully.) The first five elements of the series, calculated by the definition, are

$$1, 2, 2, 4, 8$$

(Logical Reasoning)

11. $\dfrac{2}{3}$ **or .667 or .666**

(Use Strategy: Translate from words to algebra.)

$$p = \frac{3}{5}m \qquad \boxed{1}$$

$$q = \frac{9}{10}m \qquad \boxed{2}$$

(Use Strategy: Find unknowns by division of equations.)

Thus, $\dfrac{p}{q} = \dfrac{\dfrac{3}{5}\cancel{m}}{\dfrac{9}{10}\cancel{m}}$

$$= \frac{\dfrac{3}{5}}{\dfrac{9}{10}}$$

$$= \frac{3}{5} \times \frac{10}{9} = \frac{\cancel{3}^{1}}{\cancel{5}_{1}} \times \frac{\cancel{10}^{2}}{\cancel{9}_{3}}$$

$$\frac{p}{q} = \frac{2}{3}$$

12. 60

$\left(\text{Use Strategy:}\right.$

$$\text{Average} = \frac{\text{sum of values}}{\text{total number of values}} \left.\right)$$

Given $\dfrac{40 + 40 + 40 + z}{4} = 45 \qquad \boxed{1}$

Multiplying $\boxed{1}$ by 4,

$$40 + 40 + 40 + z = 180$$

$$120 + z = 180$$

$$z = 60$$

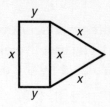

13. 36

(Use Strategy: Translate from words to algebra.) When the given diagram has been labeled as above, then we know

$$3x = 39 \qquad \boxed{1}$$
$$xy = 65 \qquad \boxed{2}$$

From $\boxed{1}$ we have

$$x = 13 \qquad \boxed{3}$$

Substituting $\boxed{3}$ into $\boxed{2}$, we have

$$13y = 65$$
$$\text{or} \qquad y = 5 \qquad \boxed{4}$$

The perimeter of the rectangle

$$= 2x + 2y$$
$$= 2(13) + 2(5)$$
$$= 36$$

14. 44

(Use Strategy: Use the given information effectively.)

Game	Darrin	Tom
1	69	43
2	59	60
3	72	55
4	70	68
5	78	73
Totals	348	299

We need the scores at the end of the first four games. We have been given the totals for all five games.

(Use Strategy: Find unknowns by subtraction.)

Darrin's Total = 348 $\boxed{1}$
Darrin's Game 5 = 78 $\boxed{2}$
Tom's Total = 299 $\boxed{3}$
Tom's Game 5 = 73 $\boxed{4}$

Subtract $\boxed{2}$ from $\boxed{1}$. We get

Darrin's Total for 1st four games = 348 − 78
$$= 270 \qquad \boxed{5}$$

Subtract $\boxed{4}$ from $\boxed{3}$. We get

Tom's total for 1st four games = 299 − 73
$$= 226 \qquad \boxed{6}$$

Subtracting $\boxed{6}$ from $\boxed{5}$, we have

Number of points Tom was behind Darrin after the first four games = 270 − 226
$$= 44$$

(Use Strategy: subtraction and logical reasoning)

15. $\dfrac{1}{4}$ or .25

(Use Strategy: Use the given information effectively.)

The 17 slips, numbered from 1 to 17, consist of $\boxed{1}$
8 even numbers (2,4,6, . . . 16) and $\boxed{2}$
9 odd numbers (1,3,5, . . . 17). $\boxed{3}$

Subtracting 5 even-numbered slips from $\boxed{2}$ leaves

8 − 5 = 3 even-numbered slips. $\boxed{4}$

Adding $\boxed{3}$ and $\boxed{4}$ we have

$$9 + 3 = 12 \text{ slips remaining} \quad \boxed{5}$$

We need $\dfrac{\text{even-numbered slips}}{\text{total numbered slips}}$ $\boxed{6}$

Substituting $\boxed{4}$ and $\boxed{5}$ into $\boxed{6}$, we have

$$\frac{3}{12} = \frac{1}{4}$$

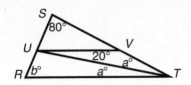

Dividing $\boxed{1}$ by $\boxed{2}$, we have

$$\text{Rose's daily rate} = \frac{\$44}{8\,\text{days}}$$

$$\text{Rose's daily rate} = \frac{\$11}{2\,\text{days}} \qquad \boxed{3}$$

Given: Total earnings to equal $99 $\qquad\boxed{4}$

Substituting $\boxed{1}$ from $\boxed{4}$, we get

Amount left to be earned = $55 $\qquad\boxed{5}$

We know

(daily rate)(days worked) = money earned $\qquad\boxed{6}$

Substituting $\boxed{3}$ and $\boxed{5}$ into $\boxed{6}$, we get

$$\left(\frac{\$11}{2\,\text{days}}\right)(\text{days worked}) \quad \$55 \qquad \boxed{7}$$

Multiplying $\boxed{7}$ by $\frac{2}{11}$ days, we have

$$\frac{2\,\cancel{\text{days}}}{\cancel{11}}\left(\frac{\cancel{11}}{2\,\cancel{\text{days}}}\right)(\text{days worked}) \quad (\cancel{55})\overset{5}{}\frac{2}{\cancel{11}}\,\text{days}$$

$$\text{days worked} = 10\,\text{days}$$

18. 48

Given: Areas of all 12 triangles are the same $\qquad\boxed{1}$

Area of outlined region = 256 $\qquad\boxed{2}$

Area of square $ABCD = 128$ $\qquad\boxed{3}$

(Use Strategy: The whole equals the sum of the parts.)

By looking at the diagram, we observe

Area of 8 triangles (I, II, ..., VIII) = area of outlined region − area of square $ABCD$.

16. 60

Given: $UV \parallel RT$ $\qquad\boxed{1}$

From $\boxed{1}$ we get $a = 20$, since alternate interior angles are equal $\qquad\boxed{2}$

(Use Strategy: The whole equals the sum of its parts.) From the diagram we see that

$$\angle STR = a + a \qquad \boxed{3}$$

Substituting $\boxed{2}$ into $\boxed{3}$, we have

$$\angle STR = 20 + 20 = 40 \qquad \boxed{4}$$

We know that the sum of the angles in a triangle = 180; thus

$$\angle R + \angle S + \angle STR = 180 \quad \boxed{5}$$

We are given, in the diagram, that

$$\angle R = b \qquad \boxed{6}$$
$$\angle S = 80 \qquad \boxed{7}$$

Substituting $\boxed{6}$, $\boxed{7}$, and $\boxed{4}$ into $\boxed{5}$, we get

$$b + 80 + 40 = 180$$
$$b + 120 = 180$$
$$b = 60$$

17. 10

(Use Strategy: Translate from words to algebra.)

Given: Rose's earnings = $44 $\qquad\boxed{1}$

Rose's time worked = 8 days $\qquad\boxed{2}$

(Use Strategy: Find unknowns by division.)

Substituting $\boxed{2}$ and $\boxed{3}$ into the above, we get

Area of 8 triangles (I, ... , VIII)

$$= 256 - 128$$
$$= 128 \qquad \boxed{4}$$

Using $\boxed{1}$, we get

Area of each of the 12 triangles =

$$\frac{\text{Area of 8 triangles}}{8}$$

Substituting $\boxed{4}$ into the above, we get

Area of each of the 12 triangles $= \dfrac{128}{8}$

Area of each of the 12 triangles $= 16 \boxed{5}$

(Use Strategy: The whole equals the sum of its parts.)

Shaded area = area ΔV + area ΔVI + area ΔXI $\qquad \boxed{6}$

Substituting $\boxed{1}$ and $\boxed{5}$ into $\boxed{6}$, we get

Shaded area $= 16 + 16 + 16 = 48$

Explanatory Answers for Math Practice Test 2 (continued)

Section 4

As you read these solutions, do the following if you answered the math question incorrectly:

When a specific Strategy is referred to in the solution, study that strategy, which you will find in "Math Strategies" (beginning on page 257).

1. Choice C is correct. **(Use Strategy: Translate from words to algebra.)** The key is to be able to translate English sentences into mathematical equations.

Let p = price of one frying pan
m = price of one coffee mug
We are given

$$p + 2m = \$27 \qquad \boxed{1}$$
$$p + m = \$23 \qquad \boxed{2}$$

Subtract equation $\boxed{2}$ from equation $\boxed{1}$ to get

$$m = \$4 \qquad \boxed{3}$$

Substitute equation $\boxed{3}$ into equation $\boxed{2}$

$$p + \$4 = \$23$$

Subtract $4 from both sides of the above equation:

$$p = \$19$$

2. Choice E is correct. **(Use Strategy: Translate from words to algebra.)**

Each tile is a square with perimeter = 2 feet

Each side of the tile is $\frac{1}{4}$(2 feet) = $\frac{1}{2}$ foot $\qquad \boxed{1}$

The area of each tile is (Side)^2.

Using $\boxed{1}$, we get area of each tile

$$= \left(\frac{1}{2}\right)^2 = \frac{1}{4} \text{ square foot} \qquad \boxed{2}$$

The area of the floor is $b \times h =$
$$8 \text{ feet} \times 6 \text{ feet} =$$
$$48 \text{ square feet} \qquad \boxed{3}$$

(Use Strategy: Use the given information effectively.)

The number of tiles necessary, at minimum, to cover the floor

$$= \frac{\text{Area of floor}}{\text{Area of 1 tile}} \qquad \boxed{4}$$

Substituting $\boxed{2}$ and $\boxed{3}$ into $\boxed{4}$ we get:

The number of tiles necessary, at minimum, to cover the floor

$$= \frac{48}{\frac{1}{4}} = \$48 \times \frac{4}{1}$$

The number of tiles necessary, at minimum, to cover the floor

$$= 192$$

3. Choice E is correct.

The only restriction is that 9 and 12 must each divide Q without a remainder. $\boxed{1}$

(Use Strategy: Use numerics to help find the answer.)

Choose specific values for Q that satisfy $\boxed{1}$.

EXAMPLE 1

$$Q = 36$$

Then, Q will divide 36 and 72.

EXAMPLE 2

$$Q = 108$$

Then, Q will divide neither 36 nor 72. Clearly, the answer to this question depends on the specific value of Q.

4. Choice B is correct. Since $DC \perp AC$, $\angle DCB$ is a right angle and has a measure of 90°. **(Use Strategy: The whole equals the sum of its parts.)** Since the sum of the angles of a $\triangle$ is 180°, we have

$$\angle DBC + 90 + 20 = 180$$
$$\angle DBC = 70 \qquad \boxed{1}$$

Since $EB \perp BD$, $\angle DBE$ is a right angle and has a measure of 90°. $\boxed{2}$

(Use Strategy: The whole equals the sum of its parts.) The whole straight $\angle ABC$ is = to the sum of its parts. Thus

$$\angle DBC + \angle DBE + x = 180 \quad \boxed{3}$$

Substituting $\boxed{1}$ and $\boxed{2}$ into $\boxed{3}$, we have

$$70 + 90 + x = 180$$
$$x = 20$$

5. Choice E is correct. **(Use Strategy: Use the given information effectively.)**

Given: x $\qquad \boxed{1}$
$\qquad 11 - x$ $\qquad \boxed{2}$
$\qquad x - 4$ $\qquad \boxed{3}$

as the lengths of the three sides of a triangle.

We know that the sum of any two sides of a triangle is greater than the third. $\boxed{4}$

First, we use $\boxed{1} + \boxed{2} > \boxed{3}$. We have

$$x + 11 - x > x - 4$$
$$11 > x - 4$$
$$15 > x \qquad \boxed{5}$$

Next, we use $\boxed{2} + \boxed{3} > \boxed{1}$. We have

$$11 - x + x - 4 > x$$
$$7 > x \qquad \boxed{6}$$

To satisfy $\boxed{6}$ and $\boxed{5}$, we choose $\boxed{6}$.

$$7 > x, \text{ or } x < 7, \text{ satisfies both } \boxed{7}$$

Finally, we use $\boxed{1} + \boxed{3} > \boxed{2}$. We have

$$x + x - 4 > 11 - x$$
$$2x - 4 > 11 - x$$
$$3x > 15$$
$$x > 5, \text{ or } 5 < x \qquad \boxed{8}$$

(Use Strategy: Know how to manipulate inequalities.) Combining $\boxed{7}$ and $\boxed{8}$, we get

$$5 < x < 7$$

6. Choice B is correct.

Given: $\qquad a, b$ are integers $\qquad \boxed{1}$

$\qquad$ Average of $a, b,$ and 4 is 6 $\boxed{2}$

(Use Strategy:

$$\text{Average} = \frac{\text{Sum of values}}{\text{Total number of values}} \Big)$$

Using $\boxed{2}$, we have

$$\frac{a+b+4}{3} = 6 \qquad \boxed{3}$$

(Use Strategy: Find unknowns by multiplication.)

Multiply $\boxed{3}$ by 3. We get

$$\cancel{3}\left(\frac{a+b+4}{\cancel{3}}\right) = (6)3$$

$$a+b+4 = 18$$

$$a+b = 14 \qquad \boxed{4}$$

Using $\boxed{1}$ and $\boxed{4}$, the possibilities are:

$a + b$	ab	
$1 + 13$	13	Choice A
$2 + 12$	24	
$3 + 11$	33	
$4 + 10$	40	Choice C
$5 + 9$	45	
$6 + 8$	48	Choice D
$7 + 7$	49	Choice E

Checking all the choices, we find that only Choice B, 14, is not a possible value of ab.

7. Choice D is correct. **(Use Strategy: Use the given information effectively.)**

$$\frac{1}{n^2}\left(\frac{m^5 n^3}{m^3}\right)^2 = \frac{1}{n^2} = (m^2 n^3)^2 = \frac{m^4 n^6}{n^2} = m^4 n^4$$

8. Choice C is correct. Label the females F_1, F_2, and F_3 and the males M_1, M_2, and M_3. The total number of combinations of three people (such as F_1–F_2–M_1 or F_1–M_2–M_3) is 6 combinations taken 3 at a time, or $_6C_3$, which is equal to $\frac{6\times5\times4}{3\times2\times1} = 20$. There are 9 favorable combinations (trios that include

exactly two men): M_1–M_2–F_1, M_1–M_2–F_2, M_1–M_2–F_3, M_1–M_3–F_1, M_1–M_3–F_2, M_1–M_3–F_3, M_2–M_3–F_1, M_2–M_3–F_2, and M_2–M_3–F_3. The probability of exactly two males in the room is:

$$\frac{\text{Favorable Combinations}}{\text{Total Combinations}} = \frac{9}{20}$$

9. Choice E is correct. **(Use Strategy: Use new definitions carefully.)**

Since W, X, Y, and Z are distinct digits from 0 to 9, the largest possible sum of $W + X + Y = 7 + 8 + 9 = 24$. $\qquad \boxed{1}$

By definition, $W + X + Y = 5Z$ $\qquad \boxed{2}$

Substituting $\boxed{1}$ into $\boxed{2}$, we get

largest value of $5Z = 24$

(Use Strategy: When all choices must be tested, start with Choice E and work backward.) Look at the choices, starting with Choice E.

If $Z = 5$, then $5Z = 25$, which is larger than 24. Thus, Choice E is correct.

10. Choice C is correct. **(Use Strategy: The whole equals the sum of its parts.)** From the diagram, we see that each straight angle is equal to the sum of two smaller angles. Thus,

$$m = 180 - x \qquad \boxed{1}$$
$$n = 180 - z \qquad \boxed{2}$$

(Use Strategy: Find unknown expressions by addition of equations.) Adding $\boxed{1}$ and $\boxed{2}$, we have

$$m + n = 180 + 180 - x - z \qquad \boxed{3}$$

We know that the sum of the angles of a triangle = 180.

Therefore, $y + x + z = 180$

or $y = 180 - x - z$ $\qquad \boxed{4}$

Substituting $\boxed{4}$ into $\boxed{3}$, we have

$$m + n = 180 + y$$

Accordingly, Choice C is the correct choice.

11. Choice C is correct. **(Use Strategy: Translate from words to algebra.)**

We know that the volume of a cube $= e^3$.

We are told that $e^3 < 25$.

(Use Strategy: Use the given information effectively.)

Since e is a positive integer (which was given),

$$e \text{ can be: } 1 \rightarrow 1^3 = 1$$
$$2 \rightarrow 2^3 = 8$$
$$3 \rightarrow 3^3 = 27$$
$$\text{etc.}$$

For $e = 2$, the volume is 8, which is < 25. Any larger e will have a volume > 25. Thus, area of one face $= e^2 = 2^2 = 4$
Total area $= 6(4) = 24$

12. Choice E is correct. **(Use Strategy: Translate from words to algebra.)**
Let $s =$ number of females
$n =$ number males
Then $s + n =$ total number of people.

We are given: $\dfrac{s}{n} = \dfrac{2}{3}$ or $s = \dfrac{2}{3}n$ $\boxed{1}$

and: $s = \dfrac{1}{3}(s + n) + 5$ $\boxed{2}$

Substituting $\boxed{1}$ into $\boxed{2}$, we have

$$\frac{2}{3}n = \frac{1}{3}\left(\frac{2}{3}n + n\right) + 5$$
$$\frac{2}{3}n = \frac{1}{3}\left(\frac{2}{3}n + \frac{3}{3}n\right) + 5$$
$$\frac{2}{3}n = \frac{1}{3}\left(\frac{5}{3}n\right) + 5$$
$$\frac{2}{3}n = \frac{5}{9}n + 5 \qquad \boxed{3}$$

Multiplying both sides of $\boxed{3}$ by 9, we get

$$9\left(\frac{2}{3}n\right) = 9\left(\frac{5}{9}n + 5\right)$$
$$\frac{18}{3}n = 5n + 45$$
$$6n = 5n + 45$$
$$n = 45$$

$$s = \frac{2}{3}(45) = 30$$

$$s + n = 75$$

$$
\begin{array}{ccccccc}
A & B & C & D & E & F & G
\end{array}
$$
$$
\vdash\!\!\!\overset{a}{\quad}\!\!\!+\!\!\!\overset{a}{\quad}\!\!\!+\!\!\!\overset{a}{\quad}\!\!\!+\!\!\!\overset{a}{\quad}\!\!\!+\!\!\!\overset{a}{\quad}\!\!\!+\!\!\!\overset{a}{\quad}\!\!\!\dashv
$$

13. Choice C is correct.

Given:
AG is divided into 6 equal segments. $\boxed{1}$

Radius of circle, centered at $F = \dfrac{1}{5}AG$ $\boxed{2}$

(Use Strategy: Label unknown quantities.)

Label segments with a as shown in above diagram.

Using $\boxed{2}$, radius of circle centered at
$$F = \frac{1}{5}(AG)$$
$$= \frac{1}{5}(6a)$$
$$= 1\frac{1}{5}a$$

This means from the center at F, the left tip of the radius of the circle is $1\frac{1}{5}a$ from point F. Thus the circumference hits the line between D and E.

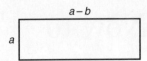

14. Choice B is correct. **(Use Strategy: Translate from words to algebra.)**

Perimeter of a rectangle
$$= 2(\text{length}) + 2(\text{width}) \quad \boxed{1}$$

Substituting from the diagram into $\boxed{1}$, we have

$$\text{Perimeter} = 2(a - b) + 2(a)$$
$$= 2a - 2b + 2a$$
$$\text{Perimeter} = 4a - 2b$$

15. Choice E is correct.

$$\begin{array}{r} AB \\ + \; BA \\ \hline CDC \end{array}$$

(Use Strategy: When testing all choices, start with Choice E.)

Let's see if $A = 2$ can work.
We get

$$\begin{array}{r} 2B \\ + \; B2 \\ \hline CDC \end{array}$$

Now for the range $B = 0,1,3,4,5,6,7$ the left C won't equal the right C. So we try $B = 8$. (Note we can't use $B = 2$ because A would equal B, which is incorrect.)

We would get:

$$\begin{array}{r} 28 \\ + \; 82 \\ \hline 110 \end{array}$$

Also, the left C doesn't equal the right C.

The only digit left for B is 9. We then get:

$$\begin{array}{r} 29 \\ + \; 92 \\ \hline 121 \end{array}$$

But then $D = A$, which is incorrect.

Thus $A = 2$ doesn't work.

16. Choice A is correct. $g(-1) = 1$, $f[g(-1)] = f(1) = 1^2 + 1 = 2$.

What You Must Do Now to Raise Your SAT Score

1. a) Follow the directions on p. 339 to determine your scaled score for the Math SAT Test you've just taken. These results will give you a good idea about whether or not you ought to study hard in order to achieve a certain score on the actual Math SAT.

   b) Using your test correct answer count as a basis, indicate for yourself your areas of strength and weakness as revealed by the "Self-Appraisal Chart" on page 391.

2. Eliminate your weaknesses in each of the SAT test areas (as revealed in the "Self-Appraisal Chart") by taking the following Giant Steps toward SAT success:

Math Part

Giant Step 1

Make good use of the Math Strategies that begin on page 257. Read again the solutions for each math question that you answered incorrectly. Refer to the Math Strategy that applies to each of your incorrect answers. Learn each of these Math Strategies thoroughly. We repeat that these strategies are crucial if you want to raise your SAT Math score substantially.

Giant Step 2

You may want to take "The 101 Most Important Math Questions You Need to Know How to Solve" test on page 21 and follow the directions after the test for a basic math skills diagnosis.

Essentials from
Dr. Gary Gruber
and the creators of MyMaxScore

*"Gruber can ring the bell on any number
of standardized exams."*
—*Chicago Tribune*

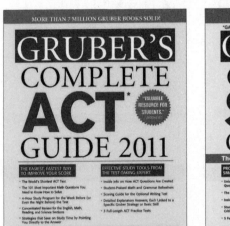

$19.99 U.S./ $23.99 CAN/ £14.99
978-1-4022-4307-3

$19.99 U.S./ £14.99
978-1-4022-5331-7

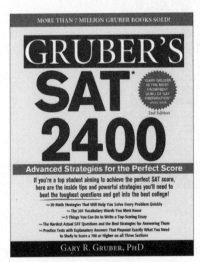

$16.99 U.S./ $19.99 CAN/ £11.99
978-1-4022-4308-0

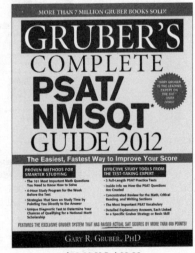

$13.99 U.S./ £9.99
978-1-4022-5334-8

"Gruber's methods make the questions
seem amazingly simple to solve."
—*Library Journal*

"Gary Gruber is the leading expert on the SAT."
—*Houston Chronicle*

$14.99 U.S./ £9.99
978-1-4022-5343-0

$14.99 U.S./ £9.99
978-1-4022-5340-9

$12.99 U.S./ £6.99
978-1-4022-6072-8

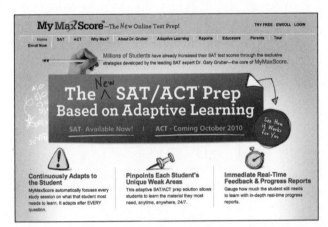